Hacker's Delight

Hacker's Delight

Henry S. Warren, Jr.

♠♥Addison-Wesley

Boston • San Francisco • New York • Toronto • Montreal
London • Munich • Paris • Madrid
Capetown • Sydney • Tokyo • Singapore • Mexico City

The publisher offers discounts on this book when ordered in quantity for special sales. For more information, please contact:

U.S. Corporate and Government Sales
(800) 382-3149
corpsales@pearsontechgroup.com

For sales outside of the U.S., please contact:
International Sales
(317) 581-3793
international@pearsontechgroup.com

Visit Addison-Wesley on the Web: www.awprofessional.com

Library of Congress Cataloging-in-Publication Data

Warren, Henry S.
    Hacker's delight / Henry S. Warren, Jr.
        p. cm.
    Includes bibliographical references and index.
    ISBN 0-201-91465-4
        1. Computer programming. I. Title.

QA76.6 .W375 2002
005.1—dc21

2002066501

ISBN 0-201-91465-4
Text printed on recycled paper
1 2 3 4 5 6 7 8 9 10—MA—0605040302
First printing, July 2002

To Joseph W. Gauld,
my high school algebra teacher,
for sparking in me a delight
in the simple things in mathematics.

CONTENTS

FOREWORD

When I first got a summer job at MIT's Project MAC almost 30 years ago, I was delighted to be able to work with the DEC PDP-10 computer, which was more fun to program in assembly language than any other computer, bar none, because of its rich yet tractable set of instructions for performing bit tests, bit masking, field manipulation, and operations on integers. Though the PDP-10 has not been manufactured for quite some years, there remains a thriving cult of enthusiasts who keep old PDP-10 hardware running and who run old PDP-10 software—entire operating systems and their applications—by using personal computers to simulate the PDP-10 instruction set. They even write new software; there is now at least one Web site whose pages are served up by a simulated PDP-10. (Come on, stop laughing—it's no sillier than keeping antique cars running.)

I also enjoyed, in that summer of 1972, reading a brand-new MIT research memo called HAKMEM, a bizarre and eclectic potpourri of technical trivia.[1] The subject matter ranged from electrical circuits to number theory, but what intrigued me most was its small catalog of ingenious little programming tricks. Each such gem would typically describe some plausible yet unusual operation on integers or bit strings (such as counting the 1-bits in a word) that could easily be programmed using either a longish fixed sequence of machine instructions or a loop, and then show how the same thing might be done much more cleverly, using just four or three or two carefully chosen instructions whose interactions are not at all obvious until explained or fathomed. For me, devouring these little programming nuggets was like eating peanuts, or rather bonbons—I just couldn't stop—and there was a certain richness to them, a certain intellectual depth, elegance, even poetry.

"Surely," I thought, "there must be more of these," and indeed over the years I collected, and in some cases discovered, a few more. "There ought to be a book of them."

I was genuinely thrilled when I saw Hank Warren's manuscript. He has systematically collected these little programming tricks, organized them thematically, and explained them clearly. While some of them may be described in terms of machine instructions, this is not a book only for assembly language programmers. The subject matter is basic structural relationships among integers and bit strings in a computer and efficient techniques for performing useful operations on them.

---

1. Why "HAKMEM"? Short for "hacks memo"; one 36-bit PDP-10 word could hold six 6-bit characters, so a lot of the names PDP-10 hackers worked with were limited to six characters. We were used to glancing at a six-character abbreviated name and instantly decoding the contractions. So naming the memo "HAKMEM" made sense at the time—at least to the hackers.

These techniques are just as useful in the C or Java programming languages as they are in assembly language.

Many books on algorithms and data structures teach complicated techniques for sorting and searching, for maintaining hash tables and binary trees, for dealing with records and pointers. They overlook what can be done with very tiny pieces of data—bits and arrays of bits. It is amazing what can be done with just binary addition and subtraction and maybe some bitwise operations; the fact that the carry chain allows a single bit to affect all the bits to its left makes addition a peculiarly powerful data manipulation operation in ways that are not widely appreciated.

Yes, there ought to be a book about these techniques. Now it is in your hands, and it's terrific. If you write optimizing compilers or high-performance code, you must read this book. You otherwise might not use this bag of tricks every single day—but if you find yourself stuck in some situation where you apparently need to loop over the bits in a word, or to perform some operation on integers and it just seems harder to code than it ought, or you really need the inner loop of some integer or bit-fiddly computation to run twice as fast, then this is the place to look. Or maybe you'll just find yourself reading it straight through out of sheer pleasure.

Guy L. Steele, Jr.
Burlington, Massachusetts
April 2002

PREFACE

*Caveat Emptor: The cost of software
maintenance increases with the square of
the programmer's creativity.*

First Law of Programmer Creativity,
Robert D. Bliss, 1992

This is a collection of small programming tricks that I have come across over many years. Most of them will work only on computers that represent integers in two's-complement form. Although a 32-bit machine is assumed when the register length is relevant, most of the tricks are easily adapted to machines with other register sizes.

This book does not deal with large tricks such as sophisticated sorting and compiler optimization techniques. Rather, it deals with small tricks that usually involve individual computer words or instructions, such as counting the number of 1-bits in a word. Such tricks often use a mixture of arithmetic and logical instructions.

It is assumed throughout that integer overflow interrupts have been masked off, so they cannot occur. C, Fortran, and even Java programs run in this environment, but Pascal and ADA users beware!

The presentation is informal. Proofs are given only when the algorithm is not obvious, and sometimes not even then. The methods use computer arithmetic, "floor" functions, mixtures of arithmetic and logical operations, and so on. Proofs in this domain are often difficult and awkward to express.

To reduce typographical errors and oversights, many of the algorithms have been executed. This is why they are given in a real programming language, even though, like every computer language, it has some ugly features. C is used for the high-level language because it is widely known, it allows the straightforward mixture of integer and bit-string operations, and C compilers that produce high-quality object code are available.

Occasionally, machine language is used. It employs a three-address format, mainly for ease of readability. The assembly language used is that of a fictitious machine that is representative of today's RISC computers.

Branch-free code is favored. This is because on many computers, branches slow down instruction fetching and inhibit executing instructions in parallel. Another problem with branches is that they may inhibit compiler optimizations such as instruction scheduling, commoning, and register allocation. That is, the compiler may be more effective at these optimizations with a program that consists of a few large basic blocks rather than many small ones.

The code sequences also tend to favor small immediate values, comparisons to zero (rather than to some other number), and instruction-level parallelism. Although much of the code would become more concise by using table lookups (from memory), this is not often mentioned. This is because loads are becoming more expensive relative to arithmetic instructions, and the table lookup methods are often not very interesting (although they *are* often practical). But there are exceptional cases.

Finally, I should mention that the term "hacker" in the title is meant in the original sense of an aficionado of computers—someone who enjoys making computers do new things, or do old things in a new and clever way. The hacker is usually quite good at his craft, but may very well not be a professional computer programmer or designer. The hacker's work may be useful or may be just a game. As an example of the latter, more than one determined hacker has written a program which, when executed, writes out an exact copy of itself.[1] This is the sense in which we use the term "hacker." If you're looking for tips on how to break into someone else's computer, you won't find them here.

Acknowledgments

First, I want to thank Bruce Shriver and Dennis Allison for encouraging me to publish this book. I am indebted to many colleagues at IBM, several of whom are cited in the Bibliography. But one deserves special mention: Martin E. Hopkins, whom I think of as "Mr. Compiler" at IBM, has been relentless in his drive to make every cycle count, and I'm sure some of his spirit has rubbed off on me. Addison-Wesley's reviewers have improved the book immensely. Most of their names are unknown to me, but the review by one whose name I did learn was truly outstanding: Guy L. Steele, Jr., completed a 50-page review that included new subject areas to address, such as bit shuffling and unshuffling, the sheep and goats operation, and many others that will have to wait for a second edition (☺). He suggested algorithms that beat the ones I used. He was extremely thorough. For example, I had erroneously written that the hexadecimal number AAAAAAAA factors as $2 \cdot 3 \cdot 17 \cdot 257 \cdot 65537$; Guy pointed out that the 3 should be a 5. He suggested improvements to style and did not shirk from mentioning minutiae. Wherever you see "parallel prefix" in this book, the material is due to Guy.

H. S. Warren, Jr.
Yorktown, New York
February 2002

---

1. The shortest such program written in C, known to the present author, is by Vlad Taeerov and Rashit Fakhreyev and is 64 characters in length:

```
main(a){printf(a,34,a="main(a){printf(a,34,a=%c%s%c,34);}",34);}
```

CHAPTER 1

INTRODUCTION

1–1 Notation

This book distinguishes between mathematical expressions of ordinary arithmetic and those that describe the operation of a computer. In "computer arithmetic," operands are bit strings, or bit vectors, of some definite fixed length. Expressions in computer arithmetic are similar to those of ordinary arithmetic, but the variables denote the contents of computer registers. The value of a computer arithmetic expression is simply a string of bits with no particular interpretation. An operator, however, interprets its operands in some particular way. For example, a comparison operator might interpret its operands as signed binary integers or as unsigned binary integers; our computer arithmetic notation uses distinct symbols to make the type of comparison clear.

The main difference between computer arithmetic and ordinary arithmetic is that in computer arithmetic, the results of addition, subtraction, and multiplication are reduced modulo 2^n, where n is the word size of the machine. Another difference is that computer arithmetic includes a large number of operations. In addition to the four basic arithmetic operations, computer arithmetic includes logical *and*, *exclusive or, compare, shift left*, and so on.

Unless specified otherwise, the word size is 32 bits, and signed integers are represented in two's-complement form.

Expressions of computer arithmetic are written similarly to those of ordinary arithmetic, except that the variables that denote the contents of computer registers are in bold-face type. This convention is commonly used in vector algebra. We regard a computer word as a vector of single bits. Constants also appear in bold-face type when they denote the contents of a computer register. (This has no analogy with vector algebra because in vector algebra the only way to write a constant is to display the vector's components.) When a constant denotes part of an instruction, such as the immediate field of a *shift* instruction, light-face type is used.

If an operator such as "+" has bold-face operands, then that operator denotes the computer's addition operation ("vector addition"). If the operands are light-faced, then the operator denotes the ordinary scalar arithmetic operation. We use a light-faced variable x to denote the arithmetic value of a bold-faced variable $\boldsymbol{x}$ under an interpretation (signed or unsigned) that should be clear from the context. Thus, if $\boldsymbol{x} = \mathbf{0x80000000}$ and $\boldsymbol{y} = \mathbf{0x80000000}$, then, under signed integer interpretation, $x = y = -2^{31}$, $x + y = -2^{32}$, and $\boldsymbol{x} + \boldsymbol{y} = \mathbf{0}$. Here, $\mathbf{0x80000000}$ is hexadecimal notation for a bit string consisting of a 1-bit followed by 31 0-bits.

Bits are numbered from the right, with the rightmost (least significant) bit being bit 0. The terms "bits," "nibbles," "bytes," "halfwords," "words," and "doublewords" refer to lengths of 1, 4, 8, 16, 32, and 64 bits, respectively.

1

Short and simple sections of code are written in computer algebra, using its assignment operator (left arrow) and occasionally an *if* statement. In this role, computer algebra is serving as little more than a machine-independent way of writing assembly language code.

Longer or more complex computer programs are written in the C++ programming language. None of the object-oriented features of C++ are used; the programs are basically in C with comments in C++ style. When the distinction is unimportant, the language is referred to simply as "C."

A complete description of C would be out of place in this book, but Table 1–1 contains a brief summary of most of the elements of C [H&S] that are used herein. This is provided for the benefit of the reader who is familiar with some procedural programming language but not with C. Table 1–1 also shows the operators of our computer-algebraic arithmetic language. Operators are listed from highest precedence (tightest binding) to lowest. In the Precedence column, L means left-associative; that is,

$$a \bullet b \bullet c = (a \bullet b) \bullet c$$

and R means right-associative. Our computer-algebraic notation follows C in precedence and associativity.

In addition to the notations described in Table 1–1, those of Boolean algebra and of standard mathematics are used, with explanations where necessary.

TABLE 1–1. EXPRESSIONS OF C AND COMPUTER ALGEBRA

Prece-dence	C	Computer Algebra	Description
	0x...	$0x\ldots, 0b\ldots$	Hexadecimal, binary constants
16	a[k]		Selecting the kth component
16		$x_0, x_1, \ldots$	Different variables, or bit selection (clarified in text)
16	f(x,...)	$f(x, \ldots)$	Function evaluation
16		abs(x)	Absolute value (but abs(-2^{31}) $= -2^{31}$)
16		nabs(x)	Negative of the absolute value
15	x++, x--		Postincrement, decrement
14	++x, --x		Preincrement, decrement
14	(*type name*) x		Type conversion
14 R		x^k	x to the kth power
14	~x	$\neg x, \bar{x}$	Bitwise *not* (one's-complement)
14	!x		Logical *not* (if $x = 0$ then $\mathbf{1}$ else $\mathbf{0}$)

TABLE 1–1. EXPRESSIONS OF C AND COMPUTER ALGEBRA, *continued*

Precedence	C	Computer Algebra	Description
14	-x	$-x$	Arithmetic negation
13 L	x*y	$x * y$	Multiplication, modulo word size
13 L	x/y	$x \div y$	Signed integer division
13 L	x/y	$x \overset{u}{\div} y$	Unsigned integer division
13 L	x%y	$\mathrm{rem}(x, y)$	Remainder (may be negative), of $(x \div y)$, signed arguments
13 L	x%y	$\mathrm{remu}(x, y)$	Remainder of $x \overset{u}{\div} y$, unsigned arguments
		$\mathrm{mod}(x, y)$	x reduced modulo y to the interval $[\mathbf{0}, \mathrm{abs}(y) - \mathbf{1}]$; signed arguments
12 L	x + y, x - y	$x + y, x - y$	Addition, subtraction
11 L	x << y, x >> y	$x \ll y, x \overset{u}{\gg} y$	Shift left, right with 0-fill ("logical" shifts)
11 L	x >> y	$x \overset{s}{\gg} y$	Shift right with sign-fill ("arithmetic" or "algebraic" shift)
11 L		$x \overset{rot}{\ll} y, x \overset{rot}{\gg} y$	Rotate shift left, right
10 L	x < y, x <= y, x > y, x >= y	$x < y, x \le y,$ $x > y, x \ge y$	Signed comparison
10 L	x < y, x <= y, x > y, x >= y	$x \overset{u}{<} y, x \overset{u}{\le} y,$ $x \overset{u}{>} y, x \overset{u}{\ge} y$	Unsigned comparison
9 L	x == y, x != y	$x = y, x \ne y$	Equality, inequality
8 L	x & y	$x \,\&\, y$	Bitwise *and*
7 L	x ^ y	$x \oplus y$	Bitwise *exclusive or*
7 L		$x \equiv y$	Bitwise *equivalence* ($\neg(x \oplus y)$)
6 L	x | y	$x \mid y$	Bitwise *or*
5 L	x && y	$x \overset{\to}{\&} y$	Conditional *and* (if $x = \mathbf{0}$ then $\mathbf{0}$ else if $y = \mathbf{0}$ then $\mathbf{0}$ else $\mathbf{1}$)
4 L	x || y	$x \overset{\to}{\mid} y$	Conditional *or* (if $x \ne \mathbf{0}$ then $\mathbf{1}$ else if $y \ne \mathbf{0}$ then $\mathbf{1}$ else $\mathbf{0}$)
3 L		$x \parallel y$	Concatenation
2 R	x = y	$x \leftarrow y$	Assignment

Our computer algebra uses other functions, in addition to "abs," "rem," and so on. These are defined where introduced.

In C, the expression x < y < z means to evaluate x < y to a 0/1-valued result, and then compare that result to z. In computer algebra, the expression $x < y < z$ means $(x < y)$ & $(y < z)$.

C has three loop control statements: while, do, and for. The while statement is written:

$$\text{while } (\textit{expression}) \text{ } \textit{statement}$$

First, *expression* is evaluated. If **true** (nonzero), *statement* is executed and control returns to evaluate *expression* again. If *expression* is **false** (0), the while-loop terminates.

The do statement is similar, except the test is at the bottom of the loop. It is written:

$$\text{do } \textit{statement} \text{ while } (\textit{expression})$$

First, *statement* is executed, and then *expression* is evaluated. If **true**, the process is repeated, and if **false**, the loop terminates.

The for statement is written:

$$\text{for } (e_1; e_2; e_3) \text{ } \textit{statement}$$

First, e_1, usually an assignment statement, is executed. Then e_2, usually a comparison, is evaluated. If **false**, the for-loop terminates. If **true**, *statement* is executed. Finally, e_3, usually an assignment statement, is executed, and control returns to evaluate e_2 again. Thus, the familiar "do i = 1 to n" is written:

```
for (i = 1; i <= n; i++)
```

(This is one of the few contexts in which we use the postincrement operator.)

1–2 Instruction Set and Execution Time Model

To permit a rough comparison of algorithms, we imagine them being coded for a machine with an instruction set similar to that of today's general purpose RISC computers, such as the Compaq Alpha, the SGI MIPS, and the IBM RS/6000. The machine is three-address and has a fairly large number of general purpose registers—that is, 16 or more. Unless otherwise specified, the registers are 32 bits long. General register 0 contains a permanent 0, and the others can be used uniformly for any purpose.

In the interest of simplicity there are no "special purpose" registers, such as a condition register or a register to hold status bits, such as "overflow." No floating-point operations are described, because that is beyond the scope of this book.

We recognize two varieties of RISC: a "basic RISC," having the instructions shown in Table 1–2, and a "full RISC," having all the instructions of the basic RISC plus those shown in Table 1–3.

TABLE 1–2. BASIC RISC INSTRUCTION SET

Opcode Mnemonic	Operands	Description
add, sub, mul, div, divu, rem, remu	RT,RA,RB	RT ← RA op RB, where op is *add, subtract, multiply, divide signed, divide unsigned, remainder signed,* or *remainder unsigned.*
addi, muli	RT,RA,I	RT ← RA op I, where op is *add* or *multiply*, and I is a 16-bit signed immediate value.
addis	RT,RA,I	RT ← RA + (I || 0x0000).
and, or, xor	RT,RA,RB	RT ← RA op RB, where op is bitwise *and, or,* or *exclusive or.*
andi, ori, xori	RT,RA,Iu	As above, except the last operand is a 16-bit unsigned immediate value.
beq, bne, blt, ble, bgt, bge	RT,target	Branch to target if RT = 0, or if RT ≠ 0, or if RT < 0, or if RT ≤ 0, or if RT > 0, or if RT ≥ 0 (signed integer interpretation of RT).
bt, bf	RT,target	Branch true/false; same as bne/beq resp.
cmpeq, cmpne, cmplt, cmple, cmpgt, cmpge, cmpltu, cmpleu, cmpgtu, cmpgeu	RT,RA,RB	RT gets the result of comparing RA with RB; 0 if **false** and 1 if **true**. Mnemonics denote *compare for equality, inequality, less than,* and so on, as for the branch instructions, and in addition, the suffix "u" denotes an unsigned comparison.
cmpieq, cmpine, cmpilt, cmpile, cmpigt, cmpige	RT,RA,I	Like cmpeq, and so on, except the second comparand is a 16-bit signed immediate value.
cmpiequ, cmpineu, cmpiltu, cmpileu, cmpigtu, cmpigeu	RT,RA,Iu	Like cmpltu, and so on, except the second comparand is a 16-bit unsigned immediate value.
ldbu, ldh, ldhu, ldw	RT,d(RA)	Load an unsigned byte, signed halfword, unsigned halfword, or word into RT from memory at location RA + d, where d is a 16-bit signed immediate value.

continues

TABLE 1–2. BASIC RISC INSTRUCTION SET, *continued*

Opcode Mnemonic	Operands	Description
mulhs, mulhu	RT,RA,RB	RT gets the high-order 32 bits of the product of RA and RB; signed and unsigned.
not	RT,RA	RT ← bitwise one's-complement of RA.
shl, shr, shrs	RT,RA,RB	RT ← RA shifted left or right by the amount given in the rightmost six bits of RB; 0-fill except for shrs, which is sign-fill. (The shift amount is treated modulo 64.)
shli, shri, shrsi	RT,RA,Iu	RT ← RA shifted left or right by the amount given in the 5-bit immediate field.
stb, sth, stw	RS,d(RA)	Store a byte, halfword, or word, from RS into memory at location RA + d, where d is a 16-bit signed immediate value.

In these brief instruction descriptions, RA and RB appearing as source operands really means the contents of those registers.

A real machine would have branch and link (for subroutine calls), branch to the address contained in a register (for subroutine returns and "switches"), and possibly some instructions for dealing with special purpose registers. It would, of course, have a number of privileged instructions and instructions for calling on supervisor services. It might also have floating-point instructions.

Some other computational instructions that a RISC computer might have are identified in Table 1–3. These are discussed in later chapters.

TABLE 1–3. ADDITIONAL INSTRUCTIONS FOR THE "FULL RISC"

Opcode Mnemonic	Operands	Description
abs, nabs	RT,RA	RT gets the absolute value, or the negative of the absolute value, of RA.
andc, eqv, nand, nor, orc	RT,RA,RB	Bitwise *and with complement* (of RB), *equivalence*, *negative and*, *negative or*, and *or with complement*.
extr	RT,RA,I,L	Extract bits I through I+L-1 of RA, and place them right-adjusted in RT, with 0-fill.
extrs	RT,RA,I,L	Like extr, but sign-fill.
ins	RT,RA,I,L	Insert bits 0 through L-1 of RA into bits I through I+L-1 of RT.
nlz	RT,RA	RT gets the number of leading 0's in RA (0 to 32).

TABLE 1–3. ADDITIONAL INSTRUCTIONS FOR THE "FULL RISC," *continued*

Opcode Mnemonic	Operands	Description
pop	RT,RA	RT gets the number of 1-bits in RA (0 to 32).
ldb	RT,d(RA)	Load a signed byte into RT from memory at location RA + d, where d is a 16-bit signed immediate value.
moveq, movne, movlt, movle, movgt, movge	RT,RA,RB	RT ← RB if RA = 0, or if RA ≠ 0, and so on, else RT is unchanged.
shlr, shrr	RT,RA,RB	RT ← RA rotate-shifted left or right by the amount given in the rightmost five bits of RB.
shlri, shrri	RT,RA,Iu	RT ← RA rotate-shifted left or right by the amount given in the 5-bit immediate field.
trpeq, trpne, trplt, trple, trpgt, trpge, trpltu, trpleu, trpgtu, trpgeu	RA,RB	*Trap* (interrupt) if RA = RB, or RA ≠ RB, and so on.
trpieq, trpine, trpilt, trpile, trpigt, trpige	RA,I	Like trpeq, and so on, except the second comparand is a 16-bit signed immediate value.
trpiequ, trpineu, trpiltu, trpileu, trpigtu, trpigeu	RA,Iu	Like trpltu, and so on, except the second comparand is a 16-bit unsigned immediate value.

It is convenient to provide the machine's assembler with a few "extended mnemonics." These are like macros whose expansion is usually a single instruction. Some possibilities are shown in Table 1–4.

TABLE 1–4. EXTENDED MNEMONICS

Extended Mnemonic	Expansion	Description
b target	beq R0,target	*Unconditional branch.*
li RT,I	See text	*Load immediate,* $-2^{31} \leq I < 2^{32}$.
mov RT,RA	ori RT,RA,0	*Move register* RA *to* RT.
neg RT,RA	sub RT,R0,RA	*Negate* (two's-complement).
subi RT,RA,I	addi RT,RA,-I	*Subtract immediate* ($I \neq -2^{15}$).

The *load immediate* instruction expands into one or two instructions, as required by the immediate value *I*. For example, if $0 \le I < 2^{16}$, an *or immediate* (ori) from R0 can be used. If $-2^{15} \le I < 0$, an *add immediate* (addi) from R0 can be used. If the rightmost 16 bits of *I* are 0, *add immediate shifted* (addis) can be used. Otherwise, two instructions are required, such as addis followed by ori. (Alternatively, in the last case a load from memory could be used, but for execution time and space estimates we assume that two elementary arithmetic instructions are used.)

Of course, which instructions belong in the basic RISC, and which belong in the full RISC is very much a matter of judgment. Quite possibly, *divide unsigned* and the *remainder* instructions should be moved to the full RISC category. *Shift right signed* is another suspicious instruction, given its low frequency of use in the SPEC benchmarks. The trouble is, in C it is easy to accidentally use these instructions, by doing a division with unsigned operands when they could just as well be signed, and by doing a shift right with a signed quantity (int) that could just as well be unsigned. Incidentally, *shift right signed* (or *shift right arithmetic,* as it is often called) does *not* do a division of a signed integer by a power of 2; you need to add 1 to the result if the dividend is negative and any nonzero bits are shifted out.

The distinction between basic and full RISC involves many other such questionable judgments, but we won't dwell on them.

The instructions are limited to two source registers and one target, which simplifies the computer (e.g., the register file requires no more than two read ports and one write port). It also simplifies an optimizing compiler, because the compiler does not need to deal with instructions that have multiple targets. The price paid for this is that a program that wants both the quotient and remainder of two numbers (not uncommon) must execute two instructions (*divide* and *remainder*). The usual machine division algorithm produces the remainder as a by-product, so many machines make them both available as a result of one execution of *divide*. Similar remarks apply to obtaining the doubleword product of two words.

The *conditional move* instructions (e.g., moveq) ostensibly have only two source operands, but in a sense they have three. Because the result of the instruction depends on the values in RT, RA, and RB, a machine that executes instructions out of order must treat RT in these instructions as both a *use* and a *set*. That is, an instruction that sets RT, followed by a *conditional move* that sets RT, must be executed in that order, and the result of the first instruction cannot be discarded. Thus, the designer of such a machine may elect to omit the *conditional move* instructions to avoid having to consider an instruction with (logically) three source operands. On the other hand, the *conditional move* instructions do save branches.

Instruction formats are not relevant to the purposes of this book, but the full RISC instruction set described above, with floating point and a few supervisory instructions added, can be implemented with 32-bit instructions on a machine with 32 general purpose registers (5-bit register fields). By reducing the immediate fields of *compare*, *load*, *store*, and *trap* instructions to 14 bits, the same holds for a machine with 64 general purpose registers (6-bit register fields).

Execution Time

We assume that all instructions execute in one cycle, except for the *multiply*, *divide*, and *remainder* instructions, for which we do not assume any particular execution time. Branches take one cycle whether they branch or fall through.

The *load immediate* instruction is counted as one or two cycles, depending on whether one or two elementary arithmetic instructions are required to generate the constant in a register.

Although *load* and *store* instructions are not often used in this book, we assume they take one cycle and ignore any load delay (time lapse between when a load instruction completes in the arithmetic unit, and when the requested data is available for a subsequent instruction).

However, knowing the number of cycles used by all the arithmetic and logical instructions is often insufficient for estimating the execution time of a program. Execution can be slowed substantially by load delays and by delays in fetching instructions. These delays, although very important and increasing in importance, are not discussed in this book. Another factor, one which improves execution time, is what is called "instruction-level parallelism," which is found in many contemporary RISC chips, particularly those for "high-end" machines.

These machines have multiple execution units and sufficient instruction-dispatching capability to execute instructions in parallel when they are independent (that is, when neither uses a result of the other, and they don't both set the same register or status bit). Because this capability is now quite common, the presence of independent operations is often pointed out in this book. Thus, we might say that such and such a formula can be coded in such a way that it requires eight instructions and executes in five cycles on a machine with unlimited instruction-level parallelism. This means that if the instructions are arranged in the proper order ("scheduled"), a machine with a sufficient number of adders, shifters, logical units, and registers can in principle execute the code in five cycles.

We do not make too much of this, because machines differ greatly in their instruction-level parallelism capabilities. For example, an IBM RS/6000 processor from ca. 1992 has a three-input adder, and can execute two consecutive *add*-type instructions in parallel even when one feeds the other (e.g., an *add* feeding a *compare*, or the base register of a *load*). As a contrary example, consider a simple computer, possibly for low-cost embedded applications, that has only one read port on its register file. Normally, this machine would take an extra cycle to do a second read of the register file for an instruction that has two register input operands. However, suppose it has a bypass so that if an instruction feeds an operand of the immediately following instruction, then that operand is available without reading the register file. On such a machine, it is actually advantageous if each instruction feeds the next—that is, if the code has no parallelism.

CHAPTER 2

BASICS

2–1 Manipulating Rightmost Bits

Some of the formulas in this section find application in later chapters.

Use the following formula to turn off the rightmost 1-bit in a word, producing 0 if none (e.g., $0101\,1000 \Rightarrow 0101\,0000$):

$$x \,\&\, (x - 1)$$

This may be used to determine if an unsigned integer is a power of 2; apply the formula followed by a 0-test on the result.

Similarly, the following formula can be used to test if an unsigned integer is of the form $2^n - 1$ (including 0 or all 1's):

$$x \,\&\, (x + 1)$$

Use the following formula to isolate the rightmost 1-bit, producing 0 if none (e.g., $0101\,1000 \Rightarrow 0000\,1000$):

$$x \,\&\, (-x)$$

Use the following formula to isolate the rightmost 0-bit, producing 0 if none (e.g., $10100111 \rightarrow 0000\,1000$):

$$\neg x \,\&\, (x + 1)$$

Use one of the following formulas to form a mask that identifies the trailing 0's, producing all 1's if $x = 0$ (e.g., $0101\,1000 \Rightarrow 00000111$):

$$\neg x \,\&\, (x - 1), \quad \text{or}$$
$$\neg(x \mid -x), \quad \text{or}$$
$$(x \,\&\, -x) - 1$$

The first formula has some instruction-level parallelism.

Use the following formula to form a mask that identifies the rightmost 1-bit and the trailing 0's, producing all 1's if $x = 0$ (e.g., $0101\,1000 \Rightarrow 0000\,1111$):

$$x \oplus (x - 1)$$

Use the following formula to right-propagate the rightmost 1-bit, producing all 1's if $x = 0$ (e.g., $0101\,1000 \Rightarrow 0101\,1111$):

$$x \mid (x - 1)$$

Use the following formula to turn off the rightmost contiguous string of 1-bits (e.g., $0101\,1000 \Rightarrow 0100\,0000$):

$$((x \mid (x - 1)) + 1) \,\&\, x$$

This may be used to see if a nonnegative integer is of the form $2^j - 2^k$ for some $j \geq k \geq 0$; apply the formula followed by a 0-test of the result.

These formulas all have duals in the following sense. Read what the formula does, interchanging 1's and 0's in the description. Then, in the formula, replace $x - 1$ with $x + 1$, $x + 1$ with $x - 1$, $-x$ with $\neg(x + 1)$, & with |, and | with &. Leave x and $\neg x$ alone. Then the result is a valid description and formula. For example, the dual of the first formula in this section reads as follows:

Use the following formula to turn on the rightmost 0-bit in a word, producing all 1's if none (e.g., $10100111 \Rightarrow 10101111$):

$$x \mid (x + 1)$$

There is a simple test to determine whether or not a given function can be implemented with a sequence of *add*'s, *subtract*'s, *and*'s, *or*'s, and *not*'s [War]. We may, of course, expand the list with other instructions that can be composed from the basic list, such as *shift left* by a fixed amount (which is equivalent to a sequence of *add*'s), or *multiply*. However, we exclude instructions that cannot be composed from the list. The test is contained in the following theorem.

> THEOREM. *A function mapping words to words can be implemented with word-parallel add, subtract, and, or, and not instructions if and only if each bit of the result depends only on bits at and to the right of each input operand.*

That is, imagine trying to compute the rightmost bit of the result by looking only at the rightmost bit of each input operand. Then, try to compute the next bit to the left by looking only at the rightmost two bits of each input operand, and so forth. If you are successful in this, then the function can be computed with a sequence of *add*'s, *and*'s, and so on. If the function cannot be computed in this right-to-left manner, then it cannot be implemented with a sequence of such instructions.

The interesting part of this is the latter statement, and it is simply the contrapositive of the observation that the functions *add*, *subtract*, *and*, *or*, and *not* can all be computed in the right-to-left manner, so any combination of them must have this property.

To see the "if" part of the theorem, we need a construction that is a little awkward to explain. We illustrate it with a specific example. Suppose that a function of two variables x and y has the right-to-left computability property, and suppose that bit 2 of the result r is given by

$$r_2 = x_2 \mid (x_0 \mathbin{\&} y_1). \tag{1}$$

We number bits from right to left, 0 to 31. Because bit 2 of the result is a function of bits at and to the right of bit 2 of the input operands, bit 2 of the result is "right-to-left computable."

Arrange the computer words x, x shifted left two, and y shifted left one, as shown below. Also, add a mask that isolates bit 2.

$$
\begin{array}{cccccc}
x_{31} & x_{30} & \cdots & x_3 & x_2 & x_1 & x_0 \\
x_{29} & x_{28} & \cdots & x_1 & x_0 & 0 & 0 \\
y_{30} & y_{29} & \cdots & y_2 & y_1 & y_0 & 0 \\
0 & 0 & \cdots & 0 & 1 & 0 & 0 \\
0 & 0 & \cdots & 0 & r_2 & 0 & 0
\end{array}
$$

Now, form the word-parallel *and* of lines 2 and 3, *or* the result with row 1 (following Equation (1)), and *and* the result with the mask (row 4 above). The result is a word of all 0's except for the desired result bit in position 2. Perform similar computations for the other bits of the result, *or* the 32 resulting words together, and the result is the desired function.

This construction does not yield an efficient program; rather, it merely shows that it can be done with instructions in the basic list.

Using the theorem, we immediately see that there is no sequence of such instructions that turns off the leftmost 1-bit in a word, because to see if a certain 1-bit should be turned off, we must look to the left to see if it is the leftmost one. Similarly, there can be no such sequence for performing a right shift, or a rotate shift, or a left shift by a variable amount, or for counting the number of trailing 0's in a word (to count trailing 0's, the rightmost bit of the result will be 1 if there are an odd number of trailing 0's, and we must look to the left of the rightmost position to determine that).

A novel application of the sort of bit twiddling discussed above is the problem of finding the next higher number after a given number that has the same number of 1-bits. You are forgiven if you are asking, "Why on earth would anyone want to compute that?" It has application where bit strings are used to represent subsets. The possible members of a set are listed in a linear array, and a subset is represented by a word or sequence of words in which bit i is on if member i is in the subset. Set unions are computed by the logical *or* of the bit strings, intersections by *and*'s, and so on.

You might want to iterate through all the subsets of a given size. This is easily done if you have a function that maps a given subset to the next higher number (interpreting the subset string as an integer) with the same number of 1-bits.

A concise algorithm for this operation was devised by R. W. Gosper [HAK, item 175].[1] Given a word x that represents a subset, the idea is to find the rightmost contiguous group of 1's in x and the following 0's, and "increment" that quantity to the next value that has the same number of 1's. For example, the string xxx0 1111 0000, where xxx represents arbitrary bits, becomes xxx1 0000 0111. The algorithm first identifies the "smallest" 1-bit in x, with $s = x \& -x$, giving 0000 0001 0000. This is added to x, giving $r =$ xxx1 0000 0000. The 1-bit here is one bit of the result. For the other bits, we need to produce a right-adjusted string of $n - 1$ 1's, where n is the size of the rightmost group of 1's in x. This can be done by first forming the *exclusive or* of r and x, which gives 0001 1111 0000 in our example.

This has two too many 1's, and needs to be right-adjusted. This can be accomplished by dividing it by s, which right-adjusts it (s is a power of 2), and shifting it right two more positions to discard the two unwanted bits. The final result is the *or* of this and r.

In computer algebra notation, the result is y in

$$s \leftarrow x \& -x$$
$$r \leftarrow s + x \qquad\qquad (2)$$
$$y \leftarrow r \mid (((x \oplus r) \overset{u}{\gg} 2) \overset{u}{\div} s)$$

A complete C procedure is given in Figure 2–1. It executes in seven basic RISC instructions, one of which is division. (Do not use this procedure with $x = 0$; that causes division by 0.)

```
unsigned snoob(unsigned x) {
    unsigned smallest, ripple, ones;
                                  // x = xxx0 1111 0000
    smallest = x & -x;           //       0000 0001 0000
    ripple = x + smallest;       //       xxx1 0000 0000
    ones = x ^ ripple;           //       0001 1111 0000
    ones = (ones >> 2)/smallest; //       0000 0000 0111
    return ripple | ones;        //       xxx1 0000 0111
}
```

FIGURE 2–1. Next higher number with same number of 1-bits.

---

1. A variation of this algorithm appears in [H&S] sec. 7.6.7.

If division is slow but you have a fast way to compute the *number of trailing zeros* function ntz(x), the *number of leading zeros* function nlz(x), or *population count* (pop(x) is the number of 1-bits in x), then the last line of Equation (2) can be replaced with one of the following:

$$y \leftarrow r \mid ((x \oplus r) \overset{u}{\gg} (2 + \text{ntz}(x)))$$

$$y \leftarrow r \mid ((x \oplus r) \overset{u}{\gg} (33 - \text{nlz}(s)))$$

$$y \leftarrow r \mid ((1 \ll (\text{pop}(x \oplus r) - 2)) - 1)$$

2–2 Addition Combined with Logical Operations

We assume the reader is familiar with the elementary identities of ordinary algebra and Boolean algebra. Below is a selection of similar identities involving addition and subtraction combined with logical operations:

a. $\quad -x = \neg x + 1$

b. $\qquad = \neg(x - 1)$

c. $\quad \neg x = -x - 1$

d. $\quad -\neg x = x + 1$

e. $\quad \neg -x = x - 1$

f. $\quad x + y = x - \neg y - 1$

g. $\qquad = (x \oplus y) + 2(x \& y)$

h. $\qquad = (x \mid y) + (x \& y)$

i. $\qquad = 2(x \mid y) - (x \oplus y)$

j. $\quad x - y = x + \neg y + 1$

k. $\qquad = (x \oplus y) - 2(\neg x \& y)$

l. $\qquad = (x \& \neg y) - (\neg x \& y)$

m. $\qquad = 2(x \& \neg y) - (x \oplus y)$

n. $\quad x \oplus y = (x \mid y) - (x \& y)$

o. $\quad x \& \neg y = (x \mid y) - y$

p. $\qquad = x - (x \& y)$

q. $\quad \neg(x - y) = y - x - 1$

r. $\qquad = \neg x + y$

s. $\quad x \equiv y = (x \& y) - (x \mid y) - 1$

t. $\qquad = (x \& y) + \neg(x \mid y)$

u. $\quad x \mid y = (x \& \neg y) + y$

v. $\quad x \& y = (\neg x \mid y) - \neg x$

Equation (d) may be applied to itself repeatedly, giving $-\neg-\neg x = x + 2$, and so on. Similarly, from (e) we have $\neg-\neg-x = x - 2$. So we can add or subtract any constant, using only the two forms of complementation.

Equation (f) is the dual of (j), where (j) is the well-known relation that shows how to build a subtracter from an adder.

Equations (g) and (h) are from HAKMEM memo [HAK, item 23]. Equation (g) forms a sum by first computing the sum with carries ignored $(x \oplus y)$, and then adding in the carries. Equation (h) is simply modifying the addition operands so that the combination $0 + 1$ never occurs at any bit position; it is replaced with $1 + 0$.

It can be shown that in the ordinary addition of binary numbers with each bit independently equally likely to be 0 or 1, a carry occurs at each position with probability about 0.5. However, for an adder built by preconditioning the inputs using (g), the probability is about 0.25. This observation is probably not of value in building an adder, because for that purpose the important characteristic is the maximum number of logic circuits the carry must pass through, and using (g) reduces the number of stages the carry propagates through by only one.

Equations (k) and (l) are duals of (g) and (h), for subtraction. That is, (k) has the interpretation of first forming the difference ignoring the borrows $(x \oplus y)$, and then subtracting the borrows. Similarly, Equation (l) is simply modifying the subtraction operands so that the combination $1 - 1$ never occurs at any bit position; it is replaced with $0 - 0$.

Equation (n) shows how to implement *exclusive or* in only three instructions on a basic RISC. Using only *and-or-not* logic requires four instructions $((x \mid y) \& \neg(x \& y))$. Similarly, (u) and (v) show how to implement *and* and *or* in three other elementary instructions, whereas using DeMorgan's laws requires four.

2–3 Inequalities among Logical and Arithmetic Expressions

Inequalities among binary logical expressions whose values are interpreted as unsigned integers are nearly trivial to derive. Here are two examples:

$$(x \oplus y) \overset{u}{\leqq} (x \mid y), \quad \text{and}$$

$$(x \& y) \overset{u}{\leqq} (x \equiv y).$$

These can be derived from a list of all binary logical operations, shown in Table 2–1.

Let $f(x, y)$ and $g(x, y)$ represent two columns in Table 2–1. If for each row in which $f(x, y)$ is 1, $g(x, y)$ also is 1, then for all (x, y), $f(x, y) \overset{u}{\leqq} g(x, y)$. Clearly, this extends to word-parallel logical operations. One can easily read off such relations (most of which are trivial) as $(x \& y) \overset{u}{\leqq} x \overset{u}{\leqq} (x \mid \neg y)$, and so on. Furthermore, if two columns have a row in which one entry is 0 and the other is 1, and another row in which the entries are 1 and 0, respectively, then no inequality relation exists between the corresponding logical expressions. So the question of

TABLE 2–1. THE 16 BINARY LOGICAL OPERATIONS

x	y	0	$x \& y$	$x \& \neg y$	x	$\neg x \& y$	y	$x \oplus y$	$x \mid y$	$\neg(x \mid y)$	$x \equiv y$	$\neg y$	$x \mid \neg y$	$\neg x$	$\neg x \mid y$	$\neg(x \& y)$	1
0	0	0	0	0	0	0	0	0	0	1	1	1	1	1	1	1	1
0	1	0	0	0	0	1	1	1	1	0	0	0	0	1	1	1	1
1	0	0	0	1	1	0	0	1	1	0	0	1	1	0	0	1	1
1	1	0	1	0	1	0	1	0	1	0	1	0	1	0	1	0	1

whether or not $f(x, y) \overset{u}{\leq} g(x, y)$ is completely and easily solved for all binary logical functions f and g.

Use caution when manipulating these relations. For example, for ordinary arithmetic, if $x + y \leq a$ and $z \leq x$, then $z + y \leq a$. But this inference is not valid if "+" is replaced with *or*.

Inequalities involving mixed logical and arithmetic expressions are more interesting. Below is a small selection.

a. $(x \mid y) \overset{u}{\geq} \max(x, y)$

b. $(x \& y) \overset{u}{\leq} \min(x, y)$

c. $(x \mid y) \overset{u}{\leq} x + y$ if the addition does not overflow

d. $(x \mid y) \overset{u}{>} x + y$ if the addition overflows

e. $|x - y| \overset{u}{\leq} (x \oplus y)$

The proofs of these are quite simple, except possibly for the relation $|x - y| \overset{u}{\leq} (x \oplus y)$. By $|x - y|$ we mean the absolute value of $x - y$, which may be computed within the domain of unsigned numbers as $\max(x, y) - \min(x, y)$. This relation may be proven by induction on the length of x and y (the proof is a little easier if you extend them on the left rather than on the right).

2–4 Absolute Value Function

If your machine does not have an instruction for computing the absolute value, this computation can usually be done in three or four branch-free instructions. First, compute $y \leftarrow x \overset{s}{\gg} 31$, and then one of the following:

abs	nabs
$(x \oplus y) - y$	$y - (x \oplus y)$
$(x + y) \oplus y$	$(y - x) \oplus y$
$x - (2x \& y)$	$(2x \& y) - x$

By "$2x$" we mean, of course, $x + x$ or $x \ll 1$.

If you have a fast multiply by a variable whose value is ±1, the following will do:

$$((x \overset{s}{\gg} 30) \mid 1) * x$$

2–5 Sign Extension

By "sign extension," we mean to consider a certain bit position in a word to be the sign bit, and we wish to propagate that to the left, ignoring any other bits present. The standard way to do this is with *shift left logical* followed by *shift right signed*. However, if these instructions are slow or nonexistent on your machine, it may be done with one of the following, where we illustrate by propagating bit position 7 to the left:

$$((x + 0x00000080) \; \& \; 0x000000FF) - 0x00000080$$

$$((x \; \& \; 0x000000FF) \oplus 0x00000080) - 0x00000080$$

The "+" above can also be "–" or "⊕." The second formula is particularly useful if you know that the unwanted high-order bits are all 0's, because then the *and* can be omitted.

2–6 Shift Right Signed from Unsigned

If your machine does not have the *shift right signed* instruction, it may be computed using the formulas shown below. The first formula is from [GM], and the second is based on the same idea. Assuming the machine has mod 64 shifts, the first four formulas hold for $0 \le n \le 31$, and the last holds for $0 \le n \le 63$. The last formula holds for any n if by "holds" we mean "treats the shift amount to the same modulus as does the logical shift."

When n is a variable, each formula requires five or six instructions on a basic RISC.

$$((x + 0x80000000) \overset{u}{\gg} n) - (0x80000000 \overset{u}{\gg} n)$$

$$t \leftarrow 0x80000000 \overset{u}{\gg} n; \qquad ((x \overset{u}{\gg} n) \oplus t) - t$$

$$t \leftarrow (x \; \& \; 0x80000000) \overset{u}{\gg} n; \; (x \overset{u}{\gg} n) - (t + t)$$

$$(x \overset{u}{\gg} n) \mid (-(x \overset{u}{\gg} 31) \ll 31 - n)$$

$$t \leftarrow -(x \overset{u}{\gg} 31); \qquad ((x \oplus t) \overset{u}{\gg} n) \oplus t$$

In the first two formulas, an alternative for the expression $0x80000000 \overset{u}{\gg} n$ is $1 \ll 31 - n$.

If n is a constant, the first two formulas require only three instructions on many machines. If $n = 31$, the function can be done in two instructions with $-(x \overset{u}{\gg} 31)$.

2–7 *Sign* Function

The *sign*, or *signum*, function is defined by

$$\text{sign}(x) = \begin{cases} -1, & x < 0, \\ 0, & x = 0, \\ 1, & x > 0. \end{cases}$$

It may be calculated with four instructions on most machines [Hop]:

$$(x \overset{s}{\gg} 31) \mid (-x \overset{u}{\gg} 31)$$

If you don't have *shift right signed*, then use the substitute noted at the end of Section 2–6, giving the following nicely symmetric formula (five instructions):

$$-(x \overset{u}{\gg} 31) \mid (-x \overset{u}{\gg} 31)$$

Comparison predicate instructions permit a three-instruction solution, with either

$$\begin{aligned} &(x > 0) - (x < 0), \text{ or} \\ &(x \ge 0) - (x \le 0). \end{aligned} \tag{3}$$

Finally, we note that the formula $(-x \overset{u}{\gg} 31) - (x \overset{u}{\gg} 31)$ almost works; it fails only for $x = -2^{31}$.

2–8 *Three-Valued Compare* Function

The *three-valued compare* function, a slight generalization of the *sign* function, is defined by

$$\text{cmp}(x, y) = \begin{cases} -1, & x < y, \\ 0, & x = y, \\ 1, & x > y. \end{cases}$$

There are both signed and unsigned versions, and unless otherwise specified, this section applies to both.

Comparison predicate instructions permit a three-instruction solution, an obvious generalization of Equations (3):

$$(x > y) - (x < y), \quad \text{or}$$
$$(x \geq y) - (x \leq y).$$

A solution for unsigned integers on PowerPC is shown below [CWG]. On this machine, "carry" is "not borrow."

```
subf   R5,Ry,Rx    # R5 <-- Rx - Ry.
subfc  R6,Rx,Ry    # R6 <-- Ry - Rx, set carry.
subfe  R7,Ry,Rx    # R7 <-- Rx - Ry + carry, set carry.
subfe  R8,R7,R5    # R8 <-- R5 - R7 + carry, (set carry).
```

If limited to the instructions of the basic RISC, there does not seem to be any particularly good way to compute this function. The comparison predicates $x < y$, $x \leq y$, and so on, require about five instructions (see Section 2–11), leading to a solution in about 12 instructions (using a small amount of commonality in computing $x < y$ and $x > y$). On the basic RISC it's probably preferable to use compares and branches (six instructions executed worst case if compares can be commoned).

2–9 Transfer of Sign

The *transfer of sign* function, called ISIGN in Fortran, is defined by

$$\text{ISIGN}(x, y) = \begin{cases} \text{abs}(x), & y \geq 0, \\ -\text{abs}(x), & y < 0. \end{cases}$$

This function can be calculated (modulo 2^{32}) with four instructions on most machines:

$$t \leftarrow y \overset{s}{\gg} 31; \qquad\qquad\qquad t \leftarrow (x \oplus y) \overset{s}{\gg} 31;$$
$$\text{ISIGN}(x, y) = (\text{abs}(x) \oplus t) - t \qquad \text{ISIGN}(x, y) = (x \oplus t) - t$$
$$= (\text{abs}(x) + t) \oplus t \qquad\qquad\qquad = (x + t) \oplus t$$

2–10 Decoding a "Zero Means 2**n" Field

Sometimes a 0 or negative value does not make much sense for a quantity, so it is encoded in an n-bit field with a 0 value being understood to mean 2^n, and a non-zero value having its normal binary interpretation. An example is the length field of PowerPC's *load string word immediate* (lswi) instruction, which occupies five bits. It is not useful to have an instruction that loads zero bytes, when the length is an immediate quantity, but it is definitely useful to be able to load 32 bytes. The length field could be encoded with values from 0 to 31 denoting lengths from 1 to 32, but the "zero means 32" convention results in simpler logic when the processor must also support a corresponding instruction with a variable (in-register) length that employs straight binary encoding (e.g., PowerPC's lswx instruction).

It is trivial to encode an integer in the range 1 to 2^n into the "zero means 2^n" encoding—simply mask the integer with $2^n - 1$. To do the decoding without a test-and-branch is not quite as simple, but below are some possibilities (no doubt overdone), illustrated for a 3-bit field. They all require three instructions, not counting possible loads of constants.

$$((x - 1)\ \&\ 7) + 1 \qquad ((x + 7)\ |\ -8) + 9 \qquad 8 - (-x\ \&\ 7)$$

$$((x + 7)\ \&\ 7) + 1 \qquad ((x + 7)\ |\ 8) - 7 \qquad -(-x\ |\ -8)$$

$$((x - 1)\ |\ -8) + 9 \qquad ((x - 1)\ \&\ 8) + x$$

2–11 Comparison Predicates

A "comparison predicate" is a function that compares two quantities, producing a single bit result of 1 if the comparison is **true**, and 0 if the comparison is **false**. Below we show branch-free expressions to evaluate the result into the sign position. To produce the 1/0 value used by some languages (e.g., C), follow the code with a *shift right* of 31. To produce the $-1/0$ result used by some other languages (e.g., Basic), follow the code with a *shift right signed* of 31.

These formulas are, of course, not of interest on machines such as MIPS, the Compaq Alpha, and our model RISC, which have comparison instructions that compute many of these predicates directly, placing a 0/1-valued result in a general purpose register.

A machine instruction that computes the negative of the absolute value is handy here. We show this function as "nabs." Unlike absolute value, it is well defined in that it never overflows. Machines that do not have "nabs" but have the more usual "abs" can use $-\text{abs}(x)$ for $\text{nabs}(x)$. If x is the maximum negative number, this overflows twice, but the result is correct. (We assume that the absolute value and the negation of the maximum negative number is itself.) Because some machines have neither "abs" nor "nabs," we give an alternative that does not use them.

The "nlz" function is the number of leading zeros in its argument. The "doz" function (*difference or zero*) is described on page 37.

$x = y$: $\text{abs}(x - y) - 1$

$\text{abs}(x - y + \textbf{0x8000\,0000})$

$\text{nlz}(x - y) \ll 26$

$-(\text{nlz}(x - y) \overset{u}{\gg} 5)$

$\neg(x - y \mid y - x)$

$x \neq y$: $\text{nabs}(x - y)$

$\text{nlz}(x - y) - 32$

$x - y \mid y - x$

$x < y$: $(x - y) \oplus [(x \oplus y) \,\&\, ((x - y) \oplus x)]$

$(x \,\&\, \neg y) \mid ((x \equiv y) \,\&\, (x - y))$

$\text{nabs}(\text{doz}(y, x))$ [GSO]

$x \leq y$: $(x \mid \neg y) \,\&\, ((x \oplus y) \mid \neg(y - x))$

$((x \equiv y) \overset{s}{\gg} 1) + (x \,\&\, \neg y)$ [GSO]

$x \overset{u}{<} y$: $(\neg x \,\&\, y) \mid ((x \equiv y) \,\&\, (x - y))$

$(\neg x \,\&\, y) \mid ((\neg x \mid y) \,\&\, (x - y))$

$x \overset{u}{\leq} y$: $(\neg x \mid y) \,\&\, ((x \oplus y) \mid \neg(y - x))$

For $x > y$, $x \geq y$, and so on, interchange x and y in the formulas for $x < y$, $x \leq y$, and so on. The *add* of **0x8000 0000** may be replaced with any instruction that inverts the high-order bit (in x, y, or $x - y$).

Another class of formulas can be derived from the observation that the predicate $x < y$ is given by the sign of $x/2 - y/2$, and the subtraction in that expression cannot overflow. The result can be fixed up by subtracting 1 in the cases in which the shifts discard essential information, as follows:

$$x < y: \qquad (x \overset{s}{\gg} 1) - (y \overset{s}{\gg} 1) - (\neg x \,\&\, y \,\&\, 1)$$

$$x \overset{u}{<} y: \qquad (x \overset{u}{\gg} 1) - (y \overset{u}{\gg} 1) - (\neg x \,\&\, y \,\&\, 1)$$

These execute in seven instructions on most machines (six if it has *and not*), which is no better than what we have above (five to seven instructions, depending upon the fullness of the set of logic instructions).

The formulas above involving "nlz" are due to [Shep], and his formula for the $x = y$ predicate is particularly useful because a minor variation of it gets the predicate evaluated to a 1/0-valued result with only three instructions:

$$\text{nlz}(x - y) \overset{u}{\gg} 5.$$

Signed comparisons to 0 are frequent enough to deserve special mention. Below are some formulas for these, mostly derived directly from the above. Again, the result is in the sign position.

$$x = 0: \qquad \mathrm{abs}(x) - 1$$
$$\mathrm{abs}(x + \mathbf{0x80000000})$$
$$\mathrm{nlz}(x) \ll 26$$
$$-(\mathrm{nlz}(x) \overset{u}{\gg} 5)$$
$$\neg(x \mid -x)$$
$$\neg x \mathbin{\&} (x - 1)$$

$$x \neq 0: \qquad \mathrm{nabs}(x)$$
$$\mathrm{nlz}(x) - \mathbf{32}$$
$$x \mid -x$$
$$(x \overset{u}{\gg} 1) - x \qquad\qquad [\mathrm{CWG}]$$

$$x < 0: \qquad x$$

$$x \leq 0: \qquad x \mid (x - 1)$$
$$x \mid \neg{-}x$$

$$x > 0: \qquad x \oplus \mathrm{nabs}(x)$$
$$(x \overset{s}{\gg} 1) - x$$
$$-x \mathbin{\&} \neg x$$

$$x \geq 0: \qquad \neg x$$

Signed comparisons can be obtained from their unsigned counterparts by biasing the signed operands upwards by 2^{31} and interpreting the results as unsigned integers. The reverse transformation also works. Thus we have

$$x < y = x + 2^{31} \overset{u}{<} y + 2^{31},$$

$$x \overset{u}{<} y = x - 2^{31} < y - 2^{31}.$$

Similar relations hold for $\leq$, $\overset{u}{\leq}$, and so on. Addition and subtraction of 2^{31} are equivalent, as they amount to inverting the sign bit.

Another way to get signed comparisons from unsigned is based on the fact that if x and y have the same sign, then $x < y = x \overset{u}{<} y$, whereas if they have opposite signs, then $x < y = x \overset{u}{>} y$ [Lamp]. Again, the reverse transformation also works, so we have

$$x < y = (x \overset{u}{<} y) \oplus x_{31} \oplus y_{31} \quad \text{and}$$

$$x \overset{u}{<} y = (x < y) \oplus x_{31} \oplus y_{31},$$

where x_{31} and y_{31} are the sign bits of x and y, respectively. Similar relations hold for $\leq$, $\overset{u}{\leq}$, and so on.

Using either of these devices enables computing all the usual comparison predicates other than $=$ and $\neq$ in terms of any one of them, with at most three additional instructions on most machines. For example, let us take $x \overset{u}{\leq} y$ as primitive, because it is one of the simplest to implement (it is the carry bit from $y - x$). Then the other predicates can be obtained as follows:

$$x < y \;=\; \neg(y + 2^{31} \overset{u}{\leq} x + 2^{31})$$

$$x \leq y \;=\; x + 2^{31} \overset{u}{\leq} y + 2^{31}$$

$$x > y \;=\; \neg(x + 2^{31} \overset{u}{\leq} y + 2^{31})$$

$$x \geq y \;=\; y + 2^{31} \overset{u}{\leq} x + 2^{31}$$

$$x \overset{u}{<} y \;=\; \neg(y \overset{u}{\leq} x)$$

$$x \overset{u}{>} y \;=\; \neg(x \overset{u}{\leq} y)$$

$$x \overset{u}{\geq} y \;=\; y \overset{u}{\leq} x$$

Comparison Predicates from the Carry Bit

If the machine can easily deliver the carry bit into a general purpose register, this may permit concise code for some of the comparison predicates. Below are listed several of these relations. The notation carry(*expression*) means the carry bit generated by the outermost operation in *expression*. We assume the carry bit for the subtraction $x - y$ is what comes out of the adder for $x + \bar{y} + 1$, which is the complement of "borrow."

$x = y$:   carry$(0 - (x - y))$, or carry$((x + y) + 1)$, or

            carry$((x - y - 1) + 1)$

$x \neq y$:   carry$((x - y) - 1)$, i.e., carry$((x - y) + (-1))$

$x < y$: $\neg$carry$((x + 2^{31}) - (y + 2^{31}))$

$x \leq y$:   carry$((y + 2^{31}) - (x + 2^{31}))$

$x \overset{u}{<} y$: $\neg$carry$(x - y)$

$x \overset{u}{\leq} y$:   carry$(y - x)$

$x = 0$:   carry$(0 - x)$, or carry$(\bar{x} + 1)$

$x \neq 0$:   carry$(x - 1)$, i.e., carry$(x + (-1))$

$x < 0$:   carry$(x + x)$

$x \leq 0$:   carry$(2^{31} - (x + 2^{31}))$

For $x > y$, use the complement of the expression for $x \leq y$, and similarly for other relations involving "greater than."

The GNU Superoptimizer has been applied to the problem of computing predicate expressions on the IBM RS/6000 computer and its close relative PowerPC [GK]. The RS/6000 has instructions for abs(x), nabs(x), doz(x, y), and a number of forms of *add* and *subtract* that use the carry bit. It was found that the RS/6000 can compute all the integer predicate expressions with three or fewer elementary (one-cycle) instructions, a result that surprised even the architects of the machine. "All" includes the six two-operand signed comparisons and the four two-operand unsigned comparisons, all of these with the second operand being 0, and all in forms that produce a 1/0 result or a −1/0 result. PowerPC, which lacks abs(x), nabs(x), and doz(x, y), can compute all the predicate expressions in four or fewer elementary instructions.

How the Computer Sets the Comparison Predicates

Most computers have a way of evaluating the integer comparison predicates to a 1-bit result. The result bit may be placed in a "condition register" or, for some machines (such as our RISC model), in a general purpose register. In either case, the facility is often implemented by subtracting the comparison operands and then performing a small amount of logic on the result bits to determine the 1-bit comparison result.

Below is the logic for these operations. It is assumed that the machine computes $x - y$ as $x + \bar{y} + 1$, and the following quantities are available in the result:

C_o, the carry out of the high-order position
C_i, the carry into the high-order position
N, the sign bit of the result
Z, which equals 1 if the result, exclusive of C_o, is all-0, and is otherwise 0

Then we have the following in Boolean algebra notation (juxtaposition denotes *and*, + denotes *or*):

$$
\begin{array}{rll}
V: & C_i \oplus C_o & \text{(signed overflow)} \\
x = y: & Z & \\
x \neq y: & \bar{Z} & \\
x < y: & N \oplus V & \\
x \leq y: & (N \oplus V) + Z & \\
x > y: & (N \equiv V)\bar{Z} & \\
x \geq y: & N \equiv V & \\
x \overset{u}{<} y: & \bar{C_o} & \\
x \overset{u}{\leq} y: & \bar{C_o} + Z & \\
x \overset{u}{>} y: & C_o\bar{Z} & \\
x \overset{u}{\geq} y: & C_o & \\
\end{array}
$$

2–12 Overflow Detection

"Overflow" means that the result of an arithmetic operation is too large or too small to be correctly represented in the target register. This section discusses methods that a programmer might use to detect when overflow has occurred, without using the machine's "status bits" that are often supplied expressly for this purpose. This is important because some machines do not have such status bits (e.g., MIPS), and because even if the machine is so equipped, it is often difficult or impossible to access the bits from a high-level language.

Signed Add/Subtract

When overflow occurs on integer addition and subtraction, contemporary machines invariably discard the high-order bit of the result and store the low-order bits that the adder naturally produces. Signed integer overflow of addition occurs if and only if the operands have the same sign and the sum has sign opposite to that of the operands. Surprisingly, this same rule applies even if there is a carry into the adder—that is, if the calculation is $x + y + 1$. This is important for the application of adding multiword signed integers, in which the last addition is a signed addition of two fullwords and a carry-in that may be 0 or +1.

To prove the rule for addition, let x and y denote the values of the one-word signed integers being added, let c (carry-in) be 0 or 1, and assume for simplicity a 4-bit machine. Then if the signs of x and y are different,

$$-8 \le x \le -1, \text{ and}$$
$$0 \le y \le 7,$$

or similar bounds apply if x is nonnegative and y is negative. In either case, by adding these inequalities and optionally adding in 1 for c,

$$-8 \le x + y + c \le 7.$$

This is representable as a 4-bit signed integer, and thus overflow does not occur when the operands have opposite signs.

Now suppose x and y have the same sign. There are two cases:

(a)	(b)
$-8 \le x \le -1$	$0 \le x \le 7$
$-8 \le y \le -1$	$0 \le y \le 7$

Thus,

(a)	(b)
$-16 \le x + y + c \le -1$	$0 \le x + y + c \le 15.$

Overflow occurs if the sum is not representable as a 4-bit signed integer—that is, if

$$\text{(a)} \qquad\qquad\qquad \text{(b)}$$
$$-16 \le x + y + c \le -9 \qquad 8 \le x + y + c \le 15.$$

In case (a), this is equivalent to the high-order bit of the 4-bit sum being 0, which is opposite to the sign of x and y. In case (b), this is equivalent to the high-order bit of the 4-bit sum being 1, which again is opposite to the sign of x and y.

For subtraction of multiword integers, the computation of interest is $x - y - c$, where again c is 0 or 1, with a value of 1 representing a borrow-in. From an analysis similar to the above, it can be seen that overflow in the final value of $x - y - c$ occurs if and only if x and y have opposite signs and the sign of $x - y - c$ is opposite to that of x (or, equivalently, the same as that of y).

This leads to the following expressions for the overflow predicate, with the result being in the sign position. Following these with a *shift right* or *shift right signed* of 31 produces a 1/0- or a −1/0-valued result.

$$x + y + c \qquad\qquad\qquad x - y - c$$

$$(x \equiv y)\ \&\ ((x+y+c) \oplus x) \qquad (x \oplus y)\ \&\ ((x-y-c) \oplus x)$$

$$((x+y+c) \oplus x)\ \&\ ((x+y+c) \oplus y) \qquad ((x-y-c) \oplus x)\ \&\ ((x-y-c) \equiv y)$$

By choosing the second alternative in the first column, and the first alternative in the second column (avoiding the *equivalence* operation), our basic RISC can evaluate these tests with three instructions in addition to those required to compute $x + y + c$ or $x - y - c$. A fourth instruction (*branch if negative*) may be added to branch to code where the overflow condition is handled.

If executing with overflow interrupts enabled, the programmer may wish to test to see if a certain addition or subtraction will cause overflow, in a way that does not cause it. One branch-free way to do this is as follows:

$$x + y + c \qquad\qquad\qquad x - y - c$$

$$z \leftarrow (x \equiv y)\ \&\ \text{0x80000000} \qquad z \leftarrow (x \oplus y)\ \&\ \text{0x80000000}$$

$$(x \equiv y)\ \&\ ((x \oplus z) + y + c) \equiv y \qquad (x \oplus y)\ \&\ ((x \oplus z) - y - c) \oplus y$$

The assignment to z in the left column sets $z = \text{0x80000000}$ if x and y have the same sign, and sets $z = 0$ if they differ. Then, the addition in the second expression is done with x and y having different signs, so it can't overflow. If x and y are nonnegative, the sign bit in the second expression will be 1 if and only if $(x - 2^{31}) + y + c \ge 0$—that is, iff $x + y + c \ge 2^{31}$, which is the condition for overflow in evaluating $x + y + c$. If x and y are negative, the sign bit in the second expression will be 1 iff $(x + 2^{31}) + y + c < 0$—that is, iff $x + y + c < -2^{31}$, which again is the condition for overflow. The term $x \equiv y$ ensures the correct result (0 in the sign position) if x and y have opposite signs. Similar remarks apply to the case of subtraction (right column). The code executes in nine instructions on the basic RISC.

It might seem that if the carry from addition is readily available, this might help in computing the signed overflow predicate. This does not seem to be the case. However, one method along these lines is as follows.

If x is a signed integer, then $x + 2^{31}$ is correctly represented as an unsigned number, and is obtained by inverting the high-order bit of x. Signed overflow in the positive direction occurs if $x + y \geq 2^{31}$—that is, if $(x + 2^{31}) + (y + 2^{31}) \geq 3 \cdot 2^{31}$. This latter condition is characterized by carry occurring in the unsigned add (which means that the sum is greater than or equal to 2^{32}) and the high-order bit of the sum being 1. Similarly, overflow in the negative direction occurs if the carry is 0 and the high-order bit of the sum is also 0.

This gives the following algorithm for detecting overflow for signed addition:

> Compute $(x \oplus 2^{31}) + (y \oplus 2^{31})$, giving sum s and carry c.
> Overflow occurred iff c equals the high-order bit of s.

The sum is the correct sum for the signed addition, because inverting the high-order bits of both operands does not change their sum.

For subtraction, the algorithm is the same except that in the first step a subtraction replaces the addition. We assume that the carry is that generated by computing $x - y$ as $x + \bar{y} + 1$. The subtraction is the correct difference for the signed subtraction.

These formulas are perhaps interesting, but on most machines they would not be quite as efficient as the formulas that do not even use the carry bit (e.g., overflow $= (x \equiv y) \& (s \oplus x)$ for addition, and $(x \oplus y) \& (d \oplus x)$ for subtraction, where s and d are the sum and difference, respectively, of x and y).

How the Computer Sets Overflow for Signed Add/Subtract

Machines often set "overflow" for signed addition by means of the logic "the carry into the sign position is not equal to the carry out of the sign position." Curiously, this logic gives the correct overflow indication for both addition and subtraction, assuming the subtraction $x - y$ is done by $x + \bar{y} + 1$. Furthermore, it is correct whether or not there is a carry- or borrow-in. This does not seem to lead to any particularly good methods for computing the signed overflow predicate in software, however, even though it is easy to compute the carry into the sign position. For addition and subtraction, the carry/borrow into the sign position is given by the sign bit after evaluating the following expressions (where c is **0** or **1**):

carry	borrow
$(x + y + c) \oplus x \oplus y$	$(x - y - c) \oplus x \oplus y$

In fact, these expressions give, at each position i, the carry/borrow into position i.

Unsigned Add/Subtract

The following branch-free code may be used to compute the overflow predicate for unsigned add/subtract, with the result being in the sign position. The expressions involving a right shift are probably useful only when it is known that $c = 0$. The expressions in brackets compute the carry or borrow generated from the least significant position.

$$x + y + c, \text{ unsigned}$$

$$(x \mathbin{\&} y) \mid ((x \mid y) \mathbin{\&} \neg(x + y + c))$$

$$(x \overset{u}{\gg} 1) + (y \overset{u}{\gg} 1) + [((x \mathbin{\&} y) \mid ((x \mid y) \mathbin{\&} c)) \mathbin{\&} 1]$$

$$x - y - c, \text{ unsigned}$$

$$(\neg x \mathbin{\&} y) \mid ((x \equiv y) \mathbin{\&} (x - y - c))$$

$$(\neg x \mathbin{\&} y) \mid ((\neg x \mid y) \mathbin{\&} (x - y - c))$$

$$(x \overset{u}{\gg} 1) - (y \overset{u}{\gg} 1) - [((\neg x \mathbin{\&} y) \mid ((\neg x \mid y) \mathbin{\&} c)) \mathbin{\&} 1]$$

For unsigned *add*'s and *subtract*'s, there are much simpler formulas in terms of comparisons [MIPS]. For unsigned addition, overflow (carry) occurs if the sum is less (by unsigned comparison) than either of the operands. This and similar formulas are given below. Unfortunately, there is no way in these formulas to allow for a variable c that represents the carry- or borrow-in. Instead, the program must test c, and use a different type of comparison depending upon whether c is **0** or **1**.

$x + y$, unsigned	$x + y + 1$, unsigned	$x - y$, unsigned	$x - y - 1$, unsigned
$\neg x \overset{u}{<} y$	$\neg x \overset{u}{\le} y$	$x \overset{u}{<} y$	$x \overset{u}{\le} y$
$x + y \overset{u}{<} x$	$x + y + 1 \overset{u}{\le} x$	$x - y \overset{u}{>} x$	$x - y - 1 \overset{u}{\ge} x$

The first formula for each case above is evaluated before the add/subtract that may overflow, and it provides a way to do the test without causing overflow. The second formula for each case is evaluated after the add/subtract that may overflow.

There does not seem to be a similar simple device (using comparisons) for computing the signed overflow predicate.

Multiplication

For multiplication, overflow means that the result cannot be expressed in 32 bits (it can always be expressed in 64 bits, whether signed or unsigned). Checking for overflow is simple if you have access to the high-order 32 bits of the product. Let us denote the two halves of the 64-bit product by $hi(x \times y)$ and $lo(x \times y)$. Then the overflow predicates can be computed as follows [MIPS]:

$$x \times y, \text{ unsigned} \qquad\qquad x \times y, \text{ signed}$$
$$hi(x \times y) \neq 0 \qquad\qquad hi(x \times y) \neq (lo(x \times y) \overset{s}{\gg} 31)$$

One way to check for overflow of multiplication is to do the multiplication and then check the result by dividing. But care must be taken not to divide by 0, and there is a further complication for signed multiplication. Overflow occurs if the following expressions are **true**:

Unsigned	Signed
$z \leftarrow x * y$	$z \leftarrow x * y$
$y \neq 0 \mathrel{\vec{\&}} z \overset{u}{\div} y \neq x$	$(y < 0 \mathrel{\&} x = -2^{31}) \mid (y \neq 0 \mathrel{\vec{\&}} z \div y \neq x)$

The complication arises when $x = -2^{31}$ and $y = -1$. In this case the multiplication overflows, but the machine may very well give a result of -2^{31}. This causes the division to overflow, and thus any result is possible (for some machines). Therefore, this case has to be checked separately, which is done by the term $y < 0 \mathrel{\&} x = -2^{31}$. The above expressions use the "conditional *and*" operator to prevent dividing by 0 (in C, use the && operator).

It is also possible to use division to check for overflow of multiplication without doing the multiplication (that is, without causing overflow). For unsigned integers, the product overflows iff $xy > 2^{32} - 1$, or $x > ((2^{32} - 1)/y)$, or, since x is an integer, $x > \lfloor (2^{32} - 1)/y \rfloor$. Expressed in computer arithmetic, this is

$$y \neq 0 \mathrel{\vec{\&}} x \overset{u}{>} (\text{0xFFFFFFFF} \overset{u}{\div} y).$$

For signed integers, the determination of overflow of $x * y$ is not so simple. If x and y have the same sign, then overflow occurs iff $xy > 2^{31} - 1$. If they have opposite signs, then overflow occurs iff $xy < -2^{31}$. These conditions may be tested as indicated in Table 2–2, which employs signed division.

TABLE 2–2. OVERFLOW TEST FOR SIGNED MULTIPLICATION

	$y > 0$	$y \leq 0$
$x > 0$	$x > \text{0x7FFFFFFF} \div y$	$y < \text{0x80000000} \div x$
$x \leq 0$	$x < \text{0x80000000} \div y$	$x \neq 0 \mathrel{\vec{\&}} y < \text{0x7FFFFFFF} \div x$

This test is awkward to implement because of the four cases. It is difficult to unify the expressions very much because of problems with overflow and with not being able to represent the number $+2^{31}$.

The test can be simplified if unsigned division is available. We can use the absolute values of x and y, which are correctly represented under unsigned integer interpretation. The complete test can then be computed as shown below. The variable $c = 2^{31} - 1$ if x and y have the same sign, and $c = 2^{31}$ otherwise.

$$c \leftarrow ((x \equiv y) \overset{s}{\gg} 31) + 2^{31}$$

$$x \leftarrow \text{abs}(x)$$

$$y \leftarrow \text{abs}(y)$$

$$y \neq 0 \mathbin{\overset{\rightarrow}{\&}} x \overset{u}{>} (c \overset{u}{\div} y)$$

The *number of leading zeros* instruction may be used to give an estimate of whether or not $x * y$ will overflow, and the estimate may be refined to give an accurate determination. First, consider the multiplication of unsigned numbers. It is easy to show that if x and y, as 32-bit quantities, have m and n leading 0's, respectively, then the 64-bit product has either $m + n$ or $m + n + 1$ leading 0's (or 64, if either $x = 0$ or $y = 0$). Overflow occurs if the 64-bit product has fewer than 32 leading 0's. Hence,

> $\text{nlz}(x) + \text{nlz}(y) \geq 32$: Multiplication definitely does not overflow.

> $\text{nlz}(x) + \text{nlz}(y) \leq 30$: Multiplication definitely does overflow.

For $\text{nlz}(x) + \text{nlz}(y) = 31$, overflow may or may not occur. In this case, the overflow assessment may be made by evaluating $t = x\lfloor y/2 \rfloor$. This will not overflow. Since xy is $2t$ or, if y is odd, $2t + x$, the product xy overflows if $t \geq 2^{31}$. These considerations lead to a plan for computing xy but branching to "overflow" if the product overflows. This plan is shown in Figure 2–2.

For the multiplication of signed integers, we can make a partial determination of whether or not overflow occurs from the number of leading 0's of nonnegative arguments, and the number of leading 1's of negative arguments. Let

$$m = \text{nlz}(x) + \text{nlz}(\bar{x}), \text{ and}$$

$$n = \text{nlz}(y) + \text{nlz}(\bar{y}).$$

Then, we have

> $m + n \geq 34$: Multiplication definitely does not overflow.

> $m + n \leq 31$: Multiplication definitely does overflow.

```
unsigned x, y, z, m, n, t;

m = nlz(x);
n = nlz(y);
if (m + n <= 30) goto overflow;
t = x*(y >> 1);
if ((int)t < 0) goto overflow;
z = t*2;
if (y & 1) {
    z = z + x;
    if (z < x) goto overflow;
}
// z is the correct product of x and y.
```

FIGURE 2–2. Determination of overflow of unsigned multiplication.

There are two ambiguous cases: 32 and 33. The case $m + n = 33$ overflows only when both arguments are negative and the true product is exactly 2^{31} (machine result is -2^{31}), so it can be recognized by a test that the product has the correct sign (that is, overflow occurred if $m \oplus n \oplus (m * n) < 0$). When $m + n = 32$, the distinction is not so easily made.

We will not dwell on this further, except to note that an overflow estimate for signed multiplication can also be made based on $\text{nlz(abs}(x)) + \text{nlz(abs}(y))$, but again there are two ambiguous cases (a sum of 31 or 32).

Division

For the signed division $x \div y$, overflow occurs if the following expression is **true**:

$$y = 0 \mid (x = \text{0x80000000} \& y = -1)$$

Most machines signal overflow (or trap) for the indeterminate form $0 \div 0$.

Straightforward code for evaluating this expression, including a final branch to the overflow handling code, consists of seven instructions, three of which are branches. There do not seem to be any particularly good tricks to improve on this, but below are a few possibilities:

$$[\text{abs}(y \oplus \text{0x80000000}) \mid (\text{abs}(x) \& \text{abs}(y \equiv \text{0x80000000}))] < 0$$

That is, evaluate the large expression in brackets, and branch if the result is less than 0. This executes in about nine instructions, counting the load of the constant and the final branch, on a machine that has the indicated instructions and that gets the "compare to 0" for free.

Some other possibilities are to first compute z from

$$z \leftarrow (x \oplus \text{0x80000000}) \mid (y + 1)$$

(three instructions on many machines), and then do the test and branch on $y = 0 \mid z = 0$ in one of the following ways:

$$((y \mid -y) \& (z \mid -z)) \geq 0$$

$$(\text{nabs}(y) \& \text{nabs}(z)) \geq 0$$

$$((\text{nlz}(y) \mid \text{nlz}(z)) \overset{u}{\gg} 5) \neq 0$$

These execute in nine, seven, and eight instructions, respectively, on a machine that has the indicated instructions. The last line represents a good method for PowerPC.

For the unsigned division $x \overset{u}{\div} y$, overflow occurs if and only if $y = 0$.

2–13 Condition Code Result of *Add*, *Subtract*, and *Multiply*

Many machines provide a "condition code" that characterizes the result of integer arithmetic operations. Often there is only one *add* instruction, and the characterization reflects the result for both unsigned and signed interpretation of the operands and result (but not for mixed types). The characterization usually consists of the following:

- Whether or not carry occurred (unsigned overflow)

- Whether or not signed overflow occurred

- Whether the 32-bit result, interpreted as a signed two's-complement integer and ignoring carry and overflow, is negative, 0, or positive

Some older machines give an indication of whether the infinite precision result (that is, 33-bit result for *add*'s and *subtract*'s) is positive, negative, or 0. However, this indication is not easily used by compilers of high-level languages, and so has fallen out of favor.

For addition, only nine of the 12 combinations of these events are possible. The ones that cannot occur are "no carry, overflow, result > 0," "no carry, overflow, result = 0," and "carry, overflow, result < 0." Thus, four bits are, just barely, needed for the condition code. Two of the combinations are unique in the sense that only one value of inputs produces them: Adding 0 to itself is the only way to get "no carry, no overflow, result = 0," and adding the maximum negative number to itself is the only way to get "carry, overflow, result = 0." These remarks remain true if there is a "carry in"—that is, if we are computing $x + y + 1$.

For subtraction, let us assume that to compute $x - y$ the machine actually computes $x + \bar{y} + 1$, with the carry produced as for an *add* (in this scheme the meaning of "carry" is reversed for subtraction, in that carry = 1 signifies that the result fits in a single word, and carry = 0 signifies that the result does not fit in a single word). Then for subtraction only seven combinations of events are possible.

The ones that cannot occur are the three that cannot occur for addition, plus "no carry, no overflow, result = 0," and "carry, overflow, result = 0."

If a machine's multiplier can produce a doubleword result, then two *multiply* instructions are desirable: one for signed and one for unsigned operands. (On a 4-bit machine, in hexadecimal, $\mathbf{F} \times \mathbf{F} = \mathbf{01}$ signed, and $\mathbf{F} \times \mathbf{F} = \mathbf{E1}$ unsigned). For these instructions, neither carry nor overflow can occur, in the sense that the result will always fit in a doubleword.

For a multiplication instruction that produces a one-word result (the low-order word of the doubleword result), let us take "carry" to mean that the result does not fit in a word with the operands and result interpreted as unsigned integers, and let us take "overflow" to mean that the result does not fit in a word with the operands and result interpreted as signed two's-complement integers. Then again, there are nine possible combinations of results, with the missing ones being "no carry, overflow, result > 0," "no carry, overflow, result = 0," and "carry, no overflow, result = 0." Thus, considering addition, subtraction, and multiplication together, ten combinations can occur.

2–14 Rotate Shifts

These are rather trivial. Perhaps surprisingly, this code works for n ranging from 0 to 32 inclusive, even if the shifts are mod-32.

$$\text{Rotate left } n: \quad y \leftarrow (x \ll n) \mid (x \overset{u}{\gg} (32 - n))$$

$$\text{Rotate right } n: \quad y \leftarrow (x \overset{u}{\gg} n) \mid (x \ll (32 - n))$$

2–15 Double-Length Add/Subtract

Using one of the expressions shown on page 29 for overflow of unsigned addition and subtraction, we can easily implement double-length addition and subtraction without accessing the machine's carry bit. To illustrate with double-length addition, let the operands be (x_1, x_0) and (y_1, y_0), and the result be (z_1, z_0). Subscript 1 denotes the most significant half, and subscript 0 the least significant. We assume that all 32 bits of the registers are used. The less significant words are unsigned quantities.

$$z_0 \leftarrow x_0 + y_0$$

$$c \leftarrow [(x_0 \And y_0) \mid ((x_0 \mid y_0) \And \neg z_0)] \overset{u}{\gg} 31$$

$$z_1 \leftarrow x_1 + y_1 + c$$

This executes in nine instructions. The second line can be $c \leftarrow (z_0 \overset{u}{<} x_0)$, permitting a four-instruction solution on machines that have this comparison operator in a form that gives the result as a **1** or **0** in a register, such as the "SLTU" (*Set on Less Than Unsigned*) instruction on MIPS [MIPS].

Similar code for double-length subtraction $(x - y)$ is

$$z_0 \leftarrow x_0 - y_0$$

$$b \leftarrow [(\neg x_0 \,\&\, y_0) \mid ((x_0 \equiv y_0) \,\&\, z_0)] \overset{u}{\gg} 31$$

$$z_1 \leftarrow x_1 - y_1 - b$$

This executes in eight instructions on a machine that has a full set of logical instructions. The second line can be $b \leftarrow (x_0 \overset{u}{<} y_0)$, permitting a four-instruction solution on machines that have the "SLTU" instruction.

Double-length addition and subtraction can be done in five instructions on most machines by representing the multiple-length data using only 31 bits of the least significant words, with the high-order bit being 0 except momentarily when it contains a carry or borrow bit.

2–16 Double-Length Shifts

Let (x_1, x_0) be a pair of 32-bit words to be shifted left or right as if they were a single 64-bit quantity, with x_1 being the most significant half. Let (y_1, y_0) be the result, interpreted similarly. Assume the shift amount n is a variable ranging from 0 to 63. Assume further that the machine's shift instructions are modulo 64 or greater. That is, a shift amount in the range 32 to 63 or –32 to –1 results in an all-0 word, unless the shift is a signed right shift, in which case the result is 32 sign bits from the word shifted. (This code will not work on the Intel x86 machines, which have mod-32 shifts.)

Under these assumptions the *shift left double* operation may be accomplished as follows (eight instructions):

$$y_1 \leftarrow x_1 \ll n \mid x_0 \overset{u}{\gg} (32 - n) \mid x_0 \ll (n - 32)$$

$$y_0 \leftarrow x_0 \ll n$$

The main connective in the first assignment must be *or*, not *plus*, to give the correct result when $n = 32$. If it is known that $0 \le n \le 32$, the last term of the first assignment may be omitted, giving a six-instruction solution.

Similarly, a *shift right double unsigned* operation may be done with

$$y_0 \leftarrow x_0 \overset{u}{\gg} n \mid x_1 \ll (32 - n) \mid x_1 \overset{u}{\gg} (n - 32)$$

$$y_1 \leftarrow x_1 \overset{u}{\gg} n.$$

Shift right double signed is more difficult, because of an unwanted sign propagation in one of the terms. Straightforward code follows:

$$\text{if } n < 32 \text{ then } y_0 \leftarrow x_0 \overset{u}{\gg} n \mid x_1 \ll (32 - n)$$

$$\text{else } y_0 \leftarrow x_1 \overset{s}{\gg} (n - 32)$$

$$y_1 \leftarrow x_1 \overset{s}{\gg} n$$

If your machine has the *conditional move* instructions, it is a simple matter to express this in branch-free code, in which form it takes eight instructions. If the conditional move instructions are not available, the operation may be done in ten instructions by using the familiar device of constructing a mask with the *shift right signed 31* instruction to mask the unwanted sign propagating term:

$$y_0 \leftarrow x_0 \overset{u}{\gg} n \mid x_1 \ll (32 - n) \mid [(x_1 \overset{s}{\gg} (n - 32)) \ \& \ ((32 - n) \overset{s}{\gg} 31)]$$

$$y_1 \leftarrow x_1 \overset{s}{\gg} n$$

2–17 Multibyte *Add, Subtract, Absolute Value*

Some applications deal with arrays of short integers (usually bytes or halfwords), and often execution is faster if they are operated on a word at a time. For definiteness, the examples here deal with the case of four 1-byte integers packed into a word, but the techniques are easily adapted to other packings, such as a word containing a 12-bit integer and two 10-bit integers, and so on. These techniques are of greater value on 64-bit machines, because more work is done in parallel.

Addition must be done in a way that blocks the carries from one byte into another. This can be accomplished by the following two-step method:

1. Mask out the high-order bit of each byte of each operand and *add* (there will then be no carries across byte boundaries).

2. Fix up the high-order bit of each byte with a 1-bit *add* of the two operands and the carry into that bit.

The carry into the high-order bit of each byte is of course given by the high-order bit of each byte of the sum computed in step 1. The subsequent similar method works for subtraction:

Addition

$$s \leftarrow (x \ \& \ 0x7F7F7F7F) + (y \ \& \ 0x7F7F7F7F)$$

$$s \leftarrow ((x \oplus y) \ \& \ 0x80808080) \oplus s$$

Subtraction

$$d \leftarrow (x \mid 0x80808080) - (y \ \& \ 0x7F7F7F7F)$$

$$d \leftarrow ((x \oplus y) \mid 0x7F7F7F7F) \equiv d$$

These execute in eight instructions, counting the load of **0x7F7F7F7F**, on a machine that has a full set of logical instructions. (Change the *and* and *or* of **0x80808080** to *and not* and *or not*, respectively, of **0x7F7F7F7F**.)

There is a different technique for the case in which the word is divided into only two fields. In this case, addition can be done by means of a 32-bit addition followed by subtracting out the unwanted carry. On page 28 we noted that the expression $(x + y) \oplus x \oplus y$ gives the carries into each position. Using this and similar observations about subtraction gives the following code for adding/subtracting two halfwords modulo 2^{16} (seven instructions):

Addition	Subtraction
$s \leftarrow x + y$	$d \leftarrow x - y$
$c \leftarrow (s \oplus x \oplus y)\ \&\ 0x00010000$	$b \leftarrow (d \oplus x \oplus y)\ \&\ 0x00010000$
$s \leftarrow s - c$	$d \leftarrow d + b$

Multibyte *absolute value* is easily done by complementing and adding 1 to each byte that contains a negative integer (that is, has its high-order bit on). The following code sets each byte of y equal to the absolute value of each byte of x (eight instructions):

$$a \leftarrow x\ \&\ 0x80808080 \qquad \text{// Isolate signs.}$$
$$b \leftarrow a \overset{u}{\gg} 7 \qquad \text{// Integer 1 where } x \text{ is negative.}$$
$$m \leftarrow (a - b)\ |\ a \qquad \text{// 0xFF where } x \text{ is negative.}$$
$$y \leftarrow (x \oplus m) + b \qquad \text{// Complement and add 1 where negative.}$$

The third line could as well be $m \leftarrow a + a - b$. The addition of b in the fourth line cannot carry across byte boundaries, because the quantity $x \oplus m$ has a high-order 0 in each byte.

2–18 Doz, Max, Min

The "doz" function is "difference or zero," defined as follows, for signed arguments:

$$\text{doz}(x, y) = \begin{cases} x - y, & x \geq y, \\ 0, & x < y. \end{cases}$$

It has been called "first grade subtraction," because the result is 0 if you try to take away too much. We will use it to implement max(x, y) and min(x, y). In this connection it is important to note that doz(x, y) can be negative; it is negative if the subtraction overflows. The *difference or zero* function can be used directly to implement the Fortran IDIM function, although in Fortran, results are generally undefined if overflow occurs.

There seems to be no very good way to implement $doz(x, y)$, $max(x, y)$, and $min(x, y)$ in a branch-free way that is applicable to most computers. About the best we can do is to compute $doz(x, y)$ using one of the expressions given on page 22 for the $x < y$ predicate, and then compute $max(x, y)$ and $min(x, y)$ from it, as follows:

$$d \leftarrow x - y$$

$$doz(x, y) = d \ \& \ [(d \equiv ((x \oplus y) \ \& \ (d \oplus x))) \overset{s}{\gg} 31]$$

$$max(x, y) = y + doz(x, y)$$

$$min(x, y) = x - doz(x, y)$$

This computes $doz(x, y)$ in seven instructions if the machine has *equivalence*, or eight if not, and it computes $max(x, y)$ or $min(x, y)$ in one more instruction.

The following are unsigned versions of these functions:

$$d \leftarrow x - y$$

$$dozu(x, y) = d \ \& \ \neg [((\neg x \ \& \ y) \ | \ ((x \equiv y) \ \& \ d)) \overset{s}{\gg} 31]$$

$$maxu(x, y) = y + dozu(x, y)$$

$$minu(x, y) = x - dozu(x, y)$$

The IBM RISC/6000 computer, and its predecessor the 801, has $doz(x, y)$ provided as a single instruction. It permits computing the $max(x, y)$ and $min(x, y)$ of signed integers in two instructions, and is occasionally useful in itself. Implementing $max(x, y)$ and $min(x, y)$ directly is more costly because the machine would then need paths from the output ports of the register file back to an input port, bypassing the ALU.

Machines that have *conditional move* can get destructive[2] $max(x, y)$ and $min(x, y)$ in two instructions. For example, on our full RISC, $x \leftarrow max(x, y)$ can be calculated as follows (we write the target register first):

```
cmplt   z,x,y       Set z = 1 if x < y, else 0.
movne   x,z,y       If z is nonzero, set x = y.
```

2–19 Exchanging Registers

A very old trick is that of exchanging the contents of two registers without using a third [IBM]:

$$x \leftarrow x \oplus y$$

$$y \leftarrow y \oplus x$$

$$x \leftarrow x \oplus y$$

---

2. A destructive operation is one that overwrites one or more of its arguments.

This works well on a two-address machine. The trick also works if $\oplus$ is replaced by the $\equiv$ logical operation (complement of *exclusive or*), and can be made to work in various ways with *add*'s and *subtract*'s:

$$x \leftarrow x + y \qquad\qquad x \leftarrow x - y \qquad\qquad x \leftarrow y - x$$
$$y \leftarrow x - y \qquad\qquad y \leftarrow y + x \qquad\qquad y \leftarrow y - x$$
$$x \leftarrow x - y \qquad\qquad x \leftarrow y - x \qquad\qquad x \leftarrow x + y$$

Unfortunately, each of these has an instruction that is unsuitable for a two-address machine, unless the machine has "reverse subtract."

This little trick can actually be useful in the application of double buffering, in which two pointers are swapped. The first instruction can be factored out of the loop in which the swap is done (although this negates the advantage of saving a register):

$$\text{Outside the loop:}\ \ t \leftarrow x \oplus y$$
$$\text{Inside the loop:}\ \ x \leftarrow x \oplus t$$
$$y \leftarrow y \oplus t$$

Exchanging Corresponding Fields of Registers

The problem here is to exchange the contents of two registers x and y wherever a mask bit $m_i = 1$, and to leave x and y unaltered wherever $m_i = 0$. By "corresponding" fields, we mean that no shifting is required. The 1-bits of m need not be contiguous. The straightforward method is as follows:

$$x' \leftarrow (x\ \&\ \overline{m})\ |\ (y\ \&\ m)$$
$$y \leftarrow (y\ \&\ \overline{m})\ |\ (x\ \&\ m)$$
$$x \leftarrow x'$$

By using "temporaries" for the four *and* expressions, this can be seen to require seven instructions, assuming that either m or $\overline{m}$ can be loaded with a single instruction and the machine has *and not* as a single instruction. If the machine is capable of executing the four (independent) *and* expressions in parallel, the execution time is only three cycles.

A method that is probably better (five instructions, but four cycles on a machine with unlimited instruction-level parallelism) is shown in column (a) below. It is suggested by the "three *exclusive or*" code for exchanging registers.

(a)	(b)	(c)
$x \leftarrow x \oplus y$	$x \leftarrow x \equiv y$	$t \leftarrow (x \oplus y)\ \&\ m$
$y \leftarrow y \oplus (x\ \&\ m)$	$y \leftarrow y \equiv (x\ |\ \overline{m})$	$x \leftarrow x \oplus t$
$x \leftarrow x \oplus y$	$x \leftarrow x \equiv y$	$y \leftarrow y \oplus t$

The steps in column (b) do the same exchange as that of column (a), but column (b) is useful if m does not fit in an immediate field but $\overline{m}$ does, and the machine has the *equivalence* instruction.

Still another method is shown in column (c) above [GLS1]. It also takes five instructions (again assuming one instruction must be used to load m into a register), but executes in only three cycles on a machine with sufficient instruction-level parallelism.

Exchanging Two Fields of the Same Register

Assume a register x has two fields (of the same length) that are to be swapped, without altering other bits in the register. That is, the object is to swap fields B and D, without altering fields A, C, and E, in the computer word illustrated below. The fields are separated by a shift distance k.

Straightforward code would shift D and B to their new positions, and combine the words with *and* and *or* operations, as follows:

$$t_1 = (x \mathbin{\&} m) \ll k$$

$$t_2 = (x \overset{u}{\gg} k) \mathbin{\&} m$$

$$x' = (x \mathbin{\&} m') \mid t_1 \mid t_2$$

Here, m is a mask with 1's in field D (and 0's elsewhere), and m' is a mask with 1's in fields A, C, and E. This code requires nine instructions and four cycles on a machine with unlimited instruction-level parallelism, allowing for two instructions to load the two masks.

A method that requires only seven instructions and executes in five cycles, under the same assumptions, is shown below [GLS1]. It is similar to the code in column (c) on page 39 for interchanging corresponding fields of two registers. Again, m is a mask that isolates field D.

$$t_1 = [x \oplus (x \overset{u}{\gg} k)] \mathbin{\&} m$$

$$t_2 = t_1 \ll k$$

$$x' = x \oplus t_1 \oplus t_2$$

The idea is that t_1 contains $B \oplus D$ in position D (and 0's elsewhere), and t_2 contains $B \oplus D$ in position B. This code, and the straightforward code given earlier, work correctly if B and D are "split fields"—that is, if the 1-bits of mask m are not contiguous.

Conditional Exchange

The exchange methods of the preceding two sections, which are based on *exclusive or*, degenerate into no-operations if the mask *m* is 0. Hence, they can perform an exchange of entire registers, or of corresponding fields of two registers, or of two fields of the same register, if *m* is set to all 1's if some condition *c* is **true**, and to all 0's if *c* is **false**. This gives branch-free code if *m* can be set up without branching.

2–20 Alternating among Two or More Values

Suppose a variable *x* can have only two possible values *a* and *b*, and you wish to assign to *x* the value other than its current one, and you wish your code to be independent of the values of *a* and *b*. For example, in a compiler *x* might be an opcode that is known to be either *branch true* or *branch false*, and whichever it is, you want to switch it to the other. The values of the opcodes *branch true* and *branch false* are arbitrary, probably defined by a C #define or enum declaration in a header file.

The straightforward code to do the switch is

```
if (x == a) x = b;
else x = a;
```

or, as is often seen in C programs,

```
x = x == a ? b : a;
```

A far better (or at least more efficient) way to code it is either

$$x \leftarrow a + b - x, \quad \text{or}$$
$$x \leftarrow a \oplus b \oplus x.$$

If *a* and *b* are constants, these require only one or two basic RISC instructions. Of course, overflow in calculating $a + b$ can be ignored.

This raises the question: Is there some particularly efficient way to cycle among three or more values? That is, given three arbitrary but distinct constants *a*, *b*, and *c*, we seek an easy-to-evaluate function *f* that satisfies

$$f(a) = b,$$
$$f(b) = c, \quad \text{and}$$
$$f(c) = a.$$

It is perhaps interesting to note that there is always a polynomial for such a function. For the case of three constants,

$$f(x) = \frac{(x-a)(x-b)}{(c-a)(c-b)}a + \frac{(x-b)(x-c)}{(a-b)(a-c)}b + \frac{(x-c)(x-a)}{(b-c)(b-a)}c. \tag{2}$$

(The idea is that if $x = a$, the first and last terms vanish, and the middle term simplifies to b, and so on.) This requires 14 arithmetic operations to evaluate, and, for arbitrary a, b, and c, the intermediate results exceed the computer's word size. But it is just a quadratic; if written in the usual form for a polynomial and evaluated using Horner's rule,[3] it would require only five arithmetic operations (four for a quadratic with integer coefficients, plus one for a final division). Rearranging Equation (2) accordingly gives

$$f(x) = \frac{1}{(a-b)(a-c)(b-c)}\{[(a-b)a + (b-c)b + (c-a)c]x^2$$
$$+ [(a-b)b^2 + (b-c)c^2 + (c-a)a^2]x$$
$$+ [(a-b)a^2b + (b-c)b^2c + (c-a)ac^2]\}.$$

This is getting too complicated to be interesting (or practical).

Another method, similar to Equation (2) in that just one of the three terms survives, is

$$f(x) = ((-(x = c)) \& a) + ((-(x = a)) \& b) + ((-(x = b)) \& c).$$

This takes 11 instructions if the machine has the *equal* predicate, not counting loads of constants. Because the two addition operations are combining two 0 values with a nonzero, they can be replaced with *or* or *exclusive or* operations.

The formula can be simplified by precalculating $a - c$ and $b - c$, and then using [GLS1]:

$$f(x) = ((-(x = c)) \& (a - c)) + ((-(x = a)) \& (b - c)) + c, \quad \text{or}$$
$$f(x) = ((-(x = c)) \& (a \oplus c)) \oplus ((-(x = a)) \& (b \oplus c)) \oplus c.$$

---

3. Horner's rule simply factors out x. For example, it evaluates the fourth-degree polynomial $ax^4 + bx^3 + cx^2 + dx + e$ as $x(x(x(ax + b) + c) + d) + e$. For a polynomial of degree n it takes n multiplications and n additions, and it is very suitable for the *multiply-add* instruction.

Each of these operations takes eight instructions. But on most machines these are probably no better than the straightforward C code shown below, which executes in four to six instructions for small a, b, and c.

```
if (x == a) x = b;
else if (x == b) x = c;
else x = a;
```

Pursuing this matter, there is an ingenious branch-free method of cycling among three values on machines that do not have comparison predicate instructions [GLS1]. It executes in eight instructions on most machines.

Because a, b, and c are distinct, there are two bit positions, n_1 and n_2, where the bits of a, b, and c are not all the same, and where the "odd one out" (the one whose bit differs in that position from the other two) is different in positions n_1 and n_2. This is illustrated below for the values 21, 31, and 20, shown in binary.

$$
\begin{array}{ccccc}
1 & 0 & 1 & 0 & 1 & c \\
1 & 1 & 1 & 1 & 1 & a \\
1 & 0 & 1 & 0 & 0 & b \\
& n_1 & & n_2 &
\end{array}
$$

Without loss of generality, rename a, b, and c so that a has the odd one out in position n_1 and b has the odd one out in position n_2, as shown above. Then there are two possibilities for the values of the bits at position n_1, namely $(a_{n_1}, b_{n_1}, c_{n_1}) = (0, 1, 1)$ or $(1, 0, 0)$. Similarly, there are two possibilities for the bits at position n_2, namely $(a_{n_2}, b_{n_2}, c_{n_2}) = (0, 1, 0)$ or $(1, 0, 1)$. This makes four cases in all, and formulas for each of these cases are shown below:

Case 1. $(a_{n_1}, b_{n_1}, c_{n_1}) = (0, 1, 1)$, $(a_{n_2}, b_{n_2}, c_{n_2}) = (0, 1, 0)$:

$$f(x) = x_{n_1} * (a - b) + x_{n_2} * (c - a) + b$$

Case 2. $(a_{n_1}, b_{n_1}, c_{n_1}) = (0, 1, 1)$, $(a_{n_2}, b_{n_2}, c_{n_2}) = (1, 0, 1)$:

$$f(x) = x_{n_1} * (a - b) + x_{n_2} * (a - c) + (b + c - a)$$

Case 3. $(a_{n_1}, b_{n_1}, c_{n_1}) = (1, 0, 0)$, $(a_{n_2}, b_{n_2}, c_{n_2}) = (0, 1, 0)$:

$$f(x) = x_{n_1} * (b - a) + x_{n_2} * (c - a) + a$$

Case 4. $(a_{n_1}, b_{n_1}, c_{n_1}) = (1, 0, 0)$, $(a_{n_2}, b_{n_2}, c_{n_2}) = (1, 0, 1)$:

$$f(x) = x_{n_1} * (b - a) + x_{n_2} * (a - c) + c$$

In these formulas, the left operand of each multiplication is a single bit. A multiplication by 0 or 1 may be converted into an *and* with a value of 0 or all 1's. Thus, the formulas can be rewritten as illustrated below for the first formula:

$$f(x) = ((x \ll (31-n_1)) \overset{s}{\gg} 31) \& (a-b) + ((x \ll (31-n_2)) \overset{s}{\gg} 31) \& (c-a) + b$$

Because all variables except x are constants, this can be evaluated in eight instructions on the basic RISC. Here again, the additions and subtractions can be replaced with *exclusive or*.

This idea can be extended to cycling among four or more constants. The essence of the idea is to find bit positions n_1, n_2, ..., at which the bits uniquely identify the constants. For four constants, three bit positions always suffice. Then (for four constants) solve the following equation for s, t, u, and v (that is, solve the system of four linear equations in which $f(x)$ is a, b, c, or d, and the coefficients x_{n_i} are 0 or 1):

$$f(x) = x_{n_1}s + x_{n_2}t + x_{n_3}u + v$$

If the four constants are uniquely identified by only two bit positions, the equation to solve is

$$f(x) = x_{n_1}s + x_{n_2}t + x_{n_1}x_{n_2}u + v.$$

CHAPTER 3

POWER-OF-2 BOUNDARIES

3-1 Rounding Up/Down to a Multiple of a Known Power of 2

Rounding an unsigned integer x down to, for example, the next smaller multiple of 8, is trivial: $x \mathbin{\&} -8$ does it. An alternative is $(x \overset{u}{\gg} 3) \ll 3$. These work for signed integers as well, provided "round down" means to round in the negative direction (e.g., $(-37) \mathbin{\&} (-8) = -40$).

Rounding up is almost as easy. For example, an unsigned integer x can be rounded up to the next greater multiple of 8 with either of

$$(x + 7) \mathbin{\&} -8, \quad \text{or}$$

$$x + (-x \mathbin{\&} 7).$$

These expressions are correct for signed integers as well, provided "round up" means to round in the positive direction. The second term of the second expression is useful if you want to know how much you must add to x to make it a multiple of 8 [Gold].

To round a signed integer to the nearest multiple of 8 toward 0, you can combine the two expressions above in an obvious way:

$$t \leftarrow (x \overset{s}{\gg} 31) \mathbin{\&} 7;$$

$$(x + t) \mathbin{\&} -8$$

An alternative for the first line is $t \leftarrow (x \overset{s}{\gg} 2) \overset{u}{\gg} 29$, which is useful if the machine lacks *and immediate*, or if the constant is too large for its immediate field.

Sometimes the rounding factor is given as the $\log_2$ of the alignment amount (e.g., a value of 3 means to round to a multiple of 8). In this case, code such as the following may be used, where $k = \log_2(\text{alignment amount})$:

round down:	$x \mathbin{\&} ((-1) \ll k)$
	$(x \overset{u}{\gg} k) \ll k$
round up:	$t \leftarrow (1 \ll k) - 1; \quad (x + t) \mathbin{\&} \lnot t$
	$t \leftarrow (-1) \ll k; \quad (x - t - 1) \mathbin{\&} t$

3-2 Rounding Up/Down to the Next Power of 2

We define two functions that are similar to floor and ceiling, but which are directed roundings to the closest integral power of 2, rather than to the closest integer. Mathematically, they are defined by

$$
\text{flp2}(x) = \begin{cases} \text{undefined,} & x < 0, \\ 0, & x = 0, \\ 2^{\lfloor \log_2 x \rfloor}, & \text{otherwise;} \end{cases} \qquad \text{clp2}(x) = \begin{cases} \text{undefined,} & x < 0, \\ 0, & x = 0, \\ 2^{\lceil \log_2 x \rceil}, & \text{otherwise.} \end{cases}
$$

The initial letters of the function names are intended to suggest "floor" and "ceiling." Thus, $\text{flp2}(x)$ is the greatest power of 2 that is $\leq x$, and $\text{clp2}(x)$ is the least power of 2 that is $\geq x$. These definitions make sense even when x is not an integer (e.g., $\text{flp2}(0.1) = 0.0625$). The functions satisfy several relations analogous to those involving floor and ceiling, such as those shown below, where n is an integer.

$\lfloor x \rfloor = \lceil x \rceil$ iff x is an integer $\qquad \text{flp2}(x) = \text{clp2}(x)$ iff x is a power of 2 or is 0

$\lfloor x + n \rfloor = \lfloor x \rfloor + n \qquad\qquad\qquad \text{flp2}(2^n x) = 2^n \text{flp2}(x)$

$\lceil x \rceil = -\lfloor -x \rfloor \qquad\qquad\qquad\qquad \text{clp2}(x) = 1/\text{flp2}(1/x), \; x \neq 0$

Computationally, we deal only with the case in which x is an integer, and we take it to be unsigned, so the functions are well defined for all x. We require the value computed to be the arithmetically correct value modulo 2^{32} (that is, we take $\text{clp2}(x)$ to be **0** for $x > 2^{31}$). The functions are tabulated below for a few values of x.

x	$\text{flp2}(x)$	$\text{clp2}(x)$
0	0	0
1	1	1
2	2	2
3	2	4
4	4	4
5	4	8
...	...	...
$2^{31} - 1$	2^{30}	2^{31}
2^{31}	2^{31}	2^{31}
$2^{31} + 1$	2^{31}	0
...	...	...
$2^{32} - 1$	2^{31}	0

Functions flp2 and clp2 are connected by the relations shown below. These can be used to compute one from the other, subject to the indicated restrictions.

$$\begin{aligned} \text{clp2}(x) &= 2\,\text{flp2}(x-1), & x \neq 1, \\ &= \text{flp2}(2x-1), & 1 \leq x \leq 2^{31}, \\ \text{flp2}(x) &= \text{clp2}(x \overset{u}{\div} 2 + 1), & x \neq 0, \\ &= \text{clp2}(x+1) \overset{u}{\div} 2, & x < 2^{31}. \end{aligned}$$

The round-up and round-down functions can be computed quite easily with the *number of leading zeros* instruction, as shown below. However, for these relations to hold for $x = 0$ and $x > 2^{31}$, the computer must have its shift instructions defined to produce **0** for shift amounts of –1, 32, and 63. Many machines (e.g., PowerPC) have "mod 64" shifts, which do this. In the case of –1, it is adequate if the machine shifts in the opposite direction (that is, a shift left of –1 becomes a shift right of 1).

$$\begin{aligned} \text{flp2}(x) &= \mathbf{1} \ll (\mathbf{31} - \text{nlz}(x)) \\ &= \mathbf{1} \ll (\text{nlz}(x) \oplus \mathbf{31}) \\ &= \mathbf{0x80000000} \overset{u}{\gg} \text{nlz}(x) \\ \text{clp2}(x) &= \mathbf{1} \ll (\mathbf{32} - \text{nlz}(x-1)) \\ &= \mathbf{0x80000000} \overset{u}{\gg} (\text{nlz}(x-1) - \mathbf{1}) \end{aligned}$$

Rounding Down

Figure 3–1 illustrates a branch-free algorithm that might be useful if *number of leading zeros* is not available. This algorithm is based on right-propagating the leftmost 1-bit, and executes in 12 instructions.

Figure 3–2 shows two simple loops that compute the same function. All variables are unsigned integers. The loop on the right keeps turning off the rightmost 1-bit of x until $x = 0$, and then returns the previous value of x.

```
unsigned flp2(unsigned x) {
    x = x | (x >> 1);
    x = x | (x >> 2);
    x = x | (x >> 4);
    x = x | (x >> 8);
    x = x | (x >>16);
    return x - (x >> 1);
}
```

FIGURE 3–1. Greatest power of 2 less than or equal to x, branch-free.

```
y = 0x80000000;              do {
while (y > x)                    y = x;
    y = y >> 1;                  x = x & (x - 1);
return                       } while(x != 0);
                             return y;
```

FIGURE 3–2. Greatest power of 2 less than or equal to x, simple loops.

The loop on the left executes in $4\,\text{nlz}(x) + 3$ instructions. The loop on the right, for $x \neq 0$, executes in $4\,\text{pop}(x)$ instructions,[1] if the comparison to 0 is zero-cost.

Rounding Up

The right-propagation trick yields a good algorithm for rounding up to the next power of 2. This algorithm, shown in Figure 3–3, is branch-free and runs in 12 instructions.

An attempt to compute this with the obvious loop does not work out very well:

```
y = 1;

while (y < x)        // Unsigned comparison.
    y = 2*y;
return y;
```

This code returns 1 for $x = 0$, which is probably not what you want, loops forever for $x \geq 2^{31}$, and executes in $4n + 3$ instructions, where n is the power of 2 of the returned integer. Thus, it is slower than the branch-free code, in terms of instructions executed, for $n \geq 3$ ($x \geq 8$).

```
unsigned clp2(unsigned x) {
    x = x - 1;
    x = x | (x >> 1);
    x = x | (x >> 2);
    x = x | (x >> 4);
    x = x | (x >> 8);
    x = x | (x >>16);
    return x + 1;
}
```

FIGURE 3–3. Least power of 2 greater than or equal to x.

---

1. pop(x) is the number of 1-bits in x.

3–3 Detecting a Power-of-2 Boundary Crossing

Assume memory is divided into blocks that are a power of 2 in size, starting at address 0. The blocks may be words, doublewords, pages, and so on. Then, given a starting address a and a length l, we wish to determine whether or not the address range from a to $a + l - 1$, $l \geq 2$, crosses a block boundary. The quantities a and l are unsigned and any values that fit in a register are possible.

If $l = 0$ or 1, a boundary crossing does not occur, regardless of a. If l exceeds the block size, a boundary crossing does occur, regardless of a. For very large values of l (wraparound is possible), a boundary crossing can occur even if the first and last bytes of the address range are in the same block.

There is a surprisingly concise way to detect boundary crossings on the IBM System/370 [CJS]. This method is illustrated below for a block size of 4096 bytes (a common page size).

```
O    RA,=A(-4096)
ALR  RA,RL
BO   CROSSES
```

The first instruction forms the logical *or* of RA (which contains the starting address a) and the number 0xFFFFF000. The second instruction adds in the length, and sets the machine's 2-bit condition code. For the *add logical* instruction, the first bit of the condition code is set to 1 if a carry occurred, and the second bit is set to 1 if the 32-bit register result is nonzero. The last instruction branches if both bits are set. At the branch target, RA will contain the length that extends beyond the first page (this is an extra feature that was not asked for).

If, for example, $a = 0$ and $l = 4096$, a carry occurs but the register result is 0, so the program properly does *not* branch to label CROSSES.

Let us see how this method can be adapted to RISC machines, which generally do not have *branch on carry and register result nonzero*. Using a block size of 8 for notational simplicity, the method of [CJS] branches to CROSSES if a carry occurred $((a \mid -8) + l \geq 2^{32})$ and the register result is nonzero $((a \mid -8) + l \neq 2^{32})$. Thus, it is equivalent to the predicate

$$(a \mid -8) + l > 2^{32}.$$

This in turn is equivalent to getting a carry in the final addition in evaluating $((a \mid -8) - 1) + l$. If the machine has *branch on carry*, this can be used directly, giving a solution in about five instructions counting a load of the constant -8.

If the machine does not have *branch on carry*, we can use the fact that carry occurs in $x + y$ iff $\neg x \overset{u}{<} y$ (see "Unsigned Add/Subtract" on page 29) to obtain the expression

$$\neg((a \mid -8) - 1) \overset{u}{<} l.$$

Using various identities such as $\neg(x - 1) = -x$ gives the following equivalent expressions for the "boundary crossed" predicate:

$$-(a \mid -8) \overset{u}{<} l$$

$$\neg(a \mid -8) + 1 \overset{u}{<} l$$

$$(\neg a \mathbin{\&} 7) + 1 \overset{u}{<} l$$

These can be evaluated in five or six instructions on most RISC computers.
     Using another tack, clearly an 8-byte boundary is crossed iff

$$(a \mathbin{\&} 7) + l - 1 \geq 8.$$

This cannot be directly evaluated because of the possibility of overflow (which occurs if l is very large), but it is easily rearranged to $8 - (a \mathbin{\&} 7) < l$, which can be directly evaluated on the computer (no part of it overflows). This gives the expression

$$\mathbf{8} - (a \mathbin{\&} 7) \overset{u}{<} l,$$

which can be evaluated in five instructions on most RISCs (four if it has *subtract from immediate*). If a boundary crossing occurs, the length that extends beyond the first block is given by $l - (\mathbf{8} - (a \mathbin{\&} \mathbf{7}))$, which can be calculated with one additional instruction (*subtract*).

CHAPTER 4

ARITHMETIC BOUNDS

4–1 Checking Bounds of Integers

By "bounds checking" we mean to verify that an integer x is within two bounds a and b—that is, that

$$a \leq x \leq b.$$

We first assume that all quantities are signed integers.

An important application is the checking of array indexes. For example, suppose a one-dimensional array A can be indexed by values from 1 to 10. Then, for a reference $A(i)$, a compiler might generate code to check that

$$1 \leq i \leq 10$$

and to *branch* or *trap* if this is not the case. In this section we show that this check can be done with a single comparison, by performing the equivalent check [PL8]:

$$i - 1 \overset{u}{\leq} 9.$$

This is probably better code, because it involves only one *compare-branch* (or *compare-trap*), and because the quantity $i - 1$ is probably needed anyway for the array addressing calculations.

Does the implementation

$$a \leq x \leq b \Rightarrow x - a \overset{u}{\leq} b - a$$

always work, even if overflow may occur in the subtractions? It does, provided we somehow know that $a \leq b$. In the case of array bounds checking, language rules may require that an array not have a number of elements (or number of elements along any axis) that are 0 or negative, and this rule can be verified at compile time or, for dynamic extents, at array allocation time. In such an environment, the transformation above is correct, as we will now show.

It is convenient to use a lemma, which is good to know in its own right.

LEMMA. *If a and b are signed integers and $a \leq b$, then the computed value $\mathbf{b} - \mathbf{a}$ correctly represents the arithmetic value $b - a$, if the computed value is interpreted as unsigned.*

Proof. (Assume a 32-bit machine.) Because $a \leq b$, the true difference $b - a$ is in the range 0 to $(2^{31} - 1) - (-2^{31}) = 2^{32} - 1$. If the true difference is in the

51

range 0 to $2^{31} - 1$, then the machine result is correct (because the result is representable under signed interpretation), and the sign bit is off. Hence the machine result is correct under either signed or unsigned interpretation.

If the true difference is in the range 2^{31} to $2^{32} - 1$, then the machine result will differ by some multiple of 2^{32} (because the result is not representable under signed interpretation). This brings the result (under signed interpretation) to the range -2^{31} to -1. The machine result is too low by 2^{32}, and the sign bit is on. Reinterpreting the result as unsigned increases it by 2^{32}, because the sign bit is given a weight of $+2^{31}$ rather than -2^{31}. Hence the reinterpreted result is correct.

The "bounds theorem" is

THEOREM. *If a and b are signed integers and* $a \leq b$, *then*

$$a \leq x \leq b \ = \ x - a \overset{u}{\leq} b - a. \tag{1}$$

Proof. We distinguish three cases, based on the value of x. In all cases, by the lemma, since $a \leq b$, the computed value $\boldsymbol{b} - \boldsymbol{a}$ is equal to the arithmetic value $b - a$ if $\boldsymbol{b} - \boldsymbol{a}$ is interpreted as unsigned, as it is in Equation (1).

Case 1, $x < a$: In this case, $\boldsymbol{x} - \boldsymbol{a}$ interpreted as unsigned is $x - a + 2^{32}$. Whatever the values of x and b are (within the range of 32-bit numbers),

$$x + 2^{32} > b.$$

Therefore

$$x - a + 2^{32} > b - a,$$

and hence

$$x - a \overset{u}{>} b - a.$$

In this case, both sides of Equation (1) are **false**.

Case 2, $a \leq x \leq b$: Then, arithmetically, $x - a \leq b - a$. Because $a \leq x$, by the lemma $x - a$ equals the computed value $\boldsymbol{x} - \boldsymbol{a}$ if the latter is interpreted as unsigned. Hence

$$x - a \overset{u}{\leq} b - a;$$

that is, both sides of Equation (1) are **true**.

Case 3, $x > b$: Then $x - a > b - a$. Because in this case $x > a$ (because $b > a$), by the lemma $x - a$ equals the value of $\boldsymbol{x} - \boldsymbol{a}$ if the latter is interpreted as unsigned. Hence

$$x - a \overset{u}{>} b - a;$$

that is, both sides of Equation (1) are **false**.

The theorem stated above is also true if a and b are *unsigned* integers. This is because for unsigned integers the lemma holds trivially, and the above proof is also valid.

Below is a list of similar bounds-checking transformations, with the one of the theorem above stated again. These all hold for either signed or unsigned interpretation of a, b, and x.

$$\text{if } a \le b \text{ then } a \le x \le b = x - a \overset{u}{\le} b - a = b - x \overset{u}{\le} b - a$$

$$\text{if } a \le b \text{ then } a \le x < b = x - a \overset{u}{<} b - a$$

$$\text{if } a \le b \text{ then } a < x \le b = b - x \overset{u}{<} b - a \tag{2}$$

$$\text{if } a < b \text{ then } a < x < b = x - a - 1 \overset{u}{<} b - a - 1 = b - x - 1 \overset{u}{<} b - a - 1$$

In the last rule, $b - a - 1$ may be replaced with $b + \neg a$.

There are some quite different transformations that may be useful when the test is of the form $-2^{n-1} \le x \le 2^{n-1} - 1$. This is a test to see if a signed quantity x can be correctly represented as an n-bit two's-complement integer. To illustrate with $n = 8$, the following tests are equivalent:

a. $\quad -128 \le x \le 127$

b. $\quad x + 128 \overset{u}{\le} 255$

c. $\quad (x \overset{s}{\gg} 7) + 1 \overset{u}{\le} 1$

d. $\quad x \overset{s}{\gg} 7 = x \overset{s}{\gg} 31$

e. $\quad (x \overset{s}{\gg} 7) + (x \overset{u}{\gg} 31) = 0$

f. $\quad (x \ll 24) \overset{s}{\gg} 24 = x$

g. $\quad x \oplus (x \overset{s}{\gg} 31) \le 127$

Equation (b) is simply an application of the preceding material in this section. Equation (c) is as well, after shifting x right seven positions. Equations (c)–(f) and possibly (g) are probably useful only if the constants in Equations (a) and (b) exceed the size of the immediate fields of the computer's *compare* and *add* instructions.

Another special case involving powers of 2 is

$$0 \le x \le 2^n - 1 \Leftrightarrow (x \overset{u}{\gg} n) = 0,$$

or, more generally,

$$a \le x \le a + 2^n - 1 \Leftrightarrow ((x - a) \overset{u}{\gg} n) = 0.$$

4–2 Propagating Bounds through *Add*'s and *Subtract*'s

Some optimizing compilers perform "range analysis" of expressions. This is the process of determining, for each occurrence of an expression in a program, upper and lower bounds on its value. Although this optimization is not a really big winner, it does permit improvements such as omitting the range check on a C "switch" statement and omitting some subscript bounds checks that compilers may provide as a debugging aid.

Suppose we have bounds on two variables x and y as follows, where all quantities are unsigned:

$$a \leq x \leq b, \quad \text{and} \tag{3}$$
$$c \leq y \leq d.$$

Then, how can we compute tight bounds on $x + y$, $x - y$, and $-x$? Arithmetically, of course, $a + c \leq x + y \leq b + d$; but the point is that the additions may overflow.

The way to calculate the bounds is expressed in the following:

THEOREM. *If a, b, c, d, x, and y are unsigned integers and*

$$a \overset{u}{\leq} x \overset{u}{\leq} b \quad \text{and}$$
$$c \overset{u}{\leq} y \overset{u}{\leq} d,$$

then

$$0 \overset{u}{\leq} x + y \overset{u}{\leq} 2^{32} - 1 \quad \text{if} \quad a + c \leq 2^{32} - 1 \quad \text{and} \quad b + d \geq 2^{32},$$
$$a + c \overset{u}{\leq} x + y \overset{u}{\leq} b + d \quad \text{otherwise;} \tag{4}$$

$$0 \overset{u}{\leq} x - y \overset{u}{\leq} 2^{32} - 1 \quad \text{if} \quad a - d < 0 \quad \text{and} \quad b - c \geq 0,$$
$$a - d \overset{u}{\leq} x - y \overset{u}{\leq} b - c \quad \text{otherwise;} \tag{5}$$

$$0 \overset{u}{\leq} -x \overset{u}{\leq} 2^{32} - 1 \quad \text{if} \quad a = 0 \quad \text{and} \quad b \neq 0,$$
$$-b \overset{u}{\leq} -x \overset{u}{\leq} -a \quad \text{otherwise.} \tag{6}$$

Inequalities (4) say that the bounds on $x + y$ are "normally" $a + c$ and $b + d$, but if the calculation of $a + c$ does *not* overflow and the calculation of *b* + *d* *does* overflow, then the bounds are 0 and the maximum unsigned integer. Equations (5) are interpreted similarly, but the true result of a subtraction being less than 0 constitutes an overflow (in the negative direction).

Proof. If neither *a* + *c* nor *b* + *d* overflows, then *x* + *y*, with *x* and *y* in the indicated ranges, cannot overflow, making the computed results equal to the true results, so the second inequality of (4) holds. If both *a* + *c* and *b* + *d* overflow, then so also does *x* + *y*. Now arithmetically, it is clear that

$$a + c - 2^{32} \le x + y - 2^{32} \le b + d - 2^{32}.$$

This, however, is what is calculated when the three terms overflow. Hence in this case also,

$$a + c \overset{u}{\le} x + y \overset{u}{\le} b + d.$$

If *a* + *c* does not overflow but *b* + *d* does, then

$$a + c \le 2^{32} - 1 \quad \text{and} \quad b + d \ge 2^{32}.$$

Because *x* + *y* takes on all values in the range *a* + *c* to *b* + *d*, it takes on the values $2^{32} - 1$ and 2^{32}—that is, the computed value *x* + *y* takes on the values $2^{32} - 1$ and 0 (although it doesn't take on *all* values in that range).

Lastly, the case that *a* + *c* overflows but *b* + *d* does not cannot occur, because $a \le b$ and $c \le d$.

This completes the proof of inequalities (4). The proof of (5) is similar, but "overflow" means that a true difference is less than 0.

Inequalities (6) can be proved by using (5) with $a = b = 0$, and then renaming the variables. (The expression −*x* with *x* an unsigned number means to compute the value of $2^{32} - x$, or of $\neg x + 1$ if you prefer.)

Because unsigned overflow is so easy to recognize (see "Unsigned Add/ Subtract" on page 29), these results are easily embodied in code, as shown in Figure 4–1 for addition and subtraction. The computed lower and upper limits are variables s and t, respectively.

```
s = a + c;                    s = a - d;
t = b + d;                    t = b - c;
if (s >= a && t < b) {        if (s > a && t <= b) {
   s = 0;                        s = 0;
   t = 0xFFFFFFFF; }             t = 0xFFFFFFFF; }
```

FIGURE 4–1. Propagating unsigned bounds through addition and subtraction operations.

Signed Numbers

The case of signed numbers is not so clean. As before, suppose we have bounds on two variables x and y as follows, where all quantities are *signed*:

$$a \le x \le b, \quad \text{and}$$
$$c \le y \le d. \tag{7}$$

We wish to compute tight bounds on $x + y$, $x - y$, and $-x$. The reasoning is very similar to that for the case of unsigned numbers, and the results for addition are shown below.

$$a + c < -2^{31}, b + d < -2^{31} : a + c \le x + y \le b + d$$
$$a + c < -2^{31}, b + d \ge -2^{31} : -2^{31} \le x + y \le 2^{31} - 1$$
$$-2^{31} \le a + c < 2^{31}, b + d < 2^{31} : a + c \le x + y \le b + d \tag{8}$$
$$-2^{31} \le a + c < 2^{31}, b + d \ge 2^{31} : -2^{31} \le x + y \le 2^{31} - 1$$
$$a + c \ge 2^{31}, b + d \ge 2^{31} : a + c \le x + y \le b + d$$

The first row means that if both of the additions $a + c$ and $b + d$ overflow in the negative direction, then the computed sum $x + y$ lies between the computed sums $a + c$ and $b + d$. This is because all three computed sums are too high by the same amount (2^{32}). The second row means that if the addition $a + c$ overflows in the negative direction, and the addition $b + d$ either does not overflow or overflows in the positive direction, then the computed sum $x + y$ can take on the extreme negative number and the extreme positive number (although perhaps not all values in between), which is not difficult to show. The other rows are interpreted similarly.

The rules for propagating bounds on signed numbers through the subtraction operation can easily be derived by rewriting the bounds on y as

$$-d \le -y \le -c$$

and using the rules for addition. The results are shown below.

$$a - d < -2^{31}, b - c < -2^{31} : a - d \le x - y \le b - c$$
$$a - d < -2^{31}, b - c \ge -2^{31} : -2^{31} \le x - y \le 2^{31} - 1$$
$$-2^{31} \le a - d < 2^{31}, b - c < 2^{31} : a - d \le x - y \le b - c$$
$$-2^{31} \le a - d < 2^{31}, b - c \ge 2^{31} : -2^{31} \le x - y \le 2^{31} - 1$$
$$a - d \ge 2^{31}, b - c \ge 2^{31} : a - d \le x - y \le b - c$$

The rules for negation can be derived from the rules for subtraction by taking $a = b = 0$, omitting some impossible combinations, simplifying, and renaming. The results are as follows:

$$a = -2^{31}, b = -2^{31} : -x = -2^{31}$$
$$a = -2^{31}, b \neq -2^{31} : -2^{31} \leq -x \leq 2^{31} - 1$$
$$a \neq -2^{31} : -b \leq -x \leq -a$$

C code for the case of signed numbers is a bit messy. We will consider only addition. It seems to be simplest to check for the two cases in (8) in which the computed limits are the extreme negative and positive numbers. Overflow in the negative direction occurs if the two operands are negative and the sum is nonnegative (see "Signed Add/Subtract" on page 26) Thus, to check for the condition that $a + c < -2^{31}$, we could let $s = a + c$; and then code something like "if (a < 0 && c < 0 && s >= 0) ...." It will be more efficient,[1] however, to perform logical operations directly on the arithmetic variables, with the sign bit containing the true/false result of the logical operations. Then, we write the above condition as "if ((a & c & ~s) < 0) ...." These considerations lead to the program fragment shown in Figure 4–2 below.

Here u is **true** (sign bit is 1) if the addition a + c overflows in the negative direction, and the addition b + d does *not* overflow in the negative direction. Variable v is **true** if the addition a + c does not overflow and the addition b + d overflows in the positive direction. The former condition can be expressed as "a and c have different signs, or a and s have the same sign." The "if" test is equivalent to "if (u < 0 || v < 0) —that is, if either u or v is **true**."

```
s = a + c;
t = b + d;
u = a & c & ~s & ~(b & d & ~t);
v = ((a ^ c) | ~(a ^ s)) & (~b & ~d & t);
if ((u | v) < 0) {
    s = 0x80000000;
    t = 0x7FFFFFFF; }
```

FIGURE 4–2. Propagating signed bounds through an addition operation.

---

1. In the sense of more compact, less branchy, code; faster-running code may result from checking first for the case of no overflow, assuming the limits are not likely to be large.

4–3 Propagating Bounds through Logical Operations

As in the preceding section, suppose we have bounds on two variables x and y as follows, where all quantities are unsigned:

$$a \leq x \leq b, \quad \text{and}$$
$$c \leq y \leq d. \tag{9}$$

Then what are some reasonably tight bounds on $x \mid y$, $x \& y$, $x \oplus y$, and $\neg x$?

Combining inequalities (9) with some inequalities from Section 2–3 on page 16, and noting that $\neg x = 2^{32} - 1 - x$, yields

$$\max(a, c) \leq (x \mid y) \leq b + d,$$
$$0 \leq (x \& y) \leq \min(b, d),$$
$$0 \leq (x \oplus y) \leq b + d, \quad \text{and}$$
$$\neg b \leq \neg x \leq \neg a,$$

where it is assumed that the addition $b + d$ does not overflow. These are easy to compute and might be good enough for the compiler application mentioned in the preceding section. The bounds in the first two inequalities, however, are not tight. For example, writing constants in binary, suppose

$$00010 \leq x \leq 00100, \quad \text{and}$$
$$01001 \leq y \leq 10100. \tag{10}$$

Then, by inspection (e.g., trying all 36 possibilities for x and y), we see that $01010 \leq (x \mid y) \leq 10111$. Thus, the lower bound is not $\max(a, c)$, nor is it $a \mid c$, and the upper bound is not $b + d$, nor is it $b \mid d$.

Given the values of a, b, c, and d in inequalities (9), how can one obtain tight bounds on the logical expressions? Consider first the minimum value attained by $x \mid y$. A reasonable guess might be the value of this expression with x and y both at their minima—that is, $a \mid c$. Example (10), however, shows that the minimum can be lower than this.

To find the minimum, our procedure is to start with $x = a$ and $y = c$, and then find an amount by which to increase either x or y so as to reduce the value of $x \mid y$. The result will be this reduced value. Rather than assigning a and c to x and y, however, we work directly with a and c, increasing one of them when doing so is valid and it reduces the value of $a \mid c$.

The procedure is to scan the bits of a and c from left to right. If both bits are 0, the result will have a 0 in that position. If both bits are 1, the result will have a 1 in that position (clearly, no values of x and y could make the result less). In these cases, continue the scan to the next bit position. If one scanned bit is 1 and the other is 0, then it is possible that changing the 0 to 1 and setting all the following bits in that bound's value to 0 will reduce the value of $a \mid c$. This change will not increase the value of $a \mid c$, because the result has a 1 in that position anyway, from the other bound. Therefore, form the number with the 0 changed to 1 and subsequent bits changed to 0. If that is less than or equal to the corresponding upper limit, the change can be made; do it, and the result is the *or* of the modified value with the other lower bound. If the change cannot be made (because the altered value exceeds the corresponding upper bound), continue the scan to the next bit position.

That's all there is to it. It might seem that after making the change, the scan should continue, looking for other opportunities to further reduce the value of $a \mid c$. However, even if a position is found that allows a 0 to be changed to 1, setting the subsequent bits to 0 does not reduce the value of $a \mid c$, because those bits are already 0.

C code for this algorithm is shown in Figure 4–3. We assume that the compiler will move the subexpressions ~a & c and a & ~c out of the loop. More significantly, if the *number of leading zeros* instruction is available, the program can be speeded up by initializing m with

```
m = 0x80000000 >> nlz(a ^ c);
```

This skips over initial bit positions in which a and c are both 0 or both 1. For this speedup to be effective when a ^ c is 0 (that is, when a = c), the machine's *shift right* instruction should be mod 64. If *number of leading zeros* is not available, it may be worthwhile to use some version of the flp2 function (see page 46) with argument a ^ c.

```
unsigned minOR(unsigned a, unsigned b,
               unsigned c, unsigned d) {
   unsigned m, temp;

   m = 0x80000000;
   while (m != 0) {
      if (~a & c & m) {
         temp = (a | m) & -m;
         if (temp <= b) {a = temp; break;}
      }
      else if (a & ~c & m) {
         temp = (c | m) & -m;
         if (temp <= d) {c = temp; break;}
      }
      m = m >> 1;
   }
   return a | c;
}
```

FIGURE 4–3. Minimum value of $x \mid y$ with bounds on x and y.

Now let us consider the *maximum* value attained by $x \mid y$, with the variables bounded as shown in inequalities (9). The algorithm is similar to that for the minimum, except it scans the values of bounds b and d (from left to right), looking for a position in which both bits are 1. If such a position is found, the algorithm tries to increase the value of $c \mid d$ by decreasing one of the bounds by changing the 1 to 0, and setting all subsequent bits in that bound to 1. If this is acceptable (if the resulting value is greater than or equal to the corresponding lower bound), the change is made and the result is the value of $c \mid d$ using the modified bound. If the change cannot be done, it is attempted on the other bound. If the change cannot be done to either bound, the scan continues. C code for this algorithm is shown in Figure 4–4. Here the subexpression b & d can be moved out of the loop, and the algorithm can be speeded up by initializing m with

```
m = 0x80000000 >> nlz(b & d);
```

There are two ways in which we might propagate the bounds of inequalities (9) through the expression $x \& y$: algebraic and direct computation. The algebraic method uses DeMorgan's rule:

$$x \& y = \neg(\neg x \mid \neg y)$$

Because we know how to propagate bounds precisely through *or*, and it is trivial to propagate them through *not* ($a \overset{u}{\leq} x \overset{u}{\leq} b \Leftrightarrow \neg b \overset{u}{\leq} \neg x \overset{u}{\leq} \neg a$), we have

$$\mathrm{minAND}(a, b, c, d) = \neg\mathrm{maxOR}(\neg b, \neg a, \neg d, \neg c), \quad \text{and}$$
$$\mathrm{maxAND}(a, b, c, d) = \neg\mathrm{minOR}(\neg b, \neg a, \neg d, \neg c).$$

For the direct computation method, the code is very similar to that for propagating bounds through *or*. It is shown in Figures 4–5 and 4–6.

```
unsigned maxOR(unsigned a, unsigned b,
               unsigned c, unsigned d) {
   unsigned m, temp;

   m = 0x80000000;
   while (m != 0) {
      if (b & d & m) {
         temp = (b - m) | (m - 1);
         if (temp >= a) {b = temp; break;}
         temp = (d - m) | (m - 1);
         if (temp >= c) {d = temp; break;}
      }
      m = m >> 1;
   }
   return b | d;
}
```

FIGURE 4–4. Maximum value of $x \mid y$ with bounds on x and y.

```
unsigned minAND(unsigned a, unsigned b,
                unsigned c, unsigned d) {
   unsigned m, temp;

   m = 0x80000000;
   while (m != 0) {
      if (~a & ~c & m) {
         temp = (a | m) & -m;
         if (temp <= b) {a = temp; break;}
         temp = (c | m) & -m;
         if (temp <= d) {c = temp; break;}
      }
      m = m >> 1;
   }
   return a & c;
}
```

FIGURE 4–5. Minimum value of x & y with bounds on x and y.

```
unsigned maxAND(unsigned a, unsigned b,
                unsigned c, unsigned d) {
   unsigned m, temp;

   m = 0x80000000;
   while (m != 0) {
      if (b & ~d & m) {
         temp = (b & ~m) | (m - 1);
         if (temp >= a) {b = temp; break;}
      }
      else if (~b & d & m) {
         temp = (d & ~m) | (m - 1);
         if (temp >= c) {d = temp; break;}
      }
      m = m >> 1;
   }
   return b & d;
}
```

FIGURE 4–6. Maximum value of x & y with bounds on x and y.

The algebraic method of finding bounds on expressions in terms of the functions for *and*, *or*, and *not* works for all the binary logical expressions except *exclusive or* and *equivalence*. The reason these two present a difficulty is that when expressed in terms of *and*, *or*, and *not*, there are two terms containing x and y. For example, we are to find

$$\min_{\substack{a \le x \le b \\ c \le y \le d}} (x \oplus y) = \min_{\substack{a \le x \le b \\ c \le y \le d}} ((x \& \neg y) \mid (\neg x \& y)).$$

The two operands of the *or* cannot be separately minimized (without proof that it works, which actually it does) because we seek one value of *x* and one value of *y* that minimizes the whole *or* expression.

The following expressions may be used to propagate bounds through *exclusive or*:

$$\text{minXOR}(a, b, c, d) = \text{minAND}(a, b, \neg d, \neg c) \mid \text{minAND}(\neg b, \neg a, c, d),$$

$$\text{maxXOR}(a, b, c, d) = \text{maxOR}(0, \text{maxAND}(a, b, \neg d, \neg c),$$

$$0, \text{maxAND}(\neg b, \neg a, c, d)).$$

It is straightforward to evaluate the minXOR and maxXOR functions by direct computation. The code for minXOR is the same as that for minOR (Figure 4–3) except with the two break statements removed, and the return value changed to a ^ c. The code for maxXOR is the same as that for maxOR (Figure 4–4) except with the four lines under the if clause replaced with

```
temp = (b - m) | (m - 1);
if (temp >= a) b = temp;
else {
    temp = (d - m) | (m - 1);
    if (temp >= c) d = temp;
}
```

and the return value changed to b ^ d.

Signed Bounds

If the bounds are *signed* integers, propagating them through logical expressions is substantially more complicated. The calculation is irregular if 0 is within the range *a* to *b*, or *c* to *d*. One way to calculate the lower and upper bounds for the expression *x* | *y* is shown in Table 4–1. A "+" entry means that the bound at the top of the column is greater than or equal to 0, and a "–" entry means that it is less than 0. The column labelled "minOR (signed)" contains expressions for computing the lower bound of *x* | *y*, and the last column contains expressions for computing the upper bound of *x* | *y*. One way to program this is to construct a value ranging from 0 to 15 from the sign bits of *a*, *b*, *c*, and *d*, and use a "switch" statement. Notice that not all values from 0 to 15 are used, because it is impossible to have *a* > *b* or *c* > *d*.

For signed numbers, the relation

$$a \leq x \leq b \Leftrightarrow \neg b \leq \neg x \leq \neg a$$

holds, so the algebraic method can be used to extend the results of Table 4–1 to other logical expressions (except for *exclusive or* and *equivalence*). We leave this and similar extensions to others.

TABLE 4–1. SIGNED MINOR AND MAXOR FROM UNSIGNED

a	b	c	d	minOR (signed)	maxOR (signed)
−	−	−	−	minOR(a, b, c, d)	maxOR(a, b, c, d)
−	−	−	+	a	-1
−	−	+	+	minOR(a, b, c, d)	maxOR(a, b, c, d)
−	+	−	−	c	-1
−	+	−	+	min(a, c)	maxOR($0, b, 0, d$)
−	+	+	+	minOR(a, **0xFFFFFFFF**, c, d)	maxOR($0, b, c, d$)
+	+	−	−	minOR(a, b, c, d)	maxOR(a, b, c, d)
+	+	−	+	minOR(a, b, c, **0xFFFFFFFF**)	maxOR($u, b, 0, d$)
+	+	+	+	minOR(a, b, c, d)	maxOR(a, b, c, d)

CHAPTER 5

COUNTING BITS

5–1 Counting 1-Bits

The IBM Stretch computer (ca. 1960) had a means of counting the number of 1-bits in a word as well as the number of leading 0's. It produced these two quantities as a by-product of all logical operations! The former function is sometimes called *population count* (e.g., on Stretch and the SPARCv9).

For machines that don't have this instruction, a good way to count the number of 1-bits is to first set each 2-bit field equal to the sum of the two single bits that were originally in the field, and then sum adjacent 2-bit fields, putting the results in each 4-bit field, and so on. A more complete discussion of this trick is in [RND]. The method is illustrated in Figure 5–1, in which the first row shows a computer word whose 1-bits are to be summed, and the last row shows the result (23 decimal).

This is an example of the "divide and conquer" strategy, in which the original problem (summing 32 bits) is divided into two problems (summing 16 bits), which are solved separately, and the results are combined (added, in this case). The strategy is applied recursively, breaking the 16-bit fields into 8-bit fields, and so on.

In the case at hand, the ultimate small problems (summing adjacent bits) can all be done in parallel, and combining adjacent sums can also be done in parallel in a fixed number of steps at each stage. The result is an algorithm that can be executed in $\log_2(32) = 5$ steps.

Other examples of divide and conquer are the well-known technique of binary search, a sorting method known as quicksort, and a method for reversing the bits of a word, discussed on page 101.

The method illustrated in Figure 5–1 may be committed to C code as

```
x = (x & 0x55555555) + ((x >> 1) & 0x55555555);
x = (x & 0x33333333) + ((x >> 2) & 0x33333333);
x = (x & 0x0F0F0F0F) + ((x >> 4) & 0x0F0F0F0F);
x = (x & 0x00FF00FF) + ((x >> 8) & 0x00FF00FF);
x = (x & 0x0000FFFF) + ((x >>16) & 0x0000FFFF);
```

The first line uses (x >> 1) & 0x55555555 rather than the perhaps more natural (x & 0xAAAAAAAA) >> 1 because the code shown avoids generating two large constants in a register. This would cost an instruction if the machine lacks the *and not* instruction. A similar remark applies to the other lines.

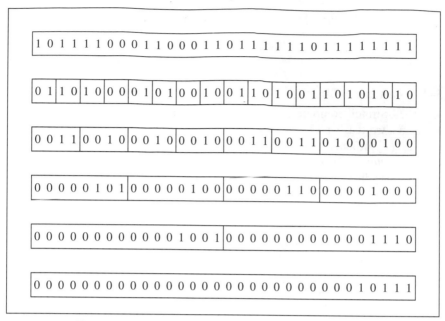

FIGURE 5–1. Counting 1-bits, "divide and conquer" strategy.

Clearly, the last *and* is unnecessary, and other *and*'s may be omitted when there is no danger that a field's sum will carry over into the adjacent field. Furthermore, there is a way to code the first line that uses one fewer instruction. This leads to the simplification shown in Figure 5–2, which executes in 21 instructions and is branch-free.

The first assignment to x is based on the first two terms of the rather surprising formula

$$\text{pop}(x) = x - \left\lfloor \frac{x}{2} \right\rfloor - \left\lfloor \frac{x}{4} \right\rfloor - \ldots - \left\lfloor \frac{x}{2^{31}} \right\rfloor. \tag{1}$$

```
int pop(unsigned x) {
    x = x - ((x >> 1) & 0x55555555);
    x = (x & 0x33333333) + ((x >> 2) & 0x33333333);
    x = (x + (x >> 4)) & 0x0F0F0F0F;
    x = x + (x >> 8);
    x = x + (x >> 16);
    return x & 0x0000003F;
}
```

FIGURE 5–2. Counting 1-bits in a word.

In Equation (1), we must have $x \geq 0$. By treating x as an unsigned integer, Equation (1) can be implemented with a sequence of 31 *shift right immediate*'s of 1, and 31 *subtract*'s. The procedure of Figure 5–2 uses the first two terms of this on each 2-bit field, in parallel.

There is a simple proof of Equation (1), which is shown below for the case of a 4-bit word. Let the word be $b_3 b_2 b_1 b_0$, where each $b_i = 0$ or 1. Then,

$$x - \left\lfloor \frac{x}{2} \right\rfloor - \left\lfloor \frac{x}{4} \right\rfloor - \left\lfloor \frac{x}{8} \right\rfloor = b_3 \cdot 2^3 + b_2 \cdot 2^2 + b_1 \cdot 2^1 + b_0 \cdot 2^0$$
$$-(b_3 \cdot 2^2 + b_2 \cdot 2^1 + b_1 \cdot 2^0)$$
$$-(b_3 \cdot 2^1 + b_2 \cdot 2^0)$$
$$-(b_3 \cdot 2^0)$$
$$= b_3(2^3 - 2^2 - 2^1 - 2^0) + b_2(2^2 - 2^1 - 2^0) + b_1(2^1 - 2^0) + b_0(2^0)$$
$$= b_3 + b_2 + b_1 + b_0.$$

Alternatively, Equation (1) can be derived by noting that bit i of the binary representation of a nonnegative integer x is given by

$$b_i = \left\lfloor \frac{x}{2^i} \right\rfloor - 2 \left\lfloor \frac{x}{2^{i+1}} \right\rfloor$$

and summing this for $i = 0$ to 31. Work it out—the last term is 0 because $x < 2^{32}$.

Equation (1) generalizes to other bases. For base ten it is

$$\text{sum\_digits}(x) = x - 9 \left\lfloor \frac{x}{10} \right\rfloor - 9 \left\lfloor \frac{x}{100} \right\rfloor - \ldots$$

where the terms are carried out until they are 0. This can be proved by essentially the same technique used above.

A variation of the above algorithm is to use a base four analogue of Equation (1) as a substitute for the second executable line of Figure 5–2:

```
x = x - 3*((x >> 2) & 0x33333333)
```

This code, however, uses the same number of instructions as the line it replaces (six), and requires a fast *multiply-by-3* instruction.

An algorithm in HAKMEM memo [HAK, item 169] counts the number of 1-bits in a word by using the first three terms of (1) to produce a word of 3-bit fields, each of which contains the number of 1-bits that were in it. It then adds adjacent 3-bit fields to form 6-bit field sums, and then adds the 6-bit fields by computing the value of the word modulo 63. Expressed in C, the algorithm is (the long constants are in octal)

```
int pop(unsigned x) {
   unsigned n;

   n = (x >> 1) & 033333333333;      // Count bits in
   x = x - n;                        // each 3-bit
   n = (n >> 1) & 033333333333;      // field.
   x = x - n;
   x = (x + (x >> 3)) & 030707070707; // 6-bit sums.
   x = modu(x, 63);                  // Add 6-bit sums.
   return x;
}
```

The last line uses the *unsigned modulus* function. (It could be either signed or unsigned if the word length were a multiple of 3). That the modulus function sums the 6-bit fields becomes clear by regarding the word x as an integer written in base 64. The remainder upon dividing a base b integer by $b - 1$ is, for $b \geq 3$, congruent mod b to the sum of the digits and, of course, is less than b. Because the sum of the digits in this case must be less than or equal to 32, $\mathrm{mod}(x, 63)$ must be equal to the sum of the digits of x, which is to say equal to the number of 1-bits in the original x.

This algorithm requires only ten instructions on the DEC PDP-10, because that machine has an instruction for computing the remainder with its second operand directly referencing a fullword in memory. On a basic RISC, it requires about 13 instructions, assuming the machine has *unsigned modulus* as one instruction (but not directly referencing a fullword immediate or memory operand). But it is probably not very fast, because division is almost always a slow operation. Also, it doesn't apply to 64-bit word lengths by simply extending the constants, although it does work for word lengths up to 62.

A variation on the HAKMEM algorithm is to use Equation (1) to count the number of 1's in each 4-bit field, working on all eight 4-bit fields in parallel [Hay1]. Then, the 4-bit sums may be converted to 8-bit sums in a straightforward way, and the four bytes can be added with a multiplication by 0x01010101. This gives

```
int pop(unsigned x) {
   unsigned n;

   n = (x >> 1) & 0x77777777;      // Count bits in
   x = x - n;                      // each 4-bit
   n = (n >> 1) & 0x77777777;      // field.
   x = x - n;
```

```
    n = (n >> 1) & 0x77777777;
    x = x - n;
    x = (x + (x >> 4)) & 0x0F0F0F0F;    // Get byte sums.
    x = x*0x01010101;                   // Add the bytes.
    return x >> 24;
}
```

This is 19 instructions on the basic RISC. It works well if the machine is two-address, because the first six lines can be done with only one *move register* instruction. Also, the repeated use of the mask 0x77777777 permits loading it into a register and referencing it with register-to-register instructions. Furthermore, most of the shifts are of only one position.

A quite different bit-counting method, illustrated in Figure 5–3, is to turn off the rightmost 1-bit repeatedly [Weg, RND], until the result is 0. It is very fast if the number of 1-bits is small, taking $2 + 5\mathrm{pop}(x)$ instructions.

This has a dual algorithm that is applicable if the number of 1-bits is expected to be large. The dual algorithm keeps turning on the rightmost 0-bit with $x = x \mid (x + 1)$, until the result is all 1's (−1). Then, it returns $32 - n$. (Alternatively, the original number x can be complemented, or n can be initialized to 32 and counted down).

A rather amazing algorithm is to rotate x left one position, 31 times, adding the 32 terms [MM]. The sum is the negative of pop(x)! That is,

$$\mathrm{pop}(x) = -\sum_{i=0}^{31} (x \overset{rot}{\ll} i),\tag{2}$$

where the additions are done modulo the word size, and the final sum is interpreted as a two's-complement integer. This is just a novelty; it would not be useful on most machines because the loop is executed 31 times and thus it requires 63 instructions plus the loop-control overhead.

```
int pop(unsigned x) {
    int n;

    n = 0;
    while (x != 0) {
        n = n + 1;
        x = x & (x - 1);
    }
    return n;
}
```

FIGURE 5–3. Counting 1-bits in a sparsely populated word.

To see why Equation (2) works, consider what happens to a single 1-bit of x. It gets rotated to all positions, and when these 32 numbers are added, a word of all 1-bits results. But this is -1. To illustrate, consider a 6-bit word size and $x = 001001$ (binary):

$$001001 \qquad x$$
$$010010 \qquad x \overset{rot}{\ll} 1$$
$$100100 \qquad x \overset{rot}{\ll} 2$$
$$001001 \qquad x \overset{rot}{\ll} 3$$
$$010010 \qquad x \overset{rot}{\ll} 4$$
$$100100 \qquad x \overset{rot}{\ll} 5$$

Of course, *rotate-right* would work just as well.

The method of Equation (1) is very similar to this "rotate and sum" method, which becomes clear by rewriting (1) as

$$\mathrm{pop}(x) = x - \sum_{i=1}^{31} (x \overset{u}{\gg} i).$$

This gives a slightly better algorithm than Equation (2) provides. It is better because it uses *shift right*, which is more commonly available than *rotate*, and because the loop can be terminated when the shifted quantity becomes 0. This reduces the loop-control code and may save a few iterations. The two algorithms are contrasted in Figure 5–4.

```
int pop(unsigned x) {
   int i, sum;

// Rotate and sum method        // Shift right & subtract

   sum = x;                      // sum = x;
   for (i = 1; i <= 31; i++) {   // while (x != 0) {
      x = rotatel(x, 1);         //    x = x >> 1;
      sum = sum + x;             //    sum = sum - x;
   }                             // }
   return -sum;                  // return sum;
}
```

FIGURE 5–4. Two similar bit-counting algorithms.

A less interesting algorithm that may be competitive with all the algorithms for pop(x) in this section is to have a table that contains pop(x) for, say, x in the range 0 to 255. The table can be accessed four times, adding the four numbers obtained. A branch-free version of the algorithm looks like this:

```
int pop(unsigned x) {                    // Table lookup.
   static char table[256] = {
      0, 1, 1, 2, 1, 2, 2, 3, 1, 2, 2, 3, 2, 3, 3, 4,
      ...
      4, 5, 5, 6, 5, 6, 6, 7, 5, 6, 6, 7, 6, 7, 7, 8};

   return table[x           & 0xFF] +
          table[(x >>  8) & 0xFF] +
          table[(x >> 16) & 0xFF] +
          table[(x >> 24)];
}
```

Item 167 in [HAK] contains a short algorithm for counting the number of 1-bits in a 9-bit quantity that is right-adjusted and isolated in a register. It works only on machines with registers of 36 or more bits. Below is a version of that algorithm that works on 32-bit machines, but only for 8-bit quantities.

```
x = x * 0x08040201;  // Make 4 copies.
x = x >> 3;          // So next step hits proper bits.
x = x & 0x11111111;  // Every 4th bit.
x = x * 0x11111111;  // Sum the digits (each 0 or 1).
x = x >> 28;         // Position the result.
```

A version for 7-bit quantities is

```
x = x * 0x02040810;  // Make 4 copies, left-adjusted.
x = x & 0x11111111;  // Every 4th bit.
x = x * 0x11111111;  // Sum the digits (each 0 or 1).
x = x >> 28;         // Position the result.
```

In these, the last two steps may be replaced with steps to compute the remainder of x modulo 15.

These are not particularly good; most programmers would probably prefer to use table lookup. The latter algorithm above, however, has a version that uses 64-bit arithmetic, which might be useful for a 64-bit machine that has fast multiplication. Its argument is a 15-bit quantity. (I don't believe there is a similar algorithm that deals with 16-bit quantities, unless it is known that not all 16 bits are 1.) The data type long long is a GNU C extension [Stall], meaning twice as long as an `int`, in our case 64 bits. The suffix `ULL` makes `unsigned long long` constants.

```
int pop(unsigned x) {
    unsigned long long y;
    y = x * 0x0002000400080010ULL;
    y = y & 0x1111111111111111ULL;
    y = y * 0x1111111111111111ULL;
    y = y >> 60;
    return y;
}
```

Counting 1-Bits in an Array

The simplest way to count the number of 1-bits in an array of fullwords, in the absence of the *population count* instruction, is to use a procedure such as that of Figure 5–2 on page 66 on each word of the array, and simply add the results.

Another way, which may be faster, is to use the first two executable lines of that procedure on groups of three words of the array, adding the three partial results. Because each partial result has a maximum value of 4 in each 4-bit field, adding three of these partial results gives a word with at most 12 in each 4-bit field, so no sum overflows into the field to its left. Next, each of these partial results may be converted into a word having four 8-bit fields with a maximum value of 24 in each field, using

```
x = (x & 0x0F0F0F0F) + ((x >> 4) & 0x0F0F0F0F);
```

As these words are produced, they may be added until the maximum value is just less than 255; this would allow summing ten such words ($\lfloor 255/24 \rfloor$). When ten such words have been added, the result may be converted into a word having two 16-bit fields, with a maximum value of 240 in each, with

```
x = (x & 0x00FF00FF) + ((x >> 8) & 0x00FF00FF);
```

Lastly, 273 such words ($\lfloor 65535/240 \rfloor$) can be added together until it is necessary to convert the sum to a word consisting of just one 32-bit field, with

```
x = (x & 0x0000FFFF) + (x >> 16);
```

In practice, the instructions added for loop control significantly detract from what is saved, so it is probably overkill to follow this procedure to the extent described. The code of Figure 5–5 applies the idea with only one intermediate level. First, it produces words containing four 8-bit partial sums. Then, after these are added together as much as possible, a fullword sum is produced. The

```
int pop_array(unsigned A[], int n) {

   int i, j, lim;
   unsigned s, s8, x;

   s = 0;
   for (i = 0; i < n; i = i + 31) {
      lim = min(n, i + 31);
      s8 = 0;
      for (j = i; j < lim; j++) {
         x = A[j];
         x = x - ((x >> 1) & 0x55555555);
         x = (x & 0x33333333) + ((x >> 2) & 0x33333333);
         x = (x + (x >> 4)) & 0x0F0F0F0F;
         s8 = s8 + x;
      }
      x = (s8 & 0x00FF00FF) + ((s8 >> 8) & 0x00FF00FF);
      x = (x & 0x0000ffff) + (x >> 16);
      s = s + x;
   }
   return s;
}
```

FIGURE 5–5. Counting 1-bits in an array.

number of words of 8-bit fields that can be added with no danger of overflow is $\lfloor 255/8 \rfloor = 31$.

This algorithm was compared to the simple loop method by compiling the two procedures with GCC to a target machine that is very similar to the basic RISC. The result is 22 instructions per word for the simple method, and 17.6 instructions per word for the method of Figure 5–5, a savings of 20%.

Applications

An application of the *population count* function is in computing the "Hamming distance" between two bit vectors, a concept from the theory of error-correcting codes. The Hamming distance is simply the number of places where the vectors differ; that is,

$$\text{dist}(x, y) = \text{pop}(x \oplus y).$$

See, for example, the chapter on error-correcting codes in [Dewd].

Another application is to allow reasonably fast direct-indexed access to a moderately sparse array A that is represented in a certain compact way. In the compact representation, only the defined, or nonzero, elements of the array are stored. There is an auxiliary bit string array *bits* of 32-bit words, which has a 1-bit for each index *i* for which $A[i]$ is defined. As a speedup device, there is also an array of words *bitsum* such that *bitsum*[*j*] is the total number of 1-bits in all the words of *bits* that precede entry *j*. This is illustrated below for an array in which elements 0, 2, 32, 47, 48, and 95 are defined.

bits	bitsum	data
0x0000 0005	0	$A[0]$
0x0001 8001	2	$A[2]$
0x8000 0000	5	$A[32]$
		$A[47]$
		$A[48]$
		$A[95]$

Given an index *i*, $0 \leq i \leq 95$, the corresponding index *sparse_i* into the data array is given by the number of 1-bits in array *bits* that precede the bit corresponding to *i*. This may be calculated as follows:

```
j = i >> 5;                      // j = i/32.
k = i & 31;                      // k = rem(i, 32);
mask = 1 << k;                   // A "1" at position k.
if ((bits[j] & mask) == 0) goto no_such_element;
mask = mask - 1;                 // 1's to right of k.
sparse_i = bitsum[j] + pop(bits[j] & mask);
```

The cost of this representation is two bits per element of the full array.

Still another application of the population function is in computing the number of trailing 0's in a word (see "Counting Trailing 0's" on page 84).

5–2 Parity

The "parity" of a string refers to whether it contains an odd or an even number of 1-bits. The string has "odd parity" if it contains an odd number of 1-bits; otherwise, it has "even parity."

Computing the Parity of a Word

Here we mean to produce a 1 if a word *x* has odd parity, and a 0 if it has even parity. This is the sum, modulo 2, of the bits of *x*—that is, the *exclusive or* of all the bits of *x*.

One way to compute this is to compute pop(*x*); the parity is the rightmost bit of the result. This is fine if you have the *population count* instruction, but if not, there are better ways than using the code for pop(*x*).

A rather direct method is to compute

$$y \leftarrow \bigoplus_{i=0}^{n-1} (x \overset{u}{\gg} i),$$

where n is the word size, and then the parity of x is given by the rightmost bit of y. (Here $\oplus$ denotes *exclusive or*, but for this formula, ordinary addition could be used.)

The parity may be computed much more quickly, for moderately large n, as follows (illustrated for $n = 32$; the shifts can be signed or unsigned):

```
y = x ^ (x >> 1);
y = y ^ (y >> 2);
y = y ^ (y >> 4);                                      (3)
y = y ^ (y >> 8);
y = y ^ (y >>16);
```

This executes in ten instructions, as compared to 62 for the first method, even if the implied loop is completely unrolled. Again, the parity bit is the rightmost bit of y. In fact, with either of these, if the shifts are unsigned, then bit i of y gives the parity of the bits of x at and to the left of i. Furthermore, because *exclusive or* is its own inverse, $x_i \oplus x_j$ is the parity of bits $i - 1$ through j, for $i \geq j$.

This is an example of the "parallel prefix," or "scan" operation, which has applications in parallel computing [KRS; HS]. Given a sufficient number of processors, it can convert certain seemingly serial processes from $O(n)$ to $O(\log_2 n)$ time. For example, if you have an array of words and you wish to compute the *exclusive or* scan operation on the entire array of bits, you can first use (3) on each word of the array, and then use essentially the same technique on the array, doing *exclusive or*'s on the words of the array. This takes more elementary (word length) *exclusive or* operations than a simple left-to-right process, and hence it is not a good idea for a uniprocessor. But on a parallel computer with a sufficient number of processors, it can do the job in $O(\log_2 n)$ rather than $O(n)$ time (where n is the number of words in the array).

A direct application of (3) is the conversion of an integer to Gray code (see page 236).

If the code (3) is changed to use left shifts, the parity of the whole word x winds up in the leftmost bit position, and bit i of y gives the parity of the bits of x at and to the *right* of position i.

If *rotate shift*'s are used, the result is a word of all 1's if the parity of x is odd, and of all 0's if even.

The following method executes in nine instructions and computes the parity of x as the integer 0 or 1 (the shifts are unsigned).

```
x = x ^ (x >> 1);
x = (x ^ (x >> 2)) & 0x11111111;
x = x*0x11111111;
p = (x >> 28) & 1;
```

After the second statement above, each hex digit of x is 0 or 1, according to the parity of the bits in that hex digit. The *multiply* adds these digits, putting the sum in the high-order hex digit. There can be no carry out of any hex column during the *add* part of the multiply, because the maximum sum of a column is 8.

The *multiply* and *shift* could be replaced by an instruction to compute the remainder after dividing x by 15, giving a (slow) solution in eight instructions, if the machine has *remainder immediate*.

Adding a Parity Bit to a 7-Bit Quantity

Item 167 in [HAK] contains a novel expression for putting even parity on a 7-bit quantity that is right-adjusted and isolated in a register. By this we mean to set the bit to the left of the seven bits, to make an 8-bit quantity with even parity. Their code is for a 36-bit machine, but it works on a 32-bit machine as well.

$$\text{modu}((x * \textbf{0x10204081}) \ \& \ \textbf{0x888888FF}, \textbf{1920})$$

Here, $\text{modu}(a, b)$ denotes the remainder of a upon division by b, with the arguments and result interpreted as unsigned integers, "$*$" denotes multiplication modulo 2^{32}, and the constant 1920 is $15 \cdot 2^7$. Actually, this computes the sum of the bits of x, and places the sum just to the left of the seven bits comprising x. For example, the expression maps **0x0000007F** to **0x000003FF**, and **0x00000055** to **0x00000255**.

Another ingenious formula from [HAK] is the following, which puts odd parity on a 7-bit integer:

$$\text{modu}((x * \textbf{0x00204081}) \ | \ \textbf{0x3DB6DB00}, \textbf{1152}),$$

where $1152 = 9 \cdot 2^7$. To understand this, it helps to know that the powers of 8 are ± 1 modulo 9. If the **0x3DB6DB00** is changed to **0xBDB6DB00**, this formula applies even parity.

These methods are not practical on today's machines, because memory is cheap but division is still slow. Most programmers would compute these functions with a simple table lookup.

Application

The parity operation is useful in multiplying bit matrices in GF(2) (in which the *add* operation is *exclusive or*).

5–3 Counting Leading 0's

There are several simple ways to count leading 0's with a binary search technique. Below is a model that has several variations. It executes in 20 to 29 instructions on the basic RISC. The comparisons are "logical" (unsigned integers).

```
if (x == 0) return(32);
n = 0;
if (x <= 0x0000FFFF) {n = n +16; x = x <<16;}
if (x <= 0x00FFFFFF) {n = n + 8; x = x << 8;}
if (x <= 0x0FFFFFFF) {n = n + 4; x = x << 4;}
if (x <= 0x3FFFFFFF) {n = n + 2; x = x << 2;}
if (x <= 0x7FFFFFFF) {n = n + 1;}
return n;
```

One variation is to replace the comparisons with *and*'s:

```
if ((x & 0xFFFF0000) == 0) {n = n +16; x = x <<16;}
if ((x & 0xFF000000) == 0) {n = n + 8; x = x << 8}
...
```

Another variation, which avoids large immediate values, is to use *shift right* instructions.

The last if statement is simply adding 1 to n if the high-order bit of x is 0, so an alternative, which saves a branch instruction, is:

```
n = n + 1 - (x >> 31);
```

The "+ 1" in this assignment can be omitted if n is initialized to 1 rather than to 0. These observations lead to the algorithm (12 to 20 instructions on the basic RISC) shown in Figure 5–6. A further improvement is possible for the case in which x begins with a 1-bit: change the first line to

```
if ((int)x <= 0) return (~x >> 26) & 32;
```

Figure 5–7 illustrates a sort of reversal of the above. It requires fewer operations the more leading 0's there are, and avoids large immediate values and large shift amounts. It executes in 12 to 20 instructions on the basic RISC.

```
int nlz(unsigned x) {
   int n;

   if (x == 0) return(32);
   n = 1;
   if ((x >> 16) == 0) {n = n +16;  x = x <<16;}
   if ((x >> 24) == 0) {n = n + 8;  x = x << 8;}
   if ((x >> 28) == 0) {n = n + 4;  x = x << 4;}
   if ((x >> 30) == 0) {n = n + 2;  x = x << 2;}
   n = n - (x >> 31);
   return n;
}
```

FIGURE 5–6. *Number of leading zeros,* binary search.

```
int nlz(unsigned x) {
   unsigned y;
   int n;

   n = 32;
   y = x >>16;  if (y != 0) {n = n -16;   x = y;}
   y = x >> 8;  if (y != 0) {n = n - 8;   x = y;}
   y = x >> 4;  if (y != 0) {n = n - 4;   x = y;}
   y = x >> 2;  if (y != 0) {n = n - 2;   x = y;}
   y = x >> 1;  if (y != 0) return n - 2;
   return n - x;
}
```

FIGURE 5–7. *Number of leading zeros,* binary search, counting down.

This algorithm is amenable to a "table assist": the last four executable lines can be replaced by

```
static char table[256] = {0,1,2,2,3,3,3,3,4,4,...,8);
return n - table[x];
```

Many algorithms can be aided by table lookup, but this will not often be mentioned here.

For compactness, this and the preceding algorithms in this section can be coded as loops. For example, the algorithm of Figure 5–7 becomes the algorithm shown in Figure 5–8. This executes in 23 to 33 basic RISC instructions, ten of which are conditional branches.

One can, of course, simply shift left one place at a time, counting, until the sign bit is on; or shift right one place at a time until the word is all 0. These algorithms are compact and work well if the number of leading 0's is expected to be small or large, respectively. One can combine the methods, as shown in Figure 5–9. We

```
int nlz(unsigned x) {
   unsigned y;
   int n, c;

   n = 32;
   c = 16;
   do {
      y = x >> c;  if (y != 0) {n = n - c;  x = y;}
      c = c >> 1;
   } while (c != 0);
   return n - x;
}
```

FIGURE 5–8. *Number of leading zeros*, binary search, coded as a loop.

```
int nlz(int x) {
   int y, n;

   n = 0;
   y = x;
L: if (x < 0) return n;
   if (y == 0) return 32 - n;
   n = n + 1;
   x = x << 1;
   y = y >> 1;
   goto L;
}
```

FIGURE 5–9. *Number of leading zeros*, working both ends at the same time.

mention this because the technique of merging two algorithms and choosing the result of whichever one stops first is more generally applicable. It leads to code that runs fast on superscalar and VLIW machines, because of the proximity of independent instructions. (These machines can execute two or more instructions simultaneously, provided they are independent.)

On the basic RISC, this executes in $\min(3 + 6\text{nlz}(x), \ 5 + 6(32 - \text{nlz}(x)))$ instructions, or 99 worst case. However, one can imagine a superscalar or VLIW machine executing the entire loop body in one cycle if the comparison results are obtained as a by-product of the shifts, or in two cycles otherwise, plus the branch overhead.

It is straightforward to convert either of the algorithms of Figure 5–6 or Figure 5–7 to a branch-free counterpart. Figure 5–10 shows a version that does the job in 28 basic RISC instructions.

If your machine has the *population count* instruction, a good way to compute the *number of leading zeros* function is given in Figure 5–11. The five assignments

```
int nlz(unsigned x) {
   int y, m, n;

   y = -(x >> 16);       // If left half of x is 0,
   m = (y >> 16) & 16;   // set n = 16. If left half
   n = 16 - m;           // is nonzero, set n = 0 and
   x = x >> m;           // shift x right 16.
                         // Now x is of the form 0000xxxx.
   y = x - 0x100;        // If positions 8-15 are 0,
   m = (y >> 16) & 8;    // add 8 to n and shift x left 8.
   n = n + m;
   x = x << m;

   y = x - 0x1000;       // If positions 12-15 are 0,
   m = (y >> 16) & 4;    // add 4 to n and shift x left 4.
   n = n + m;
   x = x << m;

   y = x - 0x4000;       // If positions 14-15 are 0,
   m = (y >> 16) & 2;    // add 2 to n and shift x left 2.
   n = n + m;
   x = x << m;

   y = x >> 14;          // Set y = 0, 1, 2, or 3.
   m = y & ~(y >> 1);    // Set m = 0, 1, 2, or 2 resp.
   return n + 2 - m;
}
```

FIGURE 5–10. *Number of leading zeros*, branch-free binary search.

```
int nlz(unsigned x) {
   int pop(unsigned x);

   x = x | (x >> 1);
   x = x | (x >> 2);
   x = x | (x >> 4);
   x = x | (x >> 8);
   x = x | (x >>16);
   return pop(~x);
}
```

FIGURE 5–11. *Number of leading zeros*, right-propagate and count 1-bits.

to x may be reversed, or in fact done in any order. This is branch-free and takes 11 instructions. Even if *population count* is not available, this algorithm may be useful. Using the 21-instruction code for counting 1-bits given in Figure 5–2 on page 66, it executes in 32 branch-free basic RISC instructions.

Floating-Point Methods

The floating-point post-normalization facilities can be used to count leading zeros. It works out quite well with IEEE-format floating-point numbers. The idea is to convert the given unsigned integer to double-precision floating-point, extract the exponent, and subtract it from a constant. Figure 5–12 illustrates a complete procedure for this.

The code uses the C++ "anonymous union" to overlay an integer with a double-precision floating-point quantity. Variable LE must be 1 for execution on a little-endian machine, and 0 for big-endian. The addition of 0.5, or some other small number, is necessary for the method to work when k = 0.

We will not attempt to assess the execution time of this code, because machines differ so much in their floating-point capabilities. For example, many machines have their floating-point registers separate from the integer registers, and on such machines data transfers through memory may be required to convert an integer to floating-point and then move the result to an integer register.

The code of Figure 5–12 is not valid C or C++ according to the ANSI standard, because it refers to the same memory locations as two different types. Thus, one cannot be sure it will work on a particular machine and compiler. It does work with IBM's XLC compiler on AIX, and with the GCC compiler on AIX and on Windows 2000, at all optimization levels (as of this writing, anyway). If the code is altered to do the overlay defining with something like

```
xx = (double)k + 0.5;
n = 1054 - (*((unsigned *)&xx + LE) >> 20);
```

it does *not* work on these systems with optimization turned on. This code, incidentally, violates a second ANSI standard, namely, that pointer arithmetic can be performed only on pointers to array elements [Cohen]. The failure, however, is due to the first violation, involving overlay defining.

```
int nlz(unsigned k) {
   union {
      unsigned asInt[2];
      double asDouble;
   };
   int n;

   asDouble = (double)k + 0.5;
   n = 1054 - (asInt[LE] >> 20);
   return n;
}
```

FIGURE 5–12. *Number of leading zeros*, using IEEE floating-point.

In spite of the flakiness of this code,[1] three variations are given below.

```
asDouble = (double)k;
n = 1054 - (asInt[LE] >> 20);
n = (n & 31) + (n >> 9);

k = k & ~(k >> 1);
asFloat = (float)k + 0.5f;
n = 158 - (asInt >> 23);

k = k & ~(k >> 1);
asFloat = (float)k;
n = 158 - (asInt >> 23);
n = (n & 31) + (n >> 6);
```

In the first variation, the problem with k = 0 is fixed not by a floating-point addition of 0.5, but by integer arithmetic on the result n (which would be 1054, or 0x41E, if the correction were not done).

The next two variations use single-precision floating-point, with the "anonymous union" changed in an obvious way. Here there is a new problem: Rounding can throw off the result when the rounding mode is either round to nearest (almost universally used) or round toward +∞. For round to nearest mode, the rounding problem occurs for k in the ranges hexadecimal FFFF FF80 to FFFF FFFF, 7FFF FFC0 to 7FFF FFFF, 3FFF FFE0 to 3FFF FFFF, and so on. In rounding, an add of 1 carries all the way to the left, changing the position of the most significant 1-bit. The correction steps used above clear the bit to the right of the most significant 1-bit, blocking the carry.

The GNU C/C++ compiler has a unique feature that allows coding any of these schemes as a macro, giving in-line code for the function references [Stall]. This feature allows statements, including declarations, to be inserted in code where an expression is called for. The sequence of statements would usually end with an expression, which is taken to be the value of the construction. Such a macro definition is shown below, for the first single-precision variation. (In C, it is customary to use uppercase for macro names.)

```
#define NLZ(k) \
    ({union {unsigned _asInt; float _asFloat;}; \
        unsigned _kk = (k) & ~((unsigned)(k) >> 1); \
        _asFloat = (float)_kk + 0.5f; \
        158 - (_asInt >> 23);})
```

The underscores are used to avoid name conflicts with parameter k; presumably, user-defined names do not begin with underscores.

---

1. The flakiness is due to the way C is used. The methods illustrated would be perfectly acceptable if coded in machine language, or generated by a compiler, for a particular machine.

Relation to the Log Function

The "nlz" function is, essentially, the "integer log base 2" function. For unsigned $x \neq 0$,

$$\lfloor \log_2(x) \rfloor = 31 - \text{nlz}(x), \text{ and}$$
$$\lceil \log_2(x) \rceil = 32 - \text{nlz}(x - 1).$$

See also Section 11–4, "Integer Logarithm," on page 215.

Another closely related function is *bitsize*, the number of bits required to represent its argument as a signed quantity in two's-complement form. We take its definition to be

$$\text{bitsize}(x) = \begin{cases} 1, & x = -1 \text{ or } 0, \\ 2, & x = -2 \text{ or } 1, \\ 3, & -4 \leq x \leq -3 \text{ or } 2 \leq x \leq 3, \\ 4, & -8 \leq x \leq -5 \text{ or } 4 \leq x \leq 7, \\ \dots & \dots \\ 32, & -2^{31} \leq x \leq -2^{30} + 1 \text{ or } 2^{30} \leq x \leq 2^{31} - 1. \end{cases}$$

From this definition, bitsize(x) = bitsize($-x - 1$). But $-x - 1 = \neg x$, so an algorithm for bitsize is (where the shift is signed)

```
x = x ^ (x >> 31);          // If (x < 0) x = -x - 1;
return 33 - nlz(x);
```

Applications

Two important applications of the *number of leading zeros* function are in simulating floating-point arithmetic operations and in various division algorithms (see Figure 9–1 on page 141, and Figure 9–3 on page 152). The instruction seems to have a miscellany of other uses.

It can be used to get the "$x = y$" predicate in only three instructions (see "Comparison Predicates" on page 21), and as an aid in computing certain elementary functions (see pages 205, 208, 214, and 218).

A novel application is to generate exponentially distributed random integers by generating uniformly distributed random integers and taking "nlz" of the result [GLS1]. The result is 0 with probability 1/2, 1 with probability 1/4, 2 with probability 1/8, and so on. Another application is as an aid in searching a word for a consecutive string of 1-bits (or 0-bits) of a certain length, a process that is used in some disk block allocation algorithms. For these last two applications, the *number of trailing zeros* function could also be used.

5–4 Counting Trailing 0's

If the *number of leading zeros* instruction is available, then the best way to count trailing 0's is, most likely, to convert it to a count *leading* 0's problem:

$$32 - \text{nlz}(\neg x \mathbin{\&} (x - 1)).$$

If *population count* is available, a slightly better method is to form a mask that identifies the trailing 0's, and count the 1-bits in it [Hay2], such as

$$\text{pop}(\neg x \mathbin{\&} (x - 1)), \text{ and}$$

$$32 - \text{pop}(x \mid -x).$$

Variations exist using other expressions for forming a mask that identifies the trailing zeros of x, such as those given in Section 2–1,"Manipulating Rightmost Bits" on page 11. These methods are also reasonable even if the machine has none of the bit-counting instructions. Using the algorithm for pop(x) given in Figure 5–2 on page 66, the first expression above executes in about $3 + 21 = 24$ instructions (branch-free).

Figure 5–13 shows an algorithm that does it directly, in 12 to 20 basic RISC instructions (for $x \neq 0$).

The n + 16 can be simplified to 17 if that helps, and if the compiler is not smart enough to do that for you (this does not affect the number of instructions as we are counting them).

Figure 5–14 shows a variation that uses smaller immediate values and simpler operations. It executes in 12 to 21 basic RISC instructions. Unlike the above procedure, when the number of trailing 0's is small, the one in Figure 5–14 executes a larger number of instructions, but also a larger number of "fall through" branches.

The line just above the `return` statement may alternatively be coded

```
n = n - ((x << 1) >> 31);
```

which saves a branch, but not an instruction.

In terms of number of instructions executed, it is hard to beat the "search tree" [Aus2]. Figure 5–15 illustrates this procedure for an 8-bit argument. This procedure executes in seven instructions for all paths except the last two (return 7 or 8), which require nine. A 32-bit version would execute in 11 to 13 instructions. Unfortunately, for large word sizes the program is quite large. The 8-bit version above is 12 lines of executable source code and would compile into about 41 instructions. A 32-bit version would be 48 lines and about 164 instructions, and a 64-bit version would be twice that.

If the number of trailing 0's is expected to be small or large, then the simple loops below are quite fast. The left-hand algorithm executes in $5 + 3\text{ntz}(x)$, and the right one in $3 + 3(32 - \text{ntz}(x))$ basic RISC instructions.

```
int ntz(unsigned x) {
   int n;

   if (x == 0) return(32);
   n = 1;
   if ((x & 0x0000FFFF) == 0) {n = n +16; x = x >>16;}
   if ((x & 0x000000FF) == 0) {n = n + 8; x = x >> 8;}
   if ((x & 0x0000000F) == 0) {n = n + 4; x = x >> 4;}
   if ((x & 0x00000003) == 0) {n = n + 2; x = x >> 2;}
   return n - (x & 1);
}
```

FIGURE 5–13. *Number of trailing zeros*, binary search.

```
int ntz(unsigned x) {
   unsigned y;
   int n;

   if (x == 0) return 32;
   n = 31;
   y = x <<16; if (y != 0) {n = n -16;   x = y;}
   y = x << 8; if (y != 0) {n = n - 8;   x = y;}
   y = x << 4; if (y != 0) {n = n - 4;   x = y;}
   y = x << 2; if (y != 0) {n = n - 2;   x = y;}
   y = x << 1; if (y != 0) {n = n - 1;}
   return n;
}
```

FIGURE 5–14. *Number of trailing zeros*, smaller immediate values.

```
int ntz(char x) {
   if (x & 15) {
      if (x & 3) {
         if (x & 1) return 0;
         else return 1;
      }
      else if (x & 4) return 2;
      else return 3;
   }
   else if (x & 0x30) {
      if (x & 0x10) return 4;
      else return 5;
   }
   else if (x & 0x40) return 6;
   else if (x) return 7;
   else return 8;
}
```

FIGURE 5–15. *Number of trailing zeros*, binary search tree.

```
int ntz(unsigned x) {
   int n;

   x = ~x & (x - 1);
   n = 0;                           // n = 32;
   while(x != 0) {                  // while (x != 0) {
      n = n + 1;                    //    n = n - 1;
      x = x >> 1;                   //    x = x + x;
   }                                // }
   return n;                        // return n;
}
```

FIGURE 5–16. *Number of trailing zeros*, simple counting loops.

It is interesting to note that if the numbers x are uniformly distributed, then the average number of trailing 0's is, very nearly, 1.0. To see this, sum the products $p_i n_i$, where p_i is the probability that there are exactly n_i trailing 0's. That is,

$$S \cong \frac{1}{2} \cdot 0 + \frac{1}{4} \cdot 1 + \frac{1}{8} \cdot 2 + \frac{1}{16} \cdot 3 + \frac{1}{32} \cdot 4 + \frac{1}{64} \cdot 5 + \dots$$

$$\cong \sum_{n=0}^{\infty} \frac{n}{2^{n+1}}.$$

To evaluate this sum, consider the following array:

$$
\begin{array}{ccccc}
1/4 & 1/8 & 1/16 & 1/32 & 1/64 \ \dots \\
    & 1/8 & 1/16 & 1/32 & 1/64 \ \dots \\
    &   & 1/16 & 1/32 & 1/64 \ \dots \\
    &   &   & 1/32 & 1/64 \ \dots \\
    &   &   &   & 1/64 \ \dots \\
    &   &   &   & \dots
\end{array}
$$

The sum of each column is a term of the series for S. Hence S is the sum of all the numbers in the array. The sum of the rows are

$$1/4 + 1/8 + 1/16 + 1/32 + \dots \ = \ 1/2$$
$$1/8 + 1/16 + 1/32 + 1/64 + \dots \ = \ 1/4$$
$$1/16 + 1/32 + 1/64 + 1/128 + \dots \ = \ 1/8$$
$$\dots$$

and the sum of these is $1/2 + 1/4 + 1/8 + \dots \ = \ 1$. The absolute convergence of the original series justifies the rearrangement.

Sometimes, a function similar to ntz(x) is wanted, but a 0 argument is a special case, perhaps an error, that should be identified with a value of the function that's easily distinguished from the "normal" values of the function. For example, let us define "the number of factors of 2 in x" to be

$$\text{nfact2}(x) = \begin{cases} \text{ntz}(x), & x \neq 0, \\ -1, & x = 0. \end{cases}$$

This can be calculated from

$$31 - \text{nlz}(x \,\&\, -x).$$

Applications

[GLS1] points out some interesting applications of the *number of trailing zeros* function. It has been named the "ruler function" by Eric Jensen, because it gives the height of a tick mark on a ruler that's divided into halves, quarters, eighths, and so on.

It has an application in R. W. Gosper's loop-detection algorithm, which will now be described in some detail because it is quite elegant and it does more than might at first seem possible.

Suppose a sequence $X_0, X_1, X_2, \ldots$ is defined by $X_{n+1} = f(X_n)$. If the range of f is finite, the sequence is necessarily periodic. That is, it consists of a leader $X_0, X_1, \ldots, X_{\mu-1}$ followed by a cycle $X_\mu, X_{\mu+1}, \ldots X_{\mu+\lambda-1}$ that repeats without limit ($X_\mu = X_{\mu+\lambda}$, $X_{\mu+1} = X_{\mu+\lambda+1}$, and so on, where λ is the period of the cycle). Given the function f, the loop-detection problem is to find the index μ of the first element that repeats, and the period λ. Loop detection has applications in testing random number generators and detecting a cycle in a linked list.

One could save all the values of the sequence as they are produced, and compare each new element with all the preceding ones. This would immediately show where the second cycle starts. But algorithms exist that are much more efficient in space and time.

Perhaps the simplest is due to R. W. Floyd [Knu2, sec. 3.1, prob. 6]. This algorithm iterates the process

$$x = f(x)$$
$$y = f(f(y))$$

with x and y initialized to X_0. After the nth step, $x = X_n$ and $y = X_{2n}$. These are compared, and if equal, it is known that X_n and X_{2n} are separated by an integral multiple of the period λ—that is, $2n - n = n$ is a multiple of λ. Then μ can be determined by regenerating the sequence from the beginning, comparing X_0 to X_n, then X_1 to X_{n+1}, and so on. Equality occurs when X_μ is compared to $X_{n+\mu}$. Finally, λ can be determined by regenerating more elements, comparing

X_μ to $X_{\mu+1}$, $X_{\mu+2}$, ... This algorithm requires only a small and bounded amount of space, but it evaluates f many times.

Gosper's algorithm [HAK, item 132; Knu2, Answers to Exercises for sec. 3.1, prob. 7] finds the period λ, but not the starting point μ of the first cycle. Its main feature is that it never backs up to reevaluate f, and it is quite economical in space and time. It is not bounded in space; it requires a table of size $\log_2(\Lambda) + 1$, where Λ is the largest possible period. This is not a lot of space; for example, if it is known a priori that $\Lambda \le 2^{32}$, then 33 words suffice.

Gosper's algorithm, coded in C, is shown in Figure 5–17. This C function is given the function f being analyzed and a starting value X_0. It returns lower and upper bounds on μ, and the period λ. (Although Gosper's algorithm cannot compute μ, it can compute lower and upper bounds μ_l and μ_u such that $\mu_u - \mu_l + 1 \le \max(\lambda - 1, 1)$.) The algorithm works by comparing X_n, for $n = 1, 2, ...$, to a subset of size $\lfloor \log_2 n \rfloor + 1$ of the elements of the sequence that precede X_n. The elements of the subset are the closest preceding X_i such that $i + 1$ ends in a 1-bit (that is, i is the even number preceding n), the closest preceding X_i such that $i + 1$ ends in exactly one 0-bit, the closest preceding X_i such that $i + 1$ ends in exactly two 0-bits, and so on.

```c
void ld_Gosper(int (*f)(int), int X0, int *mu_l,
                             int *mu_u, int *lambda) {
    int Xn, k, m, kmax, n, lgl;
    int T[33];

    T[0] = X0;
    Xn = X0;
    for (n = 1; ; n++) {
        Xn = f(Xn);
        kmax = 31 - nlz(n);             // Floor(log2 n).
        for (k = 0; k <= kmax; k++) {
            if (Xn == T[k]) goto L;
        }
        T[ntz(n+1)] = Xn;               // No match.
    }
L:
    // Compute m = max{i | i < n and ntz(i+1) = k}.

    m = ((((n >> k) - 1) | 1) << k) - 1;
    *lambda = n - m;
    lgl = 31 - nlz(*lambda - 1); // Ceil(log2 lambda) - 1.
    *mu_u = m;                          // Upper bound on mu.
    *mu_l = m - max(1, 1 << lgl) + 1;// Lower bound on mu.
}
```

FIGURE 5–17. Gosper's loop-detection algorithm.

Thus, the comparisons proceed as follows:

$$X_1 : X_0 \qquad X_7 : X_6, X_5, X_3 \qquad X_{13} : X_{12}, X_9, X_{11}, X_7$$

$$X_2 : X_0, X_1 \qquad X_8 : X_6, X_5, X_3, X_7 \qquad X_{14} : X_{12}, X_{13}, X_{11}, X_7$$

$$X_3 : X_2, X_1 \qquad X_9 : X_8, X_5, X_3, X_7 \qquad X_{15} : X_{14}, X_{13}, X_{11}, X_7$$

$$X_4 : X_2, X_1, X_3 \qquad X_{10} : X_8, X_9, X_3, X_7 \qquad X_{16} : X_{14}, X_{13}, X_{11}, X_7, X_{15}$$

$$X_5 : X_4, X_1, X_3 \qquad X_{11} : X_{10}, X_9, X_3, X_7 \qquad X_{17} : X_{16}, X_{13}, X_{11}, X_7, X_{15}$$

$$X_6 : X_4, X_5, X_3 \qquad X_{12} : X_{10}, X_9, X_{11}, X_7 \qquad X_{18} : X_{16}, X_{17}, X_{11}, X_7, X_{15}$$

It can be shown that the algorithm always terminates with n somewhere in the second cycle—that is, with $n < \mu + 2\lambda$. See [Knu2] for further details.

The ruler function reveals how to solve the Tower of Hanoi puzzle. Number the n disks from 0 to $n - 1$. At each move k, as k goes from 1 to $2^n - 1$, move disk ntz(k) the minimum permitted distance to the right, in a circular manner.

The ruler function can be used to generate a reflected binary Gray code (see Section 13–1 on page 235). Start with an arbitrary n-bit word, and at each step k, as k goes from 1 to $2^n - 1$, flip bit ntz(k).

CHAPTER 6

SEARCHING WORDS

6–1 Find First 0-Byte

The need for this function stems mainly from the way character strings are represented in the C language. They have no explicit length stored with them; instead, the end of the string is denoted by an all-0 byte. To find the length of a string, a C program uses the "strlen" (string length) function. This function searches the string, from left to right, for the 0-byte, and returns the number of bytes scanned, not counting the 0-byte.

A fast implementation of "strlen" might load and test single bytes until a word boundary is reached, and then load a word at a time into a register, and test the register for the presence of a 0-byte. On big-endian machines, we want a function that returns the index of the first 0-byte from the left. A convenient encoding is values from 0 to 3 denoting bytes 0 to 3, and a value of 4 denoting that there is no 0-byte in the word. This is the value to add to the string length, as successive words are searched, if the string length is initialized to 0. On little-endian machines, one wants the index of the first 0-byte from the right end of the register, because little-endian machines reverse the four bytes when a word is loaded into a register. Specifically, we are interested in the following functions, where "00" denotes a 0-byte, "nn" denotes a nonzero byte, and "xx" denotes a byte that may be 0 or nonzero.

$$
\text{zbytel}(x) = \begin{cases} 0, & x = 00\text{xxxxxx}, \\ 1, & x = \text{nn}00\text{xxxx}, \\ 2, & x = \text{nnnn}00\text{xx}, \\ 3, & x = \text{nnnnnn}00, \\ 4, & x = \text{nnnnnnnn}. \end{cases}
\qquad
\text{zbyter}(x) = \begin{cases} 0, & x = \text{xxxxxx}00, \\ 1, & x = \text{xxxx}00\text{nn}, \\ 2, & x = \text{xx}00\text{nnnn}, \\ 3, & x = 00\text{nnnnnn}, \\ 4, & x = \text{nnnnnnnn}. \end{cases}
$$

Our first procedure for the *find leftmost 0-byte* function, shown in Figure 6–1, simply tests each byte, in left-to-right order, and returns the result when the first 0-byte is found.

This executes in two to 11 basic RISC instructions, 11 in the case that the word has no 0-bytes (which is the important case for the "strlen" function). A very similar program will handle the problem of finding the rightmost 0-byte.

Figure 6–2 shows a branch-free procedure for this function. The idea is to convert each 0-byte to 0x80, and each nonzero byte to 0x00, and then use *number of leading zeros*. This procedure executes in eight instructions if the machine has the *number of leading zeros* and *nor* instructions. Some similar tricks are described in [Lamp].

```
int zbytel(unsigned x) {
   if                 ((x >> 24)    == 0) return 0;
   else if ((x & 0x00FF0000) == 0) return 1;
   else if ((x & 0x0000FF00) == 0) return 2;
   else if ((x & 0x000000FF) == 0) return 3;
   else return 4;
}
```

FIGURE 6–1. *Find leftmost 0-byte*, simple sequence of tests.

```
int zbytel(unsigned x) {
   unsigned y;
   int n;
                               // Original byte: 00 80 other
   y = (x & 0x7F7F7F7F) + 0x7F7F7F7F;   // 7F 7F 1xxxxxxx
   y = ~(y | x | 0x7F7F7F7F);           // 80 00 00000000
   n = nlz(y) >> 3;            // n = 0 ... 4, 4 if x
   return n;                   // has no 0-byte.
}
```

FIGURE 6–2. *Find leftmost 0-byte*, branch-free code.

The position of the *rightmost* 0-byte is given by the number of trailing 0's in the final value of y computed above, divided by 8 (with fraction discarded). Using the expression for computing the number of trailing 0's by means of the *number of leading zeros* instruction (see Section 5–4, "Counting Trailing 0's," on page 84), this can be computed by replacing the assignment to n in the procedure above with:

```
n = (32 - nlz(~y & (y - 1))) >> 3;
```

This is a 12-instruction solution, if the machine has *nor* and *and not*.

In most situations on PowerPC, incidentally, a procedure to find the rightmost 0-byte would not be needed. Instead, the words can be loaded with the *load word byte-reverse* instruction (`lwbrx`).

The procedure of Figure 6–2 is more valuable on a 64-bit machine than on a 32-bit one, because on a 64-bit machine the procedure (with obvious modifications) requires about the same number of instructions (seven or ten, depending upon how the constant is generated), whereas the technique of Figure 6–1 requires 23 instructions worst case.

If only a test for the presence of a 0-byte is wanted, then a *branch on zero* (or *nonzero*) can be inserted just after the second assignment to y.

If the "nlz" instruction is not available, there does not seem to be any really good way to compute the *find first 0-byte* function. Figure 6–3 shows a possibility (only the executable part of the code is shown).

```
                          // Original byte: 00 80 other
y = (x & 0x7F7F7F7F) + 0x7F7F7F7F;  // 7F 7F 1xxxxxxx
y = ~(y | x | 0x7F7F7F7F);          // 80 00 00000000
                                    // These steps map:
if (y == 0) return 4;               // 00000000 ==> 4,
else if (y > 0x0000FFFF)            // 80xxxxxx ==> 0,
    return (y >> 31) ^ 1;           // 0080xxxx ==> 1,
else                                // 000080xx ==> 2,
    return (y >> 15) ^ 3;           // 00000080 ==> 3.
```

FIGURE 6–3. *Find leftmost 0-byte*, not using nlz.

This executes in ten to 13 basic RISC instructions, ten in the all-nonzero case. Thus, it is probably not as good as the code of Figure 6–1, although it does have fewer branch instructions. It does not scale very well to 64-bit machines, unfortunately.

There are other possibilities for avoiding the "nlz" function. The value of y computed by the code of Figure 6–3 consists of four bytes, each of which is either 0x00 or 0x80. The remainder after dividing such a number by 0x7F is the original value with the up-to-four 1-bits moved and compressed to the four rightmost positions. Thus, the remainder ranges from 0 to 15 and uniquely identifies the original number. For example,

$$\text{remu}(\mathbf{0x80808080}, \mathbf{127}) = \mathbf{15},$$
$$\text{remu}(\mathbf{0x80000000}, \mathbf{127}) = \mathbf{8},$$
$$\text{remu}(\mathbf{0x00008080}, \mathbf{127}) = \mathbf{3}, \text{etc.}$$

This value can be used to index a table, 16 bytes in size, to get the desired result. Thus, the code beginning if (y == 0) can be replaced with

```
static char table[16] = {4, 3, 2, 2, 1, 1, 1, 1,
                         0, 0, 0, 0, 0, 0, 0, 0};
return table[y%127];
```

where y is unsigned. The number 31 can be used in place of 127, but with a different table.

These methods involving dividing by 127 or 31 are really just curiosities, because the *remainder* function is apt to require 20 cycles or more even if directly implemented in hardware. However, below are two more efficient replacements for the code in Figure 6–3 beginning with if (y == 0):

```
return table[hopu(y, 0x02040810) & 15];
return table[y*0x00204081 >> 28];
```

Here, hopu(a, b) denotes the high-order 32 bits of the unsigned product of a and b. In the second line, we assume the usual HLL convention that the value of the multiplication is the low-order 32 bits of the complete product. This might be a practical method, if either the machine has a fast multiply or the multiplication by 0x204081 is done by *shift*-and-*add*'s. It can be done in four such instructions, as suggested by

$$y(1 + 2^7 + 2^{14} + 2^{21}) = y(1 + 2^7)(1 + 2^{14}).$$

Using this 4-cycle way to do the multiplication, the total time for the procedure comes to 13 cycles (7 to compute y, plus 4 for the *shift*-and-*add*'s, plus 2 for the *shift right* of 28 and the table index), and of course it is branch-free.

These scale reasonably well to a 64-bit machine. For the "modulus" method, use

```
return table[y%511];
```

where `table` is of size 256, with values 8, 0, 1, 0, 2, 0, 1, 0, 3, 0, 1, 0, 2, 0, 1, 0, 4, ... (i.e., `table[i]` = number of trailing 0's in *i*).

For the multiplicative methods, use either

```
return table[hopu(y, 0x0204081020408100) & 255]; or
return table[(y*0x0002040810204081»56];
```

where `table` is of size 256, with values 8, 7, 6, 6, 5, 5, 5, 5, 4, 4, 4, 4, 4, 4, 4, 4, 3, ...

The multiplication by 0x20408 10204081 can be done with

$$t_1 \leftarrow y(1 + 2^7)$$
$$t_2 \leftarrow t_1(1 + 2^{14})$$
$$t_3 \leftarrow t_2(1 + 2^{28})$$

which gives a 13-cycle solution.

All these variations using the table can, of course, implement the *find right-most 0-byte* function by simply changing the data in the table.

If the machine does not have the *nor* instruction, the *not* in the second assignment to y in Figure 6–3 can be omitted, in the case of a 32-bit machine, by using one of the three `return` statements given above, with `table[i]` = 0, 0, 0, 0, 0, 0, 0, 0, 1, 1, 1, 1, 2, 2, 3, 4. This scheme does not quite work on a 64-bit machine.

Here is an interesting variation on the procedure of Figure 6–2, again aimed at machines that do not have *number of leading zeros*. Let *a*, *b*, *c*, and *d* be 1-bit variables for the predicates "the first byte of *x* is nonzero," "the second byte of *x* is nonzero," and so on. Then,

$$zbytel(x) = a + ab + abc + abcd.$$

The multiplications can be done with *and*'s, leading to the procedure shown in Figure 6–4 (only the executable code is shown).

```
y = (x & 0x7F7F7F7F) + 0x7F7F7F7F;
y = y | x;                   // Leading 1 on nonzero bytes.

t1 =  y >> 31;               // t1 = a.
t2 = (y >> 23) & t1;         // t2 = ab.
t3 = (y >> 15) & t2;         // t3 = abc.
t4 = (y >>  7) & t3;         // t4 = abcd.
return t1 + t2 + t3 + t4;
```

FIGURE 6–4. *Find leftmost 0-byte* by evaluating a polynomial.

This comes to 15 instructions on the basic RISC, which is not particularly fast, but there is a certain amount of parallelism. On a superscalar machine that can execute up to three arithmetic instructions in parallel, provided they are independent, it comes to only ten cycles.

A simple variation of this does the *find rightmost 0-byte* function, based on

$$\text{zbyter}(x) = abcd + bcd + cd + d.$$

(This requires one more *and* than the code of Figure 6–4.)

Some Simple Generalizations

Functions "zbytel" and "zbyter" can be used to search for a byte equal to any particular value, by first *exclusive or*'ing the argument x with a word consisting of the desired value replicated in each byte position. For example, to search x for an ASCII blank (0x20), search $x \oplus 0x20202020$ for a 0-byte.

Similarly, to search for a byte position in which two words x and y are equal, search $x \oplus y$ for a 0-byte.

There is nothing special about byte boundaries in the code of Figure 6–2 and its variants. For example, to search a word for a 0-value in any of the first four bits, the next 12, or the last 16, use the code of Figure 6–2 with the mask replaced by 0x77FF7FFF [PHO]. (If a field length is 1, use a 0 in the mask at that position.)

Searching for a Value in a Given Range

The code of Figure 6–2 can easily be modified to search for a byte in the range 0 to any specified value less than 128. To illustrate, the following code finds the index of the leftmost byte having value from 0 to 9:

```
y = (x & 0x7F7F7F7F) + 0x76767676;
y = y | x;
y = y | 0x7F7F7F7F;          // Bytes > 9 are 0xFF.
y = ~y;                      // Bytes > 9 are 0x00,
                             // bytes <= 9 are 0x80.
n = nlz(y) >> 3;
```

More generally, suppose you want to find the leftmost byte in a word that is in the range a to b, where the difference between a and b is less than 128. For example, the uppercase letters encoded in ASCII range from 0x41 to 0x5A. To find the first uppercase letter in a word, subtract 0x41414141 in such a way that the borrow does not propagate across byte boundaries, and then use the above code to identify bytes having value from 0 to 0x19 (0x5A – 0x41). Using the formulas for subtraction given in Section 2–17, "Multibyte *Add, Subtract, Absolute Value*," on page 36, with obvious simplifications possible with $y = $ 0x41414141, gives

```
d = (x | 0x80808080) - 0x41414141;
d = ~((x | 0x7F7F7F7F) ^ d);
y = (d & 0x7F7F7F7F) + 0x66666666;
y = y | d;
y = y | 0x7F7F7F7F;        // Bytes not from 41-5A are FF.
y = ~y;                    // Bytes not from 41-5A are 00,
                           // bytes from 41-5A are 80.
n = nlz(y) >> 3;
```

For some ranges of values, simpler code exists. For example, to find the first byte whose value is 0x30 to 0x39 (a decimal digit encoded in ASCII), simply *exclusive or* the input word with 0x30303030 and then use the code given above to search for a value in the range 0 to 9. (This simplification is applicable when the upper and lower limits have n high-order bits in common, and the lower limit ends with $8 - n$ 0's.)

These techniques can be adapted to handle ranges of 128 or larger with no additional instructions. For example, to find the index of the leftmost byte whose value is in the range 0 to 137 (0x89), simply change the line $y = y \mid x$ to $y = y$ & x in the code above for searching for a value from 0 to 9.

Similarly, changing the line $y = y \mid d$ to $y = y$ & d in the code for finding the leftmost byte whose value is in the range 0x41 to 0x5A causes it to find the leftmost byte whose value is in the range 0x41 to 0xDA.

6–2 Find First String of 1-Bits of a Given Length

The problem here is to search a word in a register for the first string of 1-bits of a given length n or longer, and to return its position, with some special indication if no such string exists. Variants are to return only the yes/no indication, and to locate the first string of exactly n 1-bits. This problem has application in disk-allocation programs, particularly for disk compaction (rearranging data on a disk so that all blocks used to store a file are contiguous). The problem was suggested to me by Albert Chang, who pointed out that it is one of the uses for the *number of leading zeros* instruction.

We assume here that the *number of leading zeros* instruction, or a suitable subroutine for that function, is available.

An algorithm that immediately comes to mind is to first count the number of leading 0's and skip over them by shifting left by the number obtained. Then count the leading 1's by inverting and counting leading 0's. If this is of sufficient length, we are done. Otherwise, shift left by the number obtained and repeat from the beginning. This algorithm might be coded as shown below. If n consecutive 1-bits are found, it returns a number from 0 to 31, giving the position of the leftmost 1-bit in the leftmost such sequence. Otherwise, it returns 32 as a "not found" indication.

```
int ffstr1(unsigned x, int n) {
   int k, p;

   p = 0;                  // Initialize position to return.
   while (x != 0) {
      k = nlz(x);          // Skip over initial 0's
      x = x << k;          // (if any).
      p = p + k;
      k = nlz(~x);         // Count first/next group of 1's.
      if (k >= n)          // If enough,
         return p;         // return.
      x = x << k;          // Not enough 1's, skip over
      p = p + k;           // them.
   }
   return 32;
}
```

This algorithm is reasonable if it is expected that the loop will not be executed very many times—for example, if it is expected that x will have long sequences of 1's and of 0's. This might very well be the expectation in the disk-allocation application. Its worst-case execution time, however, is not very good; for example, about 178 full RISC instructions executed for x = 0x5555 5555 and $n \geq 2$.

An algorithm that is better in worst-case execution time is based on a sequence of *shift left* and *and* instructions. To see how this works, consider searching for a string of eight or more consecutive 1-bits in a 32-bit word x. This might be done as follows:

$$x \leftarrow x \mathbin{\&} (x \ll 1)$$

$$x \leftarrow x \mathbin{\&} (x \ll 2)$$

$$x \leftarrow x \mathbin{\&} (x \ll 4)$$

After the first assignment, the 1's in x indicate the starting positions of strings of length 2. After the second assignment, the 1's in x indicate the starting positions of strings of length 4 (a string of length 2 followed by another string of length 2). After the third assignment, the 1's in x indicate the starting positions of strings of length 8. Executing *number of leading zeros* on this word gives the position of the first string of length 8 (or more), or 32 if none exists.

To develop an algorithm that works for any length n from 1 to 32, we will look at this a little differently. First, observe that the above three assignments may be done in any order. Reverse order will be more convenient. To illustrate the general method, consider the case $n = 10$:

$$x_1 \leftarrow x \ \& \ (x \ll 5)$$

$$x_2 \leftarrow x_1 \ \& \ (x_1 \ll 2)$$

$$x_3 \leftarrow x_2 \ \& \ (x_2 \ll 1)$$

$$x_4 \leftarrow x_3 \ \& \ (x_3 \ll 1)$$

The first statement shifts by $n/2$. After executing it, the problem is reduced to finding a string of five consecutive 1-bits in x_1. This may be done by shifting left by $\lfloor 5/2 \rfloor = 2$, *and*'ing, and searching the result for a string of length 3 $(5 - 2)$. The last two statements identify where the strings of length 3 are in x_2. The sum of the shift amounts is always $n - 1$. The algorithm is shown in Figure 6–5. The execution time ranges from 3 to 36 full RISC instructions, as n ranges from 1 to 32.

If n is often moderately large, it is not unreasonable to unroll this loop by repeating the loop body five times and omitting the test n > 1. (Five is always sufficient for a 32-bit machine.) This gives a branch-free algorithm that runs in a constant time of 20 instructions executed (the last assignment to n can be omitted). Although for small values of n the three assignments are executed more than necessary, the result is unchanged by the extra steps because variable n sticks at the value 1, and for this value the three steps have no effect on x or n. The unrolled version is faster than the looping version for n ≥ 5, in terms of number of instructions executed.

```
int ffstr1(unsigned x, int n) {
   int s;

   while (n > 1) {
      s = n >> 1;
      x = x & (x << s);
      n = n - s;
   }
   return nlz(x);
}
```

FIGURE 6–5. Find first string of n 1's, *shift*-and-*and* sequence.

A string of exactly n 1-bits can be found in six more instructions (four if *and not* is available). The quantity x computed by the algorithm of Figure 6–5 has 1-bits wherever a string of length n or more 1-bits begins. Hence, using the final value of x computed by that algorithm, the expression

$$x \mathbin{\&} \neg(x \overset{u}{\gg} 1) \mathbin{\&} \neg(x \ll 1)$$

contains a 1-bit wherever the final x contains an isolated 1-bit, which is to say wherever the original x began a string of exactly n 1-bits.

The algorithm is also easily adapted to finding strings of length n that begin at certain locations. For example, to find strings that begin at byte boundaries, simply *and* the final x with 0x80808080.

It can be used to find strings of 0-bits either by complementing x at the start, or by changing the *and*'s to *or*'s and complementing x just before invoking "nlz." For example, below is an algorithm for finding the first (leftmost) 0-byte (see Section 6–1, "Find First 0-Byte," on page 91, for a precise definition of this problem).

$$x \leftarrow x \mid (x \ll 4)$$
$$x \leftarrow x \mid (x \ll 2)$$
$$x \leftarrow x \mid (x \ll 1)$$
$$x \leftarrow \text{0x7F7F7F7F} \mid x$$
$$p \leftarrow \text{nlz}(\neg x) \overset{u}{\gg} 3$$

This executes in 12 instructions on the full RISC (not as good as the algorithm of Figure 6–2 on page 92, which executes in eight instructions).

CHAPTER 7

REARRANGING BITS AND BYTES

7–1 Reversing Bits and Bytes

By "reversing bits" we mean to reflect the contents of a register about the middle so that, for example,

$$\mathrm{rev}(0x01234567) = 0xE6A2C480.$$

By "reversing bytes" we mean a similar reflection of the four bytes of a register. Byte reversal is a necessary operation to convert data between the "little-endian" format used by DEC and Intel and the "big-endian" format used by most other manufacturers.

Bit reversal can be done quite efficiently by interchanging adjacent single bits, then interchanging adjacent 2-bit fields, and so on, as shown below [Aus1]. These five assignment statements can be executed in any order.

```
x = (x & 0x55555555) <<  1 | (x & 0xAAAAAAAA) >>  1;
x = (x & 0x33333333) <<  2 | (x & 0xCCCCCCCC) >>  2;
x = (x & 0x0F0F0F0F) <<  4 | (x & 0xF0F0F0F0) >>  4;
x = (x & 0x00FF00FF) <<  8 | (x & 0xFF00FF00) >>  8;
x = (x & 0x0000FFFF) << 16 | (x & 0xFFFF0000) >> 16;
```

A small improvement results on most machines by using fewer distinct large constants and doing the last two assignments in a more straightforward way, as is shown in Figure 7–1 (30 basic RISC instructions, branch-free).

The last assignment to x in this code does byte reversal in nine basic RISC instructions. If the machine has rotate shifts, however, this can instead be done in seven instructions with

$$x = ((x \ \& \ 0x00FF00FF) \overset{rot}{\ggg} 8) \mid ((x \overset{rot}{\lll} 8) \ \& \ 0x00FF00FF).$$

PowerPC can do the byte-reversal operation in only three instructions [Hay1]: a *rotate left* of 8, which positions two of the bytes, followed by two "rlwimi" (*rotate left word immediate then mask insert*) instructions.

```
unsigned rev(unsigned x) {
   x = (x & 0x55555555) <<  1 | (x >>  1) & 0x55555555;
   x = (x & 0x33333333) <<  2 | (x >>  2) & 0x33333333;
   x = (x & 0x0F0F0F0F) <<  4 | (x >>  4) & 0x0F0F0F0F;
   x = (x << 24) | ((x & 0xFF00) << 8) |
       ((x >> 8) & 0xFF00) | (x >> 24);
   return x;
}
```

FIGURE 7–1. Reversing bits.

Generalized Bit Reversal

[GLS1] suggests that the following sort of generalization of bit reversal, which he calls "flip," is a good candidate to consider for a computer's instruction set:

```
if (k &  1) x = (x & 0x55555555) <<  1 | (x & 0xAAAAAAAA) >>  1;
if (k &  2) x = (x & 0x33333333) <<  2 | (x & 0xCCCCCCCC) >>  2;
if (k &  4) x = (x & 0x0F0F0F0F) <<  4 | (x & 0xF0F0F0F0) >>  4;
if (k &  8) x = (x & 0x00FF00FF) <<  8 | (x & 0xFF00FF00) >>  8;
if (k & 16) x = (x & 0x0000FFFF) << 16 | (x & 0xFFFF0000) >> 16;
```

(The last two *and* operations can be omitted.) For $k = 31$, this operation reverses the bits in a word. For $k = 24$, it reverses the bytes in a word. For $k = 7$, it reverses the bits in each byte, without changing the positions of the bytes. For $k = 16$, it swaps the left and right halfwords of a word, and so on. In general, it moves the bit at position m to position $m \oplus k$. It can be implemented in hardware very similarly to the way a rotate shifter is usually implemented (five stages of MUX's, with each stage controlled by a bit of the shift amount k).

Bit-Reversing Novelties

Item 167 in [HAK] contains rather esoteric expressions for reversing 6-, 7-, and 8-bit integers. Although these expressions are designed for a 36-bit machine, the one for reversing a 6-bit integer works on a 32-bit machine, and those for 7- and 8-bit integers work on a 64-bit machine. These expressions are as follows:

6-bit: remu((x ∗ **0x0008 2082**) & **0x0112 2408, 255**)

7-bit: remu((x ∗ **0x4010 0401**) & **0x4 4221 1008, 255**)

8-bit: remu((x ∗ **0x2 0202 0202**) & **0x108 8442 2010, 1023**)

The result of all these is a "clean" integer—right-adjusted with no unused high-order bits set.

In all these cases the "remu" function can instead be "rem" or "mod," because its arguments are positive. The *remainder* function is simply summing the digits of a base 256 or base 1024 number, much like casting out nines. Hence it can be replaced with a *multiply* and a *shift right*. For example, the 6-bit formula has the following alternative on a 32-bit machine (the multiplication must be modulo 2^{32}):

$$t \leftarrow (x * \text{0x0008\,2082}) \ \& \ \text{0x0112\,2408}$$

$$(t * \text{0x0101\,0101}) \overset{u}{\gg} 24$$

These formulas are limited in their utility because they involve a remainder-ing operation (20 cycles or more) and/or some multiplications, as well as loading of large constants. The formula immediately above requires ten basic RISC instructions, two of which are *multiply*'s, which amounts to about 20 cycles on a present-day RISC. On the other hand, an adaptation of the code of Figure 7–1 to reverse 6-bit integers requires about 15 instructions, and probably about 9 to 15 cycles, depending on the amount of instruction-level parallelism in the machine. These techniques, however, do give compact code. Below are a few more techniques that might possibly be useful, all for a 32-bit machine. They involve a sort of double application of the idea from [HAK], to extend the technique to 8- and 9-bit integers on a 32-bit machine.

The following is a formula for reversing an 8-bit integer:

$$s \leftarrow (x * \text{0x0202\,0202}) \ \& \ \text{0x8442\,2010}$$

$$t \leftarrow (x * 8) \ \& \ \text{0x0000\,0420}$$

$$\text{remu}(s + t, 1023)$$

Here the "remu" cannot be changed to a *multiply* and *shift*. (You have to work these out, and look at the bit patterns, to see why.)

Here is a similar formula for reversing an 8-bit integer, which is interesting because it can be simplified quite a bit:

$$s \leftarrow (x * \text{0x0002\,0202}) \ \& \ \text{0x0104\,4010}$$

$$t \leftarrow (x * \text{0x0008\,0808}) \ \& \ \text{0x0208\,8020}$$

$$\text{remu}(s + t, 4095)$$

The simplifications are that the second product is just a *shift left* of the first product, the last mask can be generated from the second with just one instruction (*shift*), and the *remainder* can be replaced by a *multiply* and *shift*. It simplifies to 14 basic RISC instructions, two of which are *multiply*'s:

$$u \leftarrow x * \text{0x0002\,0202}$$

$$m \leftarrow \text{0x0104\,4010}$$

$$s \leftarrow u \,\&\, m$$

$$t \leftarrow (u \ll 2) \,\&\, (m \ll 1)$$

$$(\text{0x0100\,1001} * (s + t)) \overset{u}{\gg} 24$$

The following is a formula for reversing a 9-bit integer:

$$s \leftarrow (x * \text{0x0100\,1001}) \,\&\, \text{0x8410\,8010}$$

$$t \leftarrow (x * \text{0x0004\,0040}) \,\&\, \text{0x0084\,1080}$$

$$\text{remu}(s + t, 1023)$$

The second multiplication can be avoided because the product is equal to the first product shifted right six positions. The last mask is equal to the second mask shifted right eight positions. With these simplifications, this requires 12 basic RISC instructions, including the one *multiply* and one *remainder*. The *remainder* operation must be unsigned, and it cannot be changed to a *multiply* and *shift*.

The reader who studies these marvels will be able to devise similar code for other bit-permuting operations. As a simple (and artificial) example, suppose it is desired to extract every other bit from an 8-bit quantity, and compress the four bits to the right. That is, the desired transformation is

```
0000 0000 0000 0000 0000 0000 abcd efgh ==>
0000 0000 0000 0000 0000 0000 0000 bdfh
```

This may be computed as follows:

$$t \leftarrow (x * \text{0x0101\,0101}) \,\&\, \text{0x4010\,0401}$$

$$(t * \text{0x0804\,0201}) \overset{u}{\gg} 27$$

On most machines, the most practical way to do all these operations is by indexing into a table of 1-byte (or 9-bit) integers.

Incrementing a Reversed Integer

The Fast Fourier Transform (FFT) algorithm employs an integer i and its bit reversal rev(i) in a loop in which i is incremented by 1 [PB]. Straightforward coding would increment i and then compute rev(i) on each loop iteration. For small integers, computing rev(i) by table lookup is fast and practical. For large integers, however, table lookup is not practical and, as we have seen, computing rev(i) requires some 29 instructions.

If table lookup cannot be used, it is more efficient to maintain i in both normal and bit-reversed forms, incrementing them both on each loop iteration. This raises the question of how best to increment an integer that is in a register in reversed form. To illustrate, on a 4-bit machine we wish to successively step through the values (in hexadecimal)

0, 8, 4, C, 2, A, 6, E, 1, 9, 5, D, 3, B, 7, F.

In the FFT algorithm, i and its reversal are both some specific number of bits in length, almost certainly less than 32, and they are both right-justified in the register. However, we assume here that i is a 32-bit integer. After adding 1 to the reversed 32-bit integer, a *shift right* of the appropriate number of bits will make the result usable by the FFT algorithm (both i and rev(i) are used to index an array in memory).

The straightforward way to increment a reversed integer is to scan from the left for the first 0-bit, set it to 1, and set all bits to the left of it (if any) to 0's. One way to code this is

```
unsigned x, m;

m = 0x80000000;
x = x ^ m;
if ((int)x >= 0) {
    do {
        m = m >> 1;
        x = x ^ m;
    } while (x < m);
}
```

This executes in three basic RISC instructions if x begins with a 0-bit, and four additional instructions for each loop iteration. Because x begins with a 0-bit half the time, with 10 (binary) one-fourth of the time, and so on, the average number of instructions executed is approximately

$$3 \cdot \frac{1}{2} + 7 \cdot \frac{1}{4} + 11 \cdot \frac{1}{8} + 15 \cdot \frac{1}{16} + \ldots$$

$$= 4 \cdot \frac{1}{2} + 8 \cdot \frac{1}{4} + 12 \cdot \frac{1}{8} + 16 \cdot \frac{1}{16} + \ldots - 1$$

$$= 4\left(\frac{1}{2} + \frac{2}{4} + \frac{3}{8} + \frac{4}{16} + \ldots\right) - 1$$

$$= 7.$$

(In the second line we added and subtracted 1, with the first 1 in the form $1/2 + 1/4 + 1/8 + 1/16 + \ldots$. This makes the series similar to the one analyzed on page 86.) The number of instructions executed in the worst case, however, is quite large (131).

If *number of leading zeros* is available, adding 1 to a reversed integer may be done as follows:

First execute: $s \leftarrow \text{nlz}(\neg x)$

and then either: $x \leftarrow x \oplus (\text{0x8000\,0000} \overset{s}{\gg} s)$

or: $x \leftarrow ((x \ll s) + \text{0x8000\,0000}) \overset{u}{\gg} s$

Either method requires five full RISC instructions and, to properly wrap around from **0xFFFF\,FFFF** to **0**, requires that the shifts be modulo 64. (These formulas fail in this respect on the Intel x86 machines, because the shifts are modulo 32.)

7–2 Shuffling Bits

Another important permutation of the bits of a word is the "perfect shuffle" operation, which has applications in cryptography. There are two varieties, called the "outer" and "inner" perfect shuffles. They both interleave the bits in the two halves of a word in a manner similar to a perfect shuffle of a deck of 32 cards, but they differ in which card is allowed to fall first. In the outer perfect shuffle, the outer (end) bits remain in the outer positions, and in the inner perfect shuffle, bit 15 moves to the left end of the word (position 31). If the 32-bit word is (where each letter denotes a single bit)

```
abcd efgh ijkl mnop ABCD EFGH IJKL MNOP,
```

then after the outer perfect shuffle it is

```
aAbB cCdD eEfF gGhH iIjJ kKlL mMnN oOpP,
```

and after the inner perfect shuffle it is

```
AaBb CcDd EeFf GgHh IiJj KkLl MmNn OoPp.
```

Assume the word size W is a power of 2. Then the outer perfect shuffle operation can be accomplished with basic RISC instructions in $\log_2(W/2)$ steps, where each step swaps the second and third quartiles of successively smaller pieces [GLS1]. That is, a 32-bit word is transformed as follows:

```
abcd efgh ijkl mnop ABCD EFGH IJKL MNOP
abcd efgh ABCD EFGH ijkl mnop IJKL MNOP
abcd ABCD efgh EFGH ijkl IJKL mnop MNOP
abAB cdCD efEF ghGH ijIJ klKL mnMN opOP
aAbB cCdD eEfF gGhH iIjJ kKlL mMnN oOpP
```

Straightforward code for this is

```
x = (x & 0x0000FF00) << 8 | (x >> 8) & 0x0000FF00 | x & 0xFF0000FF;
x = (x & 0x00F000F0) << 4 | (x >> 4) & 0x00F000F0 | x & 0xF00FF00F;
x = (x & 0x0C0C0C0C) << 2 | (x >> 2) & 0x0C0C0C0C | x & 0xC3C3C3C3;
x = (x & 0x22222222) << 1 | (x >> 1) & 0x22222222 | x & 0x99999999;
```

which requires 42 basic RISC instructions. This can be reduced to 30 instructions, although at an increase from 17 to 21 cycles on a machine with unlimited instruction-level parallelism, by using the *exclusive or* method of exchanging two fields of a register (described on page 40). All quantities are unsigned:

```
t = (x ^ (x >> 8)) & 0x0000FF00;  x = x ^ t ^ (t << 8);
t = (x ^ (x >> 4)) & 0x00F000F0;  x = x ^ t ^ (t << 4);
t = (x ^ (x >> 2)) & 0x0C0C0C0C;  x = x ^ t ^ (t << 2);
t = (x ^ (x >> 1)) & 0x22222222;  x = x ^ t ^ (t << 1);
```

The inverse operation, the outer unshuffle, is easily accomplished by performing the swaps in reverse order:

```
t = (x ^ (x >> 1)) & 0x22222222;  x = x ^ t ^ (t << 1);
t = (x ^ (x >> 2)) & 0x0C0C0C0C;  x = x ^ t ^ (t << 2);
t = (x ^ (x >> 4)) & 0x00F000F0;  x = x ^ t ^ (t << 4);
t = (x ^ (x >> 8)) & 0x0000FF00;  x = x ^ t ^ (t << 8);
```

Using only the last two steps of either of the above two shuffle sequences shuffles the bits of each byte separately. Using only the last three steps shuffles the bits of each halfword separately, and so on. Similar remarks apply to unshuffling, except by using the *first* two or three steps.

To get the inner perfect shuffle, prepend to these sequences a step to swap the left and right halves of the register:

```
x = (x >> 16) | (x << 16);
```

(or use a *rotate* of 16 bit positions). The unshuffle sequence can be similarly modified by *appending* this line of code.

Altering the transformation to swap the *first* and *fourth* quartiles of successively smaller pieces produces the bit reversal of the inner perfect shuffle.

Perhaps worth mentioning is the special case in which the left half of the word x is all 0. In other words, we want to move the bits in the right half of x to every other bit position—that is, to transform the 32-bit word

```
0000 0000 0000 0000 ABCD EFGH IJKL MNOP
```

to

```
0A0B 0C0D 0E0F 0G0H 0I0J 0K0L 0M0N 0O0P.
```

The outer perfect shuffle code can be simplified to do this task in 22 basic RISC instructions. The code below, however, does it in only 19 basic RISC instructions, at no cost in execution time on a machine with unlimited instruction-level parallelism (12 cycles with either method). This code does not require that the left half of word x be initially cleared.

```
x = ((x & 0xFF00) << 8) | (x & 0x00FF);
x = ((x << 4) | x) & 0x0F0F0F0F;
x = ((x << 2) | x) & 0x33333333;
x = ((x << 1) | x) & 0x55555555;
```

Similarly, for the inverse of this "half shuffle" operation (a special case of *compress*; see page 116), the outer perfect unshuffle code can be simplified to do the task in 26 or 29 basic RISC instructions, depending on whether or not an initial *and* operation is required to clear the bits in the odd positions. The code below, however, does it in only 18 or 21 basic RISC instructions, and with less execution time on a machine with unlimited instruction-level parallelism (12 or 15 cycles).

```
x = x & 0x55555555;            // (If required.)
x = ((x >> 1) | x) & 0x33333333;
x = ((x >> 2) | x) & 0x0F0F0F0F;
x = ((x >> 4) | x) & 0x00FF00FF;
x = ((x >> 8) | x) & 0x0000FFFF;
```

7–3 Transposing a Bit Matrix

The transpose of a matrix A is a matrix whose columns are the rows of A and whose rows are the columns of A. Here we consider the problem of computing the transpose of a bit matrix whose elements are single bits that are packed eight per byte, with rows and columns beginning on byte boundaries. This seemingly simple transformation is surprisingly costly in instructions executed.

On most machines it would be very slow to load and store individual bits, mainly due to the code that would be required to extract and (worse yet) to store individual bits. A better method is to partition the matrix into 8×8 submatrices, load each 8×8 submatrix into registers, compute the transpose of the submatrix in registers, and then store the 8×8 result in the appropriate place in the target matrix.

This section first discusses the problem of computing the transpose of the 8×8 submatrix.

It doesn't matter whether the matrix is stored in row-major or column-major order; computing the transpose consists of the same operations in either event. Assuming for discussion that it's in row-major order, an 8×8 submatrix is loaded into eight registers with eight *load byte* instructions, addressing a column of the source matrix. That is, the addresses referenced by the *load byte* instructions are separated by multiples of the source matrix width in bytes. After the transpose of the 8×8 submatrix is computed, it is stored in a column of the target matrix—that is, it is stored with eight *store byte* instructions into locations separated by multiples of the width of the target matrix in bytes (which is different from the width of the source matrix if the matrices are not square). Thus, we are given eight 8-bit quantities right-justified in registers $a0$, $a1$, ..., $a7$, and we wish to compute eight 8-bit quantities right-justified in registers $b0$, $b1$, ..., $b7$, for use in the *store byte* instructions. This is illustrated below, where each digit and letter represents a single bit. Notice that we consider the main diagonal to run from bit 7 of byte 0 to bit 0 of byte 7. Some readers with a little-endian background may be accustomed to thinking of the main diagonal as running from bit 0 of byte 0 to bit 7 of byte 7.

```
a0 = 0123 4567              b0 = 08go wEMU
a1 = 89ab cdef              b1 = 19hp xFNV
a2 = ghij klmn              b2 = 2aiq yGOW
a3 = opqr stuv   ==>        b3 = 3bjr zHPX
a4 = wxyz ABCD              b4 = 4cks AIQY
a5 = EFGH IJKL              b5 = 5dlt BJRZ
a6 = MNOP QRST              b6 = 6emu CKS$
a7 = UVWX YZ$.              b7 = 7fnv DLT.
```

The straightforward code for this problem is to select and place each result bit individually, as follows. The multiplications and divisions represent left and right shifts, respectively.

```
b0 = (a0 & 128)     | (a1 & 128)/2  | (a2 & 128)/4  | (a3 & 128)/8 |
     (a4 & 128)/16  | (a5 & 128)/32 | (a6 & 128)/64 | (a7      )/128;
b1 = (a0 &  64)*2   | (a1 &  64)    | (a2 &  64)/2   | (a3 &  64)/4 |
     (a4 &  64)/8   | (a5 &  64)/16 | (a6 &  64)/32 | (a7 &  64)/64;
b2 = (a0 &  32)*4   | (a1 &  32)*2  | (a2 &  32)    | (a3 &  32)/2 |
     (a4 &  32)/4   | (a5 &  32)/8  | (a6 &  32)/16 | (a7 &  32)/32;
b3 = (a0 &  16)*8   | (a1 &  16)*4  | (a2 &  16)*2  | (a3 &  16)   |
     (a4 &  16)/2   | (a5 &  16)/4  | (a6 &  16)/8  | (a7 &  16)/16;
b4 = (a0 &   8)*16  | (a1 &   8)*8  | (a2 &   8)*4  | (a3 &   8)*2 |
     (a4 &   8)     | (a5 &   8)/2  | (a6 &   8)/4  | (a7 &   8)/8;
b5 = (a0 &   4)*32  | (a1 &   4)*16 | (a2 &   4)*8  | (a3 &   4)*4 |
     (a4 &   4)*2   | (a5 &   4)    | (a6 &   4)/2  | (a7 &   4)/4;
b6 = (a0 &   2)*64  | (a1 &   2)*32 | (a2 &   2)*16 | (a3 &   2)*8 |
     (a4 &   2)*4   | (a5 &   2)*2  | (a6 &   2)    | (a7 &   2)/2;
b7 = (a0      )*128 | (a1 &   1)*64 | (a2 &   1)*32 | (a3 &   1)*16|
     (a4 &   1)*8   | (a5 &   1)*4  | (a6 &   1)*2  | (a7 &   1);
```

This executes in 174 instructions on most machines (62 *and*'s, 56 *shift*'s, and 56 *or*'s). The *or*'s can of course be *add*'s. On PowerPC it can be done, perhaps surprisingly, in 63 instructions (seven *move register*'s and 56 *rotate left word immediate then mask insert*'s). We are not counting the *load byte* and *store byte* instructions, nor their addressing code.

Although there does not seem to be a *really great* algorithm for this problem, the method to be described beats the straightforward method by more than a factor of 2 on a basic RISC machine.

First, treat the 8×8-bit matrix as 16 2×2-bit matrices, and transpose each of the 16 2×2-bit matrices. Second, treat the matrix as four 2×2 submatrices whose elements are 2×2-bit matrices and transpose each of the four 2×2 submatrices. Finally, treat the matrix as a 2×2 matrix whose elements are 4×4-bit matrices, and transpose the 2×2 matrix. These transformations are illustrated below.

```
0123 4567     082a 4c6e     08go 4cks     08go wEMU
89ab cdef     193b 5d7f     19hp 5dlt     19hp xFNV
ghij klmn     goiq ksmu     2aiq 6emu     2aiq yGOW
opqr stuv     hpjr ltnv     3bjr 7fnv     3bjr zHPX
          ==>           ==>           ==>
wxyz ABCD     wEyG AICK     wEMU AIQY     4cks AIQY
EFGH IJKL     xFzH BJDL     xFNV BJRZ     5dlt BJRZ
MNOP QRST     MUOW QYS$     yGOW CKS$     6emu CKS$
UVWX YZ$.     NVPX RZT.     zHPX DLT.     7fnv DLT.
```

Rather than carrying out these steps on the eight individual bytes in eight registers, a net improvement results from first packing the bytes four to a register, performing the bit-swaps on the two registers, and then unpacking. A complete procedure is shown in Figure 7–2. Parameter A is the address of the first byte of an 8×8 submatrix of the source matrix, which is of size $8m \times 8n$ bits. Similarly, parameter B is the address of the first byte of an 8×8 submatrix in the target matrix, which is of size $8n \times 8m$ bits. That is, the full source matrix is $8m \times n$ bytes, and the full target matrix is $8n \times m$ bytes.

The line

```
t = (x ^ (x >> 7)) & 0x00AA00AA;   x = x ^ t ^ (t << 7);
```

is quite cryptic, for sure. It is swapping bits 1 and 8 (counting from the right), 3 and 10, 5 and 12, and so on, in word x, while not moving bits 0, 2, 4, and so on. The swaps are done with the *exclusive or* method of bit swapping, described on page 40. Word x, before and after the first round of swaps, is

```
0123 4567 89ab cdef ghij klmn opqr stuv
082a 4c6e 193b 5d7f goiq ksmu hpjr ltnv
```

```
void transpose8(unsigned char A[8], int m, int n,
                unsigned char B[8]) {
  unsigned x, y, t;

  // Load the array and pack it into x and y.

  x = (A[0]<<24) | (A[m]<<16) | (A[2*m]<<8) | A[3*m];
  y = (A[4*m]<<24) | (A[5*m]<<16) | (A[6*m]<<8) | A[7*m];

  t = (x ^ (x >> 7)) & 0x00AA00AA;  x = x ^ t ^ (t << 7);
  t = (y ^ (y >> 7)) & 0x00AA00AA;  y = y ^ t ^ (t << 7);

  t = (x ^ (x >>14)) & 0x0000CCCC;  x = x ^ t ^ (t <<14);
  t = (y ^ (y >>14)) & 0x0000CCCC;  y = y ^ t ^ (t <<14);

  t = (x & 0xF0F0F0F0) | ((y >> 4) & 0x0F0F0F0F);
  y = ((x << 4) & 0xF0F0F0F0) | (y & 0x0F0F0F0F);
  x = t;

  B[0]=x>>24;   B[n]=x>>16;   B[2*n]=x>>8;   B[3*n]=x;
  B[4*n]=y>>24; B[5*n]=y>>16; B[6*n]=y>>8;   B[7*n]=y;
}
```

FIGURE 7–2. Transposing an 8×8-bit matrix.

To get a realistic comparison of these methods, the naive method described on page 109 was filled out into a complete program similar to that of Figure 7–2. Both were compiled with the GNU C compiler to a target machine that is very similar to the basic RISC. The resulting number of instructions, counting all load's, store's, addressing code, prologs, and epilogs, is 219 for the naive code and 101 for Figure 7–2. (The prologs and epilogs were null, except for a *return branch* instruction.) A version of the code of Figure 7–2 adapted to a 64-bit basic RISC (in which x and y would be held in the same register) would be about 85 instructions.

The algorithm of Figure 7–2 runs from fine to coarse granularity, based on the lengths of the groups of bits that are swapped. The method can also be run from coarse to fine granularity. To do this, first treat the 8×8-bit matrix as a 2×2 matrix whose elements are 4×4-bit matrices, and transpose the 2×2 matrix. Then treat each the four 4×4 submatrices as a 2×2 matrix whose elements are 2×2-bit matrices, and transpose each of the four 2×2 submatrices, and so on. The code for this is the same as that of Figure 7–2 except with the three groups of statements that do the bit-rearranging run in reverse order.

Transposing a 32×32-Bit Matrix

The same recursive technique that was used for the 8×8-bit matrix can of course be used for larger matrices. For a 32×32-bit matrix it takes five stages.

The details are quite different from Figure 7–2 because here we assume that the entire 32×32-bit matrix does not fit in the general register space, and we seek a compact procedure that indexes the appropriate words of the bit matrix to do the bit swaps. The algorithm to be described works best if run from coarse to fine granularity.

In the first stage, treat the matrix as four 16×16-bit matrices, and transform it as follows:

$$\begin{bmatrix} A & B \\ C & D \end{bmatrix} \Rightarrow \begin{bmatrix} A & C \\ B & D \end{bmatrix}.$$

A denotes the left half of the first 16 words of the matrix, B denotes the right half of the first 16 words, and so on. It should be clear that the above transformation may be accomplished by the following swaps:

> Right half of word 0 with the left half of word 16,
> Right half of word 1 with the left half of word 17,
>
> ...
>
> Right half of word 15 with the left half of word 31.

To implement this in code, we will have an index k that ranges from 0 to 15. In a loop controlled by k, the right half of word k will be swapped with the left half of word $k + 16$.

In the second stage, treat the matrix as 16 8×8-bit matrices, and transform it as follows:

$$\begin{bmatrix} A & B & C & D \\ E & F & G & H \\ I & J & K & L \\ M & N & O & P \end{bmatrix} \Rightarrow \begin{bmatrix} A & E & C & G \\ B & F & D & H \\ I & M & K & O \\ J & N & L & P \end{bmatrix}.$$

This transformation may be accomplished by the following swaps:

> Bits 0x00FF00FF of word 0 with bits 0xFF00FF00 of word 8,
> Bits 0x00FF00FF of word 1 with bits 0xFF00FF00 of word 9, and so on.

This means that bits 0–7 (the least significant eight bits) of word 0 are swapped with bits 8–15 of word 8, and so on. The indexes of the first word in these swaps are $k = 0, 1, 2, 3, 4, 5, 6, 7, 16, 17, 18, 19, 20, 21, 22, 23$. A way to step k through these values is

$$k' = (k + 9) \ \& \ \neg 8.$$

In the loop controlled by k, bits of word k are swapped with bits of word $k + 8$.

Similarly, the third stage does the following swaps:

Bits 0x0F0F0F0F of word 0 with bits 0xF0F0F0F0 of word 4,
Bits 0x0F0F0F0F of word 1 with bits 0xF0F0F0F0 of word 5, and so on.

The indexes of the first word in these swaps are $k = 0, 1, 2, 3, 8, 9, 10, 11, 16, 17,$ $18, 19, 24, 25, 26, 27$. A way to step k through these values is

$$k' = (k + 5) \,\&\, \lnot 4.$$

In the loop controlled by k, bits of word k are swapped with bits of word $k + 4$.

These considerations are coded rather compactly in the C function shown in Figure 7-3 [GLS1]. The outer loop controls the five stages, with j taking on the values 16, 8, 4, 2, and 1. It also steps the mask m through the values 0x0000FFFF, 0x00FF00FF, 0x0F0F0F0F, 0x33333333, and 0x55555555. (The code for this, m = m ^ (m << j), is a nice little trick. It does not have an inverse, which is the main reason this code works best for coarse to fine transformations.) The inner loop steps k through the values described above. The inner loop body swaps the bits of a[k] identified by mask m with the bits of a[k+j] shifted right j and identified by m, which is equivalent to the bits of a[k+j] identified with the complement of m. The code for performing these swaps is an adaptation of the "three *exclusive or*" technique shown on page 39 column (c).

```
void transpose32(unsigned A[32]) {
    int j, k;
    unsigned m, t;

    m = 0x0000FFFF;
    for (j = 16; j != 0; j = j >> 1, m = m ^ (m << j)) {
        for (k = 0; k < 32; k = (k + j + 1) & ~j) {
            t = (A[k] ^ (A[k+j] >> j)) & m;
            A[k] = A[k] ^ t;
            A[k+j] = A[k+j] ^ (t << j);
        }
    }
}
```

FIGURE 7-3. Compact code for transposing a 32×32-bit matrix.

Based on compiling this function with the GNU C compiler to a machine very similar to the basic RISC, this compiles into 31 instructions, with 20 in the inner loop and 7 in the outer loop but not in the inner loop. Thus, it executes in $4 + 5(7 + 16 \cdot 20) = 1639$ instructions. In contrast, if this function were performed using 16 calls on the 8×8 transpose program of Figure 7-2, then it would take $16(101 + 5) = 1696$ instructions, assuming the 16 calls are "strung out."

This includes five instructions for each function call (observed in compiled code). Thus, the two methods are, on the surface anyway, very nearly equal in execution time.

On the other hand, for a 64-bit machine the code of Figure 7–3 can easily be modified to transpose a 64×64-bit matrix, and it would take about $4 + 6(7 + 32 \cdot 20) = 3886$ instructions. Doing the job with 64 executions of the 8×8 transpose method would take about $64(85 + 5) = 5760$ instructions.

The algorithm works in place, and thus if it is used to transpose a larger matrix, additional steps are required to move 32×32-bit submatrices. It can be made to put the result matrix in an area distinct from the source matrix by separating out either the first or last execution of the "for *j*-loop" and having it store the result in the other area.

About half the instructions executed by the function of Figure 7–3 are for loop control, and the function loads and stores the entire matrix five times. Would it be reasonable to reduce this overhead by unrolling the loops? It would, if you are looking for the ultimate in speed, if memory space is not a problem, if your machine's I-fetching can keep up with a large block of straight-line code, and, especially if the branches or loads are costly in execution time. The bulk of the program will be the six instructions that do the bit swaps repeated 80 times ($5 \cdot 16$). In addition, the program will need 32 *load* instructions to load the source matrix and 32 *store* instructions to store the result, for a total of at least 544 instructions.

Our GNU C compiler will not unroll loops by such large factors (16 for the inner loop, five for the outer loop). Figure 7–4 outlines a program in which the unrolling is done by hand. This program is shown as not working in place, but it executes correctly in place, if that is desired, by invoking it with identical arguments. The number of "swap" lines is 80. Our GNU C compiler for the basic RISC machine compiles this into 576 instructions (branch-free, except for the function return), counting prologs and epilogs. This machine does not have the *store multiple* and *load multiple* instructions, but it can save and restore registers two at a time with *store double* and *load double* instructions.

There is a way to squeeze a little more performance out of this if your machine has a *rotate shift* instruction (either left or right). The idea is to replace all the *swap* operations of Figure 7–4, which take six instructions each, with simpler swaps that do not involve a shift, which take four instructions each (use the swap macro given, with the shifts omitted).

First, rotate right words $A[16..31]$ (that is, $A[k]$ for $16 \leq k \leq 31$) by 16 bit positions. Second, swap the right halves of $A[0]$ with $A[16]$, $A[1]$ with $A[17]$, and so on, similarly to the code of Figure 7–4. Third, rotate right words $A[0..8]$ and $A[24..31]$ by eight bit positions, and then swap the bits indicated by a mask of 0x00FF00FF in words $A[0]$ and $A[8]$, $A[1]$ and $A[9]$, and so on, as in the code of Figure 7–4. After five stages of this, you don't quite have the transpose. Finally, you have to rotate left word $A[1]$ by one bit position, $A[2]$ by two bit positions, and

```
#define swap(a0, a1, j, m) t = (a0 ^ (a1 >>j)) & m; \
                            a0 = a0 ^ t; \
                            a1 = a1 ^ (t << j);

void transpose32(unsigned A[32], unsigned B[32]) {
   unsigned m, t;
   unsigned a0, a1, a2, a3, a4, a5, a6, a7,
            a8, a9, a10, a11, a12, a13, a14, a15,
            a16, a17, a18, a19, a20, a21, a22, a23,
            a24, a25, a26, a27, a28, a29, a30, a31;

   a0  = A[ 0];   a1  = A[ 1];   a2  = A[ 2];   a3  = A[ 3];
   a4  = A[ 4];   a5  = A[ 5];   a6  = A[ 6];   a7  = A[ 7];
   ...
   a28 = A[28];   a29 = A[29];   a30 = A[30];   a31 = A[31];

   m = 0x0000FFFF;
   swap(a0,   a16, 16, m)
   swap(a1,   a17, 16, m)
   ...
   swap(a15, a31, 16, m)
   m = 0x00FF00FF;
   swap(a0,   a8,   8, m)
   swap(a1,   a9,   8, m)
   ...
   ...
   swap(a28, a29,  1, m)
   swap(a30, a31,  1, m)

   B[ 0] = a0;    B[ 1] = a1;    B[ 2] = a2;    B[ 3] = a3;
   B[ 4] = a4;    B[ 5] = a5;    B[ 6] = a6;    B[ 7] = a7;
   ...
   B[28] = a28;   B[29] = a29;   B[30] = a30;   B[31] = a31;
}
```

FIGURE 7–4. Straight-line code for transposing a 32×32-bit matrix.

so on (31 instructions). We do not show the code, but the steps are illustrated
below for a 4×4-bit matrix.

```
abcd        abcd        abij        abij        aeim        aeim
efgh  ==>   efgh  ==>   efmn  ==>   nefm  ==>   nbfj  ==>   bfjn
ijkl        klij        klcd        klcd        kocg        cgko
mnop        opmn        opgh        hopg        hlpd        dhlp
```

The bit-rearranging part of the program of Figure 7–4 requires 480 instructions (80 swaps at six instructions each). The revised program, using *rotate*

instructions, requires 80 swaps at four instructions each, plus 80 *rotate* instructions (16 · 5) for the first five stages, plus a final 31 *rotate* instructions, for a total of 431 instructions. The prolog and epilog code would be unchanged, so using *rotate* instructions in this way saves 49 instructions.

There is another quite different method of transposing a bit matrix: apply three shearing transformations [GLS1]. If the matrix is $n \times n$, the steps are (1) rotate row i to the right i bit positions, (2) rotate column j upwards $(j + 1) \bmod n$ bit positions, (3) rotate row i to the right $(i + 1) \bmod n$ bit positions, and (4) reflect the matrix about a horizontal axis through the midpoint. To illustrate, for a 4×4-bit matrix:

```
abcd        abcd        hlpd        dhlp        aeim
efgh  ==>   hefg  ==>   kocg  ==>   cgko  ==>   bfjn
ijkl        klij        nbfj        bfjn        cgko
mnop        nopm        aeim        aeim        dhlp
```

This method is not quite competitive with the others because step (2) is costly. (To do it at reasonable cost, rotate upwards all columns that rotate by $n/2$ or more bit positions by $n/2$ bit positions [these are columns $n/2 - 1$ through $n - 2$], then rotate certain columns upwards $n/4$ bit positions, and so on.) Steps 1 and 3 require only $n - 1$ instructions each, and step 4 requires no instructions at all if the results are simply stored to the appropriate locations.

If an 8×8-bit matrix is stored in a 64-bit word in the obvious way (top row in the most significant eight bits, and so on), then the matrix transpose operation is equivalent to three outer perfect shuffles or unshuffles [GLS1]. This is a very good way to do it if your machine has shuffle or unshuffle as a single instruction, but it is not a good method on a basic RISC machine.

7–4 *Compress,* or *Generalized Extract*

The APL language includes an operation called *compress*, written B/V, where B is a Boolean vector and V is vector of the same length as B, with arbitrary elements. The result of the operation is a vector consisting of the elements of V for which the corresponding bit in B is 1. The length of the result vector is equal to the number of 1's in B.

Here we consider a similar operation on the bits of a word. Given a mask *m* and a word *x*, the bits of *x* for which the corresponding mask bit is 1 are selected and moved ("compressed") to the right. For example, if the word to be compressed is (where each letter denotes a single bit)

```
abcd efgh ijkl mnop qrst uvwx yzAB CDEF,
```

and the mask is

```
0000 1111 0011 0011 1010 1010 0101 0101,
```

then the result is

```
0000 0000 0000 0000 efgh klop qsuw zBDF.
```

This operation might also be called *generalized extract*, by analogy with the *extract* instruction found on many computers.

We are interested in code for this operation with minimum worst-case execution time, and offer the simple loop of Figure 7–5 as a straw man to be improved upon. This code has no branches in the loop, and it executes in 260 instructions worst case, including the subroutine prolog and epilog.

It is possible to improve on this by repeatedly using the parallel prefix method (see page 75) with the *exclusive or* operation [GLS1]. We will denote the parallel prefix operation by PP-XOR. The basic idea is to first identify the bits of argument x that are to be moved right an odd number of bit positions, and move those. (This operation is simplified if x is first *and*ed with the mask, to clear out irrelevant bits.) Mask bits are moved in the same way. Next, we identify the bits of x that are to be moved an odd multiple of 2 positions (2, 6, 10, and so on), and we then move these bits of x and the mask. Next, we identify and move the bits that are to be moved an odd multiple of 4 positions, then those that move an odd multiple of 8, and then those that move 16 bit positions.

Because this algorithm, believed to be original with [GLS1], is a bit difficult to understand, and because it is perhaps surprising that something along these lines can be done at all, we will describe its operation in some detail. Suppose the inputs are

$$x = abcd\ efgh\ ijkl\ mnop\ qrst\ uvwx\ yzAB\ CDEF,$$
$$m = 1000\ 1000\ 1110\ 0000\ 0000\ 1111\ 0101\ 0101,$$

```
1     1    111
9     6    333              4444  3 2  1 0
```

```
unsigned compress(unsigned x, unsigned m) {
    unsigned r, s, b;      // Result, shift, mask bit.

    r = 0;
    s = 0;
    do {
        b = m & 1;
        r = r | ((x & b) << s);
        s = s + b;
        x = x >> 1;
        m = m >> 1;
    } while (m != 0);
    return r;
}
```

FIGURE 7–5. A simple loop for the *compress* operation.

where each letter in x represents a single bit (with value 0 or 1). The numbers below each 1-bit in the mask m denote how far the corresponding bit of x must move to the right. This is the number of 0's in m to the right of the bit. As mentioned above, it is convenient to first clear out the irrelevant bits of x, giving

```
x = a000 e000 ijk0 0000 0000 uvwx 0z0B 0D0F.
```

The plan is to first determine which bits move an odd number of positions (to the right), and move those one bit position. Recall that the PP-XOR operation results in a 1-bit at each position where the number of 1's at and to the right of that position is odd. We wish to identify those bits for which the number of 0's strictly to the right is odd. This can be done by computing mk = ~m << 1 and performing PP-XOR on the result. This gives

```
mk = 1110 1110 0011 1111 1110 0001 0101 0100,
mp = 1010 0101 1110 1010 1010 0000 1100 1100.
```

Observe that mk identifies the bits of m that have a 0 immediately to the right, and mp sums these, modulo 2, from the right. Thus, mp identifies the bits of m that have an odd number of 0's to the right.

The bits that will be moved one position are those that are in positions that have an odd number of 0's strictly to the right (identified by mp) and that have a 1-bit in the original mask. This is simply mv = mp & m:

```
mv = 1000 0000 1110 0000 0000 0000 0100 0100.
```

These bits of m may be moved with the assignment

```
m = (m ^ mv) | (mv >> 1);
```

and the same bits of x may be moved with the two assignments

```
t = x & mv;
x = (x ^ t) | (t >> 1);
```

(Moving the bits of m is simpler because all the selected bits are 1's.) Here the *exclusive or* is turning off bits known to be 1 in m and x, and the *or* is turning on bits known to be 0 in m and x. The operations could also, alternatively, both be *exclusive or*, or *subtract* and *add,* respectively. The results, after moving the bits selected by mv right one position, are:

```
m = 0100 1000 0111 0000 0000 1111 0011 0011,
x = 0a00 e000 0ijk 0000 0000 uvwx 00zB 00DF.
```

Now we must prepare a mask for the second iteration, in which we identify bits that are to move an odd multiple of 2 positions to the right. Notice that the quantity mk & ~mp identifies those bits that have a 0 immediately to the right in the original mask m, and those bits that have an even number of 0's to the right in the original mask. These properties apply jointly, although not individually, to the revised mask m. (That is to say, mk identifies *all* the positions in the revised mask m that have a 0 to the immediate right and an even number of 0's to the right.) This is the quantity that, if summed from the right with PP-XOR, identifies those bits that move to the right an odd multiple of 2 positions (2, 6, 10, and so on). Therefore, the procedure is to assign this quantity to mk and perform a second iteration of the above steps. The revised value of mk is

$$mk = 0100\ 1010\ 0001\ 0101\ 0100\ 0001\ 0001\ 0000.$$

A complete C function for this operation is shown in Figure 7–6. It does the job in 127 basic RISC instructions (constant), including the subroutine prolog and epilog. Figure 7–7 shows the sequence of values taken on by certain variables at key points in the computation, with the same inputs that were used in the

```
unsigned compress(unsigned x, unsigned m) {
    unsigned mk, mp, mv, t;
    int i;

    x = x & m;              // Clear irrelevant bits.
    mk = ~m << 1;           // We will count 0's to right.

    for (i = 0; i < 5; i++) {
        mp = mk ^ (mk << 1);                // Parallel prefix.
        mp = mp ^ (mp << 2);
        mp = mp ^ (mp << 4);
        mp = mp ^ (mp << 8);
        mp = mp ^ (mp << 16);
        mv = mp & m;                        // Bits to move.
        m = m ^ mv | (mv >> (1 << i));      // Compress m.
        t = x & mv;
        x = x ^ t | (t >> (1 << i));        // Compress x.
        mk = mk & ~mp;
    }
    return x;
}
```

FIGURE 7–6. Parallel prefix method for the *compress* operation.

```
          x = abcd efgh ijkl mnop qrst uvwx yzAB CDEF
          m = 1000 1000 1110 0000 0000 1111 0101 0101
          x = a000 e000 ijk0 0000 0000 uvwx 0z0B 0D0F

i = 0,   mk = 1110 1110 0011 1111 1110 0001 0101 0100
After PP, mp = 1010 0101 1110 1010 1010 0000 1100 1100
         mv = 1000 0000 1110 0000 0000 0000 0100 0100
          m = 0100 1000 0111 0000 0000 1111 0011 0011
          x = 0a00 e000 0ijk 0000 0000 uvwx 00zB 00DF

i = 1,   mk = 0100 1010 0001 0101 0100 0001 0001 0000
After PP, mp = 1100 0110 0000 1100 1100 0000 1111 0000
         mv = 0100 0000 0000 0000 0000 0000 0011 0000
          m = 0001 1000 0111 0000 0000 1111 0000 1111
          x = 000a e000 0ijk 0000 0000 uvwx 0000 zBDF

i = 2,   mk = 0000 1000 0001 0001 0000 0001 0000 0000
After PP, mp = 0000 0111 1111 0000 1111 1111 0000 0000
         mv = 0000 0000 0111 0000 0000 1111 0000 0000
          m = 0001 1000 0000 0111 0000 0000 1111 1111
          x = 000a e000 0000 0ijk 0000 0000 uvwx zBDF

i = 3,   mk = 0000 1000 0000 0001 0000 0000 0000 0000
After PP, mp = 0000 0111 1111 1111 0000 0000 0000 0000
         mv = 0000 0000 0000 0111 0000 0000 0000 0000
          m = 0001 1000 0000 0000 0000 0111 1111 1111
          x = 000a e000 0000 0000 0000 0ijk uvwx zBDF

i = 4,   mk = 0000 1000 0000 0000 0000 0000 0000 0000
After PP, mp = 1111 1000 0000 0000 0000 0000 0000 0000
         mv = 0001 1000 0000 0000 0000 0000 0000 0000
          m = 0000 0000 0000 0000 0001 1111 1111 1111
          x = 0000 0000 0000 0000 000a eijk uvwx zBDF
```

FIGURE 7–7. Operation of the parallel prefix method for the *compress* operation.

discussion above. Observe that a by-product of the algorithm, in the last value assigned to m, is the original m with all its 1-bits compressed to the right.

We calculate that the algorithm of Figure 7–6 would execute in 169 instructions on a 64-bit basic RISC, as compared to 516 (worst case) for the algorithm of Figure 7–5.

The number of instructions required by the algorithm of Figure 7–6 can be reduced substantially if the mask m is a constant. This can occur in two situations: (1) a call to "compress(x, m)" occurs in a loop, in which the value of m is not known but it is a loop constant, and (2) the value of m is known and the code for compress is generated in advance, perhaps by a compiler.

Notice that the value assigned to x in the loop in Figure 7–6 is not used in the loop for anything other than the assignment to x. And, x is dependent only on itself and variable mv. Therefore, the subroutine can be coded with all references to x deleted, and the five values computed for mv can be saved in variables mv0, mv1, ..., mv4. Then, in situation (1) the function without references to x can be placed outside the loop in which "compress (x, m)" occurs, and the following statements can be placed in the loop:

```
x = x & m;
t = x & mv0;    x = x ^ t | (t >> 1);
t = x & mv1;    x = x ^ t | (t >> 2);
t = x & mv2;    x = x ^ t | (t >> 4);
t = x & mv3;    x = x ^ t | (t >> 8);
t = x & mv4;    x = x ^ t | (t >> 16);
```

This is only 21 instructions in the loop (the loading of the constants can be placed outside the loop), a considerable improvement over the 127 required by the full subroutine of Figure 7–7.

In situation (2), in which the value of m is known, the same sort of thing can be done, and further optimization may be possible. It might happen that one of the five masks is 0, in which case one of the five lines shown above can be omitted. For example, mask m1 is 0 if it happens that no bit moves an odd number of positions, and m4 is 0 if no bit moves more than 15 positions, and so on.

As an example, for

$$m = 0101\ 0101\ 0101\ 0101\ 0101\ 0101\ 0101\ 0101,$$

the calculated masks are

```
mv0 = 0100 0100 0100 0100 0100 0100 0100 0100
mv1 = 0011 0000 0011 0000 0011 0000 0011 0000
mv2 = 0000 1111 0000 0000 0000 1111 0000 0000
mv3 = 0000 0000 1111 1111 0000 0000 0000 0000
mv4 = 0000 0000 0000 0000 0000 0000 0000 0000
```

Because the last mask is 0, in the compiled code situation this compression operation is done in 17 instructions (not counting the loading of the masks). This is not quite as good as the code shown for this operation on page 108 (13 instructions, not counting the loading of masks), which takes advantage of the fact that alternate bits are being selected.

Using *Insert* and *Extract*

If your computer has the *insert* instruction, preferably with immediate values for the operands that identify the bit field in the target register, then in the compiled situation *insert* can often be used to do the *compress* operation with fewer instructions than the methods discussed above. Furthermore, it doesn't tie up registers holding the masks.

The target register is initialized to 0, and then, for each contiguous group of 1's in the mask m, variable x is shifted right to right-justify the next field, and the *insert* instruction is used to insert the bits of x in the appropriate place in the target register. This does the operation in $2n + 1$ instructions, where n is the number of fields (groups of consecutive 1's) in the mask. The worst case is 33 instructions, because the maximum number of fields is 16 (which occurs for alternating 1's and 0's).

An example in which the *insert* method uses substantially fewer instructions is m = 0x0010084A. Compressing with this mask requires moving bits 1, 2, 4, 8, and 16 positions. Thus, it takes the full 21 instructions for the parallel prefix method, but only 11 instructions for the *insert* method (there are five fields). A more extreme case is m = 0x80000000. Here a single bit moves 31 positions, requiring 21 instructions for the parallel prefix method, but only three instructions for the *insert* method and only one instruction (*shift right 31*) if you are not constrained to any particular scheme.

You can also use the *extract* instruction in various simple ways to do the *compress* operation with a known mask in $3n - 2$ instructions, where n is the number of fields in the mask.

Clearly, the problem of compiling optimal code for the *compress* operation with a known mask is a difficult one.

Compress Left

To compress bits to the left, obviously you can reverse the argument x and the mask, compress right, and reverse the result. Another way is to compress right and then shift left by pop($\overline{m}$). These might be satisfactory if your computer has an instruction for bit reversal or population count, but if not, the algorithm of Figure 7–6 is easily adapted: Just reverse the direction of all the shifts except the two in the expressions $1 << i$ (eight to change).

7–5 General Permutations, Sheep and Goats Operation

To do general permutations of the bits in a word, or of anything else, a central problem is how to represent the permutation. It cannot be represented very compactly. Because there are 32! permutations of the bits in a 32-bit word, at least $\lceil \log_2(32!) \rceil = 118$ bits, or three words plus 22 bits, are required to designate one permutation out of the 32!.

One interesting way to represent permutations is closely related to the compression operations discussed in Section 7–4 [GLS1]. Start with the direct method of simply listing the bit position to which each bit moves. For example, for the permutation done by a rotate left of four bit positions, the bit at position 0 (the least significant bit) moves to position 4, 1 moves to 5, ..., 31 moves to 3. This permutation can be represented by the vector of 32 5-bit indexes:

```
00100
00101
. . .
11111
00000
00001
00010
00011
```

Treating that as a bit matrix, the representation we have in mind is its transpose, except reflected about the off diagonal so the top row contains the least significant bits and the result uses little-endian bit numbering. This we store as five 32-bit words in array p:

```
p[0] = 1010 1010 1010 1010 1010 1010 1010 1010
p[1] = 1100 1100 1100 1100 1100 1100 1100 1100
p[2] = 0000 1111 0000 1111 0000 1111 0000 1111
p[3] = 0000 1111 1111 0000 0000 1111 1111 0000
p[4] = 0000 1111 1111 1111 1111 0000 0000 0000
```

Each bit of p[0] is the least significant bit of the position to which the corresponding bit of x moves, each bit of p[1] is the next more significant bit, and so on. This is similar to the encoding of the masks denoted by mv in the previous section, except that mv applies to revised masks in the compress algorithm, not to the original mask.

The compression operation we need compresses to the left all bits marked with 1's in the mask, and compresses to the right all bits marked with 0's.[1] This is sometimes called the "sheep and goats" operation (SAG), or "generalized unshuffle." It can be calculated with

```
SAG(x, m) = compress_left(x, m) | compress(x, ~m).
```

---

1. If big-endian bit numbering is used, compress to the left all bits marked with 0's, and to the right all bits marked with 1's.

With SAG as a fundamental operation, and a permutation p described as above, the bits of a word x can be permuted by p in the following 15 steps:

```
x    = SAG(x,     p[0]);
p[1] = SAG(p[1],  p[0]);
p[2] = SAG(p[2],  p[0]);
p[3] = SAG(p[3],  p[0]);
p[4] = SAG(p[4],  p[0]);

x    = SAG(x,     p[1]);
p[2] = SAG(p[2],  p[1]);
p[3] = SAG(p[3],  p[1]);
p[4] = SAG(p[4],  p[1]);

x    = SAG(x,     p[2]);
p[3] = SAG(p[3],  p[2]);
p[4] = SAG(p[4],  p[2]);

x    = SAG(x,     p[3]);
p[4] = SAG(p[4],  p[3]);

x    = SAG(x,     p[4]);
```

In these steps, SAG is used to perform a stable binary radix sort. Array p is used as 32 5-bit keys to sort the bits of x. In the first step, all bits of x for which p[0] = 1 are moved to the left half of the resulting word, and all those for which p[0] = 0 are moved to the right half. Other than this, the order of the bits is not changed (that is, the sort is "stable"). Then all the keys that will be used for the next round of sorting are similarly sorted. The sixth line is sorting x based on the second least significant bit of the key, and so on.

Similarly to the situation of compressing, if a certain permutation p is to be used on a number of words x, then a considerable savings results by precomputing most of the steps above. The permutation array is revised to

```
p[1] = SAG(p[1], p[0]);
p[2] = SAG(SAG(p[2], p[0]), p[1]);
p[3] = SAG(SAG(SAG(p[3], p[0]), p[1]), p[2]);
p[4] = SAG(SAG(SAG(SAG(p[4], p[0]), p[1]), p[2]), p[3]);
```

and then each permutation is done with

```
x = SAG(x, p[0]);
x = SAG(x, p[1]);
x = SAG(x, p[2]);
x = SAG(x, p[3]);
x = SAG(x, p[4]);
```

A more direct (but perhaps less interesting) way to do general permutations of the bits in a word is to represent a permutation as a sequence of 32 5-bit indexes.

The kth index is the bit number in the source from which the kth bit of the result comes. (This is a "comes from" list, whereas the SAG method uses a "goes to" list.) These could be packed six to a 32-bit word, thus requiring six words to hold all 32 bit indexes. An instruction can be implemented in hardware such as

$$\texttt{bitgather Rt,Rx,Ri,}$$

where register $\texttt{Rt}$ is a target register (and also a source), register $\texttt{Rx}$ contains the bits to be permuted, and register $\texttt{Ri}$ contains six 5-bit indexes (and two unused bits). The operation of the instruction is

$$t \leftarrow (t \ll 6) \mid x_{i_0} x_{i_1} x_{i_2} x_{i_3} x_{i_4} x_{i_5}.$$

In words, the contents of the target register are shifted left six bit positions, and six bits are selected from word x and placed in the vacated six positions of t. The bits selected are given by the six 5-bit indexes in word i, taken in left-to-right order. The bit numbering in the indexes could be either little- or big-endian, and the operation would probably be as described for either type of machine.

To permute a word, use a sequence of six such instructions, all with the same $\texttt{Rt}$ and $\texttt{Rx}$, but different index registers. In the first index register of the sequence, only indexes i_4 and i_5 are significant, as the bits selected by the other four indexes are shifted out of the left end of $\texttt{Rt}$.

An implementation of this instruction would most likely allow index values to be repeated, so the instruction can be used to do more than permute bits. It can be used to repeat any selected bit any number of times in the target register. The SAG operation lacks this generality.

It is not unduly difficult to implement this as a fast (e.g., one cycle) instruction. The bit selection circuit consists of six 32:1 MUX's. If these are built from five stages of 2:1 MUX's in today's technology ($6 \cdot 31 = 186$ MUX's in all), the instruction would be faster than a 32-bit *add* instruction [MD].

Permuting bits has applications in cryptography, and the closely related operation of permuting subwords (e.g., permuting the bytes in a word) has applications in computer graphics. Both of these applications are more likely to deal with 64-bit words, or possibly with 128, than with 32. The SAG and *bitgather* methods apply with obvious changes to these larger word sizes.

To encrypt or decrypt a message with the Data Encryption Standard (DES) algorithm requires a large number of permutation-like mappings. First, key generation is done, once per session. This involves 17 permutation-like mappings. The first, called "permuted choice 1," maps from a 64-bit quantity to a 56-bit quantity (it selects the 56 non-parity bits from the key and permutes them). This is followed by 16 permutation-like mappings from 56 bits to 48 bits, all using the same mapping, called "permuted choice 2."

Following key generation, each block of 64 bits in the message is subjected to 34 permutation-like operations. The first and last operations are 64-bit permutations, one being the inverse of the other. There are 16 permutations with repetitions that map 32-bit quantities to 48 bits, all using the same mapping. Finally, there are 16 32-bit permutations, all using the same permutation. The total number of distinct mappings is six. They are all constants and are given in [DES].

DES is obsolete, as it was proved to be insecure in 1998 by the Electronic Frontier Foundation, using special hardware. The National Institute of Standards and Technology (NIST) has endorsed a temporary replacement called Triple DES, which consists of DES run serially three times on each 64-bit block, each time with a different key (that is, the key length is 192 bits, including 24 parity bits). Hence it takes three times as many permutation operations as does DES to encrypt or decrypt.

However, the "permanent" replacement for DES and Triple DES, the Advanced Encryption Standard (previously known as the Rijndael algorithm [AES]), involves *no* bit-level permutations. The closest it comes to a permutation is a simple rotation of 32-bit words by a multiple of 8-bit positions. Other encryption methods proposed or in use generally involve far fewer bit-level permutations than DES.

To compare the two permutation methods discussed here, the *bitgather* method has the advantages of (1) simpler preparation of the index words from the raw data describing the permutation, (2) simpler hardware, and (3) more general mappings. The SAG method has the advantages of (1) doing the permutation in five rather than six instructions, (2) having only two source registers in its instruction format (which might fit better in some RISC architectures), (3) scaling better to permute a doubleword quantity, and (4) permuting subwords more efficiently.

Item (3) is discussed in [LSY]. The SAG instruction allows for doing a general permutation of a two-word quantity with two executions of the SAG instruction, a few basic RISC instructions, and two full permutations of single words. The *bitgather* instruction allows for doing it by executing *three* full permutations of single words plus a few basic RISC instructions. This does not count preprocessing of the permutation to produce new quantities that depend only on the permutation. We leave it to the reader to discover these methods.

Regarding item (4), to permute, for example, the four bytes of a word with *bitgather* requires executing six instructions, the same as for a general bit permutation by *bitgather*. But with SAG it can be done in only two instructions, rather than the five required for a general bit permutation by SAG. The gain in efficiency applies even when the subwords are not a power of 2 in size; the number of steps required is $\lceil \log_2 n \rceil$, where n is the number of subwords, not counting a possible non-participating group of bits that stays at one end or the other.

[LSY] discusses the SAG and *bitgather* instructions (called "GRP" and "PPERM," respectively), other possible permutation instructions based on networks, and permuting by table lookup.

7–6 Rearrangements and Index Transformations

Many simple rearrangements of the bits in a computer word correspond to even simpler transformations of the coordinates, or indexes, of the bits [GLS1]. These correspondences apply to rearrangements of the elements of any one-dimensional array, provided the number of array elements is an integral power of 2. For programming purposes, they are useful primarily when the array elements are a computer word or larger in size.

As an example, the outer perfect shuffle of the elements of an array A of size eight, with the result in array B, consists of the following moves:

$$A_0 \rightarrow B_0; \qquad A_1 \rightarrow B_2; \qquad A_2 \rightarrow B_4; \qquad A_3 \rightarrow B_6;$$
$$A_4 \rightarrow B_1; \qquad A_5 \rightarrow B_3; \qquad A_6 \rightarrow B_5; \qquad A_7 \rightarrow B_7;$$

Each B-index is the corresponding A-index rotated left one position, using a 3-bit rotator. The outer perfect *unshuffle* is of course accomplished by rotating *right* each index. Some similar correspondences are shown in Table 7–1. Here n is the number of array elements, "lsb" means least significant bit, and the rotations of indexes are done with a $\log_2 n$-bit rotator.

TABLE 7–1. REARRANGEMENTS AND INDEX TRANSFORMATIONS

Rearrangement	Index Transformation	
	Array Index, or Big-endian Bit Numbering	Little-endian Bit Numbering
Reversal	Complement	Complement
Bit flip, or generalized reversal (page 102)	*Exclusive or* with a constant	*Exclusive or* with a constant
Rotate left k positions	Subtract k (mod n)	Add k (mod n)
Rotate right k positions	Add k (mod n)	Subtract k (mod n)
Outer perfect shuffle	Rotate left one position	Rotate right one position
Outer perfect unshuffle	Rotate right one position	Rotate left one position
Inner perfect shuffle	Rotate left one, then complement lsb	Complement lsb, then rotate right one
Inner perfect unshuffle	Complement lsb, then rotate right	Rotate left one, then complement lsb
Transpose of an 8×8-bit matrix held in a 64-bit word	Rotate (left or right) three positions	Rotate (left or right) three positions
FFT unscramble	Reverse bits	Reverse bits

CHAPTER 8

MULTIPLICATION

8–1 Multiword Multiplication

This may be done with, basically, the traditional grade-school method. Rather than develop an array of partial products, however, it is more efficient to add each new row, as it is being computed, into a row that will become the product.

If the multiplicand is m words, and the multiplier is n words, then the product occupies $m + n$ words (or fewer), whether signed or unsigned.

In applying the grade-school scheme, we would like to treat each 32-bit word as a single digit. This works out well if an instruction that gives the 64-bit product of two 32-bit integers is available. Unfortunately, even if the machine has such an instruction, it is not readily accessible from most high-level languages. In fact, many modern RISC machines do not have this instruction in part *because* it isn't accessible from high-level languages and thus would not often be used. (Another reason is that the instruction would be one of a very few that give a two-register result.)

Our procedure is shown in Figure 8–1. It uses halfwords as the "digits." Parameter w gets the result, and u and v are the multiplier and multiplicand, respectively. Each is an array of halfwords, with the first halfword (w[0], u[0], and v[0]) being the least significant digit. This is "little-endian" order. Parameters m and n are the number of halfwords in u and v, respectively.

The picture below may help in understanding. There is no relation between m and n; either may be the larger.

$$
\begin{array}{r}
u_{m-1} u_{m-2} \ \cdots \ \ \cdots \ \ u_1 \ u_0 \\
\times \ v_{n-1} \ \cdots \ v_1 \ v_0 \\
\hline
w_{m+n-1} \ w_{m+n-2} \ \cdots \ \cdots \ \cdots \ w_1 \ w_0
\end{array}
$$

The procedure follows Algorithm M of [Knu2, sec. 4.3.1], but is coded in C and modified to perform signed multiplication. Observe that the assignment to t in the upper half of Figure 8–1 cannot overflow, because the maximum value that could be assigned to t is $(2^{16} - 1)^2 + 2(2^{16} - 1) = 2^{32} - 1$.

Multiword multiplication is simplest for unsigned operands. In fact, the code of Figure 8–1 performs unsigned multiplication if the "correction" steps (the lines

```
void mulmns(unsigned short w[], unsigned short u[],
   unsigned short v[], int m, int n) {
   unsigned int k, t, b;
   int i, j;

   for (i = 0; i < m; i++)
      w[i] = 0;

   for (j = 0; j < n; j++) {
      k = 0;
      for (i = 0; i < m; i++) {
         t = u[i]*v[j] + w[i + j] + k;
         w[i + j] = t;              // (I.e., t & 0xFFFF).
         k = t >> 16;
      }
      w[j + m] = k;
   }

   // Now w[] has the unsigned product. Correct by
   // subtracting v*2**16m if u < 0, and
   // subtracting u*2**16n if v < 0.

   if ((short)u[m - 1] < 0) {
      b = 0;                        // Initialize borrow.
      for (j = 0; j < n; j++) {
         t = w[j + m] - v[j] - b;
         w[j + m] = t;
         b = t >> 31;
      }
   }
   if ((short)v[n - 1] < 0) {
      b = 0;
      for (i = 0; i < m; i++) {
         t = w[i + n] - u[i] - b;
         w[i + n] = t;
         b = t >> 31;
      }
   }
   return;
}
```

FIGURE 8–1. Multiword integer multiplication, signed.

between the three-line comment and the "return" statement) are omitted. An unsigned version can be extended to signed in three ways:

1. Take the absolute value of each input operand, perform unsigned multiplication, and then negate the result if the input operands had different signs.

2. Perform the multiplication using unsigned elementary multiplication except when multiplying one of the high-order halfwords, in which case use signed × unsigned or signed × signed multiplication.

3. Perform unsigned multiplication and then correct the result somehow.

The first method requires passing over as many as $m + n$ input halfwords, to compute their absolute value. Or, if one operand is positive and one is negative, the method requires passing over as many as $\max(m, n) + m + n$ halfwords, to complement the negative input operand and the result. Perhaps more serious, the algorithm would alter its inputs (which we assume are passed by address), which may be unacceptable in some applications. Alternatively, it could allocate temporary space for them, or it could alter them and later change them back. All these alternatives are unappealing.

The second method requires three kinds of elementary multiplication (unsigned × unsigned, unsigned × signed, and signed × signed) and requires sign extension of partial products on the left, with 0's or 1's, making each partial product take longer to compute and add to the running total.

We choose the third method. To see how it works, let u and v denote the values of the two signed integers being multiplied, and let them be of lengths M and N bits, respectively. Then the steps in the upper half of Figure 8–1 erroneously interpret u as an unsigned quantity, having value $u + 2^M u_{M-1}$, where u_{M-1} is the sign bit of u. That is, $u_{M-1} = 1$ if u is negative, and $u_{M-1} = 0$ otherwise. Similarly, the program interprets v as having value $v + 2^N v_{N-1}$.

The program computes the product of these unsigned numbers—that is, it computes

$$(u + 2^M u_{M-1})(v + 2^N v_{N-1}) = uv + 2^M u_{M-1}v + 2^N v_{N-1}u + 2^{M+N}u_{M-1}v_{N-1}.$$

To get the desired result (uv), we must subtract from the unsigned product the value $2^M u_{M-1}v + 2^N v_{N-1}u$. There is no need to subtract the term $2^{M+N}u_{M-1}v_{N-1}$, because we know that the result can be expressed in $M + N$ bits, so there is no need to compute any product bits more significant than bit position $M + N - 1$. These two subtractions are performed by the steps below the three-line comment in Figure 8–1. They require passing over a maximum of $m + n$ halfwords.

It might be tempting to use the program of Figure 8–1 by passing it an array of fullword integers—that is, by "lying across the interface." Such a program will work on a little-endian machine, but not on a big-endian one. If we had stored the arrays in the reverse order, with u[0] being the most significant halfword (and the program altered accordingly), the "lying" program would work on a big-endian machine, but not on a little-endian one.

8–2 High-Order Half of 64-Bit Product

Here we consider the problem of computing the high-order 32 bits of the product of two 32-bit integers. This is the function of our basic RISC instructions *multiply high signed* (mulhs) and *multiply high unsigned* (mulhu).

For unsigned multiplication, the algorithm in the upper half of Figure 8–1 works well. Rewrite it for the special case $m = n = 2$, with loops unrolled, obvious simplifications made, and the parameters changed to 32-bit unsigned integers.

For signed multiplication, it is not necessary to code the "correction steps" in the lower half of Figure 8–1. These can be omitted if proper attention is paid to whether the intermediate results are signed or unsigned (declaring them to be signed causes the right shifts to be sign-propagating shifts). The resulting algorithm is shown in Figure 8–2. For an unsigned version, simply change all the int declarations to unsigned.

The algorithm requires 16 basic RISC instructions in either the signed or unsigned version, four of which are multiplications.

```
int mulhs(int u, int v) {
   unsigned u0, v0, w0;
   int u1, v1, w1, w2, t;

   u0 = u & 0xFFFF;  u1 = u >> 16;
   v0 = v & 0xFFFF;  v1 = v >> 16;
   w0 = u0*v0;
   t  = u1*v0 + (w0 >> 16);
   w1 = t & 0xFFFF;
   w2 = t >> 16;
   w1 = u0*v1 + w1;
   return u1*v1 + w2 + (w1 >> 16);
}
```

FIGURE 8–2. *Multiply high signed.*

8–3 High-Order Product Signed from/to Unsigned

Assume that the machine can readily compute the high-order half of the 64-bit product of two *unsigned* 32-bit integers, but we wish to perform the corresponding operation on *signed* integers. We could use the procedure of Figure 8–2, but that requires four multiplications; the procedure to be given [BGN] is much more efficient than that.

The analysis is a special case of that done to convert Knuth's Algorithm M from an unsigned to a signed multiplication routine (Figure 8–1). Let x and y denote the two 32-bit signed integers that we wish to multiply together. The machine will interpret x as an *unsigned* integer, having the value $x + 2^{32}x_{31}$, where x_{31} is the most significant bit of x (that is, x_{31} is the integer 1 if x is negative, and 0 otherwise). Similarly, y under unsigned interpretation has the value $y + 2^{32}y_{31}$.

Although the result we want is the high-order 32 bits of xy, the machine computes

$$(x + 2^{32}x_{31})(y + 2^{32}y_{31}) = xy + 2^{32}(x_{31}y + y_{31}x) + 2^{64}x_{31}y_{31}.$$

To get the desired result, we must subtract from this the quantity $2^{32}(x_{31}y + y_{31}x) + 2^{64}x_{31}y_{31}$. Because we know that the result can be expressed in 64 bits, we can perform the arithmetic modulo 2^{64}. This means that we can safely ignore the last term, and compute the signed high-order product as shown below (seven basic RISC instructions).

$$
\begin{aligned}
p &\leftarrow \text{mulhu}(x, y) && \text{// } \textit{multiply high unsigned} \text{ instruction.} \\
t_1 &\leftarrow (x \overset{s}{\gg} 31) \mathbin{\&} y && \text{// } t_1 = x_{31}y. \\
t_2 &\leftarrow (y \overset{s}{\gg} 31) \mathbin{\&} x && \text{// } t_2 = y_{31}x. \\
p &\leftarrow p - t_1 - t_2 && \text{// } p = \text{desired result.}
\end{aligned}
\tag{1}
$$

Unsigned from Signed

The reverse transformation follows easily. The resulting program is the same as (1) except with the first instruction changed to *multiply high signed* and the last operation changed to $p \leftarrow p + t_1 + t_2$.

8–4 Multiplication by Constants

It is nearly a triviality that one can multiply by a constant with a sequence of *shift left* and *add* instructions. For example, to multiply x by 13 (binary 1101), one can code

$$
\begin{aligned}
t_1 &\leftarrow x \ll 2 \\
t_2 &\leftarrow x \ll 3 \\
r &\leftarrow t_1 + t_2 + x
\end{aligned}
$$

where r gets the result.

In this section, left shifts are denoted by multiplication by a power of 2, so the above plan is written $r \leftarrow 8x + 4x + x$, which is intended to show four instructions on the basic RISC and most machines.

What we want to convey here is that there is more to this subject than meets the eye. First of all, there are other considerations besides simply the number of *shift*'s and *add*'s required to do a multiplication by a given constant. To illustrate, below are two plans for multiplying by 45 (binary 101101).

$$
\begin{array}{ll}
t \leftarrow 4x & t_1 \leftarrow 4x \\[4pt]
r \leftarrow x + t & t_2 \leftarrow 8x \\[4pt]
t \leftarrow 2t & t_3 \leftarrow 32x \\[4pt]
r \leftarrow r + t & r \leftarrow t_1 + x \\[4pt]
t \leftarrow 4t & t_3 \leftarrow t_3 + t_2 \\[4pt]
r \leftarrow r + t & r \leftarrow r + t_3
\end{array}
$$

The plan on the left uses a variable t that holds x shifted left by a number of positions that corresponds to a 1-bit in the multiplier. Each shifted value is obtained from the one before it. This plan has these advantages:

- It requires only one working register other than the input x and the output r.

- Except for the first two, it uses only 2-address instructions.

- The shift amounts are relatively small.

The same properties are retained when the plan is applied to any multiplier.

The scheme on the right does all the *shift*'s first, with x as the operand. It has the advantage of increased parallelism. On a machine with sufficient instruction-level parallelism, the scheme on the right executes in three cycles, whereas the scheme on the left, running on a machine with unlimited parallelism, requires four.

In addition to these details, it is nontrivial to find the minimum number of operations to accomplish multiplication by a constant, where by an "operation" we mean an instruction from a typical computer's set of *add* and *shift* instructions. In what follows, we assume this set consists of *add*, *subtract*, *shift left* by any constant amount, and *negate*. We assume the instruction format is three-address. However, the problem is no easier if one is restricted to only *add* (adding a number to itself, and then adding the sum to itself, and so on, accomplishes a shift left of any amount), or if one augments the set by instructions such as the HP PA-RISC's *shift and add* instructions. (These shift the contents of a register left by one, two, or three positions, add it to a second register, and put the result in a third register. Thus, it can multiply by 3, 5, or 9 in a single, presumably fast, instruction.) We also assume that only the least significant 32 bits of the product are wanted.

The first improvement to the basic binary decomposition scheme suggested above is to use *subtract* to shorten the sequence when the multiplier contains a group of three or more consecutive 1-bits. For example, to multiply by 28 (binary 11100), we can compute $32x - 4x$ (three instructions) rather than $16x + 8x + 4x$ (five instructions). On two's-complement machines, the result is correct even if the intermediate result of $32x$ overflows and the final result does not.

To multiply by a constant m with the basic binary decomposition scheme (using only *shift*'s and *add*'s) requires

$$2\text{pop}(m) - 1 - \delta$$

instructions, where $\delta = 1$ if m ends in a 1-bit (is odd), and $\delta = 0$ otherwise. If *subtract* is also used, it requires

$$4\text{g}(m) + 2\text{s}(m) - 1 - \delta$$

instructions, where $\text{g}(m)$ is the number of groups of two or more consecutive 1-bits in m, $\text{s}(m)$ is the number of "singleton" 1-bits in m, and δ has the same meaning as before.

For a group of size 2, it makes no difference which method is used.

The next improvement is to treat specially groups that are separated by a single 0-bit. For example, consider $m = 55$ (binary 110111). The group method calculates this as $(64x - 16x) + (8x - x)$, which requires six instructions. Calculating it as $64x - 8x - x$, however, requires only four. Similarly, we can multiply by binary 110111011 as illustrated by the formula $512x - 64x - 4x - x$ (six instructions).

The formulas above give an upper bound on the number of operations required to multiply a variable x by any given number m. Another bound can be obtained based on the size of m in bits—that is, on $n = \lfloor \log_2 m \rfloor + 1$.

> THEOREM. *Multiplication of a variable x by an n-bit constant m, $m \geq 1$, can be accomplished with at most n instructions of the type add, subtract, and shift left by any given amount.*

Proof. (Induction on n.) Multiplication by 1 can be done in 0 instructions, so the theorem holds for $n = 1$. For $n > 1$, if m ends in a 0-bit, then multiplication by m can be accomplished by multiplying by the number consisting of the left $n - 1$ bits of m (that is, by $m/2$), in $n - 1$ instructions, followed by a *shift left* of the result by one position. This uses n instructions altogether.

If m ends in binary 01, then mx can be calculated by multiplying x by the number consisting of the left $n - 2$ bits of m, in $n - 2$ instructions, followed by a *left shift* of the result by 2, and an *add* of x. This requires n instructions altogether.

If m ends in binary 11, then consider the cases in which it ends in 0011, 0111, 1011, and 1111. Let t be the result of multiplying x by the left $n - 4$ bits of m. If m

ends in 0011, then $mx = 16t + 2x + x$, which requires $(n - 4) + 4 = n$ instructions. If m ends in 0111, then $mx = 16t + 8x - x$, which requires n instructions. If m ends in 1111, then $mx = 16t + 16x - x$, which requires n instructions. The remaining case is that m ends in 1011.

It is easy to show that mx can be calculated in n instructions if m ends in 001011, 011011, or 111011. The remaining case is 101011.

This reasoning can be continued, with the "remaining case" always being of the form $101010...10101011$. Eventually, the size of m will be reached, and the only remaining case is the number $101010...10101011$. This n-bit number contains $n/2 + 1$ 1-bits. By a previous observation, it can multiply x with $2(n/2 + 1) - 2 = n$ instructions.

Thus, in particular, on a 32-bit machine multiplication by any constant can be done in at most 32 instructions, by the method described above. By inspection, it is easily seen that for n even, the n-bit number $101010...101011$ requires n instructions, and for n odd, the n-bit number $1010101...010110$ requires n instructions, so the bound is tight.

The methodology described so far is not too hard to work out by hand, or to incorporate into an algorithm such as might be used in a compiler. But such an algorithm would not always produce the best code, because further improvement is sometimes possible. This can result from factoring the multiplier m or some intermediate quantity along the way of computing mx. For example, consider again $m = 45$ (binary 101101). The methods described above require six instructions. Factoring 45 as $5 \cdot 9$, however, gives a four-instruction solution:

$$t \leftarrow 4x + x$$
$$r \leftarrow 8t + t$$

Factoring may be combined with additive methods. For example, multiplication by 106 (binary 1101010) requires seven instructions by the additive methods, but writing it as $7 \cdot 15 + 1$ leads to a five-instruction solution.

With factoring, the maximum number of instructions needed to multiply by an n-bit constant is, to the writer's knowledge, an open problem. For large n it may be less than the bound of n proved above. For example, $m = $ 0xAAAAAAAB requires 32 instructions without factoring, but writing this value as $2 \cdot 5 \cdot 17 \cdot 257 \cdot 65537 + 1$ gives a ten-instruction solution. (Ten instructions, however, is probably not typical of large numbers. The factorization reflects the simple bit pattern of alternate 1's and 0's.)

This should give an idea of the combinatorics involved in this seemingly simple problem. Knuth [Knu2, sec. 4.6.3] discusses the closely related problem of computing a^m using a minimum number of multiplications. This is analogous to the problem of multiplying by m using only addition instructions. A compiler algorithm for computing mx is described in [Bern].

CHAPTER 9

INTEGER DIVISION

9–1 Preliminaries

This chapter and the following one give a number of tricks and algorithms involving "computer division" of integers. In mathematical formulas we use the expression x/y to denote ordinary rational division, $x \div y$ to denote signed computer division of integers (truncating toward 0), and $x \overset{u}{\div} y$ to denote unsigned computer division of integers. Within C code, x/y of course denotes computer division, unsigned if either operand is unsigned, and signed if both operands are signed.

Division is a complex process, and the algorithms involving it are often not very elegant. It is even a matter of judgment as to just how signed integer division should be defined. Most high-level languages and most computer instruction sets define the result to be the rational result truncated toward 0. This and two other possibilities are illustrated below.

		truncating	modulus	floor
$7 \div 3$	=	2 rem 1	2 rem 1	2 rem 1
$(-7) \div 3$	=	-2 rem -1	-3 rem 2	-3 rem 2
$7 \div (-3)$	=	-2 rem 1	-2 rem 1	-3 rem -2
$(-7) \div (-3)$	=	2 rem -1	3 rem 2	2 rem -1

The relation $dividend = quotient * divisor + remainder$ holds for all three possibilities. We define "modulus" division by requiring that the remainder be nonnegative.[1] We define "floor" division by requiring that the quotient be the "floor" of the rational result. For positive divisors, modulus and floor division are equivalent. A fourth possibility, seldom used, rounds the quotient to the nearest integer.

One advantage of modulus and floor division is that most of the tricks simplify. For example, division by 2^n can be replaced by a *shift right signed* of n positions, and the remainder of dividing x by 2^n is given by the logical *and* of x and $2^n - 1$. I suspect that modulus and floor division more often give the result you want. For example, suppose you are writing a program to graph an integer-valued function, and the values range from *imin* to *imax*. You want to set up the extremes of the ordinate to be the smallest multiples of 10 that include *imin* and *imax*. Then the

---

1. I know I will be taken to task for this nomenclature, because there is no universal agreement that "modulus" implies "nonnegative." Knuth's "mod" operator [Knu1] is the remainder of floor division, which is negative (or 0) if the divisor is negative. Several programming languages use "mod" for the remainder of truncating division. However, in mathematics "modulus" is sometimes used for the magnitude of a complex number (nonnegative), and in congruence theory the modulus is generally assumed to be positive.

extreme values are simply $(imin \div 10) * 10$ and $((imax + 9) \div 10) * 10$ if modulus or floor division is used. If conventional division is used, you must evaluate something like:

```
if (imin >= 0) gmin = (imin/10)*10;
else           gmin = ((imin - 9)/10)*10;
if (imax >= 0) gmax = ((imax + 9)/10)*10;
else           gmax = (imax/10)*10;
```

Besides the quotient being more useful with modulus or floor division than with truncating division, we speculate that the nonnegative remainder is probably wanted more often than a remainder that can be negative.

It is hard to choose between modulus and floor division, because they differ only when the divisor is negative, which is unusual. Appealing to existing high-level languages does not help, because they almost universally use truncating division for x/y when the operands are signed integers. A few give floating-point numbers, or rational numbers, for the result. Looking at remainders, there is confusion. In Fortran 90, the MOD function gives the remainder of truncating division and MODULO gives the remainder of floor division (which can be negative). Similarly, in Common Lisp and ADA, REM is the remainder of truncating division, and MOD is the remainder of floor division. In PL/I, MOD is always nonnegative (it is the remainder of modulus division). In Pascal, A mod B is defined only for B > 0, and then it is the nonnegative value (the remainder of either modulus or floor division).

Anyway, we cannot change the world even if we knew how we wanted to change it,[2] so in what follows we will use the usual definition (truncating) for $x \div y$.

A nice property of truncating division is that it satisfies

$$(-n) \div d = n \div (-d) = -(n \div d), \quad \text{for } d \neq 0.$$

However, care must be exercised when applying this to transform programs, because if n or d is the maximum negative number, $-n$ or $-d$ cannot be represented in 32 bits. The operation $(-2^{31}) \div (-1)$ is an overflow (the result cannot be expressed as a signed quantity in two's-complement notation), and on most machines the result is undefined or the operation is suppressed.

Signed integer (truncating) division is related to ordinary rational division by

$$n \div d = \begin{cases} \lfloor n/d \rfloor, & \text{if } d \neq 0, nd \geq 0, \\ \lceil n/d \rceil, & \text{if } d \neq 0, nd < 0. \end{cases} \tag{1}$$

---

2. Some do try. IBM's PL.8 language uses modulus division, and Knuth's MMIX machine's division instruction uses floor division [MMIX].

Unsigned integer division—that is, division in which both n and d are interpreted as unsigned integers—satisfies the upper portion of (1).

In the discussion that follows, we make use of the following elementary properties of arithmetic, which we don't prove here. See [Knu1] and [GKP] for interesting discussions of the floor and ceiling functions.

THEOREM D1. *For x real, k an integer,*

$$\lfloor x \rfloor = -\lceil -x \rceil \qquad\qquad \lceil x \rceil = -\lfloor -x \rfloor$$
$$x - 1 < \lfloor x \rfloor \le x \qquad\qquad x \le \lceil x \rceil < x + 1$$
$$\lfloor x \rfloor \le x < \lfloor x \rfloor + 1 \qquad\qquad \lceil x \rceil - 1 < x \le \lceil x \rceil$$
$$x \ge k \Leftrightarrow \lfloor x \rfloor \ge k \qquad\qquad x \le k \Leftrightarrow \lceil x \rceil \le k$$
$$x > k \Rightarrow \lfloor x \rfloor \ge k \qquad\qquad x < k \Rightarrow \lceil x \rceil \le k$$
$$x \le k \Rightarrow \lfloor x \rfloor \le k \Rightarrow x < k + 1 \qquad\qquad x \ge k \Rightarrow \lceil x \rceil \ge k \Rightarrow x > k - 1$$
$$x < k \Leftrightarrow \lfloor x \rfloor < k \qquad\qquad x > k \Leftrightarrow \lceil x \rceil > k$$

THEOREM D2. *For n, d integers, d > 0,*

$$\left\lfloor \frac{n}{d} \right\rfloor = \left\lceil \frac{n - d + 1}{d} \right\rceil \quad and \quad \left\lceil \frac{n}{d} \right\rceil = \left\lfloor \frac{n + d - 1}{d} \right\rfloor.$$

If d < 0:

$$\left\lfloor \frac{n}{d} \right\rfloor = \left\lceil \frac{n - d - 1}{d} \right\rceil \quad and \quad \left\lceil \frac{n}{d} \right\rceil = \left\lfloor \frac{n + d + 1}{d} \right\rfloor.$$

THEOREM D3. *For x real, d an integer $\ne 0$:*

$$\lfloor \lfloor x \rfloor / d \rfloor = \lfloor x / d \rfloor \quad and \quad \lceil \lceil x \rceil / d \rceil = \lceil x / d \rceil.$$

COROLLARY. *For a, b real, $b \ne 0$, d an integer $\ne 0$,*

$$\left\lfloor \left\lfloor \frac{a}{b} \right\rfloor / d \right\rfloor = \left\lfloor \frac{a}{bd} \right\rfloor \quad and \quad \left\lceil \left\lceil \frac{a}{b} \right\rceil / d \right\rceil = \left\lceil \frac{a}{bd} \right\rceil.$$

THEOREM D4. *For n, d integers, $d \ne 0$, and x real,*

$$\left\lfloor \frac{n}{d} + x \right\rfloor = \left\lfloor \frac{n}{d} \right\rfloor \quad if \quad 0 \le x < \left| \frac{1}{d} \right|, \quad and \quad \left\lceil \frac{n}{d} + x \right\rceil = \left\lceil \frac{n}{d} \right\rceil \quad if \quad -\left| \frac{1}{d} \right| < x \le 0.$$

In the theorems below, rem(n, d) denotes the remainder of n divided by d. For negative d, it is defined by rem($n, -d$) = rem(n, d), as in truncating and modulus division. We do not use rem(n, d) with $n < 0$. Thus, for our use, the remainder is always nonnegative.

THEOREM D5. *For $n \geq 0$, $d \neq 0$,*

$$\text{rem}(2n, d) = \begin{cases} 2\text{rem}(n, d) & or \\ 2\text{rem}(n, d) - |d|, \end{cases} \quad and \quad \text{rem}(2n + 1, d) = \begin{cases} 2\text{rem}(n, d) + 1 & or \\ 2\text{rem}(n, d) - |d| + 1 \end{cases}$$

(whichever value is greater than or equal to 0 and less than $|d|$).

THEOREM D6. *For $n \geq 0$, $d \neq 0$,*

$$\text{rem}(2n, 2d) = 2\text{rem}(n, d).$$

Theorems D5 and D6 are easily proved from the basic definition of remainder—that is, that for some integer q it satisfies

$$n = qd + \text{rem}(n, d) \quad \text{with} \quad 0 \leq \text{rem}(n, d) < |d|,$$

provided $n \geq 0$ and $d \neq 0$ (n and d can be non-integers, but we will use these theorems only for integers).

9–2 Multiword Division

As in the case of multiword multiplication, multiword division may be done by, basically, the traditional grade-school method. The details, however, are surprisingly complicated. Figure 9–1 is Knuth's Algorithm D [Knu2 sec. 4.3.1], coded in C. The underlying form of division it uses is $32 \overset{u}{\div} 16 \Rightarrow 32$. (Actually, the quotient of these underlying division operations is at most 17 bits long.)

The algorithm processes its inputs and outputs a halfword at a time. Of course, we would prefer to process a fullword at a time, but it seems that such an algorithm would require an instruction that does $64 \overset{u}{\div} 32 \Rightarrow 32$ division. We assume here that either the machine does not have that instruction or it is hard to access from our high-level language. Although we generally assume the machine has $32 \overset{u}{\div} 32 \Rightarrow 32$ division, for this problem $32 \overset{u}{\div} 16 \Rightarrow 16$ suffices.

Thus, for this implementation of Knuth's algorithm, the base b is 65536. See [Knu2] for most of the explanation of this algorithm.

The dividend u and the divisor v are in "little-endian" order—that is, u[0] and v[0] are the least significant digits. (The code works correctly on both big- and little-endian machines.) Parameters m and n are the number of halfwords in u and v, respectively (Knuth defines m to be the length of the quotient). The caller

```
int divmnu(unsigned short q[], unsigned short r[],
   const unsigned short u[], const unsigned short v[],
   int m, int n) {

   const unsigned b = 65536;  // Number base (16 bits).
   unsigned short *un, *vn;   // Normalized form of u, v.
   unsigned qhat;             // Estimated quotient digit.
   unsigned rhat;             // A remainder.
   unsigned p;                // Product of two digits.
   int s, i, j, t, k;

   if (m < n || n <= 0 || v[n-1] == 0)
      return 1;                  // Return if invalid param.

   if (n == 1) {                        // Take care of
      k = 0;                            // the case of a
      for (j = m - 1; j >= 0; j--) {    // single-digit
         q[j] = (k*b + u[j])/v[0];      // divisor here.
         k = (k*b + u[j]) - q[j]*v[0];
      }
      if (r != NULL) r[0] = k;
      return 0;
   }

   // Normalize by shifting v left just enough so that
   // its high-order bit is on, and shift u left the
   // same amount. We may have to append a high-order
   // digit on the dividend; we do that unconditionally.

   s = nlz(v[n-1]) - 16;        // 0 <= s <= 16.
   vn = (unsigned short *)alloca(2*n);
   for (i = n - 1; i > 0; i--)
      vn[i] = (v[i] << s) | (v[i-1] >> 16-s);
   vn[0] = v[0] << s;

   un = (unsigned short *)alloca(2*(m + 1));
   un[m] = u[m-1] >> 16-s;
   for (i = m - 1; i > 0; i--)
      un[i] = (u[i] << s) | (u[i-1] >> 16-s);
   un[0] = u[0] << s;
   for (j = m - n; j >= 0; j--) {        // Main loop.
      // Compute estimate qhat of q[j].
      qhat = (un[j+n]*b + un[j+n-1])/vn[n-1];
      rhat = (un[j+n]*b + un[j+n-1]) - qhat*vn[n-1];
again:
```

FIGURE 9–1. Multiword integer division, unsigned, *continues.*

```
    if (qhat >= b || qhat*vn[n-2] > b*rhat + un[j+n-2])
    { qhat = qhat - 1;
      rhat = rhat + vn[n-1];
      if (rhat < b) goto again;
    }

    // Multiply and subtract.
    k = 0;
    for (i = 0; i < n; i++) {
        p = qhat*vn[i];
        t = un[i+j] - k - (p & 0xFFFF);
        un[i+j] = t;
        k = (p >> 16) - (t >> 16);
    }
    t = un[j+n] - k;
    un[j+n] = t;

    q[j] = qhat;                // Store quotient digit.
    if (t < 0) {                // If we subtracted too
        q[j] = q[j] - 1;        // much, add back.
        k = 0;
        for (i = 0; i < n; i++) {
            t = un[i+j] + vn[i] + k;
            un[i+j] = t;
            k = t >> 16;
        }
        un[j+n] = un[j+n] + k;
    }
} // End j.
// If the caller wants the remainder, unnormalize
// it and pass it back.
if (r != NULL) {
    for (i = 0; i < n; i++)
        r[i] = (un[i] >> s) | (un[i+1] << 16-s);
}
return 0;
}
```

FIGURE 9–1. Multiword integer division, unsigned, *continued*.

supplies space for the quotient q and, optionally, for the remainder r. The space for the quotient must be at least m - n + 1 halfwords, and for the remainder, n halfwords. Alternatively, a value of NULL can be given for the address of the remainder to signify that the remainder is not wanted.

The algorithm requires that the most significant digit of the divisor, v[n-1], be nonzero. This simplifies the normalization steps and helps to ensure that the caller has allocated sufficient space for the quotient. The code checks that v[n-1] is nonzero, and also the requirements that $n \geq 1$ and $m \geq n$. If any of these conditions are violated, it returns with an error code (return value 1).

After these checks, the code performs the division for the simple case in which the divisor is of length 1. This case is not singled out for speed; the rest of the algorithm requires that the divisor be of length 2 or more.

If the divisor is of length 2 or more, the algorithm normalizes the divisor by shifting it left just enough so that its high-order bit is 1. The dividend is shifted left the same amount, so the quotient is not changed by these shifts. As explained by Knuth, these steps are necessary to make it easy to guess each quotient digit with good accuracy. The *number of leading zeros* function, $\mathrm{nlz}(x)$, is used to determine the shift amount.

In the normalization steps, new space is allocated for the normalized dividend and divisor. This is done because it is generally undesirable, from the caller's point of view, to alter these input arguments, and because it may be impossible to alter them—they may be constants in read-only memory. Furthermore, the dividend may need an additional high-order digit. C's "alloca" function is ideal for allocating this space. It is usually implemented very efficiently, requiring only two or three in-line instructions to allocate the space and no instructions at all to free it. The space is allocated on the program's stack, in such a way that it is freed automatically upon subroutine return.

In the main loop, the quotient digits are cranked out one per loop iteration, and the dividend is reduced until it becomes the remainder. The estimate qhat of each quotient digit, after being refined by the steps in the loop labelled again, is always either exact or too high by 1.

The next steps multiply qhat by the divisor and subtract the product from the current remainder, as in the grade school method. If the remainder is negative, it is necessary to decrease the quotient digit by 1 and either re-multiply and subtract or, more simply, adjust the remainder by adding the divisor to it. This need be done at most once, because the quotient digit was either exact or 1 too high.

Lastly, the remainder is given back to the caller if the address of where to put it is non-null. The remainder must be shifted right by the normalization shift amount s.

The "add back" steps are executed only rarely. To see this, observe that the first calculation of each estimated quotient digit qhat is done by dividing the most significant two digits of the current remainder by the most significant digit of the divisor. The steps in the "again" loop amount to refining qhat to be the result of dividing the most significant *three* digits of the current remainder by the most significant *two* digits of the divisor (proof omitted; convince yourself of this by trying some examples using $b = 10$). Note that the divisor is greater than or equal to $b/2$ (because of normalization) and the dividend is less than or equal to b times the divisor (because each remainder is less than the divisor).

How accurate is the quotient estimated by using only three dividend digits and two divisor digits? Because normalization was done, it can be shown to be quite accurate. To see this somewhat intuitively (not a formal proof), consider estimating u/v in this way for base ten arithmetic. It can be shown that the estimate is always high (or exact). Thus, the worst case occurs if truncation of the divisor to two digits decreases the divisor by as much as possible in the sense of relative error, and truncation of the dividend to three digits increases it by as little as possible (which is 0), and if the dividend is as large as possible. This occurs for the case $49900...0/5099...9$, which we estimate by $499/50 = 9.98$. The true result is approximately $499/51 \approx 9.7843$. The difference of 0.1957 reveals that the estimated quotient digit and the true quotient digit, which are the floor functions of these ratios, will differ by at most 1, and this will occur about 20% of the time (assuming the quotient digits are uniformly distributed). This in turn means that the "add back" steps will be executed about 20% of the time.

Carrying out this (non-rigorous) analysis for a general base b yields the result that the estimated and true quotients differ by at most $2/b$. For $b = 65536$, we again obtain the result that the difference between the estimated and true quotient digits is at most 1, and this occurs with probability $2/65536 \approx 0.00003$. Thus the "add back" steps are executed for only about 0.003% of the quotient digits.

An example that requires the add back step is, in decimal, 4500/501. A similar example for base 65536 is 0x7FFF 8000 0000 0000/0x8000 0000 0001.

We will not attempt to estimate the running time of this entire program, but simply note that for large m and n, the execution time is dominated by the multiply/subtract loop. On a good compiler this will compile into about 16 basic RISC instructions, one of which is *multiply*. The "for j" loop is executed n times, and the multiply/subtract loop $m - n + 1$ times, giving an execution time for this part of the program of $(15 + mul)n(m - n + 1)$ cycles, where mul is the time to multiply two 16-bit variables. The program also executes $m - n + 1$ *divide* instructions and one *number of leading zeros* instruction.

Signed Multiword Division

We do not give an algorithm specifically for signed multiword division, but merely point out that the unsigned algorithm can be adapted for this purpose as follows:

1. Negate the dividend if it is negative, and similarly for the divisor.

2. Convert the dividend and divisor to unsigned representation.

3. Use the unsigned multiword division algorithm.

4. Convert the quotient and remainder to signed representation.

5. Negate the quotient if the dividend and divisor had opposite signs.

6. Negate the remainder if the dividend was negative.

These steps sometimes require adding or deleting a most significant digit. For example, assume for simplicity that the numbers are represented in base 256 (one byte per digit), and that in the signed representation, the high-order bit of the sequence of digits is the sign bit. This is much like ordinary two's-complement representation. Then, a divisor of 255, which has signed representation 0x00FF, must be shortened in step 2 to 0xFF. Similarly, if the quotient from step 3 begins with a 1-bit, it must be provided with a leading 0-byte for correct representation as a signed quantity.

9–3 Unsigned Short Division from Signed Division

By "short division" we mean the division of one single word by another (e.g., $32 \div 32 \Rightarrow 32$). It is the form of division provided by the "/" operator, when the operands are integers, in C and many other high-level languages. C has both signed and unsigned short division, but some computers provide only signed division in their instruction repertoire. How can you implement unsigned division on such a machine? There does not seem to be any really slick way to do it, but we offer here some possibilities.

Using Signed Long Division

Even if the machine has signed long division ($64 \div 32 \Rightarrow 32$), unsigned short division is not as simple as you might think. In the XLC compiler for the IBM RS/6000, it is implemented as illustrated below for $q \leftarrow (n \overset{u}{\div} d)$.

$$\text{if } n \overset{u}{<} d \text{ then } q \leftarrow 0$$
$$\text{else if } d = 1 \text{ then } q \leftarrow n$$
$$\text{else if } d \leq 1 \text{ then } q \leftarrow 1$$
$$\text{else } q \leftarrow (0 \parallel n) \div d$$

The third line is really testing to see if $d \overset{u}{\geq} 2^{31}$. If d is algebraically less than or equal to 1 at this point, then because it is not equal to 1 (from the second line), it must be algebraically less than or equal to 0. We don't care about the case $d = 0$, so for the cases of interest, if the test on the third line evaluates to **true**, the sign bit of d is on, that is, $d \overset{u}{\geq} 2^{31}$. Because from the first line it is known that $n \overset{u}{\geq} d$, and because n cannot exceed $2^{32} - 1$, $n \overset{u}{\div} d = 1$.

The notation on the fourth line means to form the double-length integer consisting of 32 0-bits followed by the 32-bit quantity n, and divide it by d. The test for $d = 1$ (second line) is necessary to ensure that this division does not overflow (it would overflow if $n \overset{u}{\geq} 2^{31}$, and then the quotient would be undefined).

By commoning the comparisons on the second and third lines,[3] the above can be implemented in 11 instructions, three of which are branches. If it is necessary that the *divide* be executed when $d = 0$, to get the overflow interrupt, then the

---

3. One execution of the RS/6000's *compare* instruction sets multiple status bits indicating less than, greater than, or equal.

third line can be changed to "else if $d < 0$ then $q \leftarrow 1$," giving a 12-instruction solution on the RS/6000.

It is a simple matter to alter the above code so that the probable usual cases ($2 \overset{u}{\leq} d \overset{u}{<} 2^{31}$) do not go through so many tests (begin with if $d \leq 1$ ...), but the code volume increases slightly.

Using Signed Short Division

If signed long division is not available, but signed short division is, then $n \overset{u}{\div} d$ can be implemented by somehow reducing the problem to the case $n, d < 2^{31}$, and using the machine's *divide* instruction. If $d \overset{u}{\geq} 2^{31}$, then $n \overset{u}{\div} d$ can only be **0** or **1**, so this case is easily dispensed with. Then, we can reduce the dividend by using the fact that the expression $((n \overset{u}{\div} 2) \div d) \times 2$ approximates $n \overset{u}{\div} d$ with an error of only 0 or 1. This leads to the following method:

1.   if $d < 0$ then if $n \overset{u}{<} d$ then $q \leftarrow 0$

2.   else $q \leftarrow 1$

3.   else do

4. $q \leftarrow ((n \overset{u}{\div} 2) \div d) \times 2$

5. $r \leftarrow n - qd$

6.   if $r \overset{u}{\geq} d$ then $q \leftarrow q + 1$

7.   end

The test $d < 0$ on line 1 is really testing to determine if $d \overset{u}{\geq} 2^{31}$. If $d \overset{u}{\geq} 2^{31}$, then the largest the quotient could be is $(2^{32} - 1) \div 2^{31} = 1$, so the first two lines compute the correct quotient.

Line 4 represents the code *shift right unsigned 1, divide, shift left 1*. Clearly, $n \overset{u}{\div} 2 \overset{u}{<} 2^{31}$, and at this point $d \overset{u}{<} 2^{31}$ as well, so these quantities can be used in the computer's signed division instruction. (If $d = 0$, overflow will be signaled here.)

The estimate computed at line 4 is

$$q = \lfloor \lfloor n/2 \rfloor /d \rfloor \cdot 2 = \lfloor n/(2d) \rfloor \cdot 2 = \frac{n - \text{rem}(n, 2d)}{d},$$

where we have used the corollary of Theorem D3. Line 5 computes the remainder corresponding to the estimated quotient. It is

$$r = n - \frac{n - \text{rem}(n, 2d)}{d} d = \text{rem}(n, 2d).$$

Thus, $0 \leq r < 2d$. If $r < d$, then q is the correct quotient. If $r \geq d$, then adding 1 to q gives the correct quotient (the program must use an unsigned comparison here because of the possibility that $r \geq 2^{31}$).

By moving the *load immediate* of 0 into q ahead of the comparison $n \overset{u}{<} d$, and coding the assignment $q \leftarrow 1$ in line 2 as a branch to the assignment $q \leftarrow q + 1$ in line 6, this can be coded in 14 instructions on most machines, four of which are branches. It is straightforward to augment the code to produce the remainder as well: to line 1 append $r \leftarrow n$, to line 2 append $r \leftarrow n - d$, and to the "then" clause in line 6 append $r \leftarrow r - d$. (Or, at the cost of a *multiply*, simply append $r \leftarrow n - qd$ to the end of the whole sequence.)

An alternative for lines 1 and 2 is

$$\text{if } n \overset{u}{<} d \text{ then } q \leftarrow 0$$
$$\text{else if } d < 0 \text{ then } q \leftarrow 1,$$

which can be coded a little more compactly, for a total of 13 instructions, three of which are branches. But it executes more instructions in what is probably the usual case (small numbers with $n > d$).

Using predicate expressions, the program can be written

1.   if $d < 0$ then $q \leftarrow (n \overset{u}{\geq} d)$

2.   else do

3. $q \leftarrow ((n \overset{u}{\div} 2) \div d) \times 2$

4. $r \leftarrow n - qd$

5. $q \leftarrow q + (r \overset{u}{\geq} d)$

6.   end

which saves two branches if there is a way to evaluate the predicates without branching. On the Compaq Alpha they can be evaluated in one instruction (CMPULE), on MIPS they take two (SLTU, XORI). On most computers, they can be evaluated in four instructions each (three if equipped with a full set of logic instructions), by using the expression for $x \overset{u}{\leq} y$ given in "Comparison Predicates" on page 21, and simplifying because on line 1 of the program above it is known that $d_{31} = 1$, and on line 5 it is known that $d_{31} = 0$. The expression simplifies to

$$n \overset{u}{\geq} d = (n \mathbin{\&} \neg(n - d)) \overset{u}{\gg} 31 \quad \text{on line 1, and}$$

$$r \overset{u}{\geq} d = (r \mathbin{|} \neg(r - d)) \overset{u}{\gg} 31 \quad \text{on line 5.}$$

We can get branch-free code by forcing the dividend to be 0 when $d \overset{u}{\geq} 2^{31}$. Then, the divisor can be used in the machine's signed *divide* instruction, because when it is misinterpreted as a negative number, the result is set to 0, which is within 1 of being correct. We'll still handle the case of a large dividend by shifting it one position to the right before the division, and then shifting the quotient one position to the left after the division. This gives the following program (ten basic RISC instructions):

1. $t \leftarrow d \overset{s}{\gg} 31$

2. $n' \leftarrow n \;\&\; \neg t$

3. $q \leftarrow ((n' \overset{u}{\div} 2) \div d) \times 2$

4. $r \leftarrow n - qd$

5. $q \leftarrow q + (r \overset{u}{\geq} d)$

9–4 Unsigned Long Division

By "long division" we mean the division of a doubleword by a single word. For a 32-bit machine, this is $64 \overset{u}{\div} 32 \Rightarrow 32$ division, with the result unspecified in the overflow cases, including division by 0.

Some 32-bit machines provide an instruction for unsigned long division. Its full capability, however, gets little use, because only $32 \overset{u}{\div} 32 \Rightarrow 32$ division is accessible with most high-level languages. Therefore, a computer designer might elect to provide only $32 \overset{u}{\div} 32$ division, and would probably want an estimate of the execution time of a subroutine that implements the missing function. Here we give two algorithms for providing this missing function.

Hardware Shift-and-Subtract Algorithms

As a first attempt at doing long division, we consider doing what the hardware does. There are two algorithms commonly used, called *restoring* and *nonrestoring* division [H&P, sec. A-2; EL]. They are both basically "shift-and-subtract" algorithms. In the restoring version, shown below, the restoring step consists of adding back the divisor when the subtraction gives a negative result. Here x, y, and z are held in 32-bit registers. Initially, the double-length dividend is $x \parallel y$, and the divisor is z. We need a single-bit register c to hold the overflow from the subtraction.

```
do i ← 1 to 32
    c ∥ x ∥ y ← 2(x ∥ y)                          // Shift left one.
    c ∥ x ← (c ∥ x) – (0b0 ∥ z)                   // Subtract (33 bits).
    y₀ ← ¬c                                        // Set one bit of quotient.
    if c then c ∥ x ← (c ∥ x) + (0b0 ∥ z)         // Restore.
end
```

Upon completion, the quotient is in register y and the remainder is in register x.

The algorithm does *not* give a useful result in the overflow cases. For division of the doubleword quantity $x \| y$ by 0, the quotient obtained is the one's-complement of x, and the remainder obtained is y. In particular, $0 \overset{u}{\div} 0 \Rightarrow 2^{32} - 1$ rem 0. The other overflow cases are difficult to characterize.

It might be useful if, for nonzero divisors, the algorithm would give the correct quotient modulo 2^{32}, and the correct remainder. However, the only way to do this seems to be to make the register represented by $c \| x \| y$ above 97 bits long, and do the loop 64 times. This is doing $62 \overset{u}{\div} 32 \Rightarrow 64$ division. The subtractions would still be 33-bit operations, but the additional hardware and execution time make this refinement probably not worthwhile.

This algorithm is difficult to implement exactly in software, because most machines do not have the 33-bit register that we have represented by $c \| x$. Figure 9–2, however, illustrates a shift-and-subtract algorithm that reflects the hardware algorithm to some extent.

The variable t is used for a device to make the comparison come out right. We want to do a 33-bit comparison after shifting x | | y. If the first bit of x is 1 (before the shift), then certainly the 33-bit quantity is greater than the divisor (32 bits). In this case, x | t is all 1's, so the comparison gives the correct result (**true**). On the other hand, if the first bit of x is 0, then a 32-bit comparison is sufficient.

The code of the algorithm in Figure 9–2 executes in 321 to 385 basic RISC instructions, depending upon how often the comparison is **true**. If the machine has *shift left double*, the shifting operation can be done in one instruction, rather than the four used above. This would reduce the execution time to about 225 to 289 instructions (we are allowing two instructions per iteration for loop control).

```
unsigned divlu(unsigned x, unsigned y, unsigned z) {
    // Divides (x || y) by z.
    int i;
    unsigned t;

    for (i = 1; i <= 32; i++) {
        t = (int)x >> 31;          // All 1's if x(31) = 1.
        x = (x << 1) | (y >> 31);  // Shift x || y left
        y = y << 1;                // one bit.
        if ((x | t) >= z) {
            x = x - z;
            y = y + 1;
        }
    }
    return y;                       // Remainder is x.
}
```

FIGURE 9–2. *Divide long unsigned*, shift-and-subtract algorithm.

The algorithm in Figure 9–2 can be used to do $32 \div 32 \Rightarrow 32$ division by supplying x = 0. The only simplification that results is that the variable t can be omitted, as its value would always be 0.

Below is the nonrestoring hardware division algorithm (unsigned). The basic idea is that, after subtracting the divisor z from the 33-bit quantity that we denote by $c \parallel x$, there is no need to add back z if the result was negative. Instead, it suffices to *add* on the next iteration, rather than *subtract*. This is because adding z (to correct the error of having subtracted z on the previous iteration), shifting left, and subtracting z is equivalent to adding z ($2(u+z) - z = 2u + z$). The advantage to hardware is that there is only one add or subtract operation on each loop iteration, and the adder is likely to be the slowest circuit in the loop.[4] An adjustment to the remainder is needed at the end, if it is negative. (No corresponding adjustment of the quotient is required.)

The input dividend is the doubleword quantity $x \parallel y$, and the divisor is z. Upon completion, the quotient is in register y and the remainder is in register x.

$$c = 0$$
do $i \leftarrow 1$ to 32
  if $c = 0$ then do
    $c \parallel x \parallel y \leftarrow 2(x \parallel y)$ // Shift left one.
    $c \parallel x \leftarrow (c \parallel x) - (0b0 \parallel z)$ // Subtract divisor.
  end
  else do
    $c \parallel x \parallel y \leftarrow 2(x \parallel y)$ // Shift left one.
    $c \parallel x \leftarrow (c \parallel x) + (0b0 \parallel z)$ // Add divisor.
  end
  $y_0 \leftarrow \neg c$ // Set one bit of quotient.
end
if $c = 1$ then $x \leftarrow x + z$ // Adjust remainder if negative.

This does not seem to adapt very well to a 32-bit algorithm.

The 801 minicomputer (an early experimental RISC machine built by IBM) had a *divide step* instruction that essentially performed the steps in the body of the loop above. It used the machine's carry status bit to hold c, and the MQ (a 32-bit register) to hold y. A 33-bit adder/subtracter is needed for its implementation. The 801's *divide step* instruction was a little more complicated than the loop above,

---

4. Actually, the restoring division algorithm can avoid the restoring step by putting the result of the subtraction in an additional register, and writing that register into x only if the result of the subtraction (33 bits) is nonnegative. But in some implementations this may require an additional register and possibly more time.

because it performed signed division and it had an overflow check. Using it, a division subroutine can be written that consists essentially of 32 consecutive *divide step* instructions followed by some adjustments to the quotient and remainder to make the remainder have the desired sign.

Using Short Division

An algorithm for 64 ÷ 32 ⇒ 32 division can be obtained from the multiword division algorithm of Figure 9–1 on page 141, by specializing it to the case $m = 4$, $n = 2$. Several other changes are necessary. The parameters should be fullwords passed by value, rather than arrays of halfwords. The overflow condition is different; it occurs if the quotient cannot be contained in a single fullword. It turns out that many simplifications to the routine are possible. It can be shown that the guess qhat is always exact; it is exact if the divisor consists of only two halfword digits. This means that the "add back" steps can be omitted. If the "main loop" of Figure 9–1 and the loop within it are unrolled, some minor simplifications become possible.

The result of these transformations is shown in Figure 9–3. The dividend is in u1 and u0, with u1 containing the most significant word. The divisor is parameter v. The quotient is the returned value of the function. If the caller provides a non-null pointer in parameter r, the function will return the remainder in the word to which r points.

For an overflow indication, the program returns a remainder equal to the maximum unsigned integer. This is an impossible remainder for a valid division operation, because the remainder must be less than the divisor. In the overflow case, the program also returns a quotient equal to the maximum unsigned integer, which may be an adequate indicator in some cases in which the remainder is not wanted.

The strange expression (-s >> 31) in the assignment to u32 is supplied to make the program work for the case s = 0 on machines that have mod 32 shifts (e.g., Intel x86).

Experimentation with uniformly distributed random numbers suggests that the bodies of the "again" loops are each executed about 0.38 times for each execution of the function. This gives an execution time, if the remainder is not wanted, of about 52 instructions. Of these instructions, one is *number of leading zeros*, two are *divide*, and 6.5 are *multiply* (not counting the multiplications by b, which are *shift*'s). If the remainder is wanted, add six instructions (counting the store of r), one of which is *multiply*.

What about a signed version of divlu? It would probably be difficult to modify the code of Figure 9–3, step by step, to produce a signed variant. That algorithm, however, may be used for signed division by taking the absolute value of the arguments, running divlu, and then complementing the result if the signs of the original arguments differ. There is no problem with extreme values such as the maximum negative number, because the absolute value of any signed integer has a correct representation as an unsigned integer. This algorithm is shown in Figure 9–4.

```
unsigned divlu(unsigned u1, unsigned u0, unsigned v,
               unsigned *r)  {
   const unsigned b = 65536;  // Number base (16 bits).
   unsigned un1, un0,         // Norm. dividend LSD's.
            vn1, vn0,         // Norm. divisor digits.
            q1, q0,           // Quotient digits.
            un32, un21, un10, // Dividend digit pairs.
            rhat;             // A remainder.
   int s;                     // Shift amount for norm.

   if (u1 >= v) {             // If overflow, set rem.
      if (r != NULL)          // to an impossible value,
         *r = 0xFFFFFFFF;     // and return the largest
      return 0xFFFFFFFF;}     // possible quotient.

   s = nlz(v);                // 0 <= s <= 31.
   v = v << s;                // Normalize divisor.
   vn1 = v >> 16;             // Break divisor up into
   vn0 = v & 0xFFFF;          // two 16-bit digits.

   un32 = (u1 << s) | (u0 >> 32 - s) & (-s >> 31);
   un10 = u0 << s;            // Shift dividend left.

   un1 = un10 >> 16;          // Break right half of
   un0 = un10 & 0xFFFF;       // dividend into two digits.

   q1 = un32/vn1;             // Compute the first
   rhat = un32 - q1*vn1;      // quotient digit, q1.
again1:
   if (q1 >= b || q1*vn0 > b*rhat + un1) {
     q1 = q1 - 1;
     rhat = rhat + vn1;
     if (rhat < b) goto again1;}

   un21 = un32*b + un1 - q1*v;  // Multiply and subtract.

   q0 = un21/vn1;             // Compute the second
   rhat = un21 - q0*vn1;      // quotient digit, q0.
again2:
   if (q0 >= b || q0*vn0 > b*rhat + un0) {
     q0 = q0 - 1;
     rhat = rhat + vn1;
     if (rhat < b) goto again2;}

   if (r != NULL)             // If remainder is wanted,
      *r = (un21*b + un0 - q0*v) >> s;    // return it.
   return q1*b + q0;
}
```

FIGURE 9–3. *Divide long unsigned*, using fullword division instruction.

```
int divls(int u1, unsigned u0, int v, int *r) {
   int q, uneg, vneg, diff, borrow;

   uneg = u1 >> 31;           // -1 if u < 0.
   if (uneg) {                // Compute the absolute
      u0 = -u0;               // value of the dividend u.
      borrow = (u0 != 0);
      u1 = -u1 - borrow;}

   vneg = v >> 31;            // -1 if v < 0.
   v = (v ^ vneg) - vneg;     // Absolute value of v.

   if ((unsigned)u1 >= (unsigned)v) goto overflow;

   q = divlu(u1, u0, v, (unsigned *)r);

   diff = uneg ^ vneg;        // Negate q if signs of
   q = (q ^ diff) - diff;     // u and v differed.
   if (uneg && r != NULL)
      *r = -*r;

   if ((diff ^ q) < 0 && q != 0) {   // If overflow,
overflow:                     // set remainder
      if (r != NULL)          // to an impossible value,
         *r = 0x80000000;     // and return the largest
      q = 0x80000000;}        // possible neg. quotient.
   return q;
}
```

FIGURE 9–4. *Divide long signed*, using *divide long unsigned*.

It is hard to devise really good code to detect overflow in the signed case. The algorithm shown in Figure 9–4 makes a preliminary determination identical to that used by the unsigned long division routine, which ensures that $|u/v| < 2^{32}$. After that, it is necessary only to ensure that the quotient has the proper sign or is 0.

CHAPTER 10

INTEGER DIVISION
BY CONSTANTS

On many computers, division is very time consuming and is to be avoided when possible. A value of 20 or more elementary *add* times is not uncommon, and the execution time is usually the same large value even when the operands are small. This chapter gives some methods for avoiding the *divide* instruction when the divisor is a constant.

10–1 Signed Division by a Known Power of 2

Apparently, many people have made the mistake of assuming that a *shift right signed* of k positions divides a number by 2^k, using the usual truncating form of division [GLS2]. It's a little more complicated than that. The code shown below computes $q = n \div 2^k$, for $1 \le k \le 31$ [Hop].

```
shrsi  t,n,k-1      Form the integer
shri   t,t,32-k     2**k - 1 if n < 0, else 0.
add    t,n,t        Add it to n,
shrsi  q,t,k        and shift right (signed).
```

It is branch-free. It also simplifies to three instructions in the common case of division by 2 ($k = 1$). It does, however, rely on the machine's being able to shift by a large amount in a short time. The case $k = 31$ does not make too much sense, because the number 2^{31} is not representable in the machine. Nevertheless, the code does produce the correct result in that case (which is $q = -1$ if $n = -2^{31}$ and $q = 0$ for all other n).

To divide by -2^k, the above code may be followed by a *negate* instruction. There does not seem to be any better way to do it.

The more straightforward code for dividing by 2^k is

```
       bge    n,label      Branch if n >= 0.
       addi   n,n,2**k-1   Add 2**k - 1 to n,
label  shrsi  n,n,k        and shift right (signed).
```

This would be preferable on a machine with slow shifts and fast branches.

PowerPC has an unusual device for speeding up division by a power of 2 [GGS]. The *shift right signed* instructions set the machine's carry bit if the number being shifted is negative and one or more 1-bits are shifted out. That machine also has an instruction for adding the carry bit to a register, denoted `addze`. This allows division by any (positive) power of 2 to be done in two instructions:

```
shrsi  q,n,k
addze  q,q
```

A single `shrsi` of k positions does a kind of signed division by 2^k that coincides with both modulus and floor division. This suggests that one of these might be preferable to truncating division for computers and HLL's to use. That is, modulus and floor division mesh with `shrsi` better than does truncating division, permitting a compiler to translate the expression $n/2$ to an `shrsi`. Furthermore, `shrsi` followed by `neg` (negate) does modulus division by -2^k, which is a hint that maybe modulus division is best. (However, this is mainly an aesthetic issue. It is of little practical significance because division by a negative constant is no doubt extremely rare.)

10–2 Signed Remainder from Division by a Known Power of 2

If both the quotient and remainder of $n \div 2^k$ are wanted, it is simplest to compute the remainder r from $r = q * 2^k - n$. This requires only two instructions after computing the quotient q:

```
shli   r,q,k
sub    r,r,n
```

To compute only the remainder seems to require about four or five instructions. One way to compute it is to use the four-instruction sequence above for signed division by 2^k, followed by the two instructions shown immediately above to obtain the remainder. This results in two consecutive *shift* instructions that can be replaced by an *and*, giving a solution in five instructions (four if $k = 1$):

```
shrsi  t,n,k-1      Form the integer
shri   t,t,32-k     2**k - 1 if n < 0, else 0.
add    t,n,t        Add it to n,
andi   t,t,-2**k    clear rightmost k bits,
sub    r,n,t        and subtract it from n.
```

Another method is based on

$$\text{rem}(n, 2^k) = \begin{cases} n \,\&\, (2^k - 1), & n \geq 0, \\ -((\,n)\, \&\, (2^k - 1)), & n < 0. \end{cases}$$

To use this, first compute $t \leftarrow n \overset{s}{\gg} 31$, and then

$$r \leftarrow ((\text{abs}(n) \,\&\, (2^k - 1)) \oplus t) - t$$

(five instructions) or, for $k = 1$, since $(-n) \,\&\, \mathbf{1} = n \,\&\, \mathbf{1}$,

$$r \leftarrow ((n \,\&\, \mathbf{1}) \oplus t) - t$$

(four instructions). This method is not very good for $k > 1$ if the machine does not have *absolute value* (computing the remainder would then require seven instructions).

Still another method is based on

$$\mathrm{rem}(n, 2^k) = \begin{cases} n \,\&\, (2^k - 1), & n \geq 0, \\ ((n + 2^k - 1) \,\&\, (2^k - 1)) - (2^k - 1), & n < 0. \end{cases}$$

This leads to

$$t \leftarrow (n \overset{s}{\gg} k - 1) \overset{u}{\gg} 32 - k$$

$$r \leftarrow ((n + t) \,\&\, (2^k - 1)) - t$$

(five instructions for $k > 1$, four for $k = 1$).

The above methods all work for $1 \leq k \leq 31$.

Incidentally, if *shift right signed* is not available, the value that is $2^k - 1$ for $n < 0$ and 0 for $n \geq 0$ can be constructed from

$$t_1 \leftarrow n \overset{u}{\gg} 31$$

$$r \leftarrow (t_1 \ll k) - t_1,$$

which adds only one instruction.

10–3 Signed Division and Remainder by Non-Powers of 2

The basic trick is to multiply by a sort of reciprocal of the divisor d, approximately $2^{32}/d$, and then to extract the leftmost 32 bits of the product. The details, however, are more complicated, particularly for certain divisors such as 7.

Let us first consider a few specific examples. These illustrate the code that will be generated by the general method. We denote registers as follows:

n - the input integer (numerator)
M - loaded with a "magic number"
t - a temporary register
q - will contain the quotient
r - will contain the remainder

Divide by 3

```
li     M,0x55555556   Load magic number, (2**32+2)/3.
mulhs  q,M,n          q = floor(M*n/2**32).
shri   t,n,31         Add 1 to q if
add    q,q,t          n is negative.

muli   t,q,3          Compute remainder from
sub    r,n,t          r = n - q*3.
```

Proof. The *multiply high signed* operation (mulhs) cannot overflow, as the product of two 32-bit integers can always be represented in 64 bits and mulhs gives the high-order 32 bits of the 64-bit product. This is equivalent to dividing the 64-bit product by 2^{32} and taking the floor of the result, and this is true whether the product is positive or negative. Thus, for $n \geq 0$ the above code computes

$$q = \left\lfloor \frac{2^{32}+2}{3} \frac{n}{2^{32}} \right\rfloor = \left\lfloor \frac{n}{3} + \frac{2n}{3 \cdot 2^{32}} \right\rfloor.$$

Now, $n < 2^{31}$, because $2^{31} - 1$ is the largest representable positive number. Hence the "error" term $2n/(3 \cdot 2^{32})$ is less than 1/3 (and is nonnegative), so by Theorem D4 (page 139) we have $q = \lfloor n/3 \rfloor$, which is the desired result (Equation (1) on page 138).

For $n < 0$, there is an addition of 1 to the quotient. Hence the code computes

$$q = \left\lfloor \frac{2^{32}+2}{3} \frac{n}{2^{32}} \right\rfloor + 1 = \left\lfloor \frac{2^{32}n+2n+3 \cdot 2^{32}}{3 \cdot 2^{32}} \right\rfloor = \left\lceil \frac{2^{32}n+2n+1}{3 \cdot 2^{32}} \right\rceil,$$

where we have used Theorem D2. Hence

$$q = \left\lceil \frac{n}{3} + \frac{2n+1}{3 \cdot 2^{32}} \right\rceil.$$

For $-2^{31} \leq n \leq -1$,

$$-\frac{1}{3} + \frac{1}{3 \cdot 2^{32}} \leq \frac{2n+1}{3 \cdot 2^{32}} \leq -\frac{1}{3 \cdot 2^{32}}.$$

The error term is nonpositive and greater than $-1/3$, so by Theorem D4 $q = \lceil n/3 \rceil$, which is the desired result (Equation (1) on page 138).

This establishes that the quotient is correct. That the remainder is correct follows easily from the fact that the remainder must satisfy

$$n = qd + r,$$

the multiplication by 3 cannot overflow (because $-2^{31}/3 \leq q \leq (2^{31} - 1)/3$), and the *subtract* cannot overflow because the result must be in the range –2 to +2.

The *multiply immediate* can be done with two *add*'s, or a *shift* and an *add*, if either gives an improvement in execution time.

On many present-day RISC computers, the quotient can be computed as shown above in nine or ten cycles, whereas the *divide* instruction might take 20 cycles or so.

Divide by 5

For division by 5, we would like to use the same code as for division by 3, except with a multiplier of $(2^{32} + 4)/5$. Unfortunately, the error term is then too large; the result is off by 1 for about 1/5 of the values of $n \geq 2^{30}$ in magnitude. However, we can use a multiplier of $(2^{33} + 3)/5$ and add a *shift right signed* instruction. The code is

```
li     M,0x66666667  Load magic number, (2**33+3)/5.
mulhs  q,M,n          q = floor(M*n/2**32).
shrsi  q,q,1
shri   t,n,31         Add 1 to q if
add    q,q,t          n is negative.

muli   t,q,5          Compute remainder from
sub    r,n,t          r = n - q*5.
```

Proof. The `mulhs` produces the leftmost 32 bits of the 64-bit product, and then the code shifts this right by one position, signed (or "arithmetically"). This is equivalent to dividing the product by 2^{33} and then taking the floor of the result. Thus, for $n \geq 0$ the code computes

$$q = \left\lfloor \frac{2^{33} + 3}{5} \frac{n}{2^{33}} \right\rfloor = \left\lfloor \frac{n}{5} + \frac{3n}{5 \cdot 2^{33}} \right\rfloor.$$

For $0 \leq n < 2^{31}$, the error term $3n/5 \cdot 2^{33}$ is nonnegative and less than 1/5, so by Theorem D4, $q = \lfloor n/5 \rfloor$.

For $n < 0$, the above code computes

$$q = \left\lfloor \frac{2^{33} + 3}{5} \frac{n}{2^{33}} \right\rfloor + 1 = \left\lceil \frac{n}{5} + \frac{3n + 1}{5 \cdot 2^{33}} \right\rceil.$$

The error term is nonpositive and greater than –1/5, so $q = \lceil n/5 \rceil$.

That the remainder is correct follows as in the case of division by 3.

The *multiply immediate* can be done with a *shift left* of two and an *add*.

Divide by 7

Dividing by 7 creates a new problem. Multipliers of $(2^{32} + 3)/7$ and $(2^{33} + 6)/7$ give error terms that are too large. A multiplier of $(2^{34} + 5)/7$ would work, but it's too large to represent in a 32-bit signed word. We can multiply by this large number by multiplying by $(2^{34} + 5)/7 - 2^{32}$ (a negative number), and then correcting the product by inserting an add. The code is

```
li     M,0x92492493   Magic num, (2**34+5)/7 - 2**32.
mulhs  q,M,n          q = floor(M*n/2**32).
add    q,q,n          q = floor(M*n/2**32) + n.
shrsi  q,q,2          q = floor(q/4).
shri   t,n,31         Add 1 to q if
add    q,q,t          n is negative.

muli   t,q,7          Compute remainder from
sub    r,n,t          r = n - q*7.
```

Proof. It is important to note that the instruction "add q, q, n" above cannot overflow. This is because q and n have opposite signs, due to the multiplication by a negative number. Therefore, this "computer arithmetic" addition is the same as real number addition. Hence for $n \geq 0$ the above code computes

$$q = \left\lfloor \left(\left\lfloor \left(\frac{2^{34}+5}{7} - 2^{32} \right) \frac{n}{2^{32}} \right\rfloor + n \right) / 4 \right\rfloor = \left\lfloor \left\lfloor \frac{2^{34}n + 5n - 7 \cdot 2^{32}n + 7 \cdot 2^{32}n}{7 \cdot 2^{32}} \right\rfloor / 4 \right\rfloor$$

$$= \left\lfloor \frac{n}{7} + \frac{5n}{7 \cdot 2^{34}} \right\rfloor,$$

where we have used the corollary of Theorem D3.

For $0 \leq n < 2^{31}$, the error term $5n/7 \cdot 2^{34}$ is nonnegative and less than $1/7$, so $q = \lfloor n/7 \rfloor$.

For $n < 0$, the above code computes

$$q = \left\lfloor \left(\left\lfloor \left(\frac{2^{34}+5}{7} - 2^{32} \right) \frac{n}{2^{32}} \right\rfloor + n \right) / 4 \right\rfloor + 1 = \left\lceil \frac{n}{7} + \frac{5n+1}{7 \cdot 2^{34}} \right\rceil.$$

The error term is nonpositive and greater than $-1/7$, so $q = \lceil n/7 \rceil$.

The *multiply immediate* can be done with a *shift left* of three and a *subtract*.

10–4 Signed Division by Divisors ≥ 2

At this point you may wonder if other divisors present other problems. We see in this section that they do not; the three examples given illustrate the only cases that arise (for $d \geq 2$).

Some of the proofs are a bit complicated, so to be cautious, the work is done in terms of a general word size *W*.

Given a word size $W \geq 3$ and a divisor d, $2 \leq d < 2^{W-1}$, we wish to find the least integer m and integer p such that

$$\left\lfloor \frac{mn}{2^p} \right\rfloor = \left\lfloor \frac{n}{d} \right\rfloor \qquad \text{for } 0 \leq n < 2^{W-1}, \text{ and} \tag{1a}$$

$$\left\lfloor \frac{mn}{2^p} \right\rfloor + 1 = \left\lceil \frac{n}{d} \right\rceil \qquad \text{for } -2^{W-1} \leq n \leq -1, \tag{1b}$$

with $0 \leq m < 2^W$ and $p \geq W$.

The reason we want the *least* integer m is that a smaller multiplier may give a smaller shift amount (possibly zero) or may yield code similar to the "divide by 5" example, rather than the "divide by 7" example. We must have $m \leq 2^W - 1$ so the code has no more instructions than that of the "divide by 7" example (that is, we can handle a multiplier in the range 2^{W-1} to $2^W - 1$ by means of the add that was inserted in the "divide by 7" example, but we would rather not deal with larger multipliers). We must have $p \geq W$ because the generated code extracts the left half of the product mn, which is equivalent to shifting right W positions. Thus, the total right shift is W or more positions.

There is a distinction between the multiplier m and the "magic number," denoted M. The magic number is the value used in the *multiply* instruction. It is given by

$$M = \begin{cases} m, & \text{if } 0 \leq m < 2^{W-1}, \\ m - 2^W, & \text{if } 2^{W-1} \leq m < 2^W. \end{cases}$$

Because (1b) must hold for $n = -d$, $\lfloor -md/2^p \rfloor + 1 = -1$, which implies

$$\frac{md}{2^p} > 1. \tag{2}$$

Let n_c be the largest (positive) value of n such that $\text{rem}(n_c, d) = d - 1$. n_c exists because one possibility is $n_c = d - 1$. It can be calculated from $n_c = \lfloor 2^{W-1}/d \rfloor d - 1 = 2^{W-1} - \text{rem}(2^{W-1}, d) - 1$. n_c is one of the highest d admissible values of n, so

$$2^{W-1} - d \leq n_c \leq 2^{W-1} - 1, \tag{3a}$$

and clearly

$$n_c \geq d - 1. \tag{3b}$$

Because (1a) must hold for $n = n_c$,

$$\left\lfloor \frac{mn_c}{2^p} \right\rfloor = \left\lfloor \frac{n_c}{d} \right\rfloor = \frac{n_c - (d-1)}{d},$$

or

$$\frac{mn_c}{2^p} < \frac{n_c + 1}{d}.$$

Combining this with (2) gives

$$\frac{2^p}{d} < m < \frac{2^p}{d} \frac{n_c + 1}{n_c}. \tag{4}$$

Because m is to be the least integer satisfying (4), it is the next integer greater than $2^p/d$; that is,

$$m = \frac{2^p + d - \operatorname{rem}(2^p, d)}{d}. \tag{5}$$

Combining this with the right half of (4) and simplifying gives

$$2^p > n_c(d - \operatorname{rem}(2^p, d)). \tag{6}$$

The Algorithm

Thus, the algorithm to find the magic number M and the shift amount s from d is to first compute n_c, and then solve (6) for p by trying successively larger values. If $p < W$, set $p = W$ (the theorem below shows that this value of p also satisfies (6)). When the smallest $p \geq W$ satisfying (6) is found, m is calculated from (5). This is the smallest possible value of m, because we found the smallest acceptable p, and from (4) clearly smaller values of p yield smaller values of m. Finally, $s = p - W$ and M is simply a reinterpretation of m as a signed integer (which is how the mulhs instruction interprets it).

Forcing p to be at least W is justified by the following:

THEOREM DC1. *If (6) is true for some value of p, then it is true for all larger values of p.*

Proof. Suppose (6) is true for $p = p_0$. Multiplying (6) by 2 gives

$$2^{p_0 + 1} > n_c(2d - 2\operatorname{rem}(2^{p_0}, d)).$$

From Theorem D5, $\text{rem}(2^{p_0+1}, d) \geq 2\text{rem}(2^{p_0}, d) - d$. Combining gives

$$2^{p_0+1} > n_c(2d - (\text{rem}(2^{p_0+1}, d) + d)), \quad \text{or}$$
$$2^{p_0+1} > n_c(d - \text{rem}(2^{p_0+1}, d)).$$

Therefore, (6) is true for $p = p_0 + 1$, and hence for all larger values.

Thus, one could solve (6) by a binary search, although a simple linear search (starting with $p = W$) is probably preferable, because usually d is small, and small values of d give small values of p.

Proof That the Algorithm Is Feasible

We must show that (6) always has a solution and that $0 \leq m < 2^W$. (It is not necessary to show that $p \geq W$, because that is forced.)

We show that (6) always has a solution by getting an upper bound on p. As a matter of general interest, we also derive a lower bound under the assumption that p is not forced to be at least W. To get these bounds on p, observe that for any positive integer x, there is a power of 2 greater than x and less than or equal to $2x$. Hence from (6),

$$n_c(d - \text{rem}(2^p, d)) < 2^p \leq 2n_c(d - \text{rem}(2^p, d)).$$

Because $0 \leq \text{rem}(2^p, d) \leq d - 1$,

$$n_c + 1 \leq 2^p \leq 2n_c d. \tag{7}$$

From (3a) and (3b), $n_c \geq \max(2^{W-1} - d, d - 1)$. The lines $f_1(d) = 2^{W-1} - d$ and $f_2(d) = d - 1$ cross at $d = (2^{W-1} + 1)/2$. Hence $n_c \geq (2^{W-1} - 1)/2$. Because n_c is an integer, $n_c \geq 2^{W-2}$. Because $n_c, d \leq 2^{W-1} - 1$, (7) becomes

$$2^{W-2} + 1 \leq 2^p \leq 2(2^{W-1} - 1)^2,$$

or

$$W - 1 \leq p \leq 2W - 2. \tag{8}$$

The lower bound $p = W - 1$ can occur (e.g., for $W = 32, d = 3$), but in that case we set $p = W$.

If p is not forced to equal W, then from (4) and (7),

$$\frac{n_c + 1}{d} < m < \frac{2n_c d n_c + 1}{d} \frac{1}{n_c}.$$

Using (3b) gives

$$\frac{d-1+1}{d} < m < 2(n_c + 1).$$

Because $n_c \leq 2^{W-1} - 1$ (3a),

$$2 \leq m \leq 2^W - 1.$$

If p is forced to equal W, then from (4),

$$\frac{2^W}{d} < m < \frac{2^W n_c + 1}{d \, n_c}.$$

Because $2 \leq d \leq 2^{W-1} - 1$ and $n_c \geq 2^{W-2}$,

$$\frac{2^W}{2^{W-1} - 1} < m < \frac{2^W}{2} \frac{2^{W-2} + 1}{2^{W-2}}, \quad \text{or}$$

$$3 \leq m \leq 2^{W-1} + 1.$$

Hence in either case m is within limits for the code schema illustrated by the "divide by 7" example.

Proof That the Product Is Correct

We must show that if p and m are calculated from (6) and (5), then equations (1a) and (1b) are satisfied.

Equation (5) and inequality (6) are easily seen to imply (4). (In the case that p is forced to be equal to W, (6) still holds, as shown by Theorem DC1.) In what follows, we consider separately the following five ranges of values of n:

$$0 \leq n \leq n_c,$$

$$n_c + 1 \leq n \leq n_c + d - 1,$$

$$-n_c \leq n \leq -1,$$

$$-n_c - d + 1 \leq n \leq -n_c - 1, \quad \text{and}$$

$$n = -n_c - d.$$

From (4), because m is an integer,

$$\frac{2^p}{d} < m \leq \frac{2^p(n_c + 1) - 1}{d n_c}.$$

Multiplying by $n/2^p$, for $n \geq 0$ this becomes

$$\frac{n}{d} \leq \frac{mn}{2^p} \leq \frac{2^p n(n_c + 1) - n}{2^p dn_c}, \quad \text{so that}$$

$$\left\lfloor \frac{n}{d} \right\rfloor \leq \left\lfloor \frac{mn}{2^p} \right\rfloor \leq \left\lfloor \frac{n}{d} + \frac{(2^p - 1)n}{2^p dn_c} \right\rfloor.$$

For $0 \leq n \leq n_c$, $0 \leq (2^p - 1)n/(2^p dn_c) < 1/d$, so by Theorem D4,

$$\left\lfloor \frac{n}{d} + \frac{(2^p - 1)n}{2^p dn_c} \right\rfloor = \left\lfloor \frac{n}{d} \right\rfloor.$$

Hence (1a) is satisfied in this case ($0 \leq n \leq n_c$).

For $n > n_c$, n is limited to the range

$$n_c + 1 \leq n \leq n_c + d - 1, \tag{9}$$

because $n \geq n_c + d$ contradicts the choice of n_c as the largest value of n such that $\operatorname{rem}(n_c, d) = d - 1$ (alternatively, from (3a), $n \geq n_c + d$ implies $n \geq 2^{W-1}$). From (4), for $n \geq 0$,

$$\frac{n}{d} < \frac{mn}{2^p} < \frac{n}{d}\frac{n_c + 1}{n_c}.$$

By elementary algebra, this can be written

$$\frac{n}{d} < \frac{mn}{2^p} < \frac{n_c + 1}{d} + \frac{(n - n_c)(n_c + 1)}{dn_c}. \tag{10}$$

From (9), $1 \leq n - n_c \leq d - 1$, so

$$0 < \frac{(n - n_c)(n_c + 1)}{dn_c} \leq \frac{d - 1}{d}\frac{n_c + 1}{n_c}.$$

Because $n_c \geq d - 1$ (by (3b)) and $(n_c + 1)/n_c$ has its maximum when n_c has its minimum,

$$0 < \frac{(n - n_c)(n_c + 1)}{dn_c} \leq \frac{d - 1}{d}\frac{d - 1 + 1}{d - 1} = 1.$$

In (10), the term $(n_c + 1)/d$ is an integer. The term $(n - n_c)(n_c + 1)/dn_c$ is less than or equal to 1. Therefore, (10) becomes

$$\left\lfloor \frac{n}{d} \right\rfloor \leq \left\lfloor \frac{mn}{2^p} \right\rfloor \leq \frac{n_c + 1}{d}.$$

For all n in the range (9), $\lfloor n/d \rfloor = (n_c + 1)/d$. Hence (1a) is satisfied in this case ($n_c + 1 \leq n \leq n_c + d - 1$).

For $n < 0$, from (4) we have, because m is an integer,

$$\frac{2^p + 1}{d} \leq m < \frac{2^p n_c + 1}{d \quad n_c}.$$

Multiplying by $n/2^p$, for $n < 0$ this becomes

$$\frac{n \, n_c + 1}{d \quad n_c} < \frac{mn}{2^p} \leq \frac{n}{d} \frac{2^p + 1}{2^p},$$

or

$$\left\lfloor \frac{n \, n_c + 1}{d \quad n_c} \right\rfloor + 1 \leq \left\lfloor \frac{mn}{2^p} \right\rfloor + 1 \leq \left\lfloor \frac{n}{d} \frac{2^p + 1}{2^p} \right\rfloor + 1.$$

Using Theorem D2 gives

$$\left\lceil \frac{n(n_{c+1}) - dn_c + 1}{dn_c} \right\rceil + 1 \leq \left\lfloor \frac{mn}{2^p} \right\rfloor + 1 \leq \left\lceil \frac{n(2^p + 1) - 2^p d + 1}{2^p d} \right\rceil + 1,$$

$$\left\lceil \frac{n(n_c + 1) + 1}{dn_c} \right\rceil \leq \left\lfloor \frac{mn}{2^p} \right\rfloor + 1 \leq \left\lceil \frac{n(2^p + 1) + 1}{2^p d} \right\rceil.$$

Because $n + 1 \leq 0$, the right inequality can be weakened, giving

$$\left\lceil \frac{n}{d} + \frac{n + 1}{dn_c} \right\rceil \leq \left\lfloor \frac{mn}{2^p} \right\rfloor + 1 \leq \left\lceil \frac{n}{d} \right\rceil. \tag{11}$$

For $-n_c \leq n \leq -1$,

$$\frac{-n_c + 1}{dn_c} \leq \frac{n + 1}{dn_c} \leq 0, \quad \text{or}$$

$$-\frac{1}{d} < \frac{n + 1}{dn_c} \leq 0.$$

Hence by Theorem D4,

$$\left\lceil \frac{n}{d} + \frac{n+1}{dn_c} \right\rceil = \left\lceil \frac{n}{d} \right\rceil,$$

so that (1b) is satisfied in this case $(-n_c \leq n \leq -1)$.

For $n < -n_c$, n is limited to the range

$$-n_c - d \leq n \leq -n_c - 1. \tag{12}$$

(From (3a), $n < -n_c - d$ implies that $n < -2^{W-1}$, which is impossible.) Performing elementary algebraic manipulation of the left comparand of (11) gives

$$\left\lceil \frac{-n_c - 1}{d} + \frac{(n + n_c)(n_c + 1) + 1}{dn_c} \right\rceil \leq \left\lfloor \frac{mn}{2^p} \right\rfloor + 1 \leq \left\lceil \frac{n}{d} \right\rceil. \tag{13}$$

For $-n_c - d \leq n \leq -n_c - 1$,

$$\frac{(-d+1)(n_c + 1)}{dn_c} + \frac{1}{dn_c} \leq \frac{(n + n_c)(n_c + 1) + 1}{dn_c} \leq \frac{-(n_c + 1) + 1}{dn_c} = -\frac{1}{d}.$$

The ratio $(n_c + 1)/n_c$ is a maximum when n_c is a minimum; that is, $n_c = d - 1$. Therefore,

$$\frac{(-d+1)(d-1+1)}{d(d-1)} + \frac{1}{dn_c} \leq \frac{(n + n_c)(n_c + 1) + 1}{dn_c} < 0, \quad \text{or}$$

$$-1 < \frac{(n + n_c)(n_c + 1) + 1}{dn_c} < 0.$$

From (13), because $(-n_c - 1)/d$ is an integer and the quantity added to it is between 0 and –1,

$$\frac{-n_c - 1}{d} \leq \left\lfloor \frac{mn}{2^p} \right\rfloor + 1 \leq \left\lceil \frac{n}{d} \right\rceil.$$

For n in the range $-n_c - d + 1 \leq n \leq -n_c - 1$,

$$\left\lceil \frac{n}{d} \right\rceil = \frac{-n_c - 1}{d}.$$

Hence $\lfloor mn/2^p \rfloor + 1 = \lceil n/d \rceil$—that is, (1b) is satisfied.

The last case, $n = -n_c - d$, can occur only for certain values of d. From (3a), $-n_c - d \leq -2^{W-1}$, so if n takes on this value, we must have $n = -n_c - d = -2^{W-1}$, and hence $n_c = 2^{W-1} - d$. Therefore, $\operatorname{rem}(2^{W-1}, d) = \operatorname{rem}(n_c + d, d) = d - 1$ (that is, d divides $2^{W-1} + 1$).

For this case ($n = -n_c - d$), (6) has the solution $p = W - 1$ (the smallest possible value of p), because for $p = W - 1$,

$$n_c(d - \text{rem}(2^p, d)) = (2^{W-1} - d)(d - \text{rem}(2^{W-1}, d))$$
$$= (2^{W-1} - d)(d - (d - 1)) = 2^{W-1} - d < 2^{W-1} = 2^p.$$

Then from (5),

$$m = \frac{2^{W-1} + d - \text{rem}(2^{W-1}, d)}{d} = \frac{2^{W-1} + d - (d - 1)}{d} = \frac{2^{W-1} + 1}{d}.$$

Therefore,

$$\left\lfloor \frac{mn}{2^p} \right\rfloor + 1 = \left\lfloor \frac{2^{W-1}+1}{d} \frac{-2^{W-1}}{2^{W-1}} \right\rfloor + 1 = \left\lfloor \frac{-2^{W-1}-1}{d} \right\rfloor + 1$$

$$= \left\lceil \frac{-2^{W-1}-d}{d} \right\rceil + 1 = \left\lceil \frac{-2^{W-1}}{d} \right\rceil = \left\lceil \frac{n}{d} \right\rceil,$$

so that (1b) is satisfied.

This completes the proof that if m and p are calculated from (5) and (6), then Equations (1a) and (1b) hold for all admissible values of n.

10–5 Signed Division by Divisors ≤ -2

Because signed integer division satisfies $n \div (-d) = -(n \div d)$, it is adequate to generate code for $n \div |d|$ and follow it with an instruction to negate the quotient. (This does not give the correct result for $d = -2^{W-1}$, but for this and other negative powers of 2, you can use the code in Section 10–1, "Signed Division by a Known Power of 2," on page 155, followed by a negating instruction.) It will not do to negate the dividend, because of the possibility that it is the maximum negative number.

It is possible, however, to avoid the negating instruction. The scheme is to compute

$$q = \left\lfloor \frac{mn}{2^p} \right\rfloor \quad \text{if } n \leq 0, \text{ and}$$

$$q = \left\lfloor \frac{mn}{2^p} \right\rfloor + 1 \quad \text{if } n > 0.$$

Adding 1 if $n > 0$, however, is awkward (because one cannot simply use the sign bit of n), so the code will instead add 1 if $q < 0$. This is equivalent because the multiplier m is negative (as will be seen).

The code to be generated is illustrated below for the case $W = 32, d = -7$.

```
li     M,0x6DB6DB6D    Magic num, -(2**34+5)/7 + 2**32.
mulhs  q,M,n           q = floor(M*n/2**32).
sub    q,q,n           q = floor(M*n/2**32) - n.
shrsi  q,q,2           q = floor(q/4).
shri   t,q,31          Add 1 to q if
add    q,q,t           q is negative (n is positive).

muli   t,q,-7          Compute remainder from
sub    r,n,t           r = n - q*(-7).
```

This code is the same as that for division by +7, except that it uses the negative of the multiplier for +7, and a sub rather than an add after the multiply, and the shri of 31 must use q rather than n, as discussed above. (The case of $d = +7$ could also use q here, but there would be less parallelism in the code.) The *subtract* will not overflow because the operands have the same sign. This scheme, however, does not always work! Although the code above for $W = 32, d = -7$ is correct, the analogous alteration of the "divide by 3" code to produce code to divide by -3 does not give the correct result for $W = 32, n = -2^{31}$.

Let us look at the situation more closely.

Given a word size $W \geq 3$ and a divisor d, $-2^{W-1} \leq d \leq -2$, we wish to find the least (in absolute value) integer m and integer p such that

$$\left\lfloor \frac{mn}{2^p} \right\rfloor = \left\lfloor \frac{n}{d} \right\rfloor \quad \text{for } -2^{W-1} \leq n \leq 0, \text{ and} \tag{14a}$$

$$\left\lfloor \frac{mn}{2^p} \right\rfloor + 1 = \left\lceil \frac{n}{d} \right\rceil \quad \text{for } 1 \leq n < 2^{W-1}, \tag{14b}$$

with $-2^W \leq m \leq 0$ and $p \geq W$.

Proceeding similarly to the case of division by a positive divisor, let n_c be the most negative value of n such that $n_c = kd + 1$ for some integer k. n_c exists because one possibility is $n_c = d + 1$. It can be calculated from $n_c = \lfloor (-2^{W-1} - 1)/d \rfloor d + 1 = -2^{W-1} + \text{rem}(2^{W-1} + 1, d)$. n_c is one of the least $|d|$ admissible values of n, so

$$-2^{W-1} \leq n_c \leq -2^{W-1} - d - 1, \tag{15a}$$

and clearly

$$n_c \leq d + 1. \tag{15b}$$

Because (14b) must hold for $n = -d$, and (14a) must hold for $n = n_c$, we obtain, analogous to (4),

$$\frac{2^p n_c - 1}{d \quad n_c} < m < \frac{2^p}{d}. \tag{16}$$

Because m is to be the greatest integer satisfying (16), it is the next integer less than $2^p/d$—that is,

$$\boxed{m = \frac{2^p - d - \mathrm{rem}(2^p, d)}{d}.} \tag{17}$$

Combining this with the left half of (16) and simplifying gives

$$\boxed{2^p > n_c(d + \mathrm{rem}(2^p, d)).} \tag{18}$$

The proof that the algorithm suggested by (17) and (18) is feasible and that the product is correct is similar to that for a positive divisor, and will not be repeated. A difficulty arises, however, in trying to prove that $-2^W \le m \le 0$. To prove this, consider separately the cases in which d is the negative of a power of 2, or some other number. For $d = -2^k$, it is easy to show that $n_c = -2^{W-1} + 1$, $p = W + k - 1$, and $m = -2^{W-1} - 1$ (which is within range). For d not of the form -2^k, it is straightforward to alter the earlier proof.

For Which Divisors Is $m(-d) \ne -m(d)$?

By $m(d)$ we mean the multiplier corresponding to a divisor d. If $m(-d) = -m(d)$, code for division by a negative divisor can be generated by calculating the multiplier for $|d|$, negating it, and then generating code similar to that of the "divide by –7" case illustrated above.

By comparing (18) with (6) and (17) with (5), it can be seen that if the value of n_c for $-d$ is the negative of that for d, then $m(-d) = -m(d)$. Hence $m(-d) \ne m(d)$ can occur only when the value of n_c calculated for the negative divisor is the maximum negative number, -2^{W-1}. Such divisors are the negatives of the factors of $2^{W-1} + 1$. These numbers are fairly rare, as illustrated by the factorings below (obtained from Scratchpad).

$$2^{15} + 1 = 3 \cdot 11 \cdot 331$$
$$2^{31} + 1 = 3 \cdot 715{,}827{,}883$$
$$2^{63} + 1 = 3^3 \cdot 19 \cdot 43 \cdot 5419 \cdot 77{,}158{,}673{,}929$$

For *all* these factors, $m(-d) \neq m(d)$. Proof sketch: For $d > 0$ we have $n_c = 2^{W-1} - d$. Because $\text{rem}(2^{W-1}, d) = d - 1$, (6) is satisfied by $p = W - 1$ and hence also by $p = W$. For $d < 0$, however, we have $n_c = -2^{W-1}$ and $\text{rem}(2^{W-1}, d) = |d| - 1$. Hence (18) is not satisfied for $p = W - 1$ or for $p = W$, so $p > W$.

10–6 Incorporation into a Compiler

For a compiler to change division by a constant into a multiplication, it must compute the magic number M and the shift amount s, given a divisor d. The straightforward computation is to evaluate (6) or (18) for $p = W, W + 1, \ldots$ until it is satisfied. Then, m is calculated from (5) or (17). M is simply a reinterpretation of m as a signed integer, and $s = p - W$.

The scheme described below handles positive and negative d with only a little extra code, and it avoids doubleword arithmetic.

Recall that n_c is given by

$$n_c = \begin{cases} 2^{W-1} + \text{rem}(2^{W-1}, d) - 1, & \text{if } d > 0, \\ -2^{W-1} + \text{rem}(2^{W-1} + 1, d), & \text{if } d < 0. \end{cases}$$

Hence $|n_c|$ can be computed from

$$t = 2^{W-1} + \begin{cases} 0, & \text{if } d > 0, \\ 1, & \text{if } d < 0, \end{cases}$$

$$|n_c| = t - 1 - \text{rem}(t, |d|).$$

The remainder must be evaluated using unsigned division, because of the magnitude of the arguments. We have written $\text{rem}(t, |d|)$ rather than the equivalent $\text{rem}(t, d)$, to emphasize that the program must deal with two positive (and unsigned) arguments.

From (6) and (18), p can be calculated from

$$2^p > |n_c|(|d| - \text{rem}(2^p, |d|)), \tag{19}$$

and then $|m|$ can be calculated from (c.f. (5) and (17)):

$$|m| = \frac{2^p + |d| - \text{rem}(2^p, |d|)}{|d|}. \tag{20}$$

Direct evaluation of $\text{rem}(2^p, |d|)$ in (19) requires "long division" (dividing a $2W$-bit dividend by a W-bit divisor, giving a W-bit quotient and remainder), and in fact it must be *unsigned* long division. There is a way to solve (19), and in fact to do all the calculations, that avoids long division and can easily be implemented in a conventional HLL using only W-bit arithmetic. We do, however, need unsigned division and unsigned comparisons.

We can calculate rem(2^p, $|d|$) incrementally, by initializing two variables q and r to the quotient and remainder of 2^p divided by $|d|$ with $p = 2^{W-1}$, and then updating q and r as p increases.

As the search progresses—that is, when p is incremented by 1—q and r are updated from (see Theorem D5(a))

```
q = 2*q;
r = 2*r;
if (r >= abs(d)) {
    q = q + 1;
    r = r - abs(d);}
```

The left half of inequality (4) and the right half of (16), together with the bounds proved for m, imply that $q = \lfloor 2^p/|d| \rfloor < 2^W$, so q is representable as a W-bit unsigned integer. Also, $0 \le r < |d|$, so r is representable as a W-bit signed or unsigned integer. (Caution: The intermediate result $2r$ can exceed $2^{W-1} - 1$, so r should be unsigned and the comparison above should also be unsigned.)

Next, calculate $\delta = |d| - r$. Both terms of the subtraction are representable as W-bit unsigned integers, and the result is also ($1 \le \delta \le |d|$), so there is no difficulty here.

To avoid the long multiplication of (19), rewrite it as

$$\frac{2^p}{|d|} > \delta.$$

The quantity $2^p/|n_c|$ is representable as a W-bit unsigned integer (similarly to (7), from (19) it can be shown that $2^p \le 2|n_c| \cdot |d|$ and, for $d = -2^{W-1}$, $n_c = -2^{W-1} + 1$ and $p = 2W - 2$, so that $2^p/|n_c| = 2^{2W-2}/(2^{W-1} - 1) < 2^W$ for $W \ge 3$). Also, it is easily calculated incrementally (as p increases) in the same manner as for rem(2^p, $|d|$). The comparison should be unsigned, for the case $2^p/|n_c| \ge 2^{W-1}$ (which can occur, for large d).

To compute m, we need not evaluate (20) directly (which would require long division). Observe that

$$\frac{2^p + |d| - \text{rem}(2^p, |d|)}{|d|} = \left\lfloor \frac{2^p}{|d|} \right\rfloor + 1 = q + 1.$$

The loop closure test $2^p/|n_c| > \delta$ is awkward to evaluate. The quantity $2^p/|n_c|$ is available only in the form of a quotient q_1 and a remainder r_1. $2^p/|n_c|$

may or may not be an integer (it is an integer only for $d = 2^{W-2} + 1$ and a few negative values of d). The test $2^p / |n_c| \leq \delta$ may be coded as

$$q_1 < \delta \mid (q_1 = \delta \,\&\, r_1 = 0).$$

The complete procedure for computing M and s from d is shown in Figure 10–1, coded in C, for $W = 32$. There are a few places where overflow can occur, but the correct result is obtained if overflow is ignored.

To use the results of this program, the compiler should generate the li and mulhs instructions, generate the add if d > 0 and M < 0, or the sub if d < 0 and M > 0, and generate the shrsi if s > 0. Then, the shri and final add must be generated.

For $W = 32$, handling a negative divisor may be avoided by simply returning a precomputed result for $d = 3$ and $d = 715,827,883$, and using $m(-d) = -m(d)$ for other negative divisors. However, that program would not be significantly shorter, if at all, than the one given in Figure 10–1.

10–7 Miscellaneous Topics

THEOREM DC2. *The least multiplier m is odd if p is not forced to equal W.*

Proof. Assume that Equations (1a) and (1b) are satisfied with least (not forced) integer p, and m even. Then clearly m could be divided by 2 and p could be decreased by 1, and (1a) and (1b) would still be satisfied. This contradicts the assumption that p is minimal.

Uniqueness

The magic number for a given divisor is sometimes unique (e.g., for $W = 32$, $d = 7$), but often it is not. In fact, experimentation indicates that it is usually not unique. For example, for $W = 32$, $d = 6$, there are four magic numbers:

$$
\begin{aligned}
M &= 715,827,833 \quad ((2^{32}+2)/6), & s &= 0 \\
M &= 1,431,655,766 \quad ((2^{32}+2)/3), & s &= 1 \\
M &= -1,431,655,765 \quad ((2^{33}+1)/3 - 2^{32}), & s &= 2 \\
M &= -1,431,655,764 \quad ((2^{33}+4)/3 - 2^{32}), & s &= 2.
\end{aligned}
$$

However, there is the following uniqueness property:

THEOREM DC3. *For a given divisor d, there is only one multiplier m having the minimal value of p, if p is not forced to equal W.*

```
struct ms {int M;           // Magic number
          int s;};          // and shift amount.

struct ms magic(int d) {    // Must have 2 <= d <= 2**31-1
                            // or    -2**31 <= d <= -2.
    int p;
    unsigned ad, anc, delta, q1, r1, q2, r2, t;
    const unsigned two31 = 0x80000000;       // 2**31.
    struct ms mag;

    ad = abs(d);
    t = two31 + ((unsigned)d >> 31);
    anc = t - 1 - t%ad;       // Absolute value of nc.
    p = 31;                   // Init. p.
    q1 = two31/anc;           // Init. q1 = 2**p/|nc|.
    r1 = two31 - q1*anc;      // Init. r1 = rem(2**p, |nc|).
    q2 = two31/ad;            // Init. q2 = 2**p/|d|.
    r2 = two31 - q2*ad;       // Init. r2 = rem(2**p, |d|).
    do {
        p = p + 1;
        q1 = 2*q1;            // Update q1 = 2**p/|nc|.
        r1 = 2*r1;            // Update r1 = rem(2**p, |nc|.
        if (r1 >= anc) {      // (Must be an unsigned
            q1 = q1 + 1;      // comparison here).
            r1 = r1 - anc;}
        q2 = 2*q2;            // Update q2 = 2**p/|d|.
        r2 = 2*r2;            // Update r2 = rem(2**p, |d|.
        if (r2 >= ad) {       // (Must be an unsigned
            q2 = q2 + 1;      // comparison here).
            r2 = r2 - ad;}
        delta = ad - r2;
    } while (q1 < delta || (q1 == delta && r1 == 0));

    mag.M = q2 + 1;
    if (d < 0) mag.M = -mag.M; // Magic number and
    mag.s = p - 32;            // shift amount to return.
    return mag;
}
```

FIGURE 10–1. Computing the magic number for signed division.

Proof. First consider the case $d > 0$. The difference between the upper and lower limits of inequality (4) is $2^p/dn_c$. We have already proved (7) that if p is minimal, then $2^p/dn_c \leq 2$. Therefore, there can be at most two values of m satisfying (4). Let m be the smaller of these values, given by (5); then $m + 1$ is the other.

Let p_0 be the least value of p for which $m + 1$ satisfies the right half of (4) (p_0 is not forced to equal W). Then

$$\frac{2^{p_0} + d - \text{rem}(2^{p_0}, d)}{d} + 1 < \frac{2^{p_0} n_c + 1}{d} \cdot \frac{1}{n_c}.$$

This simplifies to

$$2^{p_0} > n_c(2d - \text{rem}(2^{p_0}, d)).$$

Dividing by 2 gives

$$2^{p_0 - 1} > n_c\left(d - \frac{1}{2}\text{rem}(2^{p_0}, d)\right).$$

Because $\text{rem}(2^{p_0}, d) \le 2\text{rem}(2^{p_0 - 1}, d)$ (by Theorem D5 on page 140),

$$2^{p_0 - 1} > n_c(d - \text{rem}(2^{p_0 - 1}, d)),$$

contradicting the assumption that p_0 is minimal.

The proof for $d < 0$ is similar and will not be given.

The Divisors with the Best Programs

The program for $d = 3$, $W = 32$ is particularly short, because there is no add or shrsi after the mulhs. What other divisors have this short program?

We consider only positive divisors. We wish to find integers m and p that satisfy equations (1a) and (1b), and for which $p = W$ and $0 \le m < 2^{W-1}$. Because any integers m and p that satisfy equations (1a) and (1b) must also satisfy (4), it suffices to find those divisors d for which (4) has a solution with $p = W$ and $0 \le m < 2^{W-1}$. All solutions of (4) with $p = W$ are given by

$$m = \frac{2^W + kd - \text{rem}(2^W, d)}{d}, \quad k = 1, 2, 3, \ldots.$$

Combining this with the right half of (4) and simplifying gives

$$\text{rem}(2^W, d) > kd - \frac{2^W}{n_c}. \tag{21}$$

The weakest restriction on $\text{rem}(2^W, d)$ is with $k = 1$ and n_c at its minimal value of 2^{W-2}. Hence we must have

$$\text{rem}(2^W, d) > d - 4;$$

that is, d divides $2^W + 1$, $2^W + 2$, or $2^W + 3$.

Now let us see which of these factors actually have optimal programs.

If d divides $2^W + 1$, then $\text{rem}(2^W, d) = d - 1$. Then a solution of (6) is $p = W$, because the inequality becomes

$$2^W > n_c(d - (d-1)) = n_c,$$

which is obviously true, because $n_c < 2^{W-1}$. Then in the calculation of m we have

$$m = \frac{2^W + d - (d-1)}{d} = \frac{2^W + 1}{d},$$

which is less than 2^{W-1} for $d \geq 3$ ($d \neq 2$ because d divides $2^W + 1$). Hence all the factors of $2^W + 1$ have optimal programs.

Similarly, if d divides $2^W + 2$, then $\text{rem}(2^W, d) = d - 2$. Again, a solution of (6) is $p = W$, because the inequality becomes

$$2^W > n_c(d - (d-2)) = 2n_c,$$

which is obviously true. Then in the calculation of m we have

$$m = \frac{2^W + d - (d-2)}{d} = \frac{2^W + 2}{d},$$

which exceeds $2^{W-1} - 1$ for $d = 2$, but which is less than or equal to $2^{W-1} - 1$ for $W \geq 3$, $d \geq 3$ (the case $W = 3$ and $d = 3$ does not occur, because 3 is not a factor of $2^3 + 2 = 10$). Hence all factors of $2^W + 2$, except for 2 and the cofactor of 2, have optimal programs. (The cofactor of 2 is $(2^W + 2)/2$, which is not representable as a W-bit signed integer).

If d divides $2^W + 3$, the following argument shows that d does not have an optimal program. Because $\text{rem}(2^W, d) = d - 3$, inequality (21) implies that we must have

$$n_c < \frac{2^W}{kd - d + 3}$$

for some $k = 1, 2, 3, \ldots$. The weakest restriction is with $k = 1$, so we must have $n_c < 2^W/3$.

From (3a), $n_c \geq 2^{W-1} - d$, or $d \geq 2^{W-1} - n_c$. Hence it is necessary that

$$d > 2^{W-1} - \frac{2^W}{3} = \frac{2^W}{6}.$$

Also, since 2, 3, and 4 do not divide $2^W + 3$, the smallest possible factor of $2^W + 3$ is 5. Hence the largest possible factor is $(2^W + 3)/5$. Thus, if d divides $2^W + 3$ and d has an optimal program, it is necessary that

$$\frac{2^W}{6} < d \leq \frac{2^W + 3}{5}.$$

Taking reciprocals of this with respect to $2^W + 3$ shows that the cofactor of d, $(2^W + 3)/d$, has the limits

$$5 \leq \frac{2^W + 3}{d} < \frac{(2^W + 3) \cdot 6}{2^W} = 6 + \frac{18}{2^W}.$$

For $W \geq 5$, this implies that the only possible cofactors are 5 and 6. For $W < 5$, it is easily verified that there are no factors of $2^W + 3$. Because 6 cannot be a factor of $2^W + 3$, the only possibility is 5. Therefore, the only possible factor of $2^W + 3$ that might have an optimal program is $(2^W + 3)/5$.

For $d = (2^W + 3)/5$,

$$n_c = \left\lfloor \frac{2^{W-1}}{(2^W + 3)/5} \right\rfloor \left(\frac{2^W + 3}{5} \right) - 1.$$

For $W \geq 4$,

$$2 < \frac{2^{W-1}}{(2^W + 3)/5} < 2.5,$$

so

$$n_c = 2\left(\frac{2^W + 3}{5} \right) - 1.$$

This exceeds $(2^W/3)$, so $d = (2^W + 3)/5$ does not have an optimal program. Because for $W < 4$ there are no factors of $2^W + 3$, we conclude that no factors of $2^W + 3$ have optimal programs.

In summary, all the factors of $2^W + 1$ and of $2^W + 2$, except for 2 and $(2^W + 2)/2$, have optimal programs, and no other numbers do. Furthermore, the above proof shows that algorithm *magic* (Figure 10–1 on page 174) always produces the optimal program when it exists.

Let us consider the specific cases $W = 16, 32,$ and 64. The relevant factorizations are shown below.

$$2^{16} + 1 = 65537 \text{ (prime)} \qquad 2^{32} + 1 = 641 \cdot 6,700,417$$
$$2^{16} + 2 = 2 \cdot 3^2 \cdot 11 \cdot 331 \qquad 2^{32} + 2 = 2 \cdot 3 \cdot 715,827,883$$
$$2^{64} + 1 = 274,177 \cdot 67,280,421,310,721$$
$$2^{64} + 2 = 2 \cdot 3^3 \cdot 19 \cdot 43 \cdot 5419 \cdot 77,158,673,929$$

Hence we have the results that for $W = 16,$ there are 20 divisors that have optimal programs. The ones less than 100 are 3, 6, 9, 11, 18, 22, 33, 66, and 99.

For $W = 32,$ there are six such divisors: 3, 6, 641, 6,700,417, 715,827,883, and 1,431,655,766.

For $W = 64,$ there are 126 such divisors. The ones less than 100 are 3, 6, 9, 18, 19, 27, 38, 43, 54, 57, and 86.

10–8 Unsigned Division

Unsigned division by a power of 2 is of course implemented by a single *shift right logical* instruction, and remainder by *and immediate*.

It might seem that handling other divisors will be simple: Just use the results for signed division with $d > 0,$ omitting the two instructions that add 1 if the quotient is negative. We will see, however, that some of the details are actually more complicated in the case of unsigned division.

Unsigned Divide by 3

For a non-power of 2, let us first consider unsigned division by 3 on a 32-bit machine. Because the dividend n can now be as large as $2^{32} - 1,$ the multiplier $(2^{32} + 2)/3$ is inadequate, because the error term $2n/3 \cdot 2^{32}$ (see "divide by 3" example above) can exceed 1/3. However, the multiplier $(2^{33} + 1)/3$ is adequate. The code is

```
li    M,0xAAAAAAAB  Load magic number, (2**33+1)/3.
mulhu q,M,n          q = floor(M*n/2**32).
shri  q,q,1

muli  t,q,3          Compute remainder from
sub   r,n,t          r = n - q*3.
```

An instruction that gives the high-order 32 bits of a 64-bit unsigned product is required, which we show above as `mulhu`.

To see that the code is correct, observe that it computes

$$q = \left\lfloor \frac{2^{33} + 1}{3} \frac{n}{2^{33}} \right\rfloor = \left\lfloor \frac{n}{3} + \frac{n}{3 \cdot 2^{33}} \right\rfloor.$$

For $0 \leq n < 2^{32}$, $0 \leq n/(3 \cdot 2^{33}) < 1/3$, so by Theorem D4, $q = \lfloor n/3 \rfloor$.

In computing the remainder, the *multiply immediate* can overflow if we regard the operands as signed integers, but it does not overflow if we regard them and the result as unsigned. Also, the *subtract* cannot overflow, because the result is in the range 0 to 2, so the remainder is correct.

Unsigned Divide by 7

For unsigned division by 7 on a 32-bit machine, the multipliers $(2^{32} + 3)/7$, $(2^{33} + 6)/7$, and $(2^{34} + 5)/7$ are all inadequate because they give too large an error term. The multiplier $(2^{35} + 3)/7$ is acceptable, but it's too large to represent in a 32-bit unsigned word. We can multiply by this large number by multiplying by $(2^{35} + 3)/7 - 2^{32}$ and then correcting the product by inserting an add. The code is

```
li     M,0x24924925   Magic num, (2**35+3)/7 - 2**32.
mulhu  q,M,n           q = floor(M*n/2**32).
add    q,q,n           Can overflow (sets carry).
shrxi  q,q,3           Shift right with carry bit.

muli   t,q,7           Compute remainder from
sub    r,n,t           r = n - q*7.
```

Here we have a problem: The add can overflow. To allow for this, we have invented the new instruction *shift right extended immediate* (shrxi), which treats the carry from the add and the 32 bits of register q as a single 33-bit quantity, and shifts it right with 0-fill. On the Motorola 68000 family, this can be done with two instructions: *rotate with extend* right one position, followed by a logical right shift of three (roxr actually uses the X bit, but the add sets the X bit the same as the carry bit). On most machines, it will take more. For example, on PowerPC it takes three instructions: clear rightmost three bits of q, add carry to q, and rotate right three positions.

With shrxi implemented somehow, the code above computes

$$q = \left\lfloor \left(\left\lfloor \left(\frac{2^{35}+3}{7} - 2^{32} \right) \frac{n}{2^{32}} \right\rfloor + n \right) / 2^3 \right\rfloor = \left\lfloor \frac{n}{7} + \frac{3n}{7 \cdot 2^{35}} \right\rfloor.$$

For $0 \leq n < 2^{32}$, $0 \leq 3n/(7 \cdot 2^{35}) < 1/7$, so by Theorem D4, $q = \lfloor n/7 \rfloor$.

Granlund and Montgomery [GM] have a clever scheme for avoiding the shrxi instruction. It requires the same number of instructions as the above three-instruction sequence for shrxi, but it employs only elementary instructions that almost any machine would have, and it does not cause overflow at all. It uses the identity

$$\left\lfloor \frac{q+n}{2^p} \right\rfloor = \left\lfloor \left(\left\lfloor \frac{n-q}{2} \right\rfloor + q \right) / 2^{p-1} \right\rfloor, \quad p \geq 1.$$

Applying this to our problem, with $q = \lfloor Mn/2^{32} \rfloor$ where $0 \le M < 2^{32}$, the subtraction will not overflow because

$$n - q = n - \left\lfloor \frac{Mn}{2^{32}} \right\rfloor = \left\lfloor n - \frac{Mn}{2^{32}} \right\rfloor = \left\lfloor n \left(1 - \frac{M}{2^{32}} \right) \right\rfloor,$$

so that clearly $0 \le n - q < 2^{32}$. Also, the addition will not overflow, because

$$\left\lfloor \frac{n-q}{2} \right\rfloor + q = \left\lfloor \frac{n-q}{2} + q \right\rfloor = \left\lfloor \frac{n+q}{2} \right\rfloor,$$

and $0 \le n, q < 2^{32}$.

Using this idea gives the following code for unsigned division by 7:

```
li     M,0x24924925   Magic num, (2**35+3)/7 - 2**32.
mulhu  q,M,n          q = floor(M*n/2**32).
sub    t,n,q          t = n - q.
shri   t,t,1          t = (n - q)/2.
add    t,t,q          t = (n - q)/2 + q = (n + q)/2.
shri   q,t,2          q = (n+Mn/2**32)/8 = floor(n/7).

muli   t,q,7          Compute remainder from
sub    r,n,t          r = n - q*7.
```

For this to work, the shift amount for the hypothetical `shrxi` instruction must be greater than 0. It can be shown that if $d > 1$ and the multiplier $m \ge 2^{32}$ (so that the `shrxi` instruction is needed), then the shift amount is greater than 0.

10–9 Unsigned Division by Divisors ≥ 1

Given a word size $W \ge 1$ and a divisor d, $1 \le d < 2^W$, we wish to find the least integer m and integer p such that

$$\left\lfloor \frac{mn}{2^p} \right\rfloor = \left\lfloor \frac{n}{d} \right\rfloor \quad \text{for } 0 \le n < 2^W, \tag{22}$$

with $0 \le m < 2^{W+1}$ and $p \ge W$.

In the unsigned case, the magic number M is given by

$$M = \begin{cases} m, & \text{if } 0 \le m < 2^W, \\ m - 2^W, & \text{if } 2^W \le m < 2^{W+1}. \end{cases}$$

Because (22) must hold for $n = d$, $\lfloor md/2^p \rfloor = 1$, or

$$\frac{md}{2^p} \geq 1. \tag{23}$$

As in the signed case, let n_c be the largest value of n such that $\text{rem}(n_c, d) = d - 1$. It can be calculated from $n_c = \lfloor 2^W/d \rfloor d - 1 = 2^W - \text{rem}(2^W, d) - 1$. Then

$$2^W - d \leq n_c \leq 2^W - 1, \tag{24a}$$

and

$$n_c \geq d - 1. \tag{24b}$$

These imply that $n_c \geq 2^{W-1}$.

Because (22) must hold for $n = n_c$,

$$\left\lfloor \frac{mn_c}{2^p} \right\rfloor = \left\lfloor \frac{n_c}{d} \right\rfloor = \frac{n_c - (d-1)}{d},$$

or

$$\frac{mn_c}{2^p} < \frac{n_c + 1}{d}.$$

Combining this with (23) gives

$$\frac{2^p}{d} \leq m < \frac{2^p}{d} \frac{n_c + 1}{n_c}. \tag{25}$$

Because m is to be the least integer satisfying (25), it is the next integer greater than or equal to $2^p/d$—that is,

$$\boxed{m = \frac{2^p + d - 1 - \text{rem}(2^p - 1, d)}{d}.} \tag{26}$$

Combining this with the right half of (25) and simplifying gives

$$\boxed{2^p > n_c(d - 1 - \text{rem}(2^p - 1, d)).} \tag{27}$$

The Algorithm (Unsigned)

Thus, the algorithm is to find by trial and error the least $p \geq W$ satisfying (27). Then m is calculated from (26). This is the smallest possible value of m satisfying (22) with $p \geq W$. As in the signed case, if (27) is true for some value of p, then it is true for all larger values of p. The proof is essentially the same as that of Theorem DC1, except Theorem D5(b) is used instead of Theorem D5(a).

Proof That the Algorithm Is Feasible (Unsigned)

We must show that (27) always has a solution and that $0 \leq m < 2^{W+1}$.

Because for any nonnegative integer x there is a power of 2 greater than x and less than or equal to $2x + 1$, from (27),

$$n_c(d - 1 - \text{rem}(2^p - 1, d)) < 2^p \leq 2n_c(d - 1 - \text{rem}(2^p - 1, d)) + 1.$$

Because $0 \leq \text{rem}(2^{p-1}, d) \leq d - 1$,

$$1 \leq 2^p \leq 2n_c(d - 1) + 1. \tag{28}$$

Because $n_c, d \leq 2^W - 1$, this becomes

$$1 \leq 2^p \leq 2(2^W - 1)(2^W - 2) + 1,$$

or

$$0 \leq p \leq 2W. \tag{29}$$

Thus, (27) always has a solution.

If p is not forced to equal W, then from (25) and (28),

$$\frac{1}{d} \leq m < \frac{2n_c(d - 1) + 1}{d} \frac{n_c + 1}{n_c},$$

$$1 \leq m < \frac{2d - 2 + 1/n_c}{d}(n_c + 1),$$

$$1 \leq m < 2(n_c + 1) \leq 2^{W+1}.$$

If p is forced to equal W, then from (25),

$$\frac{2^W}{d} \leq m < \frac{2^W n_c + 1}{d \quad n_c}.$$

Because $1 \le d \le 2^W - 1$ and $n_c \ge 2^{W-1}$,

$$\frac{2^W}{2^W - 1} \le m < \frac{2^W}{1} \frac{2^{W-1} + 1}{2^{W-1}},$$

$$2 \le m \le 2^W + 1.$$

Hence in either case m is within limits for the code schema illustrated by the "unsigned divide by 7" example.

Proof That the Product Is Correct (Unsigned)

We must show that if p and m are calculated from (27) and (26), then (22) is satisfied.

Equation (26) and inequality (27) are easily seen to imply (25). Inequality (25) is nearly the same as (4), and the remainder of the proof is nearly identical to that for signed division with $n \ge 0$.

10-10 Incorporation into a Compiler (Unsigned)

There is a difficulty in implementing an algorithm based on direct evaluation of the expressions used in this proof. Although $p \le 2W$, which is proved above, the case $p = 2W$ can occur (e.g., for $d = 2^W - 2$ with $W \ge 4$). When $p = 2W$, it is difficult to calculate m, because the dividend in (26) does not fit in a $2W$-bit word.

However, it can be implemented by the "incremental division and remainder" technique of algorithm *magic*. The algorithm is given in Figure 10–2 for $W = 32$. It passes back an indicator a, which tells whether or not to generate an add instruction. (In the case of signed division, the caller recognizes this by M and d having opposite signs.)

Some key points in understanding this algorithm are as follows:

- Unsigned overflow can occur at several places and should be ignored.

- $n_c = 2^W - \text{rem}(2^W, d) - 1 = (2^W - 1) - \text{rem}(2^W - d, d)$.

- The quotient and remainder of dividing 2^p by n_c cannot be updated in the same way as is done in algorithm *magic*, because here the quantity 2*r1 can overflow. Hence the algorithm has the test "if (r1 >= nc - r1)," whereas "if (2*r1 >= nc)" would be more natural. A similar remark applies to computing the quotient and remainder of $2^p - 1$ divided by d.

- $0 \le \delta \le d - 1$, so δ is representable as a 32-bit unsigned integer.

- $m = (2^p + d - 1 - \text{rem}(2^p - 1, d))/d = \lfloor (2^p - 1)/d \rfloor + 1 = q_2 + 1$.

- The subtraction of 2^W when the magic number M exceeds $2^W - 1$ is not explicit in the program; it occurs if the computation of q2 overflows.

- The "add" indicator, magu.a, cannot be set by a straightforward comparison of M to 2^{32}, or of q2 to $2^{32} - 1$, because of overflow. Instead, the program tests q2 before overflow can occur. If q2 ever gets as large as $2^{32} - 1$, so that M will be greater than or equal to 2^{32}, then magu.a is set equal to 1. If q2 stays below $2^{32} - 1$, then magu.a is left at its initial value of 0.

- Inequality (27) is equivalent to $2^p/n_c > \delta$.

- The loop test needs the condition "p < 64" because without it, overflow of q1 would cause the program to loop too many times, giving incorrect results.

10–11 Miscellaneous Topics (Unsigned)

THEOREM DC2U. *The least multiplier m is odd if p is not forced to equal W.*

THEOREM DC3U. *For a given divisor d, there is only one multiplier m having the minimal value of p, if p is not forced to equal W.*

The proofs of these theorems follow very closely the corresponding proofs for signed division.

The Divisors with the Best Programs (Unsigned)

For unsigned division, to find the divisors (if any) with optimal programs of two instructions to obtain the quotient (li, mulhu), we can do an analysis similar to that of the signed case (see "The Divisors with the Best Programs" on page 175). The result is that such divisors are the factors of 2^W or $2^W + 1$, except for $d = 1$. For the common word sizes, this leaves very few nontrivial divisors that have optimal programs for unsigned division. For $W = 16$, there are none. For $W = 32$, there are only two: 641 and 6,700,417. For $W = 64$, again there are only two: 274,177 and 67,280,421,310,721.

The case $d = 2^k$, $k = 1, 2, \ldots$, deserves special mention. In this case, algorithm *magicu* produces $p = W$ (forced), $m = 2^{32-k}$. This is the minimal value of m, but it is not the minimal value of M. Better code results if $p = W + k$ is used, if sufficient simplifications are done. Then, $m = 2^W$, $M = 0$, $a = 1$, and $s - k$. The generated code involves a multiplication by 0 and can be simplified to a single *shift right k* instruction. As a practical matter, divisors that are a power of 2 would probably be special-cased without using *magicu*. (This

```
struct mu {unsigned M;      // Magic number,
           int a;           // "add" indicator,
           int s;};         // and shift amount.

struct mu magicu(unsigned d) {
                            // Must have 1 <= d <= 2**32-1.
   int p;
   unsigned nc, delta, q1, r1, q2, r2;
   struct mu magu;

   magu.a = 0;              // Initialize "add" indicator.
   nc = -1 - (-d)%d;        // Unsigned arithmetic here.
   p = 31;                  // Init. p.
   q1 = 0x80000000/nc;      // Init. q1 = 2**p/nc.
   r1 = 0x80000000 - q1*nc;// Init. r1 = rem(2**p, nc).
   q2 = 0x7FFFFFFF/d;       // Init. q2 = (2**p - 1)/d.
   r2 = 0x7FFFFFFF - q2*d;  // Init. r2 = rem(2**p - 1, d).
   do {
      p = p + 1;
      if (r1 >= nc - r1) {
         q1 = 2*q1 + 1;              // Update q1.
         r1 = 2*r1 - nc;}           // Update r1.
      else {
         q1 = 2*q1;
         r1 = 2*r1;}
      if (r2 + 1 >= d - r2) {
         if (q2 >= 0x7FFFFFFF) magu.a = 1;
         q2 = 2*q2 + 1;             // Update q2.
         r2 = 2*r2 + 1 - d;}       // Update r2.
      else {
         if (q2 >= 0x80000000) magu.a = 1;
         q2 = 2*q2;
         r2 = 2*r2 + 1;}
      delta = d - 1 - r2;
   } while (p < 64 &&
           (q1 < delta || (q1 == delta && r1 == 0)));

   magu.M = q2 + 1;         // Magic number
   magu.s = p - 32;         // and shift amount to return
   return magu;             // (magu.a was set above).
}
```

FIGURE 10–2. Computing the magic number for unsigned division.

phenomenon does not occur for signed division, because for signed division m cannot be a power of 2. Proof: For $d > 0$, inequality (4) combined with (3b) implies that $d - 1 < 2^p/m < d$. Therefore, $2^p/m$ cannot be an integer. For $d < 0$, the result follows similarly from (16) combined with (15b)).

For unsigned division, the code for the case $m \geq 2^W$ is considerably worse than the code for the case $m < 2^W$, if the machine does not have shrxi. Hence it is of interest to have some idea of how often the large multipliers arise. For $W = 32$, among the integers less than 100, there are 31 "bad" divisors: 1, 7, 14, 19, 21, 27, 28, 31, 35, 37, 38, 39, 42, 45, 53, 54, 55, 56, 57, 62, 63, 70, 73, 74, 76, 78, 84, 90, 91, 95, and 97.

Using Signed in Place of Unsigned Multiply, and the Reverse

If your machine does not have mulhu, but it does have mulhs (or signed long multiplication), the trick given in "High-Order Product Signed from/to Unsigned," on page 132, might make our method of doing unsigned division by a constant still useful.

That section gives a seven-instruction sequence for getting mulhu from mulhs. However, for this application it simplifies, because the magic number M is known. Thus, the compiler can test the most significant bit of the magic number, and generate code such as the following for the operation "mulhu q, M, n." Here t denotes a temporary register.

```
     M₃₁ = 0                    M₃₁ = 1
mulhs  q,M,n              mulhs  q,M,n
shrsi  t,n,31             shrsi  t,n,31
and    t,t,M             and    t,t,M
add    q,q,t             add    t,t,n
                          add    q,q,t
```

Accounting for the other instructions used with mulhu, this uses a total of six to eight instructions to obtain the quotient of unsigned division by a constant, on a machine that does not have unsigned multiply.

This trick may be inverted, to get mulhs in terms of mulhu. The code is the same as that above except the mulhs is changed to mulhu and the final add in each column is changed to sub.

A Simpler Algorithm (Unsigned)

Dropping the requirement that the magic number be minimal yields a simpler algorithm. In place of (27) we can use

$$2^p \geq 2^W(d - 1 - \text{rem}(2^p - 1, d)), \tag{30}$$

and then use (26) to compute m, as before.

It should be clear that this algorithm is formally correct (that is, that the value of m computed does satisfy equation (22)), because its only difference from the previous algorithm is that it computes a value of p that, for some values of d, is unnecessarily large. It can be proved that the value of m computed from (30) and (26) is less than 2^{W+1}. We omit the proof and simply give the algorithm (Figure 10–3).

```
struct mu {unsigned M;       // Magic number,
          int a;             // "add" indicator,
          int s;};           // and shift amount.

struct mu magicu2(unsigned d) {
                             // Must have 1 <= d <= 2**32-1.
   int p;
   unsigned p32, q, r, delta;
   struct mu magu;
   magu.a = 0;               // Initialize "add" indicator.
   p = 31;                   // Initialize p.
   q = 0x7FFFFFFF/d;         // Initialize q = (2**p - 1)/d.
   r = 0x7FFFFFFF - q*d;     // Init. r = rem(2**p - 1, d).
   do {
      p = p + 1;
      if (p == 32) p32 = 1;       // Set p32 = 2**(p-32).
      else p32 = 2*p32;
      if (r + 1 >= d - r) {
         if (q >= 0x7FFFFFFF) magu.a = 1;
         q = 2*q + 1;              // Update q.
         r = 2*r + 1 - d;         // Update r.
      }
      else {
         if (q >= 0x80000000) magu.a = 1;
         q = 2*q;
         r = 2*r + 1;
      }
      delta = d - 1 - r;
   } while (p < 64 && p32 < delta);
   magu.M = q + 1;           // Magic number and
   magu.s = p - 32;          // shift amount to return
   return magu;              // (magu.a was set above).
}
```

FIGURE 10–3. Simplified algorithm for computing the magic number, unsigned division.

Alverson [Alv] gives a much simpler algorithm, discussed in the next section, but it gives somewhat large values for m. The point of algorithm *magicu2* is that it nearly always gives the minimal value for m when $d \leq 2^{W-1}$. For $W = 32$, the smallest divisor for which *magicu2* does not give the minimal multiplier is $d = 102{,}807$, for which *magicu* calculates $m = 2{,}737{,}896{,}999$ and *magicu2* calculates $m = 5{,}475{,}793{,}997$.

There is an analog of *magicu2* for signed division by positive divisors, but it does not work out very well for signed division by arbitrary divisors.

10–12 Applicability to Modulus and Floor Division

It might seem that turning modulus or floor division by a constant into multiplication would be simpler, in that the "add 1 if the dividend is negative" step could be omitted. This is not the case. The methods given above do not apply in any obvious way to modulus and floor division. Perhaps something could be worked out; it might involve altering the multiplier m slightly depending upon the sign of the dividend.

10–13 Similar Methods

Rather than coding algorithm *magic*, we can provide a table that gives the magic numbers and shift amounts for a few small divisors. Divisors equal to the tabulated ones multiplied by a power of 2 are easily handled as follows:

1. Count the number of trailing 0's in d, and let this be denoted by k.

2. Use as the lookup argument $d/2^k$ (shift right k).

3. Use the magic number found in the table.

4. Use the shift amount found in the table, increased by k.

Thus, if the table contains the divisors 3, 5, 25, and so on, divisors of 6, 10, 100, and so forth can be handled.

This procedure usually gives the smallest magic number, but not always. The smallest positive divisor for which it fails in this respect for $W = 32$ is $d = 334{,}972$, for which it computes $m = 3{,}361{,}176{,}179$ and s = 18. However, the minimal magic number for $d = 334{,}972$ is $m = 840{,}294{,}045$, with $s = 16$. The procedure also fails to give the minimal magic number for $d = -6$. In both these cases, output code quality is affected.

Alverson [Alv] is the first known to the author to state that the method described here works with complete accuracy for all divisors. Using our notation, his method for unsigned integer division by d is to set the shift amount $p = W + \lceil \log_2 d \rceil$, and the multiplier $m = \lceil 2^p/d \rceil$, and then do the division by $n \div d = \lfloor mn/2^p \rfloor$ (that is, *multiply* and *shift right*). He proves that the multiplier m is less than 2^{W+1}, and that the method gets the exact quotient for all n expressible in W bits.

Alverson's method is a simpler variation of ours in that it doesn't require trial and error to determine p, and is thus more suitable for building in hardware, which is his primary interest. His multiplier m, however, is always greater than or equal to 2^W, and thus for the software application always gives the code illustrated by the "divide by 7" example (that is, always has the add and shrxi, or the alternative four instructions). Because most small divisors can be handled with a multiplier less than 2^W, it seems worthwhile to look for these cases.

For signed division, Alverson suggests finding the multiplier for $|d|$ and a word length of $W - 1$ (then $2^{W-1} \le m < 2^W$), multiplying the dividend by it, and negating the result if the operands have opposite signs. (The multiplier must be such that it gives the correct result when the dividend is 2^{W-1}, the absolute value of the maximum negative number). It seems possible that this suggestion might give better code than what has been given here in the case that the multiplier $m \geq 2^W$. Applying it to signed division by 7 gives the following code, where we have used the relation $-x = \bar{x} + 1$ to avoid a branch:

```
abs     an,n
li      M,0x92492493   Magic number, (2**34+5)/7.
mulhu   q,M,an         q = floor(M*an/2**32).
shri    q,q,2
shrsi   t,n,31         These three instructions
xor     q,q,t          negate q if n is
sub     q,q,t          negative.
```

This is not quite as good as the code we gave for signed division by 7 (six vs. seven instructions), but it would be useful on a machine that has abs and mulhu but not mulhs.

10–14 Sample Magic Numbers

TABLE 10–1. SOME MAGIC NUMBERS FOR $W = 32$

	Signed		Unsigned		
d	M (hex)	s	M (hex)	a	s
−5	99999999	1			
−3	55555555	1			
-2^k	7FFFFFFF	$k-1$			
1	−	−	0	1	0
2^k	80000001	$k-1$	2^{32-k}	0	0
3	55555556	0	AAAAAAAB	0	1
5	66666667	1	CCCCCCCD	0	2
6	2AAAAAAB	0	AAAAAAAB	0	2
7	92492493	2	24924925	1	3
9	38E38E39	1	38E38E39	0	1
10	66666667	2	CCCCCCCD	0	3
11	2E8BA2E9	1	BA2E8BA3	0	3
12	2AAAAAAB	1	AAAAAAAB	0	3
25	51EB851F	3	51EB851F	0	3
125	10624DD3	3	10624DD3	0	3
625	68DB8BAD	8	D1B71759	0	9

TABLE 10–2. SOME MAGIC NUMBERS FOR $W = 64$

	Signed		Unsigned		
d	**M (hex)**	**s**	**M (hex)**	**a**	**s**
–5	9999 9999 9999 9999	1			
–3	5555 5555 5555 5555	1			
-2^k	7FFF FFFF FFFF FFFF	$k-1$			
1	–	–	0	1	0
2^k	8000 0000 0000 0001	$k-1$	2^{64-k}	0	0
3	5555 5555 5555 5556	0	AAAA AAAA AAAA AAAB	0	1
5	6666 6666 6666 6667	1	CCCC CCCC CCCC CCCD	0	2
6	2AAA AAAA AAAA AAAB	0	AAAA AAAA AAAA AAAB	0	2
7	4924 9249 2492 4925	1	2492 4924 9249 2493	1	3
9	1C71 C71C 71C7 1C72	0	E38E 38E3 8E38 E38F	0	3
10	6666 6666 6666 6667	2	CCCC CCCC CCCC CCCD	0	3
11	2E8B A2E8 BA2E 8BA3	1	2E8B A2E8 BA2E 8BA3	0	1
12	2AAA AAAA AAAA AAAB	1	AAAA AAAA AAAA AAAB	0	3
25	A3D7 0A3D 70A3 D70B	4	47AE 147A E147 AE15	1	5
125	20C4 9BA5 E353 F7CF	4	0624 DD2F 1A9F BE77	1	7
625	346D C5D6 3886 594B	7	346D C5D6 3886 594B	0	7

10–15 Exact Division by Constants

By "exact division," we mean division in which it is known beforehand, somehow, that the remainder is 0. Although this situation is not common, it does arise, for example, when subtracting two pointers in the C language. In C, the result of $p - q$, where p and q are pointers, is well defined and portable only if p and q point to objects in the same array [H&S, sec. 7.6.2]. If the array element size is s, the object code for the difference $p - q$ computes $(p - q)/s$.

The material in this section was motivated by [GM, sec. 9].

The method to be given applies to both signed and unsigned exact division, and is based on the following theorem.

THEOREM MI. *If a and m are relatively prime integers, then there exists an integer $\bar{a}$, $1 \le \bar{a} < m$, such that*

$$a\bar{a} \equiv 1 \pmod{m}.$$

Thus $\bar{a}$ is a multiplicative inverse of a, modulo m. There are several ways to prove this theorem; three proofs are given in [NZM, 52]. The proof below requires only a very basic familiarity with congruences.

Proof. We will prove something a little more general than the theorem. If a and m are relatively prime (and hence nonzero), then as x ranges over all m distinct values modulo m, ax takes on all m distinct values modulo m. For example, if $a = 3$ and $m = 8$, then as x ranges from 0 to 7, $ax = 0, 3, 6, 9, 12, 15, 18, 21$ or, reduced modulo 8, $ax = 0, 3, 6, 1, 4, 7, 2, 5$. Observe that all values from 0 to 7 are present in the last sequence.

To see this in general, assume that it is not true. Then there exist distinct integers that map to the same value when multiplied by a; that is, there exist x and y, with $x \not\equiv y \pmod{m}$, such that

$$ax \equiv ay \pmod{m}.$$

But then there exists an integer k such that

$$ax - ay = km, \quad \text{or}$$
$$a(x - y) = km.$$

Because a has no factor in common with m, it must be that $x - y$ is a multiple of m; that is,

$$x \equiv y \pmod{m}.$$

This contradicts the hypothesis.

Now, because ax takes on all m distinct values modulo m, as x ranges over the m values, it must take on the value 1 for some x.

The proof shows that there is only one value (modulo m) of x such that $ax \equiv 1 \pmod{m}$—that is, the multiplicative inverse is unique, apart from additive multiples of m. It also shows that there is a unique (modulo m) integer x such that $ax \equiv b \pmod{m}$, where b is any integer.

As an example, consider the case $m = 16$. Then $\overline{3} = 11$, because $3 \cdot 11 = 33 \equiv 1 \pmod{16}$. We could just as well take $\overline{3} = -5$, because $3 \cdot (-5) = -15 \equiv 1 \pmod{16}$. Similarly, $\overline{-3} = 5$, because $(-3) \cdot 5 = -15 \equiv 1 \pmod{16}$.

These observations are important because they show that the concepts apply to both signed and unsigned numbers. If we are working in the domain of unsigned integers on a 4-bit machine, we take $\overline{3} = 11$. In the domain of signed integers, we take $\overline{3} = -5$. But 11 and -5 have the same representation in two's-complement (because they differ by 16), so the same computer word contents can serve in both domains as the multiplicative inverse.

The theorem applies directly to the problem of division (signed and unsigned) by an odd integer d on a W-bit computer. Because any odd integer is relatively prime to 2^W, the theorem says that if d is odd, there exists an integer $\overline{d}$ (unique in the range 0 to $2^W - 1$ or in the range -2^{W-1} to $2^{W-1} - 1$) such that

$$d\overline{d} \equiv 1 \pmod{2^W}.$$

Hence for any integer n that is a multiple of d,

$$\frac{n}{d} = \frac{n}{d}(d\bar{d}) \equiv n\bar{d} \pmod{2^W}.$$

In other words, n/d can be calculated by multiplying n by $\bar{d}$, and retaining only the rightmost W bits of the product.

If the divisor d is even, let $d = d_o \cdot 2^k$, where d_o is odd and $k \geq 1$. Then, simply shift n right k positions (shifting out 0's), and then multiply by $\bar{d_o}$ (the shift could be done after the multiplication as well).

Below is the code for division of n by 7, where n is a multiple of 7. This code gives the correct result whether it is considered to be signed or unsigned division.

```
li    M,0xB6DB6DB7   Mult. inverse, (5*2**32 + 1)/7.
mul   q,M,n          q = n/7.
```

Computing the Multiplicative Inverse by the Euclidean Algorithm

How can we compute the multiplicative inverse? The standard method is by means of the "extended Euclidean algorithm." This is briefly discussed below as it applies to our problem, and the interested reader is referred to [NZM, 13] and to [Knu2, sec. 4.5.2] for a more complete discussion.

Given an odd divisor d, we wish to solve for x

$$dx \equiv 1 \pmod{m},$$

where, in our application, $m = 2^W$ and W is the word size of the machine. This will be accomplished if we can solve for integers x and y (positive, negative, or 0) the equation

$$dx + my = 1.$$

Toward this end, first make d positive by adding a sufficient number of multiples of m to it. (d and $d + km$ have the same multiplicative inverse.) Second, write the following equations (in which $d, m > 0$):

$$d(-1) + m(1) = m - d \quad \text{(i)}$$
$$d(1) + m(0) = d. \quad\quad \text{(ii)}$$

If $d = 1$, we are done, because (ii) shows that $x = 1$. Otherwise, compute

$$q = \left\lfloor \frac{m-d}{d} \right\rfloor.$$

Third, multiply Equation (ii) by q and subtract it from (i). This gives

$$d(-1-q) + m(1) = m - d - qd = \text{rem}(m-d, d).$$

This equation holds because we have simply multiplied one equation by a constant and subtracted it from another. If $\text{rem}(m-d, d) = 1$, we are done; this last equation is the solution and $x = -1 - q$.

Repeat this process on the last two equations, obtaining a fourth, and continue until the right-hand side of the equation is 1. The multiplier of d, reduced modulo m, is then the desired inverse of d.

Incidentally, if $m - d < d$, so that the first quotient is 0, then the third row will be a copy of the first, so that the second quotient will be nonzero. Furthermore, most texts start with the first row being

$$d(0) + m(1) = m,$$

but in our application $m = 2^W$ is not representable in the machine.

The process is best illustrated by an example. Let $m = 256$ and $d = 7$. Then the calculation proceeds as follows. To get the third row, note that $q = \lfloor 249/7 \rfloor = 35$.

```
7(-1) + 256( 1) = 249
7( 1) + 256( 0) = 7
7(-36) + 256( 1) = 4
7( 37) + 256(-1) = 3
7(-73) + 256( 2) = 1
```

Thus, the multiplicative inverse of 7, modulo 256, is –73 or, expressed in the range 0 to 255, is 183. Check: $7 \cdot 183 = 1281 \equiv 1 \pmod{256}$.

From the third row on, the integers in the right-hand column are all remainders with respect to the number above it as a divisor (d being the dividend), so they form a sequence of strictly decreasing nonnegative integers. Therefore, the sequence must end in 0 (as the above would if carried one more step). Furthermore, the value just before the 0 must be 1, for the following reason. Suppose the sequence ends in b followed by 0, with $b \neq 1$. Then, the integer preceding the b must be a multiple of b, let's say $k_1 b$, for the next remainder to be 0. The integer preceding $k_1 b$ must be of the form $k_1 k_2 b + b$, for the next remainder to be b. Continuing up the sequence, every number must be a multiple of b, including the first two (in the positions of the 249 and the 7 in the above example). But this is impossible, because the first two integers are $m - d$ and d, which are relatively prime.

This constitutes an informal proof that the above process terminates, with a value of 1 in the right-hand column, and hence it finds the multiplicative inverse of d.

To carry this out on a computer, first note that if $d < 0$, we should add 2^W to it. But with two's-complement arithmetic it is not necessary to actually do anything here; simply interpret d as an unsigned number regardless of how the application interprets it.

The computation of q must use unsigned division.

Observe that the calculations can be done modulo m, because this does not change the right-hand column (these values are in the range 0 to $m - 1$ anyway). This is important, because it enables the calculations to be done in "single precision," using the computer's modulo-2^W unsigned arithmetic.

Most of the quantities in the table need not be represented. The column of multiples of 256 need not be represented, because in solving $dx + my = 1$, we do not need the value of y. There is no need to represent d in the first column. Reduced to its bare essentials, then, the calculation of the above example is carried out as follows:

$$
\begin{array}{rr}
255 & 249 \\
1 & 7 \\
220 & 4 \\
37 & 3 \\
183 & 1
\end{array}
$$

A C program for performing this computation is shown in Figure 10–4.

The reason the loop continuation condition is (v2 > 1) rather than the more natural (v2 != 1) is that if the latter condition were used, the loop would never terminate if the program were invoked with an even argument. It is best that programs not loop forever even if misused. (If the argument d is even, v2 never takes on the value 1, but it does become 0.)

```
unsigned mulinv(unsigned d) {            // d must be odd.
   unsigned x1, v1, x2, v2, x3, v3, q;

   x1 = 0xFFFFFFFF;        v1 = -d;
   x2 = 1;                 v2 = d;
   while (v2 > 1) {
      q = v1/v2;
      x3 = x1 - q*x2;      v3 = v1 - q*v2;
      x1 = x2;             v1 = v2;
      x2 = x3;             v2 = v3;
   }
   return(x2);
}
```

FIGURE 10–4. Multiplicative inverse modulo 2^{32} by the Euclidean algorithm.

What does the program compute if given an even argument? As written, it computes a number x such that $dx \equiv 0 \pmod{2^{32}}$, which is probably not useful. However, with the minor modification of changing the loop continuation condition to (v2 != 0) and returning x1 rather than x2, it computes a number x such that $dx \equiv g \pmod{2^{32}}$, where g is the greatest common divisor of d and 2^{32}—that is, the greatest power of 2 that divides d. The modified program still computes the multiplicative inverse of d for d odd, but it requires one more iteration than the unmodified program.

As for the number of iterations (divisions) required by the above program, for d odd and less than 20, it requires a maximum of 3 and an average of 1.7. For d in the neighborhood of 1000, it requires a maximum of 11 and an average of about 6.

Computing the Multiplicative Inverse by Newton's Method

It is well known that, over the real numbers, $1/d$, for $d \neq 0$, can be calculated to ever increasing accuracy by iteratively evaluating

$$x_{n+1} = x_n(2 - dx_n), \tag{31}$$

provided the initial estimate x_0 is sufficiently close to $1/d$. The number of digits of accuracy approximately doubles with each iteration.

It is not so well known that this same formula can be used to find the multiplicative inverse in the domain of modular arithmetic on integers! For example, to find the multiplicative inverse of 3, modulo 256, start with $x_0 = 1$ (any odd number will do). Then,

$$
\begin{aligned}
x_1 &= 1(2 - 3 \cdot 1) = -1, \\
x_2 &= -1(2 - 3(-1)) = -5, \\
x_3 &= -5(2 - 3(-5)) = -85, \\
x_4 &= -85(2 - 3(-85)) = -21845 \equiv -85 \pmod{256}.
\end{aligned}
$$

The iteration has reached a fixed point modulo 256, so -85, or 171, is the multiplicative inverse of 3 (modulo 256). All calculations can be done modulo 256.

Why does this work? Because if x_n satisfies

$$dx_n \equiv 1 \pmod{m}$$

and if x_{n+1} is defined by (31), then

$$dx_{n+1} \equiv 1 \pmod{m^2}.$$

To see this, let $dx_n = 1 + km$. Then

$$\begin{aligned}
dx_{n+1} &= dx_n(2 - dx_n) \\
&= (1 + km)(2 - (1 + km)) \\
&= (1 + km)(1 - km) \\
&= 1 - k^2 m^2 \\
&\equiv 1 \ (\text{mod } m^2).
\end{aligned}$$

In our application, m is a power of 2, say 2^N. In this case, if

$$dx_n \equiv 1 \ (\text{mod } 2^N), \ \text{then}$$

$$dx_{n+1} \equiv 1 \ (\text{mod } 2^{2N}).$$

In a sense, if x_n is regarded as a sort of approximation to $\bar{d}$, then each iteration of (31) doubles the number of bits of "accuracy" of the approximation.

It happens that, modulo 8, the multiplicative inverse of any (odd) number d is d itself. Thus, taking $x_0 = d$ is a reasonable and simple initial guess at $\bar{d}$. Then, (31) will give values of $x_1, x_2, \ldots$, such that

$$dx_1 \equiv 1 \ (\text{mod } 2^6),$$

$$dx_2 \equiv 1 \ (\text{mod } 2^{12}),$$

$$dx_3 \equiv 1 \ (\text{mod } 2^{24}),$$

$$dx_4 \equiv 1 \ (\text{mod } 2^{48}), \ \text{and so on.}$$

Thus, four iterations suffice to find the multiplicative inverse modulo 2^{32} (if $x \equiv 1 \ (\text{mod } 2^{48})$ then $x \equiv 1 \ (\text{mod } 2^n)$ for $n \leq 48$). This leads to the C program in Figure 10–5, in which all computations are done modulo 2^{32}.

For about half the values of d, this program takes 4 1/2 iterations, or nine multiplications. For the other half (those for which the initial value of xn is "correct to 4 bits"—that is, $d^2 \equiv 1 \ (\text{mod } 16)$), it takes seven or fewer, usually seven, multiplications. Thus, it takes about eight multiplications on average.

```
unsigned mulinv(unsigned d) {        // d must be odd.
   unsigned xn, t;

   xn = d;
loop: t = d*xn;
      if (t == 1) return xn;
      xn = xn*(2 - t);
      goto loop;
}
```

FIGURE 10–5. Multiplicative inverse modulo 2^{32} by Newton's method.

A variation is to simply execute the loop four times, regardless of d, perhaps "strung out" to eliminate the loop control (eight multiplications). Another variation is to somehow make the initial estimate x_0 "correct to 4 bits" (that is, find x_0 that satisfies $dx_0 \equiv 1 \pmod{16}$). Then, only three loop iterations are required. Some ways to set the initial estimate are

$$x_0 \leftarrow d + 2((d+1) \,\&\, 4), \quad \text{and}$$

$$x_0 \leftarrow d^2 + d - 1.$$

Here, the multiplication by 2 is a left shift, and the computations are done modulo 2^{32} (ignoring overflow). Because the second formula uses a multiplication, it saves only one.

This concern about execution time is of course totally unimportant for the compiler application. For that application, the routine would be so seldom used that it should be coded for minimum space. But there may be applications in which it is desirable to compute the multiplicative inverse quickly.

Sample Multiplicative Inverses

We conclude this section with a listing of some multiplicative inverses in Table 10–3.

TABLE 10–3. SAMPLE MULTIPLICATIVE INVERSES

d	$\bar{d}$		
(dec)	mod 16 (dec)	mod 2^{32} (hex)	mod 2^{64} (hex)
-7	-7	4924 9249	9249 2492 4924 9249
-5	3	3333 3333	3333 3333 3333 3333
-3	5	5555 5555	5555 5555 5555 5555
-1	-1	FFFF FFFF	FFFF FFFF FFFF FFFF
1	1	1	1
3	11	AAAA AAAB	AAAA AAAA AAAA AAAB
5	13	CCCC CCCD	CCCC CCCC CCCC CCCD
7	7	B6DB 6DB7	6DB6 DB6D B6DB 6DB7
9	9	38E3 8E39	8E38 E38E 38E3 8E39
11	3	BA2E 8BA3	2E8B A2E8 BA2E 8BA3
13	5	C4EC 4EC5	4EC4 EC4E C4EC 4EC5
15	15	EEEE EEEF	EEEE EEEE EEEE EEEF
25		C28F 5C29	8F5C 28F5 C28F 5C29
125		26E9 78D5	1CAC 0831 26E9 78D5
625		3AFB 7E91	D288 CE70 3AFB 7E91

You may notice that in several cases ($d = 3, 5, 9, 11$), the multiplicative inverse of d is the same as the magic number for unsigned division by d (see Section 10–14, "Sample Magic Numbers," on page 189). This is more or less a coincidence. It happens that for these numbers, the magic number M is equal to the multiplier m, and these are of the form $(2^p + 1)/d$, with $p \geq 32$. In this case, notice that

$$Md = \left(\frac{2^p + 1}{d}\right)d \equiv 1 \pmod{2^{32}},$$

so that $M \equiv \bar{d} \pmod{2^{32}}$.

10–16 Test for Zero Remainder after Division by a Constant

The multiplicative inverse of a divisor d can be used to test for a zero remainder after division by d [GM].

Unsigned

First, consider unsigned division with the divisor d odd. Denote by $\bar{d}$ the multiplicative inverse of d. Then, because $d\bar{d} \equiv 1 \pmod{2^W}$, where W is the machine's word size in bits, $\bar{d}$ is also odd. Thus, $\bar{d}$ is relatively prime to 2^W, and as shown in the proof of theorem MI in the preceding section, as n ranges over all 2^W distinct values modulo 2^W, $n\bar{d}$ takes on all 2^W distinct values modulo 2^W.

It was shown in the preceding section that if n is a multiple of d,

$$\frac{n}{d} \equiv n\bar{d} \pmod{2^W}.$$

That is, for $n = 0, d, 2d, \ldots, \lfloor(2^W - 1)/d\rfloor d$, $n\bar{d} \equiv 0, 1, 2, \ldots, \lfloor(2^W - 1)/d\rfloor$ $\pmod{2^W}$. Therefore, for n *not* a multiple of d, the value of $n\bar{d}$, reduced modulo 2^W to the range 0 to $2^W - 1$, must exceed $\lfloor(2^W - 1)/d\rfloor$.

This can be used to test for a zero remainder. For example, to test if an integer n is a multiple of 25, multiply n by $\overline{25}$ and compare the rightmost W bits to $\lfloor(2^W - 1)/25\rfloor$. On our basic RISC:

```
li      M,0xC28F5C29   Load mult. inverse of 25.
mul     q,M,n          q = right half of M*n.
li      c,0x0A3D70A3   c = floor((2**32-1)/25).
cmpleu  t,q,c          Compare q and c, and branch
bt      t,is_mult      if n is a multiple of 25.
```

To extend this to even divisors, let $d = d_o \cdot 2^k$, where d_o is odd and $k \geq 1$. Then, because an integer is divisible by d if and only if it is divisible by d_o and by 2^k, and because n and $n\overline{d_o}$ have the same number of trailing zeros (d_o is odd), the test that n is a multiple of d is

$$\text{Set } q = \text{mod}(n\overline{d_o}, 2^W);$$

$$q \leq \lfloor (2^W - 1)/d_o \rfloor \text{ and } q \text{ ends in } k \text{ or more 0-bits,}$$

where the "mod" function is understood to reduce $n\overline{d_o}$ to the interval $[0, 2^W - 1]$.

Direct implementation of this requires two tests and conditional branches, but it can be reduced to one *compare-branch* quite efficiently if the machine has the *rotate-shift* instruction. This follows from the following theorem, in which $a \overset{rot}{\gg} k$ denotes the computer word a rotated right k positions ($0 \leq k \leq 32$).

THEOREM ZRU. $x \overset{u}{\leq} a$ and x ends   in k 0-bits   if   and   only   if $x \overset{rot}{\gg} k \overset{u}{\leq} \lfloor a/2^k \rfloor$.

Proof. (Assume a 32-bit machine.) Suppose $x \overset{u}{\leq} a$ and x ends in k 0-bits. Then, because $x \overset{u}{\leq} a$, $\lfloor x/2^k \rfloor \overset{u}{\leq} \lfloor a/2^k \rfloor$. But $\lfloor x/2^k \rfloor = x \overset{rot}{\gg} k$. Therefore, $x \overset{rot}{\gg} k \overset{u}{\leq} \lfloor a/2^k \rfloor$. If x does not end in k 0-bits, then $x \overset{rot}{\gg} k$ does not begin with k 0-bits, whereas $\lfloor a/2^k \rfloor$ does, so $x \overset{rot}{\gg} k \overset{u}{>} \lfloor a/2^k \rfloor$. Lastly, if $x \overset{u}{>} a$ and x ends in k 0-bits, then the integer formed from the first $32 - k$ bits of x must exceed that formed from the first $32 - k$ bits of a, so that $\lfloor x/2^k \rfloor \overset{u}{>} \lfloor a/2^k \rfloor$.

Using this theorem, the test that n is a multiple of d, where n and $d \geq 1$ are unsigned integers and $d = d_o \cdot 2^k$ with d_o odd, is

$$q \leftarrow \text{mod}(n\overline{d_o}, 2^W);$$

$$q \overset{rot}{\gg} k \overset{u}{\leq} \lfloor (2^W - 1)/d \rfloor.$$

Here we used $\lfloor \lfloor (2^W - 1)/d_o \rfloor / 2^k \rfloor = \lfloor (2^W - 1)/(d_o \cdot 2^k) \rfloor = \lfloor (2^W - 1)/d \rfloor$.

As an example, the following code tests an unsigned integer n to see if it is a multiple of 100:

```
li      M,0xC28F5C29   Load mult. inverse of 25.
mul     q,M,n          q = right half of M*n.
shrri   q,q,2          Rotate right two positions.
li      c,x'028F5C28'  c = floor((2**32-1)/100).
cmpleu  t,q,c          Compare q and c, and branch
bt      t,is_mult      if n is a multiple of 100.
```

Signed, Divisor ≥ 2

For signed division, it was shown in the preceding section that if n is a multiple of d, and d is odd, then

$$\frac{n}{d} \equiv n\bar{d} \pmod{2^W}.$$

Thus, for $n = \lceil -2^{W-1}/d \rceil \cdot d, \ldots, -d, 0, d, \ldots, \lfloor (2^{W-1}-1)/d \rfloor \cdot d$, we have $n\bar{d} \equiv \lceil -2^{W-1}/d \rceil, \ldots, -1, 0, 1, \ldots, \lfloor (2^{W-1}-1)/d \rfloor \pmod{2^W}$. Furthermore, because $\bar{d}$ is relatively prime to 2^W, as n ranges over all 2^W distinct values modulo 2^W, $n\bar{d}$ takes on all 2^W distinct values modulo 2^W. Therefore, n is a multiple of d if and only if

$$\lceil -2^{W-1}/d \rceil \leq \mathrm{mod}(n\bar{d}, 2^W) \leq \lfloor (2^{W-1}-1)/d \rfloor,$$

where the "mod" function is understood to reduce $n\bar{d}$ to the interval $[-2^{W-1}, 2^{W-1}-1]$.

This can be simplified a little by observing that because d is odd and, as we are assuming, positive and not equal to 1, it does not divide 2^{W-1}. Therefore,

$$\lceil -2^{W-1}/d \rceil = \lceil (-2^{W-1}+1)/d \rceil = -\lfloor (2^{W-1}-1)/d \rfloor.$$

Thus, for signed numbers, the test that n is a multiple of d, where $d = d_o \cdot 2^k$ and d_o is odd, is

Set $q = \mathrm{mod}(n\bar{d_o}, 2^W)$;

$-\lfloor (2^{W-1}-1)/d_o \rfloor \leq q \leq \lfloor (2^{W-1}-1)/d_o \rfloor$ and q ends in k or more 0-bits.

On the surface, this would seem to require three tests and branches. However, as in the unsigned case, it can be reduced to one *compare-branch* by use of the following theorem.

THEOREM ZRS. *If $a \geq 0$, the following assertions are equivalent:*

(1) $-a \leq x \leq a$ *and x ends in k or more 0-bits,*

(2) $\mathrm{abs}(x) \overset{rot}{\gg} k \overset{u}{\leq} \lfloor a/2^k \rfloor$, *and*

(3) $x + a' \overset{rot}{\gg} k \overset{u}{\leq} \lfloor 2a'/2^k \rfloor$,

where a' is a with its rightmost k bits set to 0 (that is, $a' = a \ \& \ -2^k$).

Proof. (Assume a 32-bit machine). To see that (1) is equivalent to (2), clearly the assertion $-a \leq x \leq a$ is equivalent to $\text{abs}(x) \leq a$. Then, Theorem ZRU applies, because both sides of this inequality are nonnegative.

To see that (1) is equivalent to (3), note that assertion (1) is equivalent to itself with a replaced with a'. Then, by the theorem on bounds checking on page 52, this in turn is equivalent to

$$x + a' \overset{u}{\leq} 2a'.$$

Because $x + a'$ ends in k 0-bits if and only if x does, Theorem ZRU applies, giving the result.

Using part (3) of this theorem, the test that n is a multiple of d, where n and $d \geq 2$ are signed integers and $d = d_o \cdot 2^k$ with d_o odd, is

$$\boxed{\begin{aligned} &q \leftarrow \text{mod}(n\overline{d}_o, 2^W); \\ &a' \leftarrow \lfloor (2^{W-1} - 1)/d_o \rfloor \,\&\, {-2^k}; \\ &q + a' \overset{rot}{\gg} k \overset{u}{\leq} \lfloor (2a')/2^k \rfloor. \end{aligned}}$$

(a' may be computed at compile time, because d is a constant.)

As an example, the following code tests a signed integer n to see if it is a multiple of 100. Notice that the constant $\lfloor 2a'/2^k \rfloor$ can always be derived from the constant a' by a shift of $k - 1$ bits, saving an instruction or a load from memory to develop the comparand.

```
li      M,0xC28F5C29   Load mult. inverse of 25.
mul     q,M,n          q = right half of M*n.
li      c,0x051EB850   c = floor((2**31 - 1)/25) & -4.
add     q,q,c          Add c.
shrri   q,q,2          Rotate right two positions.
shri    c,c,1          Compute const. for comparison.
cmpleu  t,q,c          Compare q and c, and
bt      t,is_mult      branch if n is a mult. of 100.
```

I think that I shall never envision
An op unlovely as division.

An op whose answer must be guessed
And then, through multiply, assessed;

An op for which we dearly pay,
In cycles wasted every day.

Division code is often hairy;
Long division's downright scary.

The proofs can overtax your brain,
The ceiling and floor may drive you insane.

Good code to divide takes a Knuthian hero,
But even God can't divide by zero!

CHAPTER 11

SOME ELEMENTARY
FUNCTIONS

11–1 Integer Square Root

By the "integer square root" function, we mean the function $\lfloor \sqrt{x} \rfloor$. To extend its range of application and to avoid deciding what to do with a negative argument, we assume x is unsigned. Thus, $0 \leq x \leq 2^{32} - 1$.

Newton's Method

For floating-point numbers, the square root is almost universally computed by Newton's method. This method begins by somehow obtaining a starting estimate g_0 of $\sqrt{a}$. Then, a series of more accurate estimates is obtained from

$$g_{n+1} = \left(g_n + \frac{a}{g_n}\right)/2.$$

The iteration converges quadratically—that is, if at some point g_n is accurate to n bits, then g_{n+1} is accurate to $2n$ bits. The program must have some means of knowing when it has iterated enough, so it can terminate.

It is a pleasant surprise that Newton's method works fine in the domain of integers. To see this, we need the following theorem:

> THEOREM. *Let* $g_{n+1} = \lfloor (g_n + \lfloor a/g_n \rfloor)/2 \rfloor$, *with* g_n, *a integers greater than* 0. *Then*
>
> (a) *if* $g_n > \lfloor \sqrt{a} \rfloor$ *then* $\lfloor \sqrt{a} \rfloor \leq g_{n+1} < g_n$, *and*
>
> (b) *if* $g_n = \lfloor \sqrt{a} \rfloor$ *then* $\lfloor \sqrt{a} \rfloor \leq g_{n+1} \leq \lfloor \sqrt{a} \rfloor + 1$.

That is, if we have an integral guess g_n to $\lfloor \sqrt{a} \rfloor$ that is too high, then the next guess g_{n+1} will be strictly less than the preceding one, but not less than $\lfloor \sqrt{a} \rfloor$. Therefore, if we start with a guess that's too high, the sequence converges monotonically. If the guess $g_n = \lfloor \sqrt{a} \rfloor$, then the next guess is either equal to g_n or is 1 larger. This provides an easy way to determine when the sequence has converged: If we start with $g_0 \geq \lfloor \sqrt{a} \rfloor$, convergence has occurred when $g_{n+1} \geq g_n$, and then the result is precisely g_n.

The case $a = 0$, however, must be treated specially, because this procedure would lead to dividing 0 by 0.

Proof. (a) Because g_n is an integer,

$$g_{n+1} = \left\lfloor \left(g_n + \left\lfloor \frac{a}{g_n} \right\rfloor \right)/2 \right\rfloor = \left\lfloor \left\lfloor g_n + \frac{a}{g_n} \right\rfloor /2 \right\rfloor = \left\lfloor \left(g_n + \frac{a}{g_n}\right)/2 \right\rfloor = \left\lfloor \frac{g_n^2 + a}{2g_n} \right\rfloor.$$

Because $g_n > \lfloor \sqrt{a} \rfloor$ and g_n is an integer, $g_n > \sqrt{a}$. Define ε by $g_n = (1 + \varepsilon)\sqrt{a}$. Then $\varepsilon > 0$ and

$$\left\lfloor \frac{g_n^2 + a}{2g_n} \right\rfloor = g_{n+1} \le \frac{g_n^2 + a}{2g_n},$$

$$\left\lfloor \frac{(1 + \varepsilon)^2 a + a}{2(1 + \varepsilon)\sqrt{a}} \right\rfloor = g_{n+1} < \frac{g_n^2 + g_n^2}{2g_n},$$

$$\left\lfloor \frac{2 + 2\varepsilon + \varepsilon^2}{2(1 + \varepsilon)} \sqrt{a} \right\rfloor = g_{n+1} < g_n,$$

$$\left\lfloor \frac{2 + 2\varepsilon}{2(1 + \varepsilon)} \sqrt{a} \right\rfloor \le g_{n+1} < g_n,$$

$$\lfloor \sqrt{a} \rfloor \le g_{n+1} < g_n.$$

(b) Because $g_n = \lfloor \sqrt{a} \rfloor$, $\sqrt{a} - 1 < g_n \le \sqrt{a}$, so that $g_n^2 \le a < (g_n + 1)^2$. Hence we have

$$\left\lfloor \frac{g_n^2 + g_n^2}{2g_n} \right\rfloor \le g_{n+1} \le \left\lfloor \frac{g_n^2 + (g_n + 1)^2}{2g_n} \right\rfloor,$$

$$\lfloor g_n \rfloor \le g_{n+1} \le \left\lfloor g_n + 1 + \frac{1}{2g_n} \right\rfloor,$$

$$\lfloor \sqrt{a} \rfloor \le g_{n+1} \le \lfloor g_n + 1 \rfloor \quad \text{(because } g_n \text{ is an integer and } \frac{1}{2g_n} < 1\text{)},$$

$$\lfloor \sqrt{a} \rfloor \le g_{n+1} \le \lfloor g_n \rfloor + 1 = \lfloor \sqrt{a} \rfloor + 1.$$

The difficult part of using Newton's method to calculate $\lfloor \sqrt{x} \rfloor$ is getting the first guess. The procedure of Figure 11–1 sets the first guess g_0 equal to the least power of 2 that is greater than or equal to $\sqrt{x}$. For example, for $x = 4$, $g_0 = 2$, and for $x = 5$, $g_0 = 4$.

```
int isqrt(unsigned x) {
   unsigned x1;
   int s, g0, g1;

   if (x <= 1) return x;
   s = 1;
   x1 = x - 1;
   if (x1 > 65535) {s = s + 8; x1 = x1 >> 16;}
   if (x1 > 255)   {s = s + 4; x1 = x1 >> 8;}
   if (x1 > 15)    {s = s + 2; x1 = x1 >> 4;}
   if (x1 > 3)     {s = s + 1;}

   g0 = 1 << s;                  // g0 = 2**s.
   g1 = (g0 + (x >> s)) >> 1;    // g1 = (g0 + x/g0)/2.

   while (g1 < g0) {             // Do while approximations
      g0 = g1;                   // strictly decrease.
      g1 = (g0 + (x/g0)) >> 1;
   }
   return g0;
}
```

FIGURE 11–1. Integer square root, Newton's method.

Because the first guess g_0 is a power of 2, it is not necessary to do a real division to get g_1; instead, a *shift right* suffices.

Because the first guess is accurate to about 1 bit, and Newton's method converges quadratically (the number of bits of accuracy doubles with each iteration), one would expect the procedure to converge within about five iterations (on a 32-bit machine), which requires four divisions (because the first iteration substitutes a *shift right*). An exhaustive experiment reveals that the maximum number of divisions is five, or four for arguments up to 16,785,407.

If *number of leading zeros* is available, then getting the first guess is very simple: Replace the first seven executable lines in the procedure above with

```
if (x <= 1) return x;
s = 16 - nlz(x - 1)/2;
```

Another alternative, if *number of leading zeros* is not available, is to compute s by means of a binary search tree. This method permits getting a slightly better value of g_0: the least power of 2 that is greater than or equal to $\lfloor \sqrt{x} \rfloor$. For some values of x, this gives a smaller value of g_0, but a value large enough so that the convergence criterion of the theorem still holds. The difference in these schemes is illustrated below.

Range of x for Figure 11–1	Range of x for Figure 11–2	First Guess g_0
0	0	0
1	1 to 3	1
2 to 4	4 to 8	2
5 to 16	9 to 24	4
17 to 64	25 to 80	8
65 to 256	81 to 288	16
...	...	...
$2^{28} + 1$ to 2^{30}	$(2^{14} + 1)^2$ to $(2^{15} + 1)^2 - 1$	2^{15}
$2^{30} + 1$ to $2^{32} - 1$	$(2^{15} + 1)^2$ to $2^{32} - 1$	2^{16}

This procedure is shown in Figure 11–2. It is convenient there to treat small values of x ($0 \le x \le 24$) specially, so that no divisions are done for them.

The worst-case execution time of the algorithm of Figure 11–1, on the basic RISC, is about $26 + (D + 6)n$ cycles, where D is the divide time in cycles and n is the number of times the *while*-loop is executed. The worst-case execution time of Figure 11–2 is about $27 + (D + 6)n$ cycles, assuming (in both cases) that the *branch* instructions take one cycle. The table below gives the average number of times the loop is executed by the two algorithms, for x uniformly distributed in the indicated range.

x	Figure 11–1	Figure 11–2
0 to 9	0.80	0
0 to 99	1.46	0.83
0 to 999	1.58	1.44
0 to 9999	2.13	2.06
0 to $2^{32} - 1$	2.97	2.97

If we assume a divide time of 20 cycles and x ranging uniformly from 0 to 9999, then both algorithms execute in about 81 cycles.

```
int isqrt(unsigned x) {
   int s, g0, g1;

   if (x <= 4224)
      if (x <= 24)
         if (x <= 3) return (x + 3) >> 2;
         else if (x <= 8) return 2;
         else return (x >> 4) + 3;
      else if (x <= 288)
         if (x <= 80) s = 3; else s = 4;
      else if (x <= 1088) x = 5; else s = 6;
   else if (x <= 1025*1025 - 1)
      if (x <= 257*257 - 1)
         if (x <= 129*129 - 1) s = 7; else s = 8;
      else if (x <= 513*513 - 1) s = 9; else s = 10;
   else if (x <= 4097*4097 - 1)
      if (x <= 2049*2049 - 1) s = 11; else s = 12;
   else if (x <= 16385*16385 - 1)
      if (x <= 8193*8193 - 1) s = 13; else s = 14;
   else if (x <= 32769*32769 - 1) s = 15; else s = 16;
   g0 = 1 << s;                 // g0 = 2**s.

   // Continue as in Figure 11-1.
```

FIGURE 11–2. Integer square root, binary search for first guess.

Binary Search

Because the algorithms based on Newton's method start out with a sort of binary search to obtain the first guess, why not do the whole computation with a binary search? This method would start out with two bounds, perhaps initialized to 0 and 2^{16}. It would make a guess at the midpoint of the bounds. If the square of the midpoint is greater than the argument x, then the upper bound is changed to be equal to the midpoint. If the square of the midpoint is less than the argument x, then the lower bound is changed to be equal to the midpoint. The process ends when the upper and lower bounds differ by 1, and the result is the lower bound.

This avoids division, but requires quite a few multiplications—16 if 0 and 2^{16} are used as the initial bounds. (The method gets one more bit of precision with each iteration.) Figure 11–3 illustrates a variation of this procedure, which uses initial values for the bounds that are slight improvements over 0 and 2^{16}. The procedure shown in Figure 11–3 also saves a cycle in the loop, for most RISC machines, by altering a and b in such a way that the comparison is $b \geq a$ rather than $b - a \geq 1$.

The predicates that must be maintained at the beginning of each iteration are $a \leq \lfloor \sqrt{x} \rfloor + 1$ and $b \geq \lfloor \sqrt{x} \rfloor$. The initial value of b should be something that's

```
int isqrt(unsigned x) {
   unsigned a, b, m;                // Limits and midpoint.

   a = 1;
   b = (x >> 5) + 8;                // See text.
   if (b > 65535) b = 65535;
   do {
      m = (a + b) >> 1;
      if (m*m > x) b = m - 1;
      else          a = m + 1;
   } while (b >= a);
   return a - 1;
}
```

FIGURE 11–3. Integer square root, simple binary search.

easy to compute and close to $\lfloor \sqrt{x} \rfloor$. Reasonable initial values are x, $x \div 4 + 1$, $x \div 8 + 2$, $x \div 16 + 4$, $x \div 32 + 8$, $x \div 64 + 16$, and so on. Expressions near the beginning of this list are better initial bounds for small x, and those near the end are better for larger x. (The value $x \div 2 + 1$ is acceptable, but probably not useful, because $x \div 4 + 1$ is everywhere a better or equal bound.)

Seven variations on the procedure shown in Figure 11–3 can be more or less mechanically generated by substituting $a + 1$ for a, or $b - 1$ for b, or by changing $m = (a + b) \div 2$ to $m = (a + b + 1) \div 2$, or some combination of these substitutions.

The execution time of the procedure shown in Figure 11–3 is about $6 + (M + 7.5)n$, where M is the multiplication time in cycles and n is the number of times the loop is executed. The table below gives the average number of times the loop is executed, for x uniformly distributed in the indicated range.

x	Average Number of Loop Iterations
0 to 9	3.00
0 to 99	3.15
0 to 999	4.68
0 to 9999	7.04
0 to $2^{32} - 1$	16.00

If we assume a multiplication time of 5 cycles and x ranging uniformly from 0 to 9999, the algorithm runs in about 94 cycles. The maximum execution time ($n = 16$) is about 206 cycles.

If *number of leading zeros* is available, the initial bounds can be set from

```
b = (1 << (33 - nlz(x))/2) - 1;
a = (b + 3)/2;
```

That is, $b = 2^{(33 - \text{nlz}(x)) \overset{u}{\div} 2} - 1$. These are very good bounds for small values of x (one loop iteration for $0 \le x \le 15$), but only a moderate improvement, for large x, over the bounds calculated in Figure 11–3. For x in the range 0 to 9999, the average number of iterations is about 5.45, which gives an execution time of about 74 cycles, using the same assumptions as above.

A Hardware Algorithm

There is a shift-and-subtract algorithm for computing the square root that is quite similar to the hardware division algorithm described in Figure 9–2 on page 149. Embodied in hardware on a 32-bit machine, this algorithm employs a 64-bit register that is initialized to 32 0-bits followed by the argument x. On each iteration, the 64-bit register is shifted left two positions, and the current result y (initially 0) is shifted left one position. Then $2y + 1$ is subtracted from the left half of the 64-bit register. If the result of the subtraction is nonnegative, it replaces the left half of the 64-bit register, and 1 is added to y (this does not require an adder, because y ends in 0 at this point). If the result of the subtraction is negative, then the 64-bit register and y are left unaltered. The iteration is done 16 times.

This algorithm was described in 1945 [JVN].

Perhaps surprisingly, this process runs in about half the time of that of the $64 \div 32 \Rightarrow 32$ hardware division algorithm cited, because it does half as many iterations and each iteration is about equally complex in the two algorithms.

To code this algorithm in software, it is probably best to avoid the use of a doubleword shift register, which requires about four instructions to shift. The algorithm in Figure 11–4 [GLS1] accomplishes this by shifting y and a mask bit m to the right. It executes in about 149 basic RISC instructions (average). The two expressions y | m could also be y + m.

The operation of this algorithm is similar to the grade-school method. It is illustrated below, for finding $\lfloor \sqrt{179} \rfloor$ on an 8-bit machine.

```
1011 0011   x0   Initially, x - 179 (0xB3).
-  1        b1

0111 0011   x1   0100 0000  y1
-  101      b2   0010 0000  y2

0010 0011   x2   0011 0000  y2
-   11 01   b3   0001 1000  y3

0010 0011   x3   0001 1000  y3   (Can't subtract).
-    1 1001 b4   0000 1100  y4

0000 1010   x4   0000 1101  y4
```

The result is 13 with a remainder of 10 left in register x.

```
int isqrt(unsigned x) {
   unsigned m, y, b;

   m = 0x40000000;
   y = 0;
   while(m != 0) {                    // Do 16 times.
      b = y | m;
      y = y >> 1;
      if (x >= b) {
         x = x - b;
         y = y | m;
      }
      m = m >> 2;
   }
   return y;
}
```

FIGURE 11–4. Integer square root, hardware algorithm.

It is possible to eliminate the if x >= b test by the usual trickery involving *shift right signed 31*. It can be proved that the high-order bit of b is always zero (in fact, $b \le 5 \cdot 2^{28}$), which simplifies the x >= b predicate (see page 22). The result is that the *if* statement group can be replaced with

```
t = (int)(x | ~(x - b)) >> 31;    // -1 if x >= b, else 0.
x = x - (b & t);
y = y | (m & t);
```

This replaces an average of three cycles with seven, assuming the machine has *or not*, but it might be worthwhile if a conditional branch in this context takes more than five cycles.

Somehow it seems that it should be easier than some hundred cycles to compute an integer square root in software. Toward this end, we offer the expressions below to compute it for very small values of the argument. These can be useful to speed up some of the algorithms given above, if the argument is expected to be small.

The expression	is correct in the range	and uses this many instructions (full RISC).
x	0 to 1	0
$x > 0$	0 to 3	1
$(x + 3) \overset{u}{\div} 4$	0 to 3	2

The expression	is correct in the range	and uses this many instructions (full RISC).
$x \overset{u}{\gg} (x \overset{u}{\div} 2)$	0 to 3	2
$x \overset{u}{\gg} (x > 1)$	0 to 5	2
$(x + 12) \overset{u}{\div} 8$	1 to 8	2
$(x + 15) \overset{u}{\div} 8$	4 to 15	2
$(x > 0) + (x > 3)$	0 to 8	3
$(x > 0) + (x > 3) + (x > 8)$	0 to 15	5

Ah, the elusive square root,
It should be a cinch to compute.
But the best we can do
Is use powers of two
And iterate the method of Newt!

11–2 Integer Cube Root

For cube roots, Newton's method does not work out very well. The iterative formula is a bit complex:

$$x_{n+1} = \frac{1}{3}\left(2x_n + \frac{a}{x_n^2}\right),$$

and there is of course the problem of getting a good starting value x_0.

However, there is a hardware algorithm, similar to the hardware algorithm for square root, that is not too bad for software. It is shown in Figure 11–5.

The three *add*'s of 1 can be replaced by *or*'s of 1, because the value being incremented is even. Even with this change, the algorithm is of questionable value for implementation in hardware, mainly because of the multiplication $y * (y + 1)$.

This multiplication is easily avoided by applying the compiler optimization of strength reduction to the y-squared term. Introduce another unsigned variable y2 that will have the value of y-squared, by updating y2 appropriately wherever y receives a new value. Just before y = 0 insert y2 = 0. Just before y = 2*y insert y2 = 4*y2. Change the assignment to b to b = (3*y2 + 3*y + 1) << s (and factor out the 3). Just before y = y + 1, insert y2 = y2 + 2*y + 1. The resulting program has no multiplications except by small constants, which can be changed

```
int icbrt(unsigned x) {
   int s;
   unsigned y, b;

   s = 30;
   y = 0;
   while(s >= 0) {                    // Do 11 times.
      y = 2*y;
      b = (3*y*(y + 1) + 1) << s;
      s = s - 3;
      if (x >= b) {
         x = x - b;
         y = y + 1;
      }
   }
   return y;
}
```

FIGURE 11–5. Integer cube root, hardware algorithm.

to *shift*'s and *add*'s. This program has three *add*'s of 1, which can all be changed to *or*'s of 1. It is faster unless your machine's *multiply* instruction takes only two or fewer cycles.

Caution: [GLS1] points out that the code of Figure 11–5, and its strength-reduced derivative, do not work if adapted in the obvious way to a 64-bit machine. The assignment to b can then overflow. This problem can be avoided by dropping the *shift left* of s from the assignment to b, inserting after the assignment to b the assignment bs = b << s, and changing the two lines if (x >= b) {x = x - b ... to if (x >= bs && b == (bs >> s)) {x = x - bs ....

11–3 Integer Exponentiation

Computing x^n by Binary Decomposition of n

A well-known technique for computing x^n, when n is a nonnegative integer, involves the binary representation of n. The technique applies to the evaluation of an expression of the form $x \bullet x \bullet x \bullet \ldots \bullet x$ where $\bullet$ is any associative operation, such as addition, multiplication including matrix multiplication, and string concatenation (as suggested by the notation ('ab')^3 = 'ababab'). As an example, suppose we wish to compute $y = x^{13}$. Because 13 expressed in binary is 1101 (that is, 13 = 8 + 4 + 1),

$$x^{13} = x^{8+4+1} = x^8 \cdot x^4 \cdot x^1.$$

Thus, x^{13} may be computed as follows:

$$t_1 \leftarrow x^2$$
$$t_2 \leftarrow t_1^2$$
$$t_3 \leftarrow t_2^2$$
$$y \leftarrow t_3 \cdot t_2 \cdot x$$

This requires five multiplications, considerably fewer than the 12 that would be required by repeated multiplication by x.

If the exponent is a variable, known to be a nonnegative integer, the technique can be employed in a subroutine, as shown in Figure 11–6.

The number of multiplications done by this method is, for exponent $n \geq 1$,

$$\lfloor \log_2 n \rfloor + \text{nbits}(n) - 1.$$

This is not always the minimal number of multiplications. For example, for $n = 27$ the binary decomposition method computes

$$x^{16} \cdot x^8 \cdot x^2 \cdot x^1,$$

which requires seven multiplications. However, the scheme illustrated by

$$((x^3)^3)^3$$

requires only six. The smallest number for which the binary decomposition method is not optimal is $n = 15$ (hint: $x^{15} = (x^3)^5$).

```
int iexp(int x, unsigned n) {
   int p, y;

   y = 1;                    // Initialize result
   p = x;                    // and p.
   while(1) {
      if (n & 1) y = p*y;    // If n is odd, mult by p.
      n = n >> 1;            // Position next bit of n.
      if (n == 0) return y;  // If no more bits in n.
      p = p*p;               // Power for next bit of n.
   }
}
```

FIGURE 11–6. Computing x^n by binary decomposition of n.

Perhaps surprisingly, there is no known simple method that, for all n, finds an optimal sequence of multiplications to compute x^n. The only known methods involve an extensive search. The problem is discussed at some length in [Knu2, sec. 4.6.3].

The binary decomposition method has a variant that scans the binary representation of the exponent in left-to-right order [Rib, 32], which is analogous to the left-to-right method of converting binary to decimal. Initialize the result y to 1, and scan the exponent from left to right. When a 0 is encountered, square y. When a 1 is encountered, square y and multiply it by x. This computes $x^{13} = x^{1101_2}$ as

$$(((1^2 \cdot x)^2 \cdot x)^2)^2 \cdot x.$$

It always requires the same number of (nontrivial) multiplications as the right-to-left method of Figure 11–6.

2^n in Fortran

The IBM XL Fortran compiler takes the definition of this function to be

$$\text{pow2}(n) = \begin{cases} 2^n, & 0 \le n \le 30, \\ -2^{31}, & n = 31, \\ 0, & n < 0 \text{ or } n \ge 32. \end{cases}$$

It is assumed that n and the result are interpreted as signed integers. The ANSI/ISO Fortran standard requires that the result be 0 if $n < 0$. The definition above for $n \ge 31$ seems reasonable in that it is the correct result modulo 2^{32}, and it agrees with what repeated multiplication would give.

The standard way to compute 2^n is to put the integer 1 in a register and shift it left n places. This does not satisfy the Fortran definition, because shift amounts are usually treated modulo 64 or modulo 32 (on a 32-bit machine), which gives incorrect results for large or negative shift amounts.

If your machine has *number of leading zeros*, pow2(n) may be computed in four instructions as follows [Shep]:

$x \leftarrow \text{nlz}(n \overset{u}{\gg} 5);$ // $x \leftarrow 32$ if $0 \le n \le 31$, $x < 32$ otherwise.

$x \leftarrow x \overset{u}{\gg} 5;$ // $x \leftarrow 1$ if $0 \le n \le 31$, 0 otherwise.

$pow2 \leftarrow x \ll n;$

The *shift right* operations are "logical" (not sign-propagating), even though n is a signed quantity.

If the machine does not have the "nlz" instruction, its use above can be replaced with one of the $x = 0$ tests given in "Comparison Predicates" on page 21, changing the expression $x \overset{u}{\gg} 5$ to $x \overset{u}{\gg} 31$. A possibly better method is to realize that the predicate $0 \le x \le 31$ is equivalent to $x \overset{u}{\le} 32$, and then simplify the expression for $x \overset{u}{\le} y$ given in the cited section; it becomes $\neg x \;\&\; (x - 32)$. This gives a solution in five instructions (four if the machine has *and not*):

$$x \leftarrow \neg n \;\&\; (n - 32); \qquad // \; x < 0 \text{ iff } 0 \le n \le 31.$$

$$x \leftarrow x \overset{u}{\gg} 31; \qquad // \; x = 1 \text{ if } 0 \le n \le 31, 0 \text{ otherwise.}$$

$$pow2 \leftarrow x \ll n;$$

11–4 Integer Logarithm

By the "integer logarithm" function we mean the function $\lfloor \log_b x \rfloor$, where x is a positive integer and b is an integer greater than or equal to 2. Usually, $b = 2$ or 10, and we denote these functions by "ilog2" and "ilog10," respectively. We use "ilog" when the base is unspecified.

It is convenient to extend the definition to $x = 0$ by defining $\text{ilog}(0) = -1$ [CJS]. There are several reasons for this definition:

- The function $\text{ilog2}(x)$ is then related very simply to the *number of leading zeros* function, $\text{nlz}(x)$, by the formula shown below, including the case $x = 0$. Thus, if one of these functions is implemented in hardware or software, the other is easily obtained.

$$\text{ilog2}(x) = 31 - \text{nlz}(x)$$

- It is easy to compute $\lceil \log(x) \rceil$ using the formula below. For $x = 1$, this formula implies that $\text{ilog}(0) = -1$.

$$\lceil \log(x) \rceil = \text{ilog}(x - 1) + 1$$

- It makes the following identity hold for $x = 1$ (but it doesn't hold for $x = 0$):

$$\text{ilog2}(x \div 2) = \text{ilog2}(x) - 1$$

- It preserves the mathematical identity:

$$\lfloor \log_{10} x \rfloor = \lfloor (\log_{10} 2) \log_2 x \rfloor$$

- It makes the result of $\text{ilog}(x)$ a small dense set of integers (-1 to 31 for $\text{ilog2}(x)$ on a 32-bit machine, with x unsigned), making it directly useful for indexing a table.

- It falls naturally out of several algorithms for computing $\text{ilog2}(x)$ and $\text{ilog10}(x)$.

Unfortunately, it isn't the right definition for "number of digits of x," which is ilog(x) + 1 for all x except $x = 0$. But it seems best to consider that anomalous.

For $x < 0$, ilog(x) is left undefined. To extend its range of utility, we define the function as mapping unsigned numbers to signed numbers. Thus, a negative argument cannot occur.

Integer Log Base 2

Computing ilog2(x) is essentially the same as computing the number of leading zeros, which is discussed in "Counting Leading 0's" on page 77. All the algorithms in that section can be easily modified to compute ilog2(x) directly, rather than by computing nlz(x) and subtracting the result from 31. (For the algorithm of Figure 5–11 on page 80, change the line `return pop(~x)` to `return pop(x) - 1`.

Integer Log Base 10

This function has application in converting a number to decimal for inclusion into a line with leading zeros suppressed. The conversion process successively divides by 10, producing the least significant digit first. It would be useful to know ahead of time where the least significant digit should be placed, to avoid putting the converted number in a temporary area and then moving it.

To compute ilog10(x), a table search is quite reasonable. This could be a binary search, but because the table is small and in many applications x is usually small, a simple linear search is probably best. This rather straightforward program is shown in Figure 11–7.

On the basic RISC, this program can be implemented to execute in about $9 + 4\lfloor \log_{10} x \rfloor$ instructions. Thus, it executes in five to 45 instructions, with perhaps 13 (for $10 \le x \le 99$) being typical.

The program in Figure 11–7 can easily be changed into an "in register" version (not using a table). The executable part of such a program is shown in Figure 11–8. This might be useful if the machine has a fast way to multiply by 10.

```
int ilog10(unsigned x) {
    int i;
    static unsigned table[11] = {0, 9, 99, 999, 9999,
        99999, 999999, 9999999, 99999999, 999999999,
        0xFFFFFFFF};

    for (i = -1; ; i++) {
        if (x <= table[i+1]) return i;
    }
}
```

FIGURE 11–7. Integer log base 10, simple table search.

```
p = 1;
for (i = -1; i <= 8; i++) {
    if (x < p) return i;
    p = 10*p;
}
return i;
```

FIGURE 11–8. Integer log base 10, repeated multiplication by 10.

This program can be implemented to execute in about $10 + 6\lfloor \log_{10} x \rfloor$ instructions on the basic RISC (counting the *multiply* as one instruction). This amounts to 16 instructions for $10 \le x \le 99$.

A binary search can be used, giving an algorithm that is loop-free and does not use a table. Such an algorithm might compare x to 10^4, then to either 10^2 or to 10^6, and so on, until the exponent n is found such that $10^n \le x < 10^{n+1}$. The paths execute in ten to 18 instructions, four or five of which are branches (counting the final unconditional branch).

The program shown in Figure 11–9 is a modification of the binary search that has a maximum of four branches on any path, and is written in a way that favors small x. It executes in six basic RISC instructions for $10 \le x \le 99$, and in 11 to 16 instructions for $x \ge 100$.

The *shift* instructions in this program are *signed* shifts (which is the reason for the (int) casts). If your machine does not have this instruction, one of the alternatives below, which use unsigned shifts, may be preferable. These are illustrated for the case of the first return statement. Unfortunately, the first two require *subtract from immediate* for efficient implementation, which most machines don't

```
int ilog10(unsigned x) {
    if (x > 99)
        if (x < 1000000)
            if (x < 10000)
                return 3 + ((int)(x - 1000) >> 31);
            else
                return 5 + ((int)(x - 100000) >> 31);
        else
            if (x < 100000000)
                return 7 + ((int)(x - 10000000) >> 31);
            else
                return 9 + ((int)((x-1000000000)&~x) >> 31);
    else
        if (x > 9) return 1;
        else        return ((int)(x - 1) >> 31);
}
```

FIGURE 11–9. Integer log base 10, modified binary search.

have. The last involves adding a large constant (two instructions), but this does not matter for the second and third `return` statements, which require adding a large constant anyway. The large constant is $2^{31} - 1000$.

```
return 3 - ((x - 1000) >> 31);
return 2 + ((999 - x) >> 31);
return 2 + ((x + 2147482648) >> 31);
```

An alternative for the fourth `return` statement is

```
return 8 + ((x + 1147483648) | x) >> 31;
```

where the large constant is $2^{31} - 10^9$. This avoids both the *and not* and the signed shift.

Alternatives for the last *if-else* construction are

```
return ((int)(x - 1) >> 31) | ((unsigned)(9 - x) >> 31);
return (x > 9) + (x > 0) - 1;
```

either of which saves a branch.

If nlz(x) or ilog2(x) is available as an instruction, there are better and more interesting ways to compute ilog10(x). For example, the program in Figure 11–10 does it in two table lookups [CJS].

From `table1` an approximation to ilog10(x) is obtained. The approximation is usually the correct value, but it is too high by 1 for $x = 0$ and for x in the range 8 to 9, 64 to 99, 512 to 999, 8192 to 9999, and so on. The second table gives the value below which the estimate must be corrected by subtracting 1.

This scheme uses a total of 73 bytes for tables, and can be coded in only six instructions on the IBM System/370 [CJS] (to achieve this, the values in `table1` must be four times the values shown). It executes in about ten instructions on a RISC that has *number of leading zeros* but no other esoteric instructions. The other methods to be discussed are variants of this.

The first variation eliminates the conditional branch that results from the *if* statement. Actually, the program in Figure 11–10 can be coded free of branches if the machine has the *set less than unsigned* instruction, but the method to be described can be used on machines that have no unusual instructions (other than *number of leading zeros*).

The method is to replace the *if* statement with a subtraction followed by a *shift right* of 31 so that the sign bit can be subtracted from y. A difficulty occurs for large x ($x \geq 2^{31} + 10^9$), which can be fixed by adding an entry to `table2`, as shown in Figure 11–11.

```
int ilog10(unsigned x) {
   int y;
   static unsigned char table1[33] = {9, 9, 9, 8, 8, 8,
      7, 7, 7, 6, 6, 6, 6, 5, 5, 5, 4, 4, 4, 3, 3, 3, 3,
      2, 2, 2, 1, 1, 1, 0, 0, 0, 0};
   static unsigned table2[10] = {1, 10, 100, 1000, 10000,
      100000, 1000000, 10000000, 100000000, 1000000000};

   y = table1[nlz(x)];
   if (x < table2[y]) y = y - 1;
   return y;
}
```

FIGURE 11–10. Integer log base 10 from log base 2, double table lookup.

```
int ilog10(unsigned x) {
   int y;
   static unsigned char table1[33] = {10, 9, 9, 8, 8, 8,
      7, 7, 7, 6, 6, 6, 6, 5, 5, 5, 4, 4, 4, 3, 3, 3, 3,
      2, 2, 2, 1, 1, 1, 0, 0, 0, 0};
   static unsigned table2[11] = {1, 10, 100, 1000, 10000,
      100000, 1000000, 10000000, 100000000, 1000000000,
      0};

   y = table1[nlz(x)];
   y = y - ((x - table2[y]) >> 31);
   return y;
}
```

FIGURE 11–11. Integer log base 10 from log base 2, double table lookup, branch-free.

This executes in about 11 instructions on a RISC that has *number of leading zeros* but is otherwise quite "basic." It can be modified to return the value 0, rather than –1, for $x = 0$ (which is preferable for the decimal conversion problem) by changing the last entry in table1 to 1 (that is, by changing "0, 0, 0, 0" to "0, 0, 0, 1").

The next variation replaces the first table lookup with a subtraction, a multiplication, and a shift. This seems likely to be possible because $\log_{10}x$ and $\log_2 x$ are related by a multiplicative constant, namely $\log_{10}2 = 0.30103....$ Thus, it may be possible to compute ilog10(x) by computing $\lfloor c \, \text{ilog2}(x) \rfloor$ for some suitable $c \approx 0.30103$, and correcting the result by using a table such as table2 in Figure 11–11.

To pursue this, let $\log_{10}2 = c + \varepsilon$, where $c > 0$ is a rational approximation to $\log_{10}2$ that is a convenient multiplier, and $\varepsilon > 0$. Then for $x \geq 1$,

$$\text{ilog}10(x) = \lfloor \log_{10}x \rfloor = \lfloor (c + \varepsilon)\log_2 x \rfloor$$
$$\lfloor c \log_2 x \rfloor \leq \text{ilog}10(x) = \lfloor c \log_2 x + \varepsilon \log_2 x \rfloor$$
$$\lfloor c \, \text{ilog}2(x) \rfloor \leq \text{ilog}10(x) \leq \lfloor c \, (\text{ilog}2(x) + 1) + \varepsilon \log_2 x \rfloor$$
$$\leq \lfloor c \, \text{ilog}2(x) + c + \varepsilon \log_2 x \rfloor$$
$$\leq \lfloor c \, \text{ilog}2(x) \rfloor + \lfloor c + \varepsilon \log_2 x \rfloor + 1.$$

Thus, if we choose c so that $c + \varepsilon \log_2 x < 1$, then $\lfloor c \, \text{ilog}2(x) \rfloor$ approximates $\text{ilog}10(x)$ with an error of 0 or +1. Furthermore, if we take $\text{ilog}2(0) = \text{ilog}10(0) = -1$, then $\lfloor c \, \text{ilog}2(0) \rfloor = \text{ilog}10(0)$ (because $0 < c \leq 1$), so we need not be concerned about this case. (There are other definitions that would work here, such as $\text{ilog}2(0) = \text{ilog}10(0) = 0$).

Because $\varepsilon = \log_{10}2 - c$, we must choose c so that

$$c + (\log_{10}2 - c)\log_2 x < 1, \text{ or}$$
$$c(\log_2 x - 1) > (\log_{10}2)\log_2 x - 1.$$

This is satisfied for $x = 1$ (because $c < 1$) and 2. For larger x, we must have

$$c > \frac{(\log_{10}2)\log_2 x - 1}{\log_2 x - 1}.$$

The most stringent requirement on c occurs when x is large. For a 32-bit machine, $x < 2^{32}$, so choosing

$$c > \frac{0.30103 \cdot 32 - 1}{32 - 1} \approx 0.27848$$

suffices. Because $c < 0.30103$ (because $\varepsilon > 0$), $c = 9/32 = 0.28125$ is a convenient value. Experimentation reveals that coarser values such as 5/16 and 1/4 are not adequate.

This leads to the scheme illustrated in Figure 11–12, which estimates low and then corrects by adding 1. It executes in about 11 instructions on a RISC that has *number of leading zeros*, counting the *multiply* as one instruction.

This can be made into a branch-free version, but again there is a difficulty with large x ($x > 2^{31} + 10^9$), which can be fixed in either of two ways. One way is to use a different multiplier (19/64) and a slightly expanded table. The program is shown in Figure 11–13 (about 11 instructions on a RISC that has *number of leading zeros*, counting the *multiply* as one instruction).

```
static unsigned table2[10] = {0, 9, 99, 999, 9999,
   99999, 999999, 9999999, 99999999, 999999999};

y = (9*(31 - nlz(x))) >> 5;
if (x > table2[y+1]) y = y + 1;
return y;
```

FIGURE 11–12. Integer log base 10 from log base 2, one table lookup.

```
int ilog10(unsigned x) {
   int y;
   static unsigned table2[11] = {0, 9, 99, 999, 9999,
      99999, 999999, 9999999, 99999999, 999999999,
      0xFFFFFFFF};

   y = (19*(31 - nlz(x))) >> 6;
   y = y + ((table2[y+1] - x) >> 31);
   return y;
}
```

FIGURE 11–13. Integer log base 10 from log base 2, one table lookup, branch-free.

The other "fix" is to *or x* into the result of the subtraction, to force the sign bit to be on for $x \geq 2^{31}$; that is, change the second executable line of Figure 11–12 to

```
y = y + (((table2[y+1] - x) | x) >> 31);
```

This is the preferable program if multiplication by 19 is substantially more difficult than multiplication by 9 (as it is for a *shift*-and-*add* sequence).

For a 64-bit machine, choosing

$$c > \frac{0.30103 \cdot 64 - 1}{64 - 1} \approx 0.28993$$

suffices. The value $19/64 = 0.296875$ is convenient, and experimentation reveals that no coarser value is adequate. The program is (branch-free version)

```
unsigned table2[20] = {0, 9, 99, 999, 9999, ...,
   9999999999999999999};
y = ((19*(63 - nlz(x)) >> 6;
y = y + ((table2[y+1] - x) >> 63);
return y;
```

CHAPTER 12

UNUSUAL BASES FOR
NUMBER SYSTEMS

This section discusses a few unusual positional number systems. They are just interesting curiosities and are probably not practical for anything. We limit the discussion to integers, but they can all be extended to include digits after the radix point—which usually, but not always, denotes non-integers.

12–1 Base –2

By using –2 as the base, both positive and negative integers can be expressed without an explicit sign or other irregularity such as having a negative weight for the most significant bit (Knu3). The digits used are 0 and 1, as in base +2; that is, the value represented by a string of 1's and 0's is understood to be

$$(a_n...a_3a_2a_1a_0) = a_n(-2)^n + ... + a_3(-2)^3 + a_2(-2)^2 + a_1(-2) + a_0.$$

From this, it can be seen that a procedure for finding the base –2, or "negabinary," representation of an integer is to successively divide the number by –2, recording the remainders. The division must be such that it always gives a remainder of 0 or 1 (the digits to be used); that is, it must be modulus division. As an example, the plan below shows how to find the base –2 representation of –3.

$$\frac{-3}{-2} = 2 \text{ rem } 1$$

$$\frac{2}{-2} = -1 \text{ rem } 0$$

$$\frac{-1}{-2} = 1 \text{ rem } 1$$

$$\frac{1}{-2} = 0 \text{ rem } 1$$

Because we have reached a 0 quotient, the process terminates (if continued, the remaining quotients and remainders would all be 0). Thus, reading the remainders upwards, we see that –3 is written 1101 in base –2.

Table 12–1 shows, on the left, how each bit pattern from 0000 to 1111 is interpreted in base –2, and on the right, how integers in the range –15 to +15 are represented.

TABLE 12–1. CONVERSIONS BETWEEN DECIMAL AND BASE –2

n (base –2)	n (decimal)	n (decimal)	n (base –2)	$-n$ (base –2)
0	0	0	0	0
1	1	1	1	11
10	–2	2	110	10
11	–1	3	111	1101
100	4	4	100	1100
101	5	5	101	1111
110	2	6	11010	1110
111	3	7	11011	1001
1000	–8	8	11000	1000
1001	–7	9	11001	1011
1010	–10	10	11110	1010
1011	–9	11	11111	110101
1100	–4	12	11100	110100
1101	–3	13	11101	110111
1110	–6	14	10010	110110
1111	–5	15	10011	110001

It is not obvious that the 2^n possible bit patterns in an n-bit word uniquely represent all integers in a certain range, but this can be shown by induction. The inductive hypothesis is that an n-bit word represents all integers in the range

$$-(2^{n+1} - 2)/3 \text{ to } (2^n - 1)/3 \text{ for } n \text{ even, and} \qquad (1a)$$

$$(-(2^n - 2)/3) \text{ to } ((2^{n+1} - 1)/3) \text{ for } n \text{ odd.} \qquad (1b)$$

Assume first that n is even. For $n = 2$, the representable integers are 10, 11, 00, and 01 in base –2, or

$$-2, -1, 0, 1.$$

This agrees with (1a), and each integer in the range is represented once and only once.

A word of $n + 1$ bits can, with a leading bit of 0, represent all the integers given by (1a). In addition, with a leading bit of 1, it can represent all these integers biased by $(-2)^n = 2^n$. The new range is

$$2^n - (2^{n+1} - 2)/3 \text{ to } 2^n + (2^n - 1)/3,$$

or

$$(2^n - 1)/3 + 1 \text{ to } (2^{n+2} - 1)/3.$$

This is contiguous to the range given by (1a), so for a word size of $n + 1$ bits, all integers in the range

$$-(2^{n+1} - 2)/3 \text{ to } (2^{n+2} - 1)/3$$

are represented once and only once. This agrees with (1b), with n replaced by $n + 1$.

The proof that (1a) follows from (1b), for n odd, and that all integers in the range are uniquely represented, is similar.

To add and subtract, the usual rules, such as $0 + 1 = 1$ and $1 - 1 = 0$, of course apply. Because 2 is written 110, and -1 is written 11, and so on, the following additional rules apply. These, together with the obvious ones, suffice.

$$1 + 1 = 110$$
$$11 + 1 = 0$$
$$1 + 1 + 1 = 111$$
$$0 - 1 = 11$$
$$11 - 1 = 10$$

When adding or subtracting, there are sometimes two carry bits. The carry bits are to be *added* to their column, even when subtracting. It is convenient to place them both over the next bit to the left, and simplify (when possible) using $11 + 1 = 0$. If 11 is carried to a column that contains two 0's, bring down a 1 and carry a 1. Below are examples.

```
        Addition                          Subtraction
  11 1 11     11                    1 11  1       1
      1  0  1  1  1      19              1  0  1  0  1      21
  + 1 1  0  1  0  1  + (-11)        - 1  0  1  1  1  0   - (-38)
  -----------------  ------         -----------------   -----
    0  1  1  0  0  0       8         1  0  0  1  1  1  1      59
```

The only carries possible are 0, 1, and 11. Overflow occurs if there is a carry (either 1 or 11) out of the high-order position. These remarks apply to both addition and subtraction.

Because there are three possibilities for the carry, a base -2 adder would be more complex than a two's-complement adder.

There are two ways to negate an integer. It may be added to itself shifted left one position (that is, multiply by -1), or it may be subtracted from 0. There is no rule as simple and convenient as the "complement and add 1" rule of two's-complement arithmetic. In two's-complement, this rule is used to build a subtracter from an adder (to compute $A - B$, form $A + \bar{B} + 1$). There does not seem to be any such simple device for base -2.

Multiplication of base -2 integers is straightforward. Just use the rule that $1 \times 1 = 1$ and 0 times either 0 or 1 is 0, and add the columns using base -2 addition.

Division, however, is quite complicated. It is a real challenge to devise a reasonable hardware division algorithm—that is, one based on repeated subtraction and shifting. Figure 12–1 shows an algorithm that is expressed, for definiteness, for an 8-bit machine. It does modulus division (nonnegative remainder).

Although this program is written in C and was tested on a binary two's-complement machine, that is immaterial—it should be viewed somewhat

```
int divbm2(int n, int d) {          // q = n/d in base -2.
   int r, dw, c, q, i;

   r = n;                           // Init. remainder.
   dw = (-128)*d;                   // Position d.
   c = (-43)*d;                     // Init. comparand.
   if (d > 0) c = c + d;
   q = 0;                           // Init. quotient.
   for (i = 7; i >= 0; i--) {
      if (d > 0 ^ (i&1) == 0 ^ r >= c) {
         q = q | (1 << i);          // Set a quotient bit.
         r = r - dw;                // Subtract d shifted.
      }
      dw = dw/(-2);                 // Position d.
      if (d > 0) c = c - 2*d;       // Set comparand for
      else c = c + d;              // next iteration.
      c = c/(-2);
   }
   return q;                        // Return quotient in
                                    // base -2.
                                    // Remainder is r,
}                                   // 0 <= r < |d|.
```

FIGURE 12–1. Division in base -2.

abstractly. The input quantities n and d, and all internal variables except for q, are simply numbers without any particular representation. The output q is a string of bits to be interpreted in base –2.

This requires a little explanation. If the input quantities were in base –2, the algorithm would be very awkward to express in an executable form. For example, the test "if (d > 0)" would have to test that the most significant bit of d is in an even position. The addition in "c = c + d" would have to be a base –2 addition. The code would be very hard to read. The way the algorithm is coded, you should think of n and d as numbers without any particular representation. The code shows the arithmetic operations to be performed, whatever encoding is used. If the numbers are encoded in base –2, as they would be in hardware that implements this algorithm, the multiplication by –128 is a left shift of seven positions, and the divisions by –2 are right shifts of one position.

As examples, the code computes values as follows:

divbm2(6, 2) = 7 (six divided by two is 111_{-2})
divbm2(–4, 3) = 2 (minus four divided by three is 10_{-2})
divbm2(–4, –3) = 6 (minus four divided by minus 3 is 110_{-2})

The step q = q | (1 << i); represents simply setting bit i of q. The next line— r = r - dw—represents reducing the remainder by the divisor d shifted left.

The algorithm is difficult to describe in detail, but we will try to give the general idea.

Consider determining the value of the first bit of the quotient, bit 7 of q. In base –2, 8-bit numbers that have their most significant bit "on" range in value from –170 to –43. Therefore, ignoring the possibility of overflow, the first (most significant) quotient bit will be 1 if (and only if) the quotient will be algebraically less than or equal to – 43.

Because $n = qd + r$ and for a positive divisor $r \leq d - 1$, for a positive divisor the first quotient bit will be 1 iff $n \leq -43d + (d-1)$, or $n < -43d + d$. For a negative divisor, the first quotient bit will be 1 iff $n \geq -43d$ ($r \geq 0$ for modulus division).

Thus, the first quotient bit is 1 iff

$$(d > 0 \ \& \ \neg(n \geq -43d + d)) \ | \ (d < 0 \ \& \ n \geq -43d).$$

Ignoring the possibility that $d = 0$, this can be written as

$$d > 0 \oplus n \geq c,$$

where $c = -43d + d$ if $d > 0$, and $c = -43d$ if $d < 0$.

This is the logic for determining a quotient bit for an odd-numbered bit position. For an even-numbered position, the logic is reversed. Hence the test includes the term (i&1) == 0. (The ^ character in the program denotes *exclusive or*.)

At each iteration, c is set equal to the smallest (closest to zero) integer that must have a 1-bit at position i after dividing by d. If the current remainder r exceeds that, then bit i of q is set to 1 and r is adjusted by subtracting the value of a 1 at that position, multiplied by the divisor d. No real multiplication is required here; d is simply positioned properly and subtracted.

The algorithm is not elegant. It is awkward to implement because there are several additions, subtractions, and comparisons, and there is even a multiplication (by a constant) that must be done at the beginning. One might hope for a "uniform" algorithm—one that does not test the signs of the arguments and do different things depending on the outcome. Such a uniform algorithm, however, probably does not exist for base –2 (or for two's-complement arithmetic). The reason for this is that division is inherently a non-uniform process. Consider the simplest algorithm of the *shift*-and-*subtract* type. This algorithm would not shift at all, but for positive arguments would simply subtract the divisor from the dividend repeatedly, counting the number of subtractions performed until the remainder is less than the divisor. But if the dividend is negative (and the divisor is positive), the process is to add the divisor repeatedly until the remainder is 0 or positive, and the quotient is the negative of the count obtained. The process is still different if the divisor is negative.

In spite of this, division *is* a uniform process for the signed-magnitude representation of numbers. With such a representation, the magnitudes are positive, so the algorithm can simply subtract magnitudes and count until the remainder is negative, and then set the sign bit of the quotient to the *exclusive or* of the arguments, and the sign bit of the remainder equal to the sign of the dividend (this gives ordinary truncating division).

The algorithm given above could be made more uniform, in a sense, by first complementing the divisor, if it is negative, and then performing the steps given as simplified by having $d > 0$. Then a correction would be performed at the end. For modulus division, the correction is to negate the quotient and leave the remainder unchanged. This moves some of the tests out of the loop, but the algorithm as a whole is still not pretty.

It is interesting to contrast the commonly used number representations and base –2 regarding the question of whether or not the computer hardware treats numbers uniformly in carrying out the four fundamental arithmetic operations. We don't have a precise definition of "uniformly," but basically it means free of operations that might or might not be done, depending on the signs of the arguments. We consider setting the sign bit of the result equal to the *exclusive or* of the signs of the arguments to be a uniform operation. Table 12–2 shows which operations treat their operands uniformly with various number representations.

One's-complement addition and subtraction are done uniformly by means of the "end around carry" trick. For addition, all bits, including the sign bit, are added in the usual binary way, and the carry out of the leftmost bit (the sign bit) is added to the least significant position. This process always terminates right away (that is, the addition of the carry cannot generate another carry out of the sign bit position).

TABLE 12–2. UNIFORM OPERATIONS IN VARIOUS NUMBER ENCODINGS

	Signed-magnitude	One's-complement	Two's-complement	Base –2
addition	no	yes	yes	yes
subtraction	no	yes	yes	yes
multiplication	yes	no	no	yes
division	yes	no	no	no

In the case of two's-complement multiplication, the entry is "yes" if only the right half of the doubleword product is desired.

We conclude this discussion of the base –2 number system with some observations about how to convert between straight binary and base –2.

To convert to binary from base –2, form a word that has only the bits with positive weight, and subtract a word that has only the bits with negative weight, using the subtraction rules of binary arithmetic. An alternative method that may be a little simpler is to extract the bits appearing in the negative weight positions, shift them one position to the left, and subtract the extracted number from the original number using the subtraction rules of ordinary binary arithmetic.

To convert to base –2 from binary, extract the bits appearing in the odd positions (positions weighted by 2^n with n odd), shift them one position to the left, and add the two numbers using the addition rules of base –2. Here are two examples:

```
     Binary from base -2              Base -2 from binary
        110111  (-13)                    110111  (55)
      - 1 0 1   (binary subtract)      + 1 0 1   (base -2 add)
      ---------                        ---------
   ...111110011  (-13)                 1001011  (55)
```

On a computer, with its fixed word size, these conversions work for negative numbers if the carries out of the high-order position are simply discarded. To illustrate, the example on the right above can be regarded as converting –9 to base –2 from binary if the word size is six bits.

The above algorithm for converting to base –2 cannot easily be implemented in software on a binary computer, because it requires doing addition in base –2. Schroeppel [HAK, item 128] overcomes this with a much more clever and useful way to do the conversions in both directions. To convert to binary, his method is

$$B \leftarrow (N \oplus \textbf{0b10}\ldots\textbf{1010}) - \textbf{0b10}\ldots\textbf{1010}.$$

To see why this works, let the base –2 number consist of the four digits *abcd*. Then, interpreted (erroneously) in straight binary, this is $8a + 4b + 2c + d$. After the *exclusive or*, interpreted in binary it is $8(1 - a) + 4b + 2(1 - c) + d$. After the (binary) subtraction of $8 + 2$, it is $-8a + 4b - 2c + d$, which is its value interpreted in base –2.

Schroeppel's formula can be readily solved for N in terms of B, so it gives a three-instruction method for converting in the other direction. Collecting these results, we have the following formulas for converting to binary, for a 32-bit machine:

$$B \leftarrow (N \,\&\, \text{0x55555555}) - (N \,\&\, \neg\text{0x55555555}),$$

$$B \leftarrow N - ((N \,\&\, \text{0xAAAAAAAA}) \ll 1),$$

$$B \leftarrow (N \oplus \text{0xAAAAAAAA}) - \text{0xAAAAAAAA},$$

and the following, for converting to base –2 from binary:

$$N \leftarrow (B + \text{0xAAAAAAAA}) \oplus \text{0xAAAAAAAA}.$$

12–2 Base –1 + i

By using $-1 + i$ as the base, where i is $\sqrt{-1}$, all *complex* integers (complex numbers with integral real and imaginary parts) can be expressed as a single "number" without an explicit sign or other irregularity. Surprisingly, this can be done using only 0 and 1 for digits, and all integers are represented uniquely. We will not prove this or much else about this number system, but will just describe it very briefly.

It is not entirely trivial to discover how to write the integer 2.[1] However, this can be determined algorithmically by successively dividing 2 by the base and recording the remainders. What does a "remainder" mean in this context? We want the remainder after dividing by $-1 + i$ to be 0 or 1, if possible (so that the digits will be 0 or 1). To see that it is always possible, assume that we are to divide an arbitrary complex integer $a + bi$ by $-1 + i$. Then, we wish to find q and r such that q is a complex integer, $r = 0$ or 1, and

$$a + bi = (q_r + q_i i)(-1 + i) + r,$$

where q_r and q_i denote the real and imaginary parts of q, respectively. Equating real and imaginary parts and solving the two simultaneous equations for q gives

$$q_r = \frac{b - a + r}{2}, \text{ and}$$

$$q_i = \frac{-a - b + r}{2}.$$

---

1. The interested reader might warm up to this challenge.

Clearly, if a and b are both even or are both odd, then by choosing $r = 0$, q is a complex integer. Furthermore, if one of a and b is even and the other is odd, then by choosing $r = 1$, q is a complex integer.

Thus, the integer 2 can be converted to base $-1 + i$ by the plan illustrated below.

Because the real and imaginary parts of the integer 2 are both even, we simply do the division, knowing that the remainder will be 0:

$$\frac{2}{-1+i} = \frac{2(-1-i)}{(-1+i)(-1-i)} = -1 - i \text{ rem } 0.$$

Because the real and imaginary parts of $-1 - i$ are both odd, again we simply divide, knowing that the remainder is 0:

$$\frac{-1-i}{-1+i} = \frac{(-1-i)(-1-i)}{(-1+i)(-1-i)} = i \text{ rem } 0.$$

Because the real and imaginary parts of i are even and odd, respectively, the remainder will be 1. It is simplest to account for this at the beginning by subtracting 1 from the dividend.

$$\frac{i-1}{-1+i} = 1 \text{ (remainder is 1).}$$

Because the real and imaginary parts of 1 are odd and even, the next remainder will be 1. Subtracting this from the dividend gives

$$\frac{1-1}{-1+i} = 0 \text{ (remainder is 1).}$$

Because we have reached a 0 quotient, the process terminates, and the base $-1 + i$ representation for 2 is seen to be 1100 (reading the remainders upwards).

Table 12–3 shows how each bit pattern from 0000 to 1111 is interpreted in base $-1 + i$, and how the real integers in the range –15 to +15 are represented.

The addition rules for base $-1 + i$ (in addition to the trivial ones involving a 0 bit) are as follows:

$$1 + 1 = 1100$$
$$1 + 1 + 1 = 1101$$
$$1 + 1 + 1 + 1 = 111010000$$
$$1 + 1 + 1 + 1 + 1 = 111010001$$
$$1 + 1 + 1 + 1 + 1 + 1 = 111011100$$
$$1 + 1 + 1 + 1 + 1 + 1 + 1 = 111011101$$
$$1 + 1 + 1 + 1 + 1 + 1 + 1 + 1 = 111000000$$

TABLE 12–3. CONVERSIONS BETWEEN DECIMAL AND BASE $-1 + i$

n (base $-1 + i$)	n (decimal)	n (decimal)	n (base $-1 + i$)	$-n$ (base $-1 + i$)
0	0	0	0	0
1	1	1	1	11101
10	$-1 + i$	2	1100	11100
11	i	3	1101	10001
100	$-2i$	4	111010000	10000
101	$1 - 2i$	5	111010001	11001101
110	$-1 - i$	6	111011100	11001100
111	$-i$	7	111011101	11000001
1000	$2 + 2i$	8	111000000	11000000
1001	$3 + 2i$	9	111000001	11011101
1010	$1 + 3i$	10	111001100	11011100
1011	$2 + 3i$	11	111001101	11010001
1100	2	12	100010000	11010000
1101	3	13	100010001	1110100001101
1110	$1 + i$	14	100011100	1110100001100
1111	$2 + i$	15	100011101	1110100000001

When adding two numbers, the largest number of carries that occurs in one column is six, so the largest sum of a column is 8 (111000000). This makes for a rather complicated adder. If one were to build a complex arithmetic machine, it would no doubt be best to keep the real and imaginary parts separate,[2] with each represented in some sensible way such as two's-complement.

12–3 Other Bases

The base $-1 - i$ has essentially the same properties as the base $-1 + i$ discussed above. If a certain bit pattern represents the number $a + bi$ in one of these bases, then the same bit pattern represents the number $a - bi$ in the other base.

The bases $1 + i$ and $1 - i$ can also represent all the complex integers, using only 0 and 1 for digits. These two bases have the same complex-conjugate relationship to each other, as do the bases $-1 \pm i$. In bases $1 \pm i$, the representation of some integers has an infinite string of 1's on the left, similar to the two's-complement representation of negative integers. This arises naturally by using

---

2. This is the way it was done at Bell Labs back in 1940 on George Stibitz's Complex Number Calculator [Irvine].

uniform rules for addition and subtraction, as in the case of two's-complement. One such integer is 2, which (in either base) is written …11101100. Thus, these bases have the rather complex addition rule $1 + 1 = …11101100$.

By grouping into pairs the bits in the base -2 representation of an integer, one obtains a base 4 representation for the positive and negative numbers, using the digits $-2, -1, 0,$ and 1. For example,

$$-14_{\text{decimal}} = 110110_{-2} = (-1)(1)(-2)_4 = -1 \cdot 4^2 + 1 \cdot 4^1 - 2 \cdot 4^0.$$

Similarly, by grouping into pairs the bits in the base $-1 + i$ representation of a complex integer, we obtain a base $-2i$ representation for the complex integers using the digits $0, 1, -1 + i,$ and i. This is a bit too complicated to be interesting.

The "quater-imaginary" system (Knu2) is similar. It represents the complex integers using $2i$ as a base, and the digits $0, 1, 2,$ and 3 (with no sign). To represent some integers, namely those with an odd imaginary component, it is necessary to use a digit to the right of the radix point. For example, i is written 10.2 in base $2i$.

12–4 What Is the Most Efficient Base?

Suppose you are building a computer and you are trying to decide what base to use to represent integers. For the registers you have available circuits that are 2-state (binary), 3-state, 4-state, and so on. Which should you use?

Let us assume that the cost of a b-state circuit is proportional to b. Thus, a 3-state circuit costs 50% more than a binary circuit, a 4-state circuit costs twice as much as a binary circuit, and so on.

Suppose you want the registers to be able to hold integers from 0 to some maximum M. Encoding integers from 0 to M in base b requires $\lceil \log_b(M + 1) \rceil$ digits (e.g., to represent all integers from 0 to 999,999 in decimal requires $\log_{10}(1,000,000) = 6$ digits).

One would expect the cost of a register to be equal to the product of the number of digits required times the cost to represent each digit:

$$c = k\log_b(M + 1) \cdot b,$$

where c is the cost of a register and k is a constant of proportionality. For a given M, we wish to find b that minimizes the cost.

The minimum of this function occurs for that value of b that makes $dc/db = 0$. Thus, we have

$$\frac{d}{db}(kb\log_b(M + 1)) = \frac{d}{db}\left(kb\frac{\ln(M + 1)}{\ln b}\right) = k\ln(M + 1)\frac{\ln b - 1}{(\ln b)^2}.$$

This is zero when $\ln b = 1$, or $b = e$.

This is not a very satisfactory result. Because $e \approx 2.718$, 2 and 3 must be the most efficient integral bases. Which is more efficient? The ratio of the cost of a base 2 register to the cost of a base 3 register is

$$\frac{c(2)}{c(3)} = \frac{k \cdot 2\log_2(M+1)}{k \cdot 3\log_3(M+1)} = \frac{2\ln(M+1)/(\ln 2)}{3\ln(M+1)/(\ln 3)} = \frac{2\ln 3}{3\ln 2} \approx 1.056.$$

Thus, base 2 is more costly than base 3, but only by a small amount.

By the same analysis, base 2 is more costly than base e by a factor of about 1.062.

CHAPTER 13

GRAY CODE

13–1 Gray Code

Is it possible to cycle through all 2^n combinations of n bits by changing only one bit at a time? The answer is "yes," and this is the defining property of Gray codes. That is, a Gray code is an encoding of the integers such that a Gray-coded integer and its successor differ in only one bit position. This concept can be generalized to apply to any base, such as decimal, but here we will discuss only binary Gray codes.

Although there are many binary Gray codes, we will discuss only one: the "reflected binary Gray code." This code is what is usually meant in the literature by the unqualified term "Gray code." We will show, usually without proof, how to do some basic operations in this representation of integers, and we will show a few surprising properties.

The reflected binary Gray code is constructed as follows. Start with the strings 0 and 1, representing the integers 0 and 1:

0

1

Reflect this about a horizontal axis at the bottom of the list, and place a 1 to the left of the new list entries, and a 0 to the left of the original list entries:

00

01

11

10

This is the reflected binary Gray code for $n = 2$. To get the code for $n = 3$, reflect this and attach a 0 or 1 as before:

000

001

011

010

110

111

101

100

From this construction, it is easy to see by induction on n that (1) each of the 2^n bit combinations appears once and only once in the list, (2) only one bit changes in going from one list entry to the next, and (3) only one bit changes when cycling around from the last entry to the first. Gray codes having this last property are called "cyclic," and the reflected binary Gray code is necessarily cyclic.

If $n > 2$, there are non-cyclic codes that take on all 2^n values once and only once. One such code is 000 001 011 010 110 100 101 111.

Figure 13–1 shows, for $n = 4$, the integers encoded in ordinary binary and in Gray code. The formulas show how to convert from one representation to the other at the bit-by-bit level (as it would be done in hardware).

As for the number of Gray codes on n bits, notice that one still has a cyclic binary Gray code after rotating the list (starting at any of the 2^n positions and cycling around) or reordering the columns. Any combination of these operations results in a distinct code. Therefore, there are at least $2^n \cdot n!$ cyclic binary Gray codes on n bits. There are more than this for $n \geq 3$.

The Gray code and binary representations have the following dual relationships, evident from the formulas given in Figure 13–1:

- Bit i of a Gray-coded integer is the parity of bit i and the bit to the left of i in the corresponding binary integer (using 0 if there is no bit to the left of i).

- Bit i of a binary integer is the parity of all the bits at and to the left of position i in the corresponding Gray-coded integer.

Converting to Gray from binary can be done in only two instructions:

$$G \leftarrow B \oplus (B \overset{u}{\gg} 1).$$

The conversion to binary from Gray is harder. One method is given by

$$B \leftarrow \overset{n-1}{\underset{i=0}{\oplus}} G \overset{u}{\gg} i.$$

We have already seen this formula in "Computing the Parity of a Word" on page 74. As mentioned there, this formula can be evaluated as illustrated below for $n = 32$.

```
B = G ^ (G >> 1);
B = B ^ (B >> 2);
B = B ^ (B >> 4);
B = B ^ (B >> 8);
B = B ^ (B >> 16);
```

Thus, in general it requires $2 \cdot \lceil \log_2 n \rceil$ instructions.

Binary	Gray
abcd	*efgh*

Binary *abcd*	Gray *efgh*	Gray from Binary	Binary from Gray
0000	0000		
0001	0001	$e = a$	$a = e$
0010	0011	$f = a \oplus b$	$b = e \oplus f$
0011	0010	$g = b \oplus c$	$c = e \oplus f \oplus g$
0100	0110	$h = c \oplus d$	$d = e \oplus f \oplus g \oplus h$
0101	0111		
0110	0101		
0111	0100		
1000	1100		
1001	1101		
1010	1111		
1011	1110		
1100	1010		
1101	1011		
1110	1001		
1111	1000		

FIGURE 13–1. 4-bit Gray code and conversion formulas.

Because it is so easy to convert from binary to Gray, it is trivial to generate successive Gray-coded integers:

```
for (i - 0; i < n; i++) {
    G = i ^ (i >> 1);
    output G;
}
```

13–2 Incrementing a Gray-Coded Integer

The logic for incrementing a 4-bit *binary* integer *abcd* can be expressed as follows, using Boolean algebra notation:

$$d' = \bar{d}$$
$$c' = c \oplus d$$
$$b' = b \oplus cd$$
$$a' = a \oplus bcd$$

Thus, one way to build a Gray-coded counter in hardware is to build a binary counter using the above logic, and convert the outputs a', b', c', d' to Gray by forming the *exclusive or* of adjacent bits, as shown under "Gray from Binary" in Figure 13–1.

A way that might be slightly better is described by the following formulas:

$$p = e \oplus f \oplus g \oplus h$$
$$h' = h \oplus \bar{p}$$
$$g' = g \oplus hp$$
$$f' = f \oplus g\bar{h}p$$
$$e' = e \oplus f\bar{g}\bar{h}p$$

That is, the general case is

$$G'_n = G_n \oplus (G_{n-1}\bar{G}_{n-2}...\bar{G}_0 p), \quad n \geq 2.$$

Because the parity p alternates between 0 and 1, a counter circuit might maintain p in a separate 1-bit register and simply invert it on each count.

In software, the best way to find the successor G' of a Gray-coded integer G is probably simply to convert G to binary, increment the binary word, and convert it back to Gray code. Another way that's interesting and almost as good is to determine which bit to flip in G. The pattern goes like this, expressed as a word to be *exclusive or*'d to G:

$$1 \ 2 \ 1 \ 4 \ 1 \ 2 \ 1 \ 8 \ 1 \ 2 \ 1 \ 4 \ 1 \ 2 \ 1 \ 16$$

The alert reader will recognize this as a mask that identifies the position of the leftmost bit that changes when incrementing the integer 0, 1, 2, 3, …, corresponding to the positions in the above list. Thus, to increment a Gray-coded integer G, the bit position to invert is given by the leftmost bit that changes when 1 is added to the binary integer corresponding to G.

This leads to the following algorithms for incrementing a Gray-coded integer G. They both first convert G to binary, which is shown as index(G).

```
B = index(G);                    B = index(G);
B = B + 1;                       M = ~B & (B + 1);
Gp = B ^ (B >> 1);               Gp = G ^ M;
```

FIGURE 13–2. Incrementing a Gray-coded integer.

A pencil-and-paper method of incrementing a Gray-coded integer is as follows:

> Starting from the right, find the first place at which the parity of bits at and to the left of the position is even. Invert the bit at this position.

Or, equivalently:

> Let p be the parity of the word G. If p is even, invert the rightmost bit.
> If p is odd, invert the bit to the left of the rightmost 1-bit.

The latter rule is directly expressed in the Boolean equations given above.

13–3 Negabinary Gray Code

If you write the integers in order in base −2, and convert them using the "shift and exclusive or" that converts to Gray from straight binary, you get a Gray code. The 3-bit Gray code has indexes that range over the 3-bit base −2 numbers, namely −2 to 5. Similarly, the 4-bit Gray code corresponding to 4-bit base −2 numbers has indexes ranging from −10 to 5. It is not a reflected Gray code, but it almost is. The 4-bit Gray code can be generated by starting with 0 and 1, reflecting this about a horizontal axis at the *top* of the list, and then reflecting it about a horizontal axis at the *bottom* of the list, and so on. It is cyclic.

To convert back to base −2 from this Gray code, the rules are of course the same as they are for converting to straight binary from ordinary reflected binary Gray code (because these operations are inverses, no matter what the interpretation of the bit strings is).

13–4 Brief History and Applications

Gray codes are named after Frank Gray, a physicist at Bell Telephone Laboratories who in the 1930's invented the method we now use for broadcasting color TV in a way that's compatible with the black-and-white transmission and reception methods then in existence; that is, when the color signal is received by a black-and-white set, the picture appears in shades of gray.

Martin Gardner [Gard] discusses applications of Gray codes involving the Chinese ring puzzle, the Tower of Hanoi puzzle, and Hamiltonian paths through graphs that represent hypercubes. He also shows how to convert from the decimal representation of an integer to a decimal Gray code representation.

Gray codes are used in position sensors. A strip of material is made with conducting and nonconducting areas, corresponding to the 1's and 0's of a Gray-coded integer. Each column has a conducting wire brush positioned to read it out.

If a brush is positioned on the dividing line between two of the quantized positions, so that its reading is ambiguous, then it doesn't matter which way the ambi-
guity is resolved. There can be only one ambiguous brush, and interpreting it as a
0 or 1 gives a position adjacent to the dividing line.

The strip can instead be a series of concentric circular tracks, giving a rotational position sensor. For this application, the Gray code must be cyclic. Such a
sensor is shown in Figure 13–3, where the four dots represent the brushes.

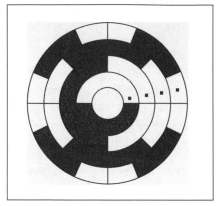

FIGURE 13–3. Rotational position sensor.

CHAPTER 14

HILBERT'S CURVE

In 1890 Giuseppe Peano discovered a planar curve[1] with the rather surprising property that it is "space-filling." The curve winds around the unit square and hits every point (x, y) at least once.

Peano's curve is based on dividing each side of the unit square into three equal parts, which divides the square into nine smaller squares. His curve traverses these nine squares in a certain order. Then, each of the nine small squares is similarly divided into nine still smaller squares, and the curve is modified to traverse all these squares in a certain order. The curve can be described using fractions expressed in base 3; in fact, that's the way Peano first described it.

In 1891 David Hilbert [Hil] discovered a variation of Peano's curve based on dividing each side of the unit square into two equal parts, which divides the square into four smaller squares. Then, each of the four small squares is similarly divided into four still smaller squares, and so on. For each stage of this division, Hilbert gives a curve that traverses all the squares. Hilbert's curve, sometimes called the "Peano-Hilbert curve," is the limit curve of this division process. It can be described using fractions expressed in base 2.

Figure 14–1 shows the first three steps in the sequence that leads to Hilbert's space-filling curve, as they were depicted in his 1891 paper.

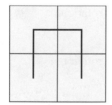 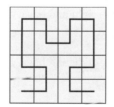 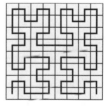

FIGURE 14–1. First three curves in the sequence defining Hilbert's curve.

Here, we do things a little differently. We use the term "Hilbert curve" for any of the curves on the sequence whose limit is the Hilbert space-filling curve. The "Hilbert curve of order n" means the nth curve in the sequence. In Figure 14–1, the curves are of order 1, 2, and 3. We shift the curves down and to the left so that the corners of the curves coincide with the intersections of the lines in the boxes above. Finally, we scale the size of the order n curve up by a factor of 2^n, so that

---

1. Recall that a *curve* is a continuous map from a one-dimensional space to an n-dimensional space.

the coordinates of the corners of the curves are integers. Thus, our order n Hilbert curve has corners at integers ranging from 0 to $2^n - 1$ in both x and y. We take the positive direction along the curve to be from $(x, y) = (0, 0)$ to $(2^n - 1, 0)$. On the next page are shown the "Hilbert curves," in our terminology, of orders 1 through 6.

14–1 A Recursive Algorithm for Generating the Hilbert Curve

To see how to generate a Hilbert curve, examine the curves in Figure 14–2. The order 1 curve goes up, right, and down. The order 2 curve follows this overall pattern. First, it makes a U-shaped curve that goes up, in net effect. Second, it takes a unit step up. Third, it takes a U-shaped curve, a step, and another U, all to the right. Finally, it takes a step down, followed by a U that goes down, in net effect.

The order 1 inverted U is converted into the order 2 Y-shaped curve.

We can regard the Hilbert curve of any order as a series of U-shaped curves of various orientations, each of which, except for the last, is followed by a unit step in a certain direction. In transforming a Hilbert curve of one order to the next, each U-shaped curve is transformed into a Y-shaped curve with the same general orientation, and each unit step is transformed to a unit step in the same direction.

The transformation of the order 1 Hilbert curve (a U curve with a net direction to the right and a clockwise rotational orientation) to the order 2 Hilbert curve goes as follows:

1. Draw a U that goes up and has a counterclockwise rotation.

2. Draw a step up.

3. Draw a U that goes to the right and has a clockwise rotation.

4. Draw a step to the right.

5. Draw a U that goes to the right and has a clockwise rotation.

6. Draw a step down.

7. Draw a U that goes down and has a counterclockwise rotation.

We can see by inspection that all U's that are oriented as the order 1 Hilbert curve are transformed in the same way. A similar set of rules can be made for transforming U's with other orientations. These rules are embodied in the recursive program shown in Figure 14–3 [Voor]. In this program, the orientation of a U curve is characterized by two integers that specify the net linear and the rotational directions, encoded as follows:

dir = 0: right	rot = +1: clockwise
dir = 1: up	rot = –1: counterclockwise
dir = 2: left	
dir = 3: down	

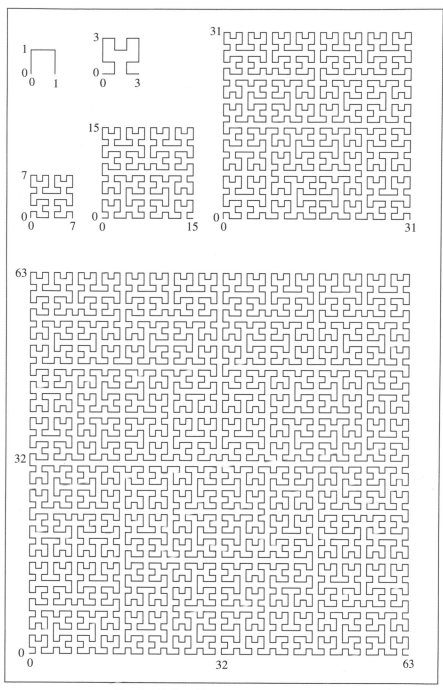

FIGURE 14–2. Hilbert curves of orders 1–6.

```
void step(int);

void hilbert(int dir, int rot, int order) {

   if (order == 0) return;

   dir = dir + rot;
   hilbert(dir, -rot, order - 1);
   step(dir);
   dir = dir - rot;
   hilbert(dir, rot, order - 1);
   step(dir);
   hilbert(dir, rot, order - 1);
   dir = dir - rot;
   step(dir);
   hilbert(dir, -rot, order - 1);
}
```

FIGURE 14–3. Hilbert curve generator.

Actually, `dir` can take on other values, but its congruency modulo 4 is what matters.

Figure 14–4 shows a driver program and function `step` that is used by program `hilbert`. This program is given the order of a Hilbert curve to construct, and it displays a list of line segments, giving for each the direction of movement, the length along the curve to the end of the segment, and the coordinates of the end of the segment. For example, for order 2 it displays

```
 0    0000    00 00
 0    0001    01 00
 1    0010    01 01
 2    0011    00 01
 1    0100    00 10
 1    0101    00 11
 0    0110    01 11
-1    0111    01 10
 0    1000    10 10
 1    1001    10 11
 0    1010    11 11
-1    1011    11 10
-1    1100    11 01
-2    1101    10 01
-1    1110    10 00
 0    1111    11 00
```

```
#include <stdio.h>
#include <stdlib.h>

int x = -1, y = 0;              // Global variables.
int i = 0;                      // Dist. along curve.
int blen;                       // Length to print.

void hilbert(int dir, int rot, int order);

void binary(unsigned k, int len, char *s) {
/* Converts the unsigned integer k to binary character
form. Result is string s of length len. */
   int i;

   s[len] = 0;
   for (i = len - 1; i >= 0; i--) {
      if (k & 1) s[i] = '1';
      else       s[i] = '0';
      k = k >> 1;
   }
}
void step(int dir) {
   char ii[33], xx[17], yy[17];

   switch(dir & 3) {
      case 0: x = x + 1; break;
      case 1: y = y + 1; break;
      case 2: x = x - 1; break;
      case 3: y = y - 1; break;
   }
   binary(i, 2*blen, ii);
   binary(x, blen, xx);
   binary(y, blen, yy);
   printf("%5d    %s    %s %s\n", dir, ii, xx, yy);
   i = i + 1;                   // Increment distance.
}
int main(int argc, char *argv[]) {
   int order;

   order = atoi(argv[1]);
   blen = order;
   step(0);                     // Print init. point.
   hilbert(0, 1, order);
   return 0;
}
```

FIGURE 14-4. Driver program for Hilbert curve generator.

14–2 Coordinates from Distance along the Hilbert Curve

To find the (x, y) coordinates of a point located at a distance s along the order n Hilbert curve, observe that the most significant two bits of the $2n$-bit integer s determine which major quadrant the point is in. This is because the Hilbert curve of any order follows the overall pattern of the order 1 curve. If the most significant two bits of s are 00, the point is somewhere in the lower left quadrant, if 01 it is in the upper left quadrant, if 10 it is in the upper right quadrant, and if 11 it is in the lower right quadrant. Thus, the most significant two bits of s determine the most significant bits of the n-bit integers x and y, as follows:

Most significant two bits of s	Most significant bits of (x, y)
00	(0, 0)
01	(0, 1)
10	(1, 1)
11	(1, 0)

In any Hilbert curve, only four of the eight possible U-shapes occur. These are shown in Table 14–1 as graphics and as maps from two bits of s to a single bit of each of x and y.

Observe from Figure 14–2 that in all cases, the U-shape represented by map A (⌐↓) becomes, at the next level of detail, a U-shape represented by maps B, A, A, or D, depending on whether the length traversed in the first-mentioned map A is 0, 1, 2, or 3, respectively. Similarly, a U-shape represented by map B (⇐⌐) becomes, at the next level of detail, a U-shape represented by maps A, B, B, or C, depending on whether the length traversed in the first-mentioned map B is 0, 1, 2, or 3, respectively.

These observations lead to the state transition table shown in Table 14–2, in which the states correspond to the mappings shown in Table 14–1.

TABLE 14–1. THE FOUR POSSIBLE MAPPINGS

A	B	C	D
⌐↓	⇐⌐	↑⌐	⌐→
00 → (0, 0)	00 → (0, 0)	00 → (1, 1)	00 → (1, 1)
01 → (0, 1)	01 → (1, 0)	01 → (1, 0)	01 → (0, 1)
10 → (1, 1)	10 → (1, 1)	10 → (0, 0)	10 → (0, 0)
11 → (1, 0)	11 → (0, 1)	11 → (0, 1)	11 → (1 0)

TABLE 14–2. STATE TRANSITION TABLE FOR COMPUTING (x, y) FROM s

If the current state is	and the next (to right) two bits of s are	then append to (x, y)	and enter state
A	00	(0, 0)	B
A	01	(0, 1)	A
A	10	(1, 1)	A
A	11	(1, 0)	D
B	00	(0, 0)	A
B	01	(1, 0)	B
B	10	(1, 1)	B
B	11	(0, 1)	C
C	00	(1, 1)	D
C	01	(1, 0)	C
C	10	(0, 0)	C
C	11	(0, 1)	B
D	00	(1, 1)	C
D	01	(0, 1)	D
D	10	(0, 0)	D
D	11	(1, 0)	A

To use the table, start in state A. The integer s should be padded with leading zeros so that its length is $2n$, where n is the order of the Hilbert curve. Scan the bits of s in pairs from left to right. The first row of Table 14–2 means that if the current state is A and the currently scanned bits of s are 00, then output (0, 0) and enter state B. Then, advance to the next two bits of s. Similarly, the second row means that if the current state is A and the scanned bits are 01, then output (0, 1) and stay in state A.

The output bits are accumulated in left-to-right order. When the end of s is reached, the n-bit output quantities x and y are defined.

As an example, suppose $n = 3$ and

$$s = 110100.$$

Because the process starts in state A and the initial bits scanned are 11, the process outputs (1, 0) and enters state D (fourth row). Then, in state D and scanning 01, the process outputs (0, 1) and stays in state D. Lastly, the process outputs (1, 1) and enters state C, although the state is now immaterial.

Thus, the output is (101, 011)—that is, $x = 5$ and $y = 3$.

A C program implementing these steps is shown in Figure 14–5. In this program, the current state is represented by an integer from 0 to 3 for states A through

```
void hil_xy_from_s(unsigned s, int n, unsigned *xp,
                                       unsigned *yp) {

    int i;
    unsigned state, x, y, row;

    state = 0;                              // Initialize.
    x = y = 0;

    for (i = 2*n - 2; i >= 0; i -= 2) {     // Do n times.
        row = 4*state | (s >> i) & 3;       // Row in table.
        x = (x << 1) | (0x936C >> row) & 1;
        y = (y << 1) | (0x39C6 >> row) & 1;
        state = (0x3E6B94C1 >> 2*row) & 3;  // New state.
    }
    *xp = x;                                // Pass back
    *yp = y;                                // results.
}
```

FIGURE 14–5. Program for computing (x, y) from s.

D, respectively. In the assignment to variable row, the current state is concatenated with the next two bits of s, giving an integer from 0 to 15, which is the applicable row number in Table 14–2. Variable row is used to access integers (expressed in hexadecimal) that are used as bit strings to represent the rightmost two columns of Table 14–2; that is, these accesses are in-register table lookups. Left-to-right in the hexadecimal values corresponds to bottom-to-top in Table 14–2.

[L&S] give a quite different algorithm. Unlike the algorithm of Figure 14–5, it scans the bits of s from right to left. It is based on the observation that one can map the least significant two bits of s to (x, y) based on the order 1 Hilbert curve, and then test the next two bits of s to the left. If they are 00, the values of x and y just computed should be interchanged, which corresponds to reflecting the order 1 Hilbert curve about the line $x = y$. (Refer to the curves of orders 1 and 2 shown in Figure 14–1 on page 241.) If these two bits are 01 or 10, the values of x and y are not changed. If they are 11, the values of x and y are interchanged and complemented. These same rules apply as one progresses leftward along the bits of s. They are embodied in Table 14–3 and the code of Figure 14–6. It is somewhat curious that the bits can be prepended to x and y first, and then the swap and complement operations can be done, including these newly prepended bits; the results are the same.

In Figure 14–6, variables x and y are uninitialized, which might cause an error message from some compilers. But the code functions correctly for whatever values x and y have initially.

The branch in the loop of Figure 14–6 can be avoided by doing the swap operation with the "three *exclusive or*" trick given in Section 2–19 on page 38.

TABLE 14–3. LAM AND SHAPIRO METHOD FOR COMPUTING (X, Y) FROM S

If the next (to left) two bits of s are	then	and prepend to (x, y)
00	Swap x and y	(0, 0)
01	No change	(0, 1)
10	No change	(1, 1)
11	Swap and complement x and y	(1, 0)

```
void hil_xy_from_s(unsigned s, int n, unsigned *xp,
                                      unsigned *yp) {

    int i, sa, sb;
    unsigned x, y, temp;

    for (i = 0; i < 2*n; i += 2) {
        sa = (s >> (i+1)) & 1;       // Get bit i+1 of s.
        sb = (s >> i) & 1;           // Get bit i of s.

        if ((sa ^ sb) == 0) {        // If sa,sb = 00 or 11,
            temp = x;                // swap x and y,
            x = y^(-sa);             // and if sa = 1,
            y = temp^(-sa);          // complement them.
        }
        x = (x >> 1) | (sa << 31);   // Prepend sa to x and
        y = (y >> 1) | ((sa ^ sb) << 31); // (sa^sb) to y.
    }
    *xp = x >> (32 - n);             // Right-adjust x and y
    *yp = y >> (32 - n);             // and return them to
}                                    // the caller.
```

FIGURE 14–6. Lam and Shapiro method for computing (x, y) from s.

The *if* block can be replaced by the following code, where swap and cmpl are unsigned integers:

```
swap = (sa ^ sb) - 1;   // -1 if should swap, else 0.
cmpl = -(sa & sb);      // -1 if should compl't, else 0.
x = x ^ y;
y = y ^ (x & swap) ^ cmpl;
x = x ^ y;
```

However, this is nine instructions, versus about two or six for the *if* block, so the branch cost would have to be quite high for this to be a good choice.

The "swap and complement" idea of [L&S] suggests a logic circuit for generating the Hilbert curve. The idea behind the circuit described below is that as you trace along the path of an order n curve, you basically map pairs of bits of s to (x, y) according to map A of Table 14–1. As the trace enters various regions, however, the mapping output gets swapped, complemented, or both. The circuit of Figure 14–7 keeps track of the swap and complement requirements of each stage, uses the appropriate mapping to map two bits of s to (x_i, y_i), and generates the swap and complement signals for the next stage.

Assume there is a register containing the path length s and circuits for incrementing it. Then, to find the next point on the Hilbert curve, first increment s and then transform it as described in Table 14–4. This is a left-to-right process, which is a bit of a problem because incrementing s is a right-to-left process. Thus, the time to generate a new point on an order n Hilbert curve is proportional to $2n$ (for incrementing s) plus n (for transforming s to (x, y)).

Figure 14–7 shows this computation as a logic circuit. In this figure, S denotes the swap signal and C denotes the complement signal.

TABLE 14–4. LOGIC FOR COMPUTING (X, Y) FROM S

If the next (to right) two bits of s are	then append to (x, y)	and set
00	$(0, 0)$*	swap = $\overline{\text{swap}}$
01	$(0, 1)$*	No change
10	$(1, 1)$*	No change
11	$(1, 0)$*	swap = $\overline{\text{swap}}$, cmpl = $\overline{\text{cmpl}}$
* Possibly swapped and/or complemented		

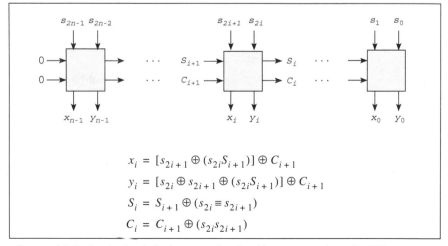

$$x_i = [s_{2i+1} \oplus (s_{2i}S_{i+1})] \oplus C_{i+1}$$
$$y_i = [s_{2i} \oplus s_{2i+1} \oplus (s_{2i}S_{i+1})] \oplus C_{i+1}$$
$$S_i = S_{i+1} \oplus (s_{2i} \equiv s_{2i+1})$$
$$C_i = C_{i+1} \oplus (s_{2i}s_{2i+1})$$

FIGURE 14–7. Logic circuit for incrementing (x, y) by one step along the Hilbert curve.

The logic circuit of Figure 14–7 suggests another way to compute (x, y) from s. Notice how the swap and complement signals propagate from left to right through the n stages. This suggests that it may be possible to use the parallel prefix operation to quickly (in $\log_2 n$ steps rather than $n - 1$) propagate the swap and complement information to each stage, and then do some word-parallel logical operations to compute x and y, using the equations in Figure 14–7. The values of x and y are intermingled in the even and odd bit positions of a word, so they have to be separated by the unshuffle operation (see page 107). This might seem a bit complicated, and likely to pay off only for rather large values of n, but let us see how it goes.

A procedure for this operation is shown in Figure 14–8 [GLS1]. The procedure operates on fullword quantities, so it first pads the input s on the left with '01' bits. This bit combination does not affect the swap and complement quantities. Next, a quantity cs (complement-swap) is computed. This word is of the form cscs . . . cs, where each c (a single bit), if 1, means that the corresponding pair of bits is to be complemented, and each s means that the corresponding pair of bits is to be swapped, following Table 14–3. In other words, these two statements map each pair of bits of s as follows:

s_{2i+1} s_{2i}	cs
0 0	01
0 1	00
1 0	00
1 1	11

This is the quantity to which we want to apply the parallel prefix operation. PP-XOR is the one to use, going from left to right, because successive 1-bits meaning to complement or to swap have the same logical properties as *exclusive or*. Two successive 1-bits cancel each other.

Both signals (complement and swap) are propagated in the same PP-XOR operation, each working with every other bit of cs.

The next four assignment statements have the effect of translating each pair of bits of s into (x, y) values, with x being in the odd (leftmost) bit positions, and y being in the even bit positions. Although the logic may seem obscure, it is not difficult to verify that each pair of bits of s is transformed by the logic of the first two Boolean equations in Figure 14–7. (Suggestion: Consider separately how the even and odd bit positions are transformed, using the fact that t and sr are 0 in the odd positions.)

The rest of the procedure is self-explanatory. It executes in 66 basic RISC instructions (constant, branch-free), versus about $19n + 10$ (average) for the code of Figure 14–6 (based on compiled code; includes prologs and epilogs, which are essentially nil). Thus, the parallel prefix method is faster for $n \geq 3$.

```
void hil_xy_from_s(unsigned s, int n, unsigned *xp,
                                      unsigned *yp) {
    unsigned comp, swap, cs, t, sr;

    s = s | (0x55555555 << 2*n);   // Pad s on left with 01
    sr = (s >> 1) & 0x55555555;    // (no change) groups.
    cs = ((s & 0x55555555) + sr)   // Compute complement &
        ^ 0x55555555;              // swap info in two-bit
                                   // groups.
    // Parallel prefix xor op to propagate both complement
    // and swap info together from left to right (there is
    // no step "cs ^= cs >> 1", so in effect it computes
    // two independent parallel prefix operations on two
    // interleaved sets of sixteen bits).

    cs = cs ^ (cs >> 2);
    cs = cs ^ (cs >> 4);
    cs = cs ^ (cs >> 8);
    cs = cs ^ (cs >> 16);
    swap = cs & 0x55555555;        // Separate the swap and
    comp = (cs >> 1) & 0x55555555; // complement bits.

    t = (s & swap) ^ comp;         // Calculate x and y in
    s = s ^ sr ^ t ^ (t << 1);     // the odd & even bit
                                   // positions, resp.
    s = s & ((1 << 2*n) - 1);      // Clear out any junk
                                   // on the left (unpad).

    // Now "unshuffle" to separate the x and y bits.

    t = (s ^ (s >> 1)) & 0x22222222; s = s ^ t ^ (t << 1);
    t = (s ^ (s >> 2)) & 0x0C0C0C0C; s = s ^ t ^ (t << 2);
    t = (s ^ (s >> 4)) & 0x00F000F0; s = s ^ t ^ (t << 4);
    t = (s ^ (s >> 8)) & 0x0000FF00; s = s ^ t ^ (t << 8);

    *xp = s >> 16;                 // Assign the two halves
    *yp = s & 0xFFFF;              // of t to x and y.
}
```

FIGURE 14–8. Parallel prefix method for computing (x, y) from s.

14–3 Distance from Coordinates on the Hilbert Curve

Given the coordinates of a point on the Hilbert curve, the distance from the origin to the point can be calculated by means of a state transition table similar to Table 14–2. Table 14–5 is such a table.

Its interpretation is similar to that of the previous section. First, x and y should be padded with leading zeros so that they are of length n bits, where n is the order of the Hilbert curve. Second, the bits of x and y are scanned from left to right, and s is built up from left to right.

A C program implementing these steps is shown in Figure 14–9.

[L&S] give an algorithm for computing s from (x, y) that is similar to their algorithm for going in the other direction (Table 14–3). It is a left-to-right algorithm, shown in Table 14–6 and Figure 14–10.

TABLE 14–5. STATE TRANSITION TABLE FOR COMPUTING s FROM (X, Y)

If the current state is	and the next (to right) two bits of (x, y) are	then append to s	and enter state
A	(0, 0)	00	B
A	(0, 1)	01	A
A	(1, 0)	11	D
A	(1, 1)	10	A
B	(0, 0)	00	A
B	(0, 1)	11	C
B	(1, 0)	01	B
B	(1, 1)	10	B
C	(0, 0)	10	C
C	(0, 1)	11	B
C	(1, 0)	01	C
C	(1, 1)	00	D
D	(0, 0)	10	D
D	(0, 1)	01	D
D	(1, 0)	11	A
D	(1, 1)	00	C

```
unsigned hil_s_from_xy(unsigned x, unsigned y, int n) {

    int i;
    unsigned state, s, row;

    state = 0;                              // Initialize.
    s = 0;

    for (i = n - 1; i >= 0; i--) {
        row = 4*state | 2*((x >> i) & 1) | (y >> i) & 1;
        s = (s << 2) | (0x361E9CB4 >> 2*row) & 3;
        state = (0x8FE65831 >> 2*row) & 3;
    }
    return s;
}
```

FIGURE 14–9. Program for computing s from (x, y).

TABLE 14–6. LAM AND SHAPIRO METHOD FOR COMPUTING s FROM (X, Y)

If the next (to right) two bits of (x, y) are	then	and append to s
$(0, 0)$	Swap x and y	00
$(0, 1)$	No change	01
$(1, 0)$	Swap and complement x and y	11
$(1, 1)$	No change	10

```
unsigned hil_s_from_xy(unsigned x, unsigned y, int n) {

   int i, xi, yi;
   unsigned s, temp;

   s = 0;                          // Initialize.
   for (i = n - 1; i >= 0; i--) {
      xi = (x >> i) & 1;           // Get bit i of x.
      yi = (y >> i) & 1;           // Get bit i of y.

      if (yi == 0) {
         temp = x;                 // Swap x and y and,
         x = y^(-xi);              // if xi = 1,
         y = temp^(-xi);           // complement them.
      }
      s = 4*s + 2*xi + (xi^yi);    // Append two bits to s.
   }
   return s;
}
```

FIGURE 14–10. Lam and Shapiro method for computing s from (x, y).

14–4 Incrementing the Coordinates on the Hilbert Curve

Given the (x, y) coordinates of a point on the order n Hilbert curve, how can one find the coordinates of the next point? One way is to convert (x, y) to s, add 1 to s, and then convert the new value of s back to (x, y), using algorithms given above.

A slightly (but not dramatically) better way is based on the fact that as one moves along the Hilbert curve, at each step either x or y, but not both, is either incremented or decremented (by 1). The algorithm to be described scans the coordinate numbers from left to right to determine the type of U-curve that the rightmost two bits are on. Then, based on the U-curve and the value of the rightmost two bits, it increments or decrements either x or y.

That's basically it, but there is a complication when the path is at the end of a U-curve (which happens once every four steps). At this point, the direction to take is determined by the *previous* bits of x and y and by the higher order U-curve with

which these bits are associated. If that point is also at the end of its U-curve, then
the previous bits and the U-curve there determine the direction to take, and so on.

Table 14–7 describes this algorithm. In this table, the A, B, C, and D denote
the U-curves as shown in Table 14–1 on page 246. To use the table, first pad x and
y with leading zeros so they are n bits long, where n is the order of the Hilbert
curve. Start in state A and scan the bits of x and y from left to right. The first row
of Table 14–7 means that if the current state is A and the currently scanned bits
are $(0, 0)$, then set a variable to indicate to increment y, and enter state B. The
other rows are interpreted similarly, with a suffix minus sign indicating to decrement the associated coordinate. A dash in the third column means do not alter the
variable that keeps track of the coordinate changes.

After scanning the last (rightmost) bits of x and y, increment or decrement the
appropriate coordinate as indicated by the final value of the variable.

A C program implementing these steps is shown in Figure 14–11. Variable
dx is initialized in such a way that if invoked many times, the algorithm cycles
around, generating the same Hilbert curve over and over again. (However, the step
that connects one cycle to the next is not a unit step.)

TABLE 14–7. TAKING ONE STEP ON THE HILBERT CURVE

If the current state is	and the next (to right) two bits of (x, y) are	then prepare to inc/dec	and enter state
A	$(0, 0)$	$y+$	B
A	$(0, 1)$	$x+$	A
A	$(1, 0)$	—	D
A	$(1, 1)$	$y-$	A
B	$(0, 0)$	$x+$	A
B	$(0, 1)$	—	C
B	$(1, 0)$	$y+$	B
B	$(1, 1)$	$x-$	B
C	$(0, 0)$	$y+$	C
C	$(0, 1)$	—	B
C	$(1, 0)$	$x-$	C
C	$(1, 1)$	$y-$	D
D	$(0, 0)$	$x+$	D
D	$(0, 1)$	$y-$	D
D	$(1, 0)$	—	A
D	$(1, 1)$	$x-$	C

```
void hil_inc_xy(unsigned *xp, unsigned *yp, int n) {

   int i;
   unsigned x, y, state, dx, dy, row, dochange;

   x = *xp;
   y = *yp;
   state = 0;                    // Initialize.
   dx = -((1 << n) - 1);         // Init. -(2**n - 1).
   dy = 0;

   for (i = n-1; i >= 0; i--) {           // Do n times.
      row = 4*state | 2*((x >> i) & 1) | (y >> i) & 1;
      dochange = (0xBDDB >> row) & 1;
      if (dochange) {
          dx = ((0x16451659 >> 2*row) & 3) - 1;
          dy = ((0x51166516 >> 2*row) & 3) - 1;
      }
      state = (0x8FE65831 >> 2*row) & 3;
   }
   *xp = *xp + dx;
   *yp = *yp + dy;
}
```

FIGURE 14–11. Program for taking one step on the Hilbert curve.

Table 14–7 can readily be implemented in logic, as shown in Figure 14–12. In this figure, the variables have the following meanings:

x_i: Bit i of input x.
y_i: Bit i of input y.
X, Y: x_i and y_i swapped and complemented, according to S_{i+1} and C_{i+1}.
I: If 1, increment; if 0, decrement (by 1).
W: If 1, increment or decrement x; if 0, increment or decrement y.
S: If 1, swap x_i and y_i.
C: If 1, complement x_i and y_i.

S and C together identify the "state" of Table 14–7, with $(C, S) = (0,0)$, $(0,1)$, $(1,0)$, and $(1,1)$ denoting states A, B, C, and D, respectively. The output signals are I_0 and W_0, which tell, respectively, whether to increment or decrement, and which variable to change. (In addition to the logic shown, an incrementer/decrementer circuit is required, with MUX's to route either x or y to the incrementer/decrementer, and a circuit to route the altered value back to the register that holds x or y. Alternatively, two incrementer/decrementer circuits could be used.)

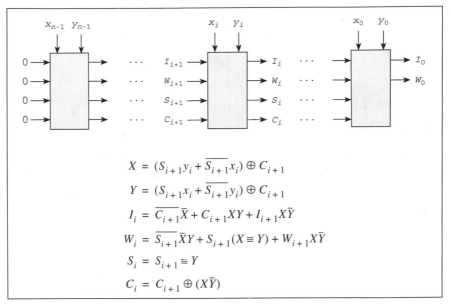

$$X = (S_{i+1} y_i + \overline{S_{i+1}} x_i) \oplus C_{i+1}$$

$$Y = (S_{i+1} x_i + \overline{S_{i+1}} y_i) \oplus C_{i+1}$$

$$I_i = \overline{C_{i+1}} \overline{X} + C_{i+1} XY + I_{i+1} X \overline{Y}$$

$$W_i = \overline{S_{i+1}} \overline{X} Y + S_{i+1}(X \equiv Y) + W_{i+1} X \overline{Y}$$

$$S_i = S_{i+1} \equiv Y$$

$$C_i = C_{i+1} \oplus (X \overline{Y})$$

FIGURE 14–12.   Logic circuit for incrementing (x, y) by one step along the Hilbert curve.

14–5   Non-recursive Generating Algorithms

The algorithms of Tables 14–2 and 14–7 provide two non-recursive algorithms for generating the Hilbert curve of any order. Either algorithm can be implemented in hardware without great difficulty. Hardware based on Table 14–2 includes a register holding s, which it increments for each step, and then converts to (x, y) coordinates. Hardware based on Table 14–7 would not have to include a register for s, but the algorithm is more complicated.

14–6   Other Space-Filling Curves

As was mentioned, Peano was first, in 1890, to discover a space-filling curve. The many variations discovered since then are often called "Peano curves." One interesting variation of Hilbert's curve was discovered by Eliakim Hastings Moore in 1900. It is "cyclic" in the sense that the end point is one step away from the starting point. The Peano curve of order 3, and the Moore curve of order 4, are shown in Figure 14–13. Moore's curve has an irregularity in that the order 1 curve is up-right-down ($\sqcap\!\!\downarrow$), but this shape does not appear in the higher-order curves. Except for this minor exception, the algorithms for dealing with Moore's curve are very similar to those for the Hilbert curve.

    The Hilbert curve has been generalized to arbitrary rectangles and to three and higher dimensions. The basic building block for a 3-dimensional Hilbert

FIGURE 14–13. Peano (left) and Moore (right) curves.

curve is shown below. It hits all eight points of a 2×2×2 cube. These and many other space-filling curves are discussed in [Sagan].

14–7 Applications

Space-filling curves have applications in image processing: compression, halftoning, and textural analysis [L&S]. Another application is to improve computer performance in ray tracing, a graphics-rendering technique. Conventionally, a scene is scanned by projecting rays across the scene in ordinary raster scan line order (left to right across the screen, and then top to bottom). When a ray hits an object in the simulated scene's database, the color and other properties of the object at that point are determined and the results are used to illuminate the pixel through which the ray was sent. (This is an oversimplification, but it's adequate for our purposes.) One problem is that the database is often large and the data on each object must be paged in and cast out as various objects are hit by the scanning ray. When the ray scans across a line, it often hits many objects that were hit in the previous scan, requiring them to be paged in again. Paging operations would be reduced if the scanning had some kind of locality property. For example, it might be helpful to scan a quadrant of the screen completely before going on to another quadrant.

The Hilbert curve seems to have the locality property we are seeking. It scans a quadrant completely before scanning another, recursively, and also does not make a long jump when going from one quadrant to another.

Douglas Voorhies [Voor] has simulated what the paging behavior would likely be for the conventional uni-directional scan line traversal, the Peano curve, and the Hilbert curve. His method is to scatter circles of a given size randomly on the screen. A scan path hitting a circle represents touching a new object, and paging it in. But when a scan leaves a circle, it is presumed that the object's data remains in memory until the scan exits a circle of radius twice that of the "object" circle. Thus, if the scan leaves the object for just a short distance and then returns to it, it is assumed that no paging operation occurred. He repeats this experiment for many different sizes of circles, on a simulated 1024×1024 screen.

Assume that entering an object circle and leaving its surrounding circle represent one paging operation. Then, clearly the normal scan line causes D paging operations in covering a (not too big) circle of diameter D pixels, because each scan line that enters it leaves its outer circle. The interesting result of Voorhies's simulation is that for the Peano curve, the number of paging operations to scan a circle is about 2.7 and, perhaps surprisingly, is independent of the circle's diameter. For the Hilbert curve the figure is about 1.4, also independent of the circle's diameter. Thus, the experiment suggests that the Hilbert curve is superior to the Peano curve, and vastly superior to the normal scan line path, in reducing paging operations. (The result that the page count is independent of the circles' diameters is probably an artifact of the outer circle's being proportional in size to the object circle.)

CHAPTER 15

FLOATING-POINT

God created the integers,
all else is the work of man.

Leopold Kronecker

Operating on floating-point numbers with integer arithmetic and logical instructions is often a messy proposition. This is particularly true for the rules and formats of the *IEEE Standard for Binary Floating-Point Arithmetic*, IEEE Std. 754-1985, commonly known as "IEEE arithmetic." It has the NaN (not a number) and infinities, which are special cases for almost all operations. It has plus and minus zero, which must compare equal to one another. It has a fourth comparison result, "unordered." The most significant bit of the fraction is not explicitly present in "normal" numbers, but it is in "denormalized" or "subnormal" numbers. The fraction is in signed-true form and the exponent is in biased form, whereas integers are now almost universally in two's-complement form. There are of course reasons for all this, but it results in programs that are full of compares and branches, and that present a challenge to implement efficiently.

We assume the reader has some familiarity with the IEEE standard, and thus summarize it here only very briefly.

15–1 IEEE Format

We will restrict our attention to the single and double formats (32- and 64-bit) described in IEEE 754. The standard also describes "single extended" and "double extended" formats, but they are only loosely described because the details are implementation-dependent (e.g., the exponent width is unspecified in the standard). The single and double formats are shown below.

Single format		
s	e	f
1	8	23

Double format		
s	e	f
1	11	52

The sign bit s is encoded as 0 for plus, 1 for minus. The biased exponent e and fraction f are magnitudes with their most significant bits on the left. The floating-point value represented is encoded as shown on the next page.

261

Single format

e	f	value
0	0	± 0
0	$\neq 0$	$\pm 2^{-126}(0.f)$
1 to 254	–	$\pm 2^{e-127}(1.f)$
255	0	$\pm \infty$
255	$\neq 0$	NaN

Double format

e	f	value
0	0	± 0
0	$\neq 0$	$\pm 2^{-1022}(0.f)$
1 to 2046	–	$\pm 2^{e-1023}(1.f)$
2047	0	$\pm \infty$
2047	$\neq 0$	NaN

As an example, consider encoding the number π in single format. In binary [Knu1],

$$\pi \approx 11.0010\ 0100\ 0011\ 1111\ 0110\ 1010\ 1000\ 1000\ 1000\ 0101\ 1010\ 0011\ 0000\ 10\ldots.$$

This is in the range of the "normalized" numbers shown in the third row of the table above. The most significant 1 in π is dropped, as the leading 1 is not stored in the encoding of normalized numbers. The exponent $e - 127$ should be 1, to get the binary point in the right place, and hence $e = 128$. Thus, the representation is

```
0 10000000 10010010000111111011011
```

or, in hexadecimal,

```
40490FDB,
```

where we have rounded the fraction to the nearest representable number.

Numbers with $1 \leq e \leq 254$ are called "normalized numbers." These are in "normal" form, meaning that their most significant bit is not explicitly stored. Nonzero numbers with $e = 0$ are called "denormalized numbers," or simply "denorms." Their most significant bit *is* explicitly stored. This scheme is sometimes called "gradual underflow." Some extreme values in the various ranges of floating-point number are shown in Table 15–1. In this table "Max integer" means the largest integer such that all integers less than or equal to it, in absolute value, are representable exactly; the next integer is rounded.

For normalized numbers, one unit in the last position (ulp) has a relative value ranging from $1/2^{24}$ to $1/2^{23}$ (about 5.96×10^{-8} to 1.19×10^{-7}) for single format, and from $1/2^{53}$ to $1/2^{52}$ (about 1.11×10^{-16} to 2.22×10^{-16}) for double format. The maximum "relative error," for round to nearest mode, is half of those figures.

The range of integers that is represented exactly is from -2^{24} to $+2^{24}$ ($-16,777,216$ to $+16,777,216$) for single format, and from -2^{53} to $+2^{53}$

TABLE 15–1. EXTREME VALUES

Single Precision			
	Hex	**Exact Value**	**Approximate Value**
Smallest denorm	0000 0001	2^{-149}	1.401×10^{-45}
Largest denorm	007F FFFF	$2^{-126}(1 - 2^{-23})$	1.175×10^{-38}
Smallest normalized	0080 0000	2^{-126}	1.175×10^{-38}
1.0	3F80 0000	1	1
Max integer	4B80 0000	2^{24}	1.677×10^{7}
Largest normalized	7F7F FFFF	$2^{128}(1 - 2^{-24})$	3.403×10^{38}
∞	7F80 0000	∞	∞
Double Precision			
Smallest denorm	0...0001	2^{-1074}	4.941×10^{-324}
Largest denorm	000F...F	$2^{-1022}(1 - 2^{-52})$	2.225×10^{-308}
Smallest normalized	0010...0	2^{-1022}	2.225×10^{-308}
1.0	3FF0...0	1	1
Max integer	4340...0	2^{53}	9.007×10^{15}
Largest normalized	7FEF...F	$2^{1024}(1 - 2^{-53})$	1.798×10^{308}
∞	7FF0...0	∞	∞

($-9,007,199,254,740,992$ to $+9,007,199,254,740,992$) for double format. Of course, certain integers outside these ranges, such as larger powers of 2, can be represented exactly; the ranges cited are the maximal ranges for which *all* integers are represented exactly

One might want to change division by a constant to multiplication by the reciprocal. This can be done with complete (IEEE) accuracy only for numbers whose reciprocals are represented exactly. These are the powers of 2 from 2^{-127} to 2^{127} for single format, and from 2^{-1023} to 2^{1023} for double format. The numbers 2^{-127} and 2^{-1023} are denormalized numbers, which are best avoided on machines that implement operations on denormalized numbers inefficiently.

15–2 Comparing Floating-Point Numbers Using Integer Operations

One of the features of the IEEE encodings is that non-NAN values are properly ordered if treated as signed magnitude integers.

To program a floating-point comparison using integer operations, it is necessary that the "unordered" result not be needed. In IEEE 754, the unordered result occurs when one or both comparands are NaNs. The methods below treat NaNs as if they were numbers greater in magnitude than infinity.

The comparisons are also much simpler if -0.0 may be treated as strictly less than $+0.0$ (which is not in accordance with IEEE 754). Assuming this is acceptable, the comparisons may be done as shown below, where $\overset{f}{<}$, $\overset{f}{\leq}$, and $\overset{f}{=}$ denote floating-point comparisons, and the $\approx$ symbol is used as a reminder that these formulas do not treat ± 0.0 quite right.

$$a \overset{f}{=} b \approx (a = b)$$

$$a \overset{f}{<} b \approx (a \geq 0 \ \& \ a < b) \mid (a < 0 \ \& \ a \overset{u}{>} b)$$

$$a \overset{f}{\leq} b \approx (a \geq 0 \ \& \ a \leq b) \mid (a < 0 \ \& \ a \overset{u}{\geq} b)$$

If -0.0 must be treated as equal to $+0.0$, there does not seem to be any very slick way to do it, but the following formulas, which follow more or less obviously from the above, are possibilities.

$$a \overset{f}{=} b \equiv (a = b) \mid (-a = a \ \& \ -b = b)$$

$$\equiv (a = b) \mid ((a \mid b) = \text{0x80000000})$$

$$\equiv (a = b) \mid (((a \mid b) \ \& \ \text{0x7FFFFFFF}) = 0)$$

$$a \overset{f}{<} b \equiv ((a \geq 0 \ \& \ a < b) \mid (a < 0 \ \& \ a \overset{u}{>} b)) \ \& \ ((a \mid b) \neq \text{0x80000000})$$

$$a \overset{f}{\leq} b \equiv (a \geq 0 \ \& \ a \leq b) \mid (a < 0 \ \& \ a \overset{u}{\geq} b) \mid ((a \mid b) = \text{0x80000000})$$

In some applications, it might be more efficient to first transform the numbers in some way, and then do a floating-point comparison with a single fixed-point comparison instruction. For example, in sorting n numbers, the transformation would be done only once to each number, whereas a comparison must be done at least $\lceil n\log_2 n \rceil$ times (in the minimax sense).

Table 15–2 gives four such transformations. For those in the left column, -0.0 compares equal to $+0.0$, and for those in the right column, -0.0 compares less than $+0.0$. In all cases, the sense of the comparison is not altered by the transformation. Variable n is signed, t is unsigned, and c may be either signed or unsigned.

The last row shows branch-free code that can be implemented on our basic RISC in four instructions for the left column, and three for the right column (these four or three instructions must be executed for each comparand).

15–3 The Distribution of Leading Digits

When IBM introduced the System/360 computer in 1964, numerical analysts were horrified at the loss of precision of single-precision arithmetic. The previous IBM computer line, the 704 - 709 - 7090 family, had a 36-bit word. For single-precision floating-point, the format consisted of a 9-bit sign and exponent field, followed by

TABLE 15–2. PRECONDITIONING FLOATING-POINT NUMBERS FOR INTEGER COMPARISONS

$-0.0 = +0.0$ (IEEE)	$-0.0 < +0.0$ (non-IEEE)
| ```
if (n >= 0) n = n+0x80000000;
else n = -n;
Use unsigned comparison.
``` | ```
if (n >= 0) n = n+0x80000000;
else n = ~n;
Use unsigned comparison.
``` |
| ```
c = 0x7FFFFFFF;
if (n < 0) n = (n ^ c) + 1;
Use signed comparison.
``` | ```
c = 0x7FFFFFFF;
if (n < 0) n = n ^ c;
Use signed comparison.
``` |
| ```
c = 0x80000000;
if (n < 0) n = c - n;
Use signed comparison.
``` | ```
c = 0x7FFFFFFF;
if (n < 0) n = c - n;
Use signed comparison.
``` |
| ```
t = n >> 31;
n = (n ^ (t >> 1)) - t;
Use signed comparison.
``` | ```
t = (unsigned)(n>>30) >> 1;
n = n ^ t;
Use signed comparison.
``` |

a 27-bit fraction in binary. The most significant fraction bit was explicitly included (in "normal" numbers), so quantities were represented with a precision of 27 bits.

The S/360 has a 32-bit word. For single-precision, IBM chose to have an 8-bit sign and exponent field followed by a 24-bit fraction. This drop from 27 to 24 bits was bad enough, but it gets worse. To keep the exponent range large, a unit in the 7-bit exponent of the S/360 format represents a factor of 16. Thus, the fraction is in base 16, and this format came to be called "hexadecimal" floating-point. The leading digit can be any number from 1 to 15 (binary 0001 to 1111). Numbers with leading digit 1 have only 21 bits of precision (because of the three leading 0's), but they should constitute only 1/15 (6.7%) of all numbers.

No, it's worse than that! There was a flurry of activity to show, both analytically and empirically, that leading digits are *not* uniformly distributed. In hexadecimal floating-point, one would expect 25% of the numbers to have leading digit 1, and hence only 21 bits of precision.

Let us consider the distribution of leading digits in decimal. Suppose you have a large set of numbers with units, such as length, volume, mass, speed, and so on, expressed in "scientific" notation (e.g., 6.022×10^{23}). If the leading digit of a large number of such numbers has a well-defined distribution function, then it must be independent of the units—whether inches or centimeters, pounds or kilograms, and so on. Thus, if you multiply all the numbers in the set by any constant, the distribution of leading digits should be unchanged. For example, considering multiplying by 2, we conclude that the number of numbers with leading digit 1 (those from 1.0 to 1.999... times 10 to some power) must equal the number of numbers with leading digit 2 or 3 (those from 2.0 to 3.999... times 10 to some power), because it shouldn't matter if our unit of length is inches or half inches, or our unit of mass is kilograms or half kilograms, and so on.

Let $f(x)$, for $1 \le x < 10$, be the probability density function for the leading digits of the set of numbers with units. $f(x)$ has the property that

$$\int_a^b f(x)\,dx$$

is the proportion of numbers that have leading digits ranging from a to b. Referring to the figure below, for a small increment Δx in x, f must satisfy

$$f(1) \cdot \Delta x = f(x) \cdot x\Delta x$$

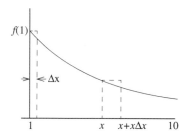

because $f(1) \cdot \Delta x$ is, approximately, the proportion of numbers ranging from 1 to $1 + \Delta x$ (ignoring a multiplier of a power of 10), and $f(x) \cdot x\Delta x$ is the approximate proportion of numbers ranging from x to $x + x\Delta x$. Because the latter set is the first set multiplied by x, their proportions must be equal. Thus, the probability density function is a simple inverse relationship,

$$f(x) = f(1)/x.$$

Because the area under the curve from $x = 1$ to $x = 10$ must be 1 (all numbers have leading digits from 1.000... to 9.999...), it is easily shown that

$$f(1) = 1/\ln 10.$$

The proportion of numbers with leading digits in the range a to b, with $1 \le a \le b < 10$, is

$$\int_a^b \frac{dx}{x \ln 10} = \left. \frac{\ln x}{\ln 10} \right|_a^b = \frac{\ln b/a}{\ln 10} = \log_{10}\frac{b}{a}.$$

Thus, in decimal, the proportion of numbers with leading digit 1 is $\log_{10}(2/1) \approx 0.30103$, and the proportion of numbers with leading digit 9 is $\log_{10}(10/9) \approx 0.0458$.

For base 16, the proportion of numbers with leading digits in the range a to b, with $1 \le a \le b < 16$, is similarly derived to be $\log_{16}(b/a)$. Hence the proportion of numbers with leading digit 1 is $\log_{16}(2/1) = 1/\log_2 16 = 0.25$.

15–4 Table of Miscellaneous Values

Table 15–3 shows the IEEE representation of miscellaneous values that may be of interest. The values that are not exact are rounded to the nearest representable value.

TABLE 15–3. MISCELLANEOUS VALUES

Decimal	Single Format (Hex)	Double Format (Hex)
$-\infty$	FF80 0000	FFF0 0000 0000 0000
-2.0	C000 0000	C000 0000 0000 0000
-1.0	BF80 0000	BFF0 0000 0000 0000
-0.5	BF00 0000	BFE0 0000 0000 0000
-0.0	8000 0000	8000 0000 0000 0000
$+0.0$	0000 0000	0000 0000 0000 0000
Smallest positive denorm	0000 0001	0000 0000 0000 0001
Largest denorm	007F FFFF	000F FFFF FFFF FFFF
Least positive normalized	0080 0000	0010 0000 0000 0000
$\pi/180$ (0.01745...)	3C8E FA35	3F91 DF46 A252 9D39
0.1	3DCC CCCD	3FB9 9999 9999 999A
$\log_{10} 2$ (0.3010...)	3E9A 209B	3FD3 4413 509F 79FF
$1/e$ (0.3678...)	3EBC 5AB2	3FD7 8B56 362C EF38
$1/\ln 10$ (0.4342...)	3EDE 5BD9	3FDB CB7B 1526 E50E
0.5	3F00 0000	3FE0 0000 0000 0000
$\ln 2$ (0.6931...)	3F31 7218	3FE6 2E42 FEFA 39EF
$1/\sqrt{2}$ (0.7071...)	3F35 04F3	3FE6 A09E 667F 3BCD
$1/\ln 3$ (0.9102...)	3F69 0570	3FED 20AE 03BC C153
1.0	3F80 0000	3FF0 0000 0000 0000
$\ln 3$ (1.0986...)	3F8C 9F54	3FF1 93EA 7AAD 030B
$\sqrt{2}$ (1.414...)	3FB5 04F3	3FF6 A09E 667F 3BCD
$1/\ln 2$ (1.442...)	3FB8 AA3B	3FF7 1547 652B 82FE
$\sqrt{3}$ (1.732...)	3FDD B3D7	3FFB B67A E858 4CAA
2.0	4000 0000	4000 0000 0000 0000

continues

TABLE 15–3. MISCELLANEOUS VALUES, *continued*

Decimal	Single Format (Hex)	Double Format (Hex)
ln 10 (2.302...)	4013 5D8E	4002 6BB1 BBB5 5516
e (2.718...)	402D F854	4005 BF0A 8B14 5769
3.0	4040 0000	4008 0000 0000 0000
π (3.141...)	4049 0FDB	4009 21FB 5444 2D18
$\sqrt{10}$ (3.162...)	404A 62C2	4009 4C58 3ADA 5B53
$\log_2 10$ (3.321...)	4054 9A78	400A 934F 0979 A371
4.0	4080 0000	4010 0000 0000 0000
5.0	40A0 0000	4014 0000 0000 0000
6.0	40C0 0000	4018 0000 0000 0000
2π (6.283...)	40C9 0FDB	4019 21FB 5444 2D18
7.0	40E0 0000	401C 0000 0000 0000
8.0	4100 0000	4020 0000 0000 0000
9.0	4110 0000	4022 0000 0000 0000
10.0	4120 0000	4024 0000 0000 0000
11.0	4130 0000	4026 0000 0000 0000
12.0	4140 0000	4028 0000 0000 0000
13.0	4150 0000	402A 0000 0000 0000
14.0	4160 0000	402C 0000 0000 0000
15.0	4170 0000	402E 0000 0000 0000
16.0	4180 0000	4030 0000 0000 0000
$180/\pi$ (57.295...)	4265 2EE1	404C A5DC 1A63 C1F8
$2^{23} - 1$	4AFF FFFE	415F FFFF C000 0000
2^{23}	4B00 0000	4160 0000 0000 0000
$2^{24} - 1$	4B7F FFFF	416F FFFF E000 0000
2^{24}	4B80 0000	4170 0000 0000 0000
$2^{31} - 1$	4F00 0000	41DF FFFF FFC0 0000
2^{31}	4F00 0000	41E0 0000 0000 0000
$2^{32} - 1$	4F80 0000	41EF FFFF FFE0 0000
2^{32}	4F80 0000	41F0 0000 0000 0000
2^{52}	5980 0000	4330 0000 0000 0000
2^{63}	5F00 0000	43E0 0000 0000 0000

TABLE 15–3. MISCELLANEOUS VALUES, *continued*

Decimal	Single Format (Hex)	Double Format (Hex)
2^{64}	5F80 0000	43F0 0000 0000 0000
Largest normalized	7F7F FFFF	7FEF FFFF FFFF FFFF
∞	7F80 0000	7FF0 0000 0000 0000
"Smallest" SNaN	7F80 0001	7FF0 0000 0000 0001
"Largest" SNaN	7FBF FFFF	7FF7 FFFF FFFF FFFF
"Smallest" QNaN	7FC0 0000	7FF8 0000 0000 0000
"Largest" QNaN	7FFF FFFF	7FFF FFFF FFFF FFFF

IEEE 754 does not specify how the signaling and quiet NaNs are distinguished. Table 15–3 uses the convention employed by PowerPC, the AMD 29050, the Intel x86 and I860, and the Fairchild Clipper: The most significant fraction bit is 0 for signaling and 1 for quiet NaN's. The Compaq Alpha, HP PA-RISC, and MIPS computers use the same bit to make the distinction, but in the opposite sense (0 = quiet, 1 = signaling).

CHAPTER 16

FORMULAS FOR PRIMES

16–1 Introduction

Like many young students, I once became fascinated with prime numbers, and tried to find a formula for them. I didn't know exactly what operations would be considered valid in a "formula," or exactly what function I was looking for—a formula for the nth prime in terms of n, or in terms of the previous prime(s), or a formula that produces primes but not all of them, and so on. Nevertheless, in spite of these ambiguities, I would like to discuss a little of what is known about this problem. We will see that (a) there *are* formulas for primes, and (b) none of them are very satisfying.

Much of this subject relates to the present work in that it deals with formulas similar to those of some of our programming tricks, albeit in the domain of real number arithmetic rather than "computer arithmetic." But let us first review a few highlights from the history of this subject.

In 1640, Fermat conjectured that the formula

$$F_n = 2^{2^n} + 1$$

always produces a prime, and numbers of this form have come to be called "Fermat numbers." It is true that F_n is prime for n ranging from 0 to 4, but Euler found in 1732 that

$$F_5 = 2^{2^5} + 1 = 641 \cdot 6700417.$$

(We have seen these factors before in connection with dividing by a constant on a 32-bit machine). Then, F. Landry showed in 1880 that

$$F_6 = 2^{2^6} + 1 = 274177 \cdot 67280421310721.$$

F_n is now known to be composite for many larger values of n, such as all n from 7 to 16 inclusive. For no value of $n > 4$ is it known to be prime [H&W]. So much for rash conjectures.[1]

---

1. However, this is the only conjecture of Fermat known to be wrong [Wells].

Incidentally, why would Fermat be led to the double exponential? He knew that if m has an odd factor other than 1, then $2^m + 1$ is composite. For if $m = ab$ with b odd and not equal to 1, then

$$2^{ab} + 1 = (2^a + 1)(2^{a(b-1)} - 2^{a(b-2)} + 2^{a(b-3)} - \ldots + 1).$$

Knowing this, he must have wondered about $2^m + 1$ with m not containing any odd factors (other than 1)—that is, $m = 2^n$. He tried a few values of n and found that $2^{2^n} + 1$ seemed to be prime.

Certainly everyone would agree that a polynomial qualifies as a "formula." One rather amazing polynomial was discovered by Leonhard Euler in 1772. He found that

$$f(n) = n^2 + n + 41$$

is prime-valued for every n from 0 to 39. His result can be extended. Because

$$f(-n) = n^2 - n + 41 = f(n - 1),$$

$f(-n)$ is prime-valued for every n from 1 to 40; that is, $f(n)$ is prime-valued for every n from -1 to -40. Therefore,

$$f(n - 40) = (n - 40)^2 + (n - 40) + 41 = n^2 - 79n + 1601$$

is prime-valued for every n from 0 to 79. (However, it is lacking in aesthetic appeal because it is nonmonotonic and it repeats; that is, for $n = 0, 1, \ldots, 79$, $n^2 - 79n + 1601 = 1601, 1523, 1447, \ldots, 43, 41, 41, 43, \ldots, 1447, 1523, 1601$.)

In spite of this success, it is now known that there is no polynomial $f(n)$ that produces a prime for every n (aside from constant polynomials such as $f(n) = 5$). In fact, any nontrivial "polynomial in exponentials" is composite infinitely often. More precisely, as stated in [H&W],

> THEOREM. *If* $f(n) = P(n, 2^n, 3^n, \ldots, k^n)$ *is a polynomial in its arguments, with integral coefficients, and* $f(n) \to \infty$ *when* $n \to \infty$, *then* $f(n)$ *is composite for an infinity of values of* n.

Thus, a formula such as $n^2 \cdot 2^n + 2n^3 + 2n + 5$ must produce an infinite number of composites. On the other hand, the theorem says nothing about formulas containing terms such as 2^{2^n}, n^n, and $n!$.

A formula for the nth prime in terms of n can be obtained by using the floor function and a magic number

$$a = 0.203005000700011000013\ldots.$$

The number a is, in decimal, the first prime written in the first place after the decimal point, the second prime written in the next two places, the third prime written in the next three places, and so on. There is always room for the nth prime, because $p_n < 10^n$. We will not prove this, except to point out that it is known that there is always a prime between n and $2n$ (for $n \geq 2$), and hence certainly at least one between n and $10n$, from which it follows that $p_n < 10^n$. The formula for the nth prime is

$$p_n = \left\lfloor 10^{\frac{n^2+n}{2}} a \right\rfloor - 10^n \left\lfloor 10^{\frac{n^2-n}{2}} a \right\rfloor,$$

where we have used the relation $1 + 2 + 3 + \ldots + n = (n^2 + n)/2$. For example,

$$p_3 = \lfloor 10^6 a \rfloor - 10^3 \lfloor 10^3 a \rfloor$$
$$= 203005 - 203000$$
$$= 5.$$

This is a pretty cheap trick, as it requires knowledge of the result to define a. The formula would be interesting if there were some way to define a independently of the primes, but no one knows of such a definition.

Obviously, this technique can be used to obtain a formula for many sequences, but it begs the question.

16–2 Willans's Formulas

C. P. Willans gives the following formula for the nth prime [Will]:

$$p_n = 1 + \sum_{m=1}^{2^n} \left\lfloor \sqrt[n]{\frac{n}{\sum_{x=1}^{m} \left\lfloor \cos^2 \pi \frac{(x-1)! + 1}{x} \right\rfloor}} \right\rfloor^{-1/n}.$$

The derivation starts from Wilson's theorem, which states that p is prime or 1 if and only if $(p-1)! \equiv -1 \pmod{p}$. Thus,

$$\frac{(x-1)! + 1}{x}$$

is an integer for x prime or $x = 1$ and is fractional for all composite x. Hence

$$F(x) = \left\lfloor \cos^2 \pi \frac{(x-1)! + 1}{x} \right\rfloor = \begin{cases} 1, & x \text{ prime or } 1, \\ 0, & x \text{ composite.} \end{cases} \qquad (1)$$

Thus, if $\pi(m)$ denotes[2] the number of primes $\leq m$,

$$\pi(m) = -1 + \sum_{x=1}^{m} F(x). \tag{2}$$

Observe that $\pi(p_n) = n$, and furthermore,

$$\pi(m) < n, \text{ for } m < p_n, \text{ and}$$
$$\pi(m) \geq n, \text{ for } m \geq p_n.$$

Therefore, the number of values of m from 1 to ∞ for which $\pi(m) < n$ is $p_n - 1$. That is,

$$p_n = 1 + \sum_{m=1}^{\infty} (\pi(m) < n), \tag{3}$$

where the summand is a "predicate expression" (0/1-valued).

Because we have a formula for $\pi(m)$, Equation (3) constitutes a formula for the nth prime as a function of n. But it has two features that might be considered unacceptable: an infinite summation and the use of a "predicate expression," which is not in standard mathematical usage.

It has been proved that for $n \geq 1$ there is at least one prime between n and $2n$. Therefore, the number of primes $\leq 2^n$ is at least n—that is, $\pi(2^n) \geq n$. Thus, the predicate $\pi(m) < n$ is 0 for $m \geq 2^n$, so the upper limit of the summation above can be replaced with 2^n.

Willans has a rather clever substitute for the predicate expression. Let

$$\mathrm{LT}(x, y) = \left\lfloor \sqrt[x]{\frac{y}{1+x}} \right\rfloor, \text{ for } x = 0, 1, 2, \ldots; \ y = 1, 2, \ldots.$$

Then, if $x < y$, $1 \leq y/(1+x) \leq y$, so $1 \leq \sqrt[x]{y/(1+x)} \leq \sqrt[x]{y} < 2$. Furthermore, if $x \geq y$, then $0 < y/(1+x) < 1$, so $0 \leq \sqrt[x]{y/(1+x)} < 1$. Applying the floor function, we have

$$\mathrm{LT}(x, y) = \begin{cases} 1, & \text{for } x < y, \\ 0, & \text{for } x \geq y, \end{cases}$$

That is, $\mathrm{LT}(x, y)$ is the predicate $x < y$ (for x and y in the given ranges).

---

2. Our apologies for the two uses of π in close proximity, but it's standard notation and shouldn't cause any difficulty.

Substituting, Equation (3) can be written

$$p_n = 1 + \sum_{m=1}^{2^n} LT(\pi(m), n)$$

$$= 1 + \sum_{m=1}^{2^n} \left\lfloor \sqrt[n]{\frac{n}{1 + \pi(m)}} \right\rfloor.$$

Further substituting Equation (2) for $\pi(m)$ in terms of $F(x)$, and Equation (1) for $F(x)$, gives the formula shown at the beginning of this section.

Second Formula

Willans then gives another formula:

$$p_n = \sum_{m=1}^{2^n} mF(m) \lfloor 2^{-|\pi(m) - n|} \rfloor.$$

Here, F and π are the functions used in his first formula. Thus, $mF(m) = m$ if m is prime or 1, and 0 otherwise. The third factor in the summand is the predicate $\pi(m) = n$. The summand is 0 except for one term, which is the nth prime. For example,

$$p_4 = 1 \cdot 1 \cdot 0 + 2 \cdot 1 \cdot 0 + 3 \cdot 1 \cdot 0 + 4 \cdot 0 \cdot 0 + 5 \cdot 1 \cdot 0 + 6 \cdot 0 \cdot 0 + 7 \cdot 1 \cdot 1$$
$$+ 8 \cdot 0 \cdot 1 + 9 \cdot 0 \cdot 1 + 10 \cdot 0 \cdot 1 + 11 \cdot 1 \cdot 0 + \ldots + 16 \cdot 0 \cdot 0$$
$$= 7.$$

Third Formula

Willans goes on to present another formula for the nth prime that does not use any "nonanalytic"[3] functions such as floor and absolute value. He starts by noting that for $x = 2, 3, \ldots$, the function

$$\frac{((x-1)!)^2}{x} = \begin{cases} \text{an integer} + \dfrac{1}{x} & \text{when } x \text{ is prime,} \\ \text{an integer, when } x \text{ is composite or 1.} \end{cases}$$

---

3. This is my terminology, not Willans's.

The first part follows from

$$\frac{((x-1)!)^2}{x} = \frac{((x-1)!+1)\cdot((x-1)!-1)}{x} + \frac{1}{x}$$

and x divides $(x-1)!+1$, by Wilson's theorem. Thus, the predicate "x is prime," for $x \geq 2$, is given by

$$H(x) = \frac{\sin^2 \pi \dfrac{((x-1)!)^2}{x}}{\sin^2 \dfrac{\pi}{x}}.$$

From this it follows that

$$\pi(m) = \sum_{x=2}^{m} H(x), \text{ for } m = 2, 3, \dots.$$

This cannot be converted to a formula for p_n by the methods used in the first two formulas, because they use the floor function. Instead, Willans suggests the following formula[4] for the predicate $x < y$, for $x, y \geq 1$:

$$LT(x, y) = \sin\left(\frac{\pi}{2} \cdot 2^e\right), \text{ where}$$

$$e = \prod_{i=0}^{y-1} (x - i).$$

Thus, if $x < y$, $e = x(x-1)\dots(0)(-1)\dots(x-(y-1)) = 0$, so that $LT(x, y) = \sin(\pi/2) = 1$. If $x \geq y$, the product does not include 0, so $e \geq 1$, so that $LT(x, y) = \sin((\pi/2) \cdot (\text{an even number})) = 0$.

Finally, as in the first of Willans's formulas,

$$p_n = 2 + \sum_{m=2}^{2^n} LT(\pi(m), n).$$

---

4. We have slightly simplified his formula.

Written out in full, this is the rather formidable

$$p_n = 2 + \sum_{m=2}^{2^n} \sin\left(\frac{\pi}{2} \cdot 2^{\left(\prod_{i=0}^{n-1}\sum_{x=2}^{m}\frac{\sin^2\pi\frac{((x-1)!)^2}{x}}{\sin^2\frac{\pi}{x}} - i\right)}\right).$$

Fourth Formula

Willans then gives a formula for p_{n+1} in terms of p_n:

$$p_{n+1} = 1 + p_n + \sum_{i=1}^{2p_n}\prod_{j=1}^{i} f(p_n + j),$$

where $f(x)$ is the predicate "x is composite," for $x \geq 2$; that is,

$$f(x) = \left\lfloor \cos^2\pi\frac{((x-1)!)^2}{x} \right\rfloor.$$

Alternatively, one could use $f(x) = 1 - H(x)$, to keep the formula free of floor functions.

As an example of this formula, let $p_n = 7$. Then,

$$
\begin{aligned}
p_{n+1} &= 1 + 7 + f(8) + f(8)f(9) + f(8)f(9)f(10) \\
&\quad + f(8)f(9)f(10)f(11) + \ldots + f(8)f(9)\ldots f(14) \\
&= 1 + 7 + 1 + 1{\cdot}1 + 1{\cdot}1{\cdot}1 + 1{\cdot}1{\cdot}1{\cdot}0 + \ldots + 1{\cdot}1{\cdot}1\,0{\cdot}1{\cdot}0{\cdot}1 \\
&= 11.
\end{aligned}
$$

16–3 Wormell's Formula

C. P. Wormell [Wor] improves on Willans's formulas by avoiding both trigonometric functions and the floor function. Wormell's formula can in principle be evaluated by a simple computer program that uses only integer arithmetic. The derivation does not use Wilson's theorem. Wormell starts with, for $x \geq 2$,

$$B(x) = \prod_{a=2}^{x}\prod_{b=2}^{x}(x - ab)^2 = \begin{cases} \text{a positive integer, if } x \text{ is prime,} \\ 0, \text{ if } x \text{ is composite.} \end{cases}$$

Thus, the number of primes $\leq m$ is given by

$$\pi(m) = \sum_{x=2}^{m} \frac{1 + (-1)^{2^{B(x)}}}{2}$$

because the summand is the predicate "x is prime."

Observe that, for $n \geq 1$, $a \geq 0$,

$$\prod_{r=1}^{n} (1 - r + a)^2 = \begin{cases} 0, \text{ when } a < n, \\ \text{a positive integer, when } a \geq n. \end{cases}$$

Repeating a trick above, the predicate $a < n$ is

$$(a < n) = \frac{1 - (-1)^{2^{\prod_{r=1}^{n}(1-r+a)^2}}}{2}.$$

Because

$$p_n = 2 + \sum_{m=2}^{2^n} (\pi(m) < n),$$

we have, upon factoring constants out of summations,

$$p_n = \frac{3}{2} + 2^{n-1} - \frac{1}{2} \sum_{m=2}^{2^n} (-1)^2 \left(\prod_{r=1}^{n} \left| 1 - r + \frac{(m-1)}{2} + \frac{1}{2} \sum_{x=2}^{m} (-1)^{2^{\prod_{a=2}^{x} \prod_{b=2}^{x} (x-ab)^2}} \right| \right)^2.$$

As promised, Wormell's formula does not use trigonometric functions. However, as he points out, if the powers of -1 were expanded using $(-1)^n = \cos \pi n$, they would reappear.

16–4 Formulas for Other Difficult Functions

Let us have a closer look at what Willans and Wormell have done. We postulate the rules below as defining what we mean by the class of functions that can be represented by "formulas," which we will call "formula functions." Here, $\bar{x}$ is

shorthand for $x_1, x_2, ..., x_n$ for any $n \geq 1$. The domain of values is the integers
... $-2, -1, 0, 1, 2, ...$.

1. The constants ... $-1, 0, 1, ...$ are formula functions.

2. The projection functions $f(\bar{x}) = x_i$, for $1 \leq i \leq n$, are formula functions.

3. The expressions $x + y$, $x - y$, and xy are formula functions, if x and y are.

4. The class of formula functions is closed under composition (substitution).
    That is, $f(g_1(\bar{x}), g_2(\bar{x}), ..., g_m(\bar{x}))$ is a formula function if f and g_i are, for
    $i = 1, ..., m$.

5. Bounded sums and products, written

$$\sum_{i=a(\bar{x})}^{b(\bar{x})}{}' f(i, \bar{x}) \qquad \prod_{i=a(\bar{x})}^{b(\bar{x})}{}' f(i, \bar{x}),$$

are formula functions, if a, b, and f are, and $a(\bar{x}) \leq b(\bar{x})$.

Sums and products are required to be bounded to preserve the computational
character of formulas; that is, formulas can be evaluated by plugging in values for
the arguments and carrying out a finite number of calculations. The reason for the
prime on the Σ and Π is explained later in this chapter.

When forming new formula functions using composition, we supply paren-
theses when necessary according to well-established conventions.

Notice that division is not included in the list above; that's too complicated to
be uncritically accepted as a "formula function." Even so, the above list is not
minimal. It might be fun to find a minimal starting point, but we won't dwell on
that here.

This definition of "formula function" is close to the definition of "elementary
function" given in [Cut]. However, the domain of values used in [Cut] is the nonnegative integers (as is usual in recursive function theory). Also, [Cut] requires the
bounds on the iterated sum and product to be 0 and $x - 1$ (where x is a variable),
and allows the range to be vacuous (in which case the sum is defined as 0 and the
product is defined as 1).

In what follows, we show that the class of formula functions is quite extensive,
including most of the functions ordinarily encountered in mathematics. But it
doesn't include every function that is easy to define and has an elementary character.

Our development is slightly encumbered, compared to similar developments
in recursive function theory, because here variables can take on negative values.
However, the possibility of a value's being negative can often be accommodated
by simply squaring some expression that would otherwise appear in the first
power. Our insistence that iterated sums and products not be vacuous is another
slight encumbrance.

Here, a "predicate" is simply a 0/1-valued function, whereas in recursive function theory a predicate is a true/false-valued function, and every predicate has an associated "characteristic function" that is 0/1-valued. We associate 1 with true and 0 with false, as is universally done in programming languages and in computers (in what their *and* and *or* instructions do); in logic and recursive function theory, the association is often the opposite.

The following are formula functions:

1. $a^2 = aa$, $a^3 = aaa$, and so on.

2. The predicate $a = b$:

$$(a = b) = \prod_{j=0}^{(a-b)^2}{}'(1 - j).$$

3. $(a \neq b) = 1 - (a = b)$.

4. The predicate $a \geq b$:

$$(a \geq b) = \sum_{i=0}^{(a-b)^2}{}'((a - b) = i)$$
$$= \sum_{i=0}^{(a-b)^2}{}' \prod_{j=0}^{((a-b)-i)^2}{}'(1 - j).$$

We can now explain why we do not use the convention that a vacuous iterated sum/product has the value 0/1. If we did, we would have such shams as

$$(a = b) = \sum_{i=0}^{-(a-b)^2} 1 \qquad \text{and} \qquad (a \geq b) = \prod_{i=a}^{b-1} 0.$$

The comparison predicates are key to everything that follows, and we don't wish to have them based on anything quite that artificial.

5. $(a > b) = (a \geq b + 1)$.

6. $(a \leq b) = (b \geq a)$.

7. $(a < b) = (b > a)$.

8. $|a| = (2(a \geq 0) - 1)a$.

9. $\max(a, b) = (a \geq b)(a - b) + b$.

10. $\min(a, b) = (a \geq b)(b - a) + a$.

Now we can fix the iterated sums and products so that they give the conventional and useful result when the range is vacuous.

11. $\displaystyle\sum_{i=a(\bar{x})}^{b(\bar{x})} f(i, \bar{x}) = (b(\bar{x}) \geq a(\bar{x})) \sum_{i=a(\bar{x})}^{\max(a(\bar{x}),\, b(\bar{x}))} {}' f(i, \bar{x})$.

12. $\displaystyle\prod_{i=a(\bar{x})}^{b(\bar{x})} f(i, \bar{x}) = 1 + (b(\bar{x}) \geq a(\bar{x}))(-1 + \prod_{i=a(\bar{x})}^{\max(a(\bar{x}),\, b(\bar{x}))} {}' f(i, \bar{x}))$.

From now on we will use Σ and Π without the prime. All functions thus defined are total (defined for all values of the arguments).

13. $\displaystyle n! = \prod_{i=1}^{n} i$.

This gives $n! = 1$ for $n \leq 0$.

In what follows, P and Q denote predicates.

14. $\neg P(\bar{x}) = 1 - P(\bar{x})$.

15. $P(\bar{x}) \mathbin{\&} Q(\bar{x}) = P(\bar{x})Q(\bar{x})$.

16. $P(\bar{x}) \mathbin{|} Q(\bar{x}) = 1 - (1 - P(\bar{x}))(1 - Q(\bar{x}))$.

17. $P(\bar{x}) \oplus Q(\bar{x}) = (P(\bar{x}) - Q(\bar{x}))^2$.

18. if $P(\bar{x})$ then $f(\bar{y})$ else $g(\bar{z}) = P(\bar{x})f(\bar{y}) + (1 - P(\bar{x}))g(\bar{z})$.

19. $\displaystyle a^n = $ if $n \geq 0$ then $\prod_{i=1}^{n} a$ else 0.

This gives, arbitrarily and perhaps incorrectly for a few cases, the result 0 for $n < 0$, and the result 1 for 0^0.

20. $\displaystyle (m \leq \forall x \leq n)P(x, \bar{y}) = \prod_{x=m}^{n} P(x, \bar{y})$.

21. $\displaystyle (m \leq \exists x \leq n)P(x, \bar{y}) = 1 - \prod_{x=m}^{n} (1 - P(x, \bar{y}))$.

$\forall$ is vacuously true, $\exists$ is vacuously false.

22. $\displaystyle (m \leq \min x \leq n)P(x, \bar{y}) = m + \sum_{i=m}^{n} \prod_{j=m}^{i} (1 - P(j, \bar{y}))$.

The value of this expression is the least x in the range m to n such that the predicate is true, or m if the range is vacuous, or $n + 1$ if the predicate is false throughout the (nonvacuous) range. The operation is called "bounded minimalization" and it is a very powerful tool for developing new formula functions. It is a sort of functional inverse, as illustrated by the next formula. That minimalization can be done by a sum of products is due to Goodstein [Good].

23. $\lfloor \sqrt{n} \rfloor = (0 \le \min k \le |n|)((k+1)^2 > n)$.

This is the "integer square root" function, which we define to be 0 for $n < 0$, just to make it a total function.

24. $d|n = (-|n| \le \exists q \le |n|)(n = qd)$.

This is the "d divides n" predicate, according to which $0|0$ but $\neg(0|n)$ for $n \ne 0$.

25. $n \div d = $ if $n \ge 0$ then $(-n \le \min q \le n)(0 \le \exists r \le |d| - 1)(n = qd + r)$

else $(n \le \min q \le -n)(-|d| + 1 \le \exists r \le 0)(n = qd + r)$.

This is the conventional truncating form of integer division. For $d = 0$ it gives a result of $|n| + 1$, arbitrarily.

26. $\text{rem}(n, d) = n - (n \div d)d$.

This is the conventional remainder function. If $\text{rem}(n, d)$ is nonzero, it has the sign of the numerator n. If $d = 0$, the remainder is n.

27. $\text{isprime}(n) = n \ge 2 \ \& \ \neg(2 \le \exists d \le |n| - 1)(d|n)$.

28. $\pi(n) = \sum_{i=1}^{n} \text{isprime}(i)$.

(Number of primes $\le n$.)

29. $p_n = (1 \le \min k \le 2^n)(\pi(k) = n)$.

30. $\text{exponent}(p, n) = (0 \le \min x \le |n|)\neg(p^{x+1}|n)$.

This is the exponent of a given prime factor p of n, for $n \ge 1$.

31. For $n \ge 0$:

$$2^n = \prod_{i=1}^{n} 2, \qquad 2^{2^n} = \prod_{i=1}^{2^n} 2, \qquad 2^{2^{2^n}} = \prod_{i=1}^{2^{2^n}} 2, \text{ etc.}$$

32. The nth digit after the decimal point in the decimal expansion of $\sqrt{2}$:
$\text{rem}(\lfloor \sqrt{2} \cdot 10^{2n} \rfloor, 10)$.

Thus, the class of formula functions is quite large. It is limited, though, by the following theorem (at least):

THEOREM. *If f is a formula function, then there is a constant k such that*

$$f(\bar{x}) \le 2^{2^{\cdot^{\cdot^{2^{\max(|x_1|, \ldots, |x_n|)}}}}}$$

where there are k 2's.

This can be proved by showing that each application of one of the rules 1–5 (on page 279) preserves the theorem. For example, if $f(\bar{x}) = c$ (rule 1), then for some h,

$$f(\bar{x}) \leq 2^{2^{\cdot\cdot2}}\}h,$$

where there are h 2's. Therefore,

$$f(\bar{x}) \leq 2^{2^{\cdot\cdot2^{\max(|x_1|,\ \dots,\ |x_n|)}}}\}h + 2,$$

because $\max(|x_1|, \dots, |x_n|) \geq 0$.

For $f(\bar{x}) = x_i$ (rule 2), $f(\bar{x}) \leq \max(|x_1|, \dots, |x_n|)$, so the theorem holds with $k = 0$.

For rule 3, let

$$f(\bar{x}) \leq 2^{2^{\cdot\cdot2^{\max(|x_1|,\ \dots,\ |x_n|)}}}\}k_1 \qquad \text{and} \qquad g(\bar{x}) \leq 2^{2^{\cdot\cdot2^{\max(|x_1|,\ \dots,\ |x_n|)}}}\}k_2.$$

Then, clearly

$$f(\bar{x}) \pm g(\bar{x}) \leq 2 \cdot 2^{2^{\cdot\cdot2^{\max(|x_1|,\ \dots,\ |x_n|)}}}\}\max(k_1, k_2)$$

$$\leq 2^{2^{\cdot\cdot2^{\max(|x_1|,\ \dots,\ |x_n|)}}}\}\max(k_1, k_2) + 1.$$

Similarly, it can be shown that the theorem holds for $f(x, y) = xy$.

The proofs that rules 4 and 5 preserve the theorem are a bit tedious but not difficult, and are omitted.

From the theorem, it follows that the function

$$f(x) = 2^{2^{\cdot\cdot2^x}}\}x \tag{4}$$

is not a formula function, because for sufficiently large x, Equation (4) exceeds the value of the same expression with any fixed number k of 2's.

For those interested in recursive function theory, we point out that Equation (4) is primitive recursive. Furthermore, it is easy to show directly from the definition of primitive recursion that formula functions are primitive recursive. Therefore, the class of formula functions is a proper subset of the primitive recursive functions. The interested reader is referred to [Cut].

In summary, this section shows that not only is there a formula in elementary functions for the nth prime, but also for a good many other functions encountered in mathematics. Furthermore, our "formula functions" are not based on trigonometric functions, the floor function, absolute value, powers of -1, or even division. The only sneaky maneuver is to use the fact that the product of a lot of numbers is 0 if any one of them is 0, which is used in the formula for the predicate $a = b$.

It is true, however, that once you see them, they are not interesting. The quest for "interesting" formulas for primes should go on. For example, [Rib] cites the amazing theorem of W. H. Mills (1947) that there exists a θ such that the expression

$$\left\lfloor \theta^{3^n} \right\rfloor$$

is prime-valued for all $n \geq 1$. Actually, there are an infinite number of such values (e.g., 1.3063778838+ and 1.4537508625483+). Furthermore, there is nothing special about the "3"; the theorem is true if the 3 is replaced with any integer ≥ 3 (for different values of θ). Better yet, the 3 can be replaced with 2 if it is true that there is always a prime between n^2 and $(n + 1)^2$, which is almost certainly true, but has never been proved. And furthermore, ... well, the interested reader is referred to [Rib] and to [Dud] for more fascinating formulas of this type.

ARITHMETIC TABLES FOR A 4-BIT MACHINE

In the tables in Appendix A, underlining denotes signed overflow.

TABLE A–1. ADDITION

										-8	-7	-6	-5	-4	-3	-2	-1
		0	1	2	3	4	5	6	7	8	9	A	B	C	D	E	F
	0	0	1	2	3	4	5	6	7	8	9	A	B	C	D	E	F
	1	1	2	3	4	5	6	7	8	9	A	B	C	D	E	F	10
	2	2	3	4	5	6	7	8	9	A	B	C	D	E	F	10	11
	3	3	4	5	6	7	8	9	A	B	C	D	E	F	10	11	12
	4	4	5	6	7	8	9	A	B	C	D	E	F	10	11	12	13
	5	5	6	7	8	9	A	B	C	D	E	F	10	11	12	13	14
	6	6	7	8	9	A	B	C	D	E	F	10	11	12	13	14	15
	7	7	8	9	A	B	C	D	E	F	10	11	12	13	14	15	16
-8	8	8	9	A	B	C	D	E	F	10	11	12	13	14	15	16	17
-7	9	9	A	B	C	D	E	F	10	11	12	13	14	15	16	17	18
-6	A	A	B	C	D	E	F	10	11	12	13	14	15	16	17	18	19
-5	B	B	C	D	E	F	10	11	12	13	14	15	16	17	18	19	1A
-4	C	C	D	E	F	10	11	12	13	14	15	16	17	18	19	1A	1B
-3	D	D	E	F	10	11	12	13	14	15	16	17	18	19	1A	1B	1C
-2	E	E	F	10	11	12	13	14	15	16	17	18	19	1A	1B	1C	1D
-1	F	F	10	11	12	13	14	15	16	17	18	19	1A	1B	1C	1D	1E

The table for subtraction (Table A–2) assumes that the carry bit for $a - b$ is set as it would be for $a + \bar{b} + 1$, so that carry is equivalent to "not borrow."

TABLE A–2. SUBTRACTION (ROW – COLUMN)

										-8	-7	-6	-5	-4	-3	-2	-1
		0	1	2	3	4	5	6	7	8	9	A	B	C	D	E	F
	0	10	F	E	D	C	B	A	9	8	7	6	5	4	3	2	1
	1	11	10	F	E	D	C	B	A	9	8	7	6	5	4	3	2
	2	12	11	10	F	E	D	C	B	A	9	8	7	6	5	4	3
	3	13	12	11	10	F	E	D	C	B	A	9	8	7	6	5	4
	4	14	13	12	11	10	F	E	D	C	B	A	9	8	7	6	5
	5	15	14	13	12	11	10	F	E	D	C	B	A	9	8	7	6
	6	16	15	14	13	12	11	10	F	E	D	C	B	A	9	8	7
	7	17	16	15	14	13	12	11	10	F	E	D	C	B	A	9	8
-8	8	18	17	16	15	14	13	12	11	10	F	E	D	C	B	A	9
-7	9	19	18	17	16	15	14	13	12	11	10	F	E	D	C	B	A
-6	A	1A	19	18	17	16	15	14	13	12	11	10	F	E	D	C	B
-5	B	1B	1A	19	18	17	16	15	14	13	12	11	10	F	E	D	C
-4	C	1C	1B	1A	19	18	17	16	15	14	13	12	11	10	F	E	D
-3	D	1D	1C	1B	1A	19	18	17	16	15	14	13	12	11	10	F	E
-2	E	1E	1D	1C	1B	1A	19	18	17	16	15	14	13	12	11	10	F
-1	F	1F	1E	1D	1C	1B	1A	19	18	17	16	15	14	13	12	11	10

For multiplication (Tables A–3 and A–4), overflow means that the result cannot be expressed as a 4-bit quantity. For signed multiplication (Table A–3), this is equivalent to the first five bits of the 8-bit result not being all 1's or all 0's.

TABLE A–3. SIGNED MULTIPLICATION

		0	1	2	3	4	5	6	7	-8 8	-7 9	-6 A	-5 B	-4 C	-3 D	-2 E	-1 F
	0	0	0	0	0	0	0	0	0	0	0	0	0	0	0	0	0
	1	0	1	2	3	4	5	6	7	F8	F9	FA	FB	FC	FD	FE	FF
	2	0	2	4	6	8	A	C	E	F0	F2	F4	F6	F8	FA	FC	FE
	3	0	3	6	9	C	F	12	15	E8	EB	EE	F1	F4	F7	FA	FD
	4	0	4	8	C	10	14	18	1C	E0	E4	E8	EC	F0	F4	F8	FC
	5	0	5	A	F	14	19	1E	23	D8	DD	E2	E7	EC	F1	F6	FB
	6	0	6	C	12	18	1E	24	2A	D0	D6	DC	E2	E8	EE	F4	FA
	7	0	7	E	15	1C	23	2A	31	C8	CF	D6	DD	E4	EB	F2	F9
-8	8	0	F8	F0	E8	E0	D8	D0	C8	40	38	30	28	20	18	10	8
-7	9	0	F9	F2	EB	E4	DD	D6	CF	38	31	2A	23	1C	15	E	7
-6	A	0	FA	F4	EE	E8	E2	DC	D6	30	2A	24	1E	18	12	C	6
-5	B	0	FB	F6	F1	EC	E7	E2	DD	28	23	1E	19	14	F	A	5
-4	C	0	FC	F8	F4	F0	EC	E8	E4	20	1C	18	14	10	C	8	4
-3	D	0	FD	FA	F7	F4	F1	EE	EB	18	15	12	F	C	9	6	3
-2	E	0	FE	FC	FA	F8	F6	F4	F2	10	E	C	A	8	6	4	2
-1	F	0	FF	FE	FD	FC	FB	FA	F9	8	7	6	5	4	3	2	1

TABLE A–4. UNSIGNED MULTIPLICATION

	0	1	2	3	4	5	6	7	8	9	A	B	C	D	E	F
0	0	0	0	0	0	0	0	0	0	0	0	0	0	0	0	0
1	0	1	2	3	4	5	6	7	8	9	A	B	C	D	E	F
2	0	2	4	6	8	A	C	E	10	12	14	16	18	1A	1C	1E
3	0	3	6	9	C	F	12	15	18	1B	1E	21	24	27	2A	2D
4	0	4	8	C	10	14	18	1C	20	24	28	2C	30	34	38	3C
5	0	5	A	F	14	19	1E	23	28	2D	32	37	3C	41	46	4B
6	0	6	C	12	18	1E	24	2A	30	36	3C	42	48	4E	54	5A
7	0	7	E	15	1C	23	2A	31	38	3F	46	4D	54	5B	62	69
8	0	8	10	18	20	28	30	38	40	48	50	58	60	68	70	78
9	0	9	12	1B	24	2D	36	3F	48	51	5A	63	6C	75	7E	87
A	0	A	14	1E	28	32	3C	46	50	5A	64	6E	78	82	8C	96
B	0	B	16	21	2C	37	42	4D	58	63	6E	79	84	8F	9A	A5
C	0	C	18	24	30	3C	48	54	60	6C	78	84	90	9C	A8	B4
D	0	D	1A	27	34	41	4E	5B	68	75	82	8F	9C	A9	B6	C3
E	0	E	1C	2A	38	46	54	62	70	7E	8C	9A	A8	B6	C4	D2
F	0	F	1E	2D	3C	4B	5A	69	78	87	96	A5	B4	C3	D2	E1

Tables A–5 and A–6 are for conventional truncating division. Table A–5 shows a result of 8 with overflow for the case of the maximum negative number divided by –1, but on most machines the result in this case is undefined, or the operation is suppressed.

TABLE A–5. SIGNED SHORT DIVISION (ROW ÷ COLUMN)

									-8	-7	-6	-5	-4	-3	-2	-1
		0	1	2	3	4	5	6	7	8	9	A	B	C	D	E	F
	0	–	0	0	0	0	0	0	0	0	0	0	0	0	0	0	0
	1	–	1	0	0	0	0	0	0	0	0	0	0	0	0	0	F
	2	–	2	1	0	0	0	0	0	0	0	0	0	0	0	F	E
	3	–	3	1	1	0	0	0	0	0	0	0	0	0	F	F	D
	4	–	4	2	1	1	0	0	0	0	0	0	0	F	F	E	C
	5	–	5	2	1	1	1	0	0	0	0	0	F	F	F	E	B
	6	–	6	3	2	1	1	1	0	0	0	F	F	F	E	D	A
	7	–	7	3	2	1	1	1	1	0	F	F	F	F	E	D	9
-8	8	–	8	C	E	E	F	F	F	1	1	1	1	2	2	4	8
-7	9	–	9	D	E	F	F	F	F	0	1	1	1	1	2	3	7
-6	A	–	A	D	E	F	F	F	0	0	0	1	1	1	2	3	6
-5	B	–	B	E	F	F	F	0	0	0	0	0	1	1	1	2	5
-4	C	–	C	E	F	F	0	0	0	0	0	0	0	1	1	2	4
-3	D	–	D	F	F	0	0	0	0	0	0	0	0	0	1	1	3
-2	E	–	E	F	0	0	0	0	0	0	0	0	0	0	0	1	2
-1	F	–	F	0	0	0	0	0	0	0	0	0	0	0	0	0	1

TABLE A–6. UNSIGNED SHORT DIVISION (ROW ÷ COLUMN)

	0	1	2	3	4	5	6	7	8	9	A	B	C	D	E	F
0	–	0	0	0	0	0	0	0	0	0	0	0	0	0	0	0
1	–	1	0	0	0	0	0	0	0	0	0	0	0	0	0	0
2	–	2	1	0	0	0	0	0	0	0	0	0	0	0	0	0
3	–	3	1	1	0	0	0	0	0	0	0	0	0	0	0	0
4	–	4	2	1	1	0	0	0	0	0	0	0	0	0	0	0
5	–	5	2	1	1	1	0	0	0	0	0	0	0	0	0	0
6	–	6	3	2	1	1	1	0	0	0	0	0	0	0	0	0
7	–	7	3	2	1	1	1	1	0	0	0	0	0	0	0	0
8	–	8	4	2	2	1	1	1	1	0	0	0	0	0	0	0
9	–	9	4	3	2	1	1	1	1	1	0	0	0	0	0	0
A	–	A	5	3	2	2	1	1	1	1	1	0	0	0	0	0
B	–	B	5	3	2	2	1	1	1	1	1	1	0	0	0	0
C	–	C	6	4	3	2	2	1	1	1	1	1	1	0	0	0
D	–	D	6	4	3	2	2	1	1	1	1	1	1	1	0	0
E	–	E	7	4	3	2	2	2	1	1	1	1	1	1	1	0
F	–	F	7	5	3	3	2	2	1	1	1	1	1	1	1	1

Tables A–7 and A–8 give the remainder associated with conventional truncating division. Table A–7 shows a result of 0 for the case of the maximum negative number divided by –1, but on most machines the result for this case is undefined, or the operation is suppressed.

TABLE A–7. REMAINDER FOR SIGNED SHORT DIVISION (ROW ÷ COLUMN)

		0	1	2	3	4	5	6	7	-8 8	-7 9	-6 A	-5 B	-4 C	-3 D	-2 E	-1 F
	0	–	0	0	0	0	0	0	0	0	0	0	0	0	0	0	0
	1	–	0	1	1	1	1	1	1	1	1	1	1	1	1	1	0
	2	–	0	0	2	2	2	2	2	2	2	2	2	2	2	0	0
	3	–	0	1	0	3	3	3	3	3	3	3	3	3	0	1	0
	4	–	0	0	1	0	4	4	4	4	4	4	4	0	1	0	0
	5	–	0	1	2	1	0	5	5	5	5	5	0	1	2	1	0
	6	–	0	0	0	2	1	0	6	6	6	0	1	2	0	0	0
	7	–	0	1	1	3	2	1	0	7	0	1	2	3	1	1	0
-8	8	–	0	0	E	0	D	E	F	0	F	E	D	0	E	0	0̲
-7	9	–	0	F	F	D	E	F	0	9	0	F	E	D	F	F	0
-6	A	–	0	0	0	E	F	0	A	A	A	0	F	E	0	0	0
-5	B	–	0	F	E	F	0	B	B	B	B	B	0	F	E	F	0
-4	C	–	0	0	F	0	C	C	C	C	C	C	C	0	F	0	0
-3	D	–	0	F	0	D	D	D	D	D	D	D	D	D	0	F	0
-2	E	–	0	0	E	E	E	E	E	E	E	E	E	E	0	0	0
-1	F	–	0	F	F	F	F	F	F	F	F	F	F	F	F	0

TABLE A–8. REMAINDER FOR UNSIGNED SHORT DIVISION (ROW ÷ COLUMN)

	0	1	2	3	4	5	6	7	8	9	A	B	C	D	E	F
0	–	0	0	0	0	0	0	0	0	0	0	0	0	0	0	0
1	–	0	1	1	1	1	1	1	1	1	1	1	1	1	1	1
2	–	0	0	2	2	2	2	2	2	2	2	2	2	2	2	2
3	–	0	1	0	3	3	3	3	3	3	3	3	3	3	3	3
4	–	0	0	1	0	4	4	4	4	4	4	4	4	4	4	4
5	–	0	1	2	1	0	5	5	5	5	5	5	5	5	5	5
6	–	0	0	0	2	1	0	6	6	6	6	6	6	6	6	6
7	–	0	1	1	3	2	1	0	7	7	7	7	7	7	7	7
8	–	0	0	2	0	3	2	1	0	8	8	8	8	8	8	8
9	–	0	1	0	1	4	3	2	1	0	9	9	9	9	9	9
A	–	0	0	1	2	0	4	3	2	1	0	A	A	A	A	A
B	–	0	1	2	3	1	5	4	3	2	1	0	B	B	B	B
C	–	0	0	0	0	2	0	5	4	3	2	1	0	C	C	C
D	–	0	1	1	1	3	1	6	5	4	3	2	1	0	D	D
E	–	0	0	2	2	4	2	0	6	5	4	3	2	1	0	E
F	–	0	1	0	3	0	3	1	7	6	5	4	3	2	1	0

APPENDIX B

NEWTON'S METHOD

To review Newton's method very briefly, we are given a differentiable function f of a real variable x and we wish to solve the equation $f(x) = 0$ for x. Given a current estimate x_n of a root of f, Newton's method gives us a better estimate x_{n+1}, under suitable conditions, according to the formula

$$x_{n+1} = x_n - \frac{f(x_n)}{f'(x_n)}.$$

Here, $f'(x_n)$ is the derivative of f at $x = x_n$. The derivation of this formula can be read off the figure below (solve for x_{n+1}).

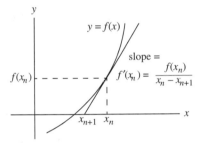

The method works very well for simple, well-behaved functions such as polynomials, provided the first estimate is quite close. Once an estimate is sufficiently close, the method converges quadratically. That is, if r is the exact value of the root, and x_n is a sufficiently close estimate, then

$$|x_{n+1} - r| \le (x_n - r)^2.$$

Thus, the number of digits of accuracy doubles with each iteration (e.g., if $|x_n - r| \le 0.001$, then $|x_{n+1} - r| \le 0.000001$).

If the first estimate is way off, then the iterations may converge very slowly, may diverge to infinity, may converge to a root other than the one closest to the first estimate, or may loop among certain values indefinitely.

This discussion has been quite vague because of phrases like "suitable conditions," "well-behaved," and "sufficiently close." For a more precise discussion, consult almost any first-year calculus textbook.

In spite of the caveats surrounding this method, it is occasionally useful in the domain of integers. To see whether or not the method applies to a particular function, you have to work it out, such as is done in Section 11–1, "Integer Square Root," on page 203.

Table B–1 gives a few iterative formulas derived from Newton's method, for computing certain numbers. The first column shows the number it is desired to compute. The second column shows a function that has that number as a root. The third column shows the right-hand side of Newton's formula corresponding to that function.

It is not always easy, incidentally, to find a good function to use. There are, of course, many functions that have the desired quantity as a root, and only a few of them lead to a useful iterative formula. Usually, the function to use is a sort of inverse of the desired computation. For example, to find $\sqrt{a}$ use $f(x) = x^2 - a$; to find $\log_2 a$ use $f(x) = 2^x - a$, and so on.[1]

TABLE B–1. NEWTON'S METHOD FOR COMPUTING CERTAIN NUMBERS

Quantity to Be Computed	Function	Iterative Formula
$\sqrt{a}$	$x^2 - a$	$\frac{1}{2}\left(x_n + \dfrac{a}{x_n}\right)$
$\sqrt[3]{a}$	$x^3 - a$	$\frac{1}{3}\left(2x_n + \dfrac{a}{x_n^2}\right)$
$\dfrac{1}{\sqrt{a}}$	$x^{-2} - a$	$\dfrac{x_n}{2}(3 - ax_n^2)$
$\dfrac{1}{a}$	$x^{-1} - a$	$x_n(2 - ax_n)$
$\log_2 a$	$2^x - a$	$x_n + \dfrac{1}{\ln 2}\left(\dfrac{a}{2^{x_n}} - 1\right)$

The iterative formula for $\log_2 a$ converges (to $\log_2 a$) even if the multiplier $1/\ln 2$ is altered somewhat (for example, to 1, or to 2). However, it then converges more slowly. A value of 3/2 or 23/16 might be useful in some applications ($1/\ln 2 \approx 1.4427$).

---

1. Newton's method for the special case of the square root function was known to Babylonians about 4,000 years ago.

BIBLIOGRAPHY

[AES] *Advanced Encryption Standard (AES)*, National Institute of Standards and Technology, FIPS PUB 197 (November 2001). Available at http:// csrc.nist.gov/publications/fips/fips197/fips-197.pdf.

[Alv] Alverson, Robert. "Integer Division Using Reciprocals." In *Proceedings IEEE 10th Symposium on Computer Arithmetic*, June 26–28, 1991, Grenoble, France, 186–190.

[Aus1] Found in a REXX interpreter subroutine written by Marc A. Auslander.

[Aus2] Auslander, Marc A. Private communication.

[Bern] Bernstein, Robert. "Multiplication by Integer Constants." *Software— Practice and Experience 16*, 7 (July 1986), 641–652.

[BGN] Burks, Arthur W., Goldstine, Herman H., and von Neumann, John. "Preliminary Discussion of the Logical Design of an Electronic Computing Instrument, Second Edition" (1947). In *Papers of John von Neumann on Computing and Computing Theory*, Volume 12 in the Charles Babbage Institute Reprint Series for the History of Computing, MIT Press, 1987.

[CJS] Stephenson, Christopher J. Private communication.

[Cohen] These rules were pointed out by Norman H. Cohen.

[Cut] Cutland, Nigel J. *Computability: An Introduction to Recursive Function Theory*. Cambridge University Press, 1980.

[CWG] Hoxey, Karim, Hay, and Warren (Editors). *The PowerPC Compiler Writer's Guide*. Warthman Associates, 1996.

[DES] *Data Encryption Standard (DES)*, National Institute of Standards and Technology, FIPS PUB 46-2 (December 1993). Available at http:// www.itl.nist.gov/fipspubs/fip46-2.htm.

[Dewd] Dewdney, A. K. *The Turing Omnibus*. Computer Science Press, 1989.

[Dud] Dudley, Underwood. "History of a Formula for Primes." *American Mathematics Monthly 76* (1969), 23–28.

[EL]   Ercegovac, Miloš D. and Lang, Tomás. *Division and Square Root: Digit-Recurrence Algorithms and Implementations.* Kluwer Academic Publishers, 1994.

[Gard]   Gardner, Martin. "Mathematical Games" column in *Scientific American 227*, 2 (August 1972), 106–109.

[GGS]   Gregoire, Dennis G., Groves, Randall D., and Schmookler, Martin S. *Single Cycle Merge/Logic Unit*, US Patent No. 4,903,228, February 20, 1990.

[GK]   Granlund, Torbjörn and Kenner, Richard. "Eliminating Branches Using a Superoptimizer and the GNU C Compiler." In *Proceedings of the 5th ACM SIGPLAN Conference on Programming Language Design and Implementation* (PLDI), July 1992, 341–352.

[GKP]   Graham, Ronald L., Knuth, Donald E., and Patashnik, Oren. *Concrete Mathematics: A Foundation for Computer Science, Second Edition.* Addison-Wesley, 1994.

[GLS1]   Steele, Guy L., Jr. Private communication.

[GLS2]   Steele, Guy L., Jr. "Arithmetic Shifting Considered Harmful." AI Memo 378, MIT Artificial Intelligence Laboratory (September 1976); also in *SIGPLAN Notices 12*, 11 (November 1977), 61–69.

[GM]   Granlund, Torbjörn and Montgomery, Peter L. "Division by Invariant Integers Using Multiplication." In *Proceedings of the ACM SIGPLAN '94 Conference on Programming Language Design and Implementation* (PLDI), August 1994, 61–72.

[Gold]   The second expression is due to Richard Goldberg.

[Good]   Goodstein, Prof. R. L. "Formulae for Primes." *The Mathematical Gazette 51* (1967), 35–36.

[GSO]   Found by the GNU Superoptimizer.

[HAK]   Beeler, M., Gosper, R. W., and Schroeppel, R. *HAKMEM*, MIT Artificial Intelligence Laboratory AIM 239, February 1972.

[Hay1]   Hay, R. W. Private communication.

[Hay2] The first expression was found in a compiler subroutine written by R. W. Hay.

[Hil]   Hilbert, David. "Ueber die stetige Abbildung einer Linie auf ein Flächenstück." *Mathematischen Annalen 38* (1891), 459–460.

[Hop]   Hopkins, Martin E. Private communication.

[HS]   Hillis, W. Daniel and Steele, Guy L., Jr. "Data Parallel Algorithms." *Comm. ACM 29*, 12 (December 1986) 1170–1183.

[H&P]   Hennessy, John L. and Patterson, David A. *Computer Architecture: A Quantitative Approach*. Morgan Kaufmann, 1990.

[H&S]   Harbison, Samuel P. and Steele, Guy L., Jr. *C: A Reference Manual, Fourth Edition*. Prentice-Hall, 1995.

[H&W]   Hardy, G. H. and Wright, E. M. *An Introduction to the Theory of Numbers*, Fourth Edition. Oxford University Press, 1960.

[IBM]   From an IBM programming course, 1961.

[Irvine] Irvine, M. M. "Early Digital Computers at Bell Telephone Laboratories." *IEEE Annals of the History of Computing 23*, 3 (July-September 2001), 22–42.

[JVN]   von Neumann, John. "First Draft of a Report on the EDVAC." In *Papers of John von Neumann on Computing and Computing Theory*, Volume 12 in the Charles Babbage Institute Reprint Series for the History of Computing, MIT Press, 1987.

[Ken]   Found in a GNU C compiler for the RS/6000 that was ported by Richard Kenner. He attributes this to a 1992 PLDI conference paper by him and Torbjörn Granlund.

[Knu1] Knuth, Donald E. *The Art of Computer Programming, Volume 1, Third Edition: Fundamental Algorithms*. Addison-Wesley, 1997.

[Knu2] Knuth, Donald E. *The Art of Computer Programming, Volume 2, Third Edition: Seminumerical Algorithms*. Addison-Wesley, 1998.

[Knu3]   The idea of using a negative integer as the base of a number system for
         arithmetic has been independently discovered by many people. The earli-
         est reference given by Knuth is to Vittorio Grünwald in 1885. Knuth him-
         self submitted a paper on the subject in 1955 to a "science talent search"
         for high-school seniors. For other early references, see Knuth, Volume 2.

[KRS]   Kruskal, Clyde P., Rudolph, Larry, and Snir, Marc. "The Power of Paral-
         lel Prefix." *IEEE Transactions on Computers C-34*, 10 (October 1985),
         965–968.

[Lamp]   Lamport, Leslie. "Multiple Byte Processing with Full-Word Instruc-
         tions." *Communications of the ACM 18*, 8 (August 1975), 471–475.

[LSY]   Lee, Ruby B., Shi, Zhijie, and Yang, Xiao. "Efficient Permutation
         Instructions for Fast Software Cryptography." *IEEE Micro 21*, 6
         (November/December 2001), 56–69.

[L&S]   Lam, Warren M. and Shapiro, Jerome M. "A Class of Fast Algorithms for
         the Peano-Hilbert Space-Filling Curve." In *Proceedings ICIP 94*, 1
         (1994), 638–641.

[MD]   Denneau, Monty. Private communication.

[MIPS]   Kane, Gerry and Heinrich, Joe. *MIPS RISC Architecture*. Prentice-Hall,
         1992.

[MM]   Morton, Mike. "Quibbles & Bits." *Computer Language 7*, 12 (December
         1990), 45–55.

[MMIX]   Part of a forthcoming edition of *The Art of Computer Programming*.
         Available at http://www-cs-faculty.stanford.edu/~knuth/taocp.html.

[NZM]   Niven, Ivan, Zuckerman, Herbert S., and Montgomery, Hugh L. *An
         Introduction to the Theory of Numbers*, Fifth Edition. John Wiley &
         Sons, Inc., 1991.

[PB]   Purdom, Paul Walton Jr., and Brown, Cynthia A. *The Analysis of
         Algorithms*. Holt, Rinehart and Winston, 1985.

[PHO]   Oden, Peter H. Private communication.

[PL8]   I learned this trick from the PL.8 compiler.

[Rib]   Ribenboim, Paulo. *The Little Book of Big Primes.* Springer-Verlag, 1991.

[RND]   Reingold, Edward M., Nievergelt, Jurg, and Deo, Narsingh. *Combinatorial Algorithms: Theory and Practice.* Prentice-Hall, 1977.

[Sagan] Sagan, Hans. *Space-Filling Curves.* Springer-Verlag, 1994. A wonderful book, thoroughly recommended to anyone even slightly interested in the subject.

[Shep]   Shepherd, Arvin D. Private communication.

[Stall] Stallman, Richard M. *Using and Porting GNU CC.* Free Software Foundation, 1998.

[Voor]   Voorhies, Douglas. "Space-Filling Curves and a Measure of Coherence." *Graphics Gems II,* AP Professional (1991).

[War]   Warren, H. S., Jr. "Functions Realizable with Word-Parallel Logical and Two's-Complement Addition Instructions." *Communications of the ACM 20*, 6 (June 1977), 439–441.

[Weg]   The earliest reference to this that I know of is: Wegner, P. A. "A Technique for Counting Ones in a Binary Computer." *Communications of the ACM 3*, 5 (May 1960), 322.

[Wells] Wells, David. *The Penguin Dictionary of Curious and Interesting Numbers.* Penguin Books, 1997.

[Will]   Willans, C. P. "On Formulae for the nth Prime Number." *The Mathematical Gazette 48* (1964), 413–415.

[Wor]   Wormell, C. P. "Formulae for Primes." *The Mathematical Gazette 51* (1967), 36–38.

INDEX

Numbers

0-bits
    counting. *See* counting bits.
    isolating, 11
    trailing 0's
        counting, 74, 84–87
        identifying, 11
    turning on, 12
0-bytes, finding, 91–95
1-bits
    counting. *See* counting bits.
    identifying, 11
    isolating, 11
    right-propagating, 12
    rightmost, turning off, 11–12

A

absolute value
    computing, 17–18
    multibyte, 36–37
    negative of, 21
add instruction
    condition codes, 33–34
    propagating arithmetic bounds, 54–57
addition
    arithmetic tables, 285
    double-length, 34–35
    and logical operations, 15–16
    multibyte, 36–37
    of negabinary numbers, 225–226
    overflow detection, 26–28
    in various number encodings, 228–229
Advanced Encryption Standard, 126
alternating among values, 41–44
Alverson's method, 188–189
and, in three instructions, 16
arithmetic, computer *vs.* ordinary, 1
arithmetic bounds
    checking, 51–53
    of expressions, 54–55

propagating through
    add and subtract instructions, 54–57
    logical operations, 58–63
range analysis, 54
searching for values in, 95–96
arithmetic tables, 285–288
arrays
    checking bounds. *See* arithmetic
        bounds.
    counting 1-bits, 72–73
    indexes, checking. *See* arithmetic
        bounds.
    indexing a sparse array, 73–74
    rearranging, 127
    of short integers, 36–37
    shuffling/unshuffling, 127

B

base $-1 + i$ number system, 230–232
base $-1 - i$ number system, 232–233
base -2 number system, 223–230, 239
big-endian format, converting to little-
    endian, 101
binary decomposition, integer exponentia-
    tion, 212–214
binary search
    counting leading 0's, 77–80
    integer logarithm, 215–221
    integer square root, 203–210
bit matrices, multiplying, 77
bit numbering, 1
bit operations
    compress operation, 93, 104, 108,
        116–123
    computing parity. *See* parity.
    counting bits. *See* counting bits.
    cycling through bit combinations. *See*
        Gray code.
    extracting alternate bits, 104
    finding strings of 1-bits, 96–99